Paying
for the
Past

Paying for the Past

The Struggle
over Reparations
for Surviving
Victims of the
Nazi Terror

Christian Pross

Translated by
Belinda Cooper

**The Johns Hopkins
University Press**
Baltimore and London

Translation prepared with the generous assistance of Inter Nationes.
Originally published as *Wiedergutmachung: Der Kleinkrieg gegen die Opfer* © 1988
Athenäum Verlag. Sponsored by the Hamburger Institut für Sozialforschung
English translation © 1998 The Johns Hopkins University Press

The Johns Hopkins University Press
2715 North Charles Street
Baltimore, Maryland 21218–4363
The Johns Hopkins Press Ltd., London

Library of Congress Cataloging-in-Publication Data will be found at the end of this book.
A catalog record for this book is available from the British Library.
ISBN 0-8018-5824-0

Contents

Preface to the English-Language Edition

This book requires some preliminary explanation for English-speaking readers unfamiliar with conditions in Germany. It arose out of historical interest in the profound consequences of the Holocaust for (West) German society, which confronted my generation, growing up after the war, at every turn. And it reflected a public political debate in the 1980s about the sincerity of reparations, especially with regard to the "forgotten victims," victims of persecution who had fallen through the cracks of reparations law—forced laborers, Sinti and Roma (Gypsies), victims of forced sterilization, communists, homosexuals, draft resisters, and deserters. After a wave of research by young amateur historians in the early 1980s revealed hitherto undiscovered material on Nazi crimes against these minorities, members of these groups began to step forward publicly for the first time since the end of World War II. The Green Party organized a hearing in the Bundestag on the persecution of Gypsies. Victims of forced sterilization, who had kept silent for decades out of shame and fear of renewed discrimination, spoke out publicly and organized their own association.

A year after the first edition of this book appeared, in 1988, the Berlin Wall fell. In the face of this profound historic event, debates on the Holocaust and on reparations for the "forgotten victims" of Nazism faded into the background. The book, which had at first made something of a splash, also vanished from the scene. However, certain events in recent years have lent it new currency. In Chile, Argentina, South Africa, and the countries of the former East Bloc, decades of dictatorship have come to an end. Sober realizations have replaced the early revolutionary euphoria; the ruins left by totalitarian regimes weigh upon their successor societies like a nightmare. Hopes of radical change and new beginnings, kept alive by resistance fighters and victims of the regimes, have been disappointed. In general, representatives of the old regimes have managed to reorganize rapidly and move all too gracefully on the parquet of the new order, while the victims have been reduced to social insignificance.

There have been some half-hearted attempts to bring the perpetrators to justice, but they have generally ended in acquittal or mild punishment.

Failure to punish the wrongdoers of criminal regimes is a pathogenic retraumatizing factor for the surviving victims. It is known that news of the acquittal of concentration camp guards by German courts sometimes led to violent psychological reactions in concentration camp survivors. Studies in Argentina have shown that failure to punish wrongdoers and the continued political influence of the military—responsible for many crimes committed under the dictatorship—have driven victims to psychotherapy. Similar effects can be observed in former East German political prisoners.

The Nuremberg trials immediately after World War II, the trial of Adolf Eichmann in Jerusalem, and the Auschwitz trial in Frankfurt in the 1960s bore tremendous significance for victims of the Holocaust, providing a measure of justice and satisfaction. Whether the international criminal tribunal in the Hague will do the same for survivors of the horrors in the former Yugoslavia remains to be seen. Whether the Truth and Reconciliation Commission in South Africa can heal apartheid's wounds is also a question to be answered by history. In all these debates in countries just emerging from dictatorship, societies have been looking to historical models of reparations and justice for the victims. German reparations for the victims of Nazism represent both a model and a warning. That contradiction is the subject of this book.

The starting point of the book was a collection of medical evaluations in the possession of a German émigré doctor living in Paris, S. Pierre Kaplan. I first made his acquaintance in 1983 while researching the fate of Jewish doctors at a Berlin hospital during the Third Reich. Kaplan had survived underground as a member of the French resistance; after the war, as an expert medical advisor to the German embassy in Paris, he had examined many concentration camp survivors for the reparations program. The opinions of German medical evaluators and officials of reparations offices quoted in his reports gave me my first taste of the bureaucratic pettiness and veiled hostility confronting the victims. I hoped to determine the background of this attitude on the part of Germans and delved ever more deeply into the history of reparations, the development of the laws, and the domestic political debates that accompanied them. The study I had originally planned, on medical examination and evaluation of concentration camp survivors by German doctors, became a study on reparations in general. I attempted to immerse myself in the social atmosphere of the 1950s and 1960s, reading countless press reports from the period. The reports on Germany in *Aufbau*, the most important newspaper in the United States published by German emigrants who had fled Nazi Germany, were a valuable aid.

As I wrote the book, I found myself in the midst of a renewed political debate on reparations for the "forgotten victims." At the behest of the vice-president of the Berlin House of Deputies, Hilde Schramm, I became a member of an expert commission of the House of Deputies formed to develop proposals for a hardship fund for these victims. In this capacity, I met almost all the surviving functionaries of the victims' organizations and the judicial, political, and medical figures who had been personally involved in the heated public debates on reparations in the immediate postwar period. They had at their disposal extensive archives that helped fill the gaps in my knowledge left by the fact that access to the files of the reparations offices was prohibited. Thus I obtained a wealth of oral history and documentary material that brought to life the history of reparations; with its help, I could recreate the causes of the small-mindedness with which the reparations program was frequently administered.

In addition, I stumbled upon a particularly explosive issue. The federal government was just completing publication of a multivolume chronicle of reparations that would record this "achievement of the century" from the government's point of view for coming generations. Problems arose with the final volume, in which the participants looked back upon and summarized events. The federal Ministry of Finance wished to silence critical commentators such as Otto Küster, Martin Hirsch, and Kurt Steinitz.

Otto Küster, a lawyer, can be considered one of the fathers and pioneers of the reparations laws. He was a scrappy, passionate moralist and a sworn enemy of the first federal minister of finance, Fritz Schäffer, an opponent of reparations. Due to the machinations of Schäffer and other politicians hostile to reparations, Küster was politically sidelined in the 1950s. He was one of the few who had the courage, in the dismal postwar years, to stand up to the cartel of former Nazis and opportunists who dominated the German political scene at the time.

In 1985, I visited Otto Küster at his law offices in Stuttgart. He was already well over eighty, but unbowed. He still represented persecutees in reparations cases before the Supreme Court of Appeals and found himself in constant conflict with some of the authoritarian judges. Küster and Kurt May, head of the United Restitution Organization, gave me the keys to understanding both the history of reparations in Germany and the more recent debates about it.

When I began to study the government's multivolume work carefully and compare it with publications by Küster and other participants, I discovered so many inconsistencies, distortions, superficialities, and prejudices, including even veiled anti-Semitism, in the official work that large parts of my book became a response to it. I became involved in a sort of minor *Historikerstreit* with the *éminence grise* of the federal Ministry of Finance, Ernst Féaux de la Croix, the source of the worst historical falsehoods and omissions. In particular, Féaux de la Croix failed to mention the key role played by Küster, as well as the scandalous circumstances surrounding his neutralization.

Féaux de la Croix had risen to become the top reparations official in Schäffer's Finance Ministry. This was already his second career, however. His first had been as an expert on nationality questions in the Nazi Ministry of Justice. In my opinion, one could not simply accept the fact that the federal government had appointed a former Nazi official as chronicler of the history of reparations for Nazi crimes, while censoring people like Küster.

Because of the rejection of his manuscript for the sixth volume of the government chronicle, Küster broke even with a former ally, the lawyer Walter Schwarz, the co-editor of the chronicle. Like Küster, Schwarz was one of the fathers of reparations. However, unlike Küster, he saw reparations as a unique historical achievement, a successful compromise between the rights of the victims and the concessions possible by the perpetrators and their legal successors. Falling somewhere between the two was Kurt May, a man who, as head of the largest legal assistance organization for Jewish victims, had done the best he could for his clients and acknowledged both the historical achievement of reparations and the shortcomings of the authorities' often petty behavior.

Shortly before Küster's death in 1989, the federal Ministry of Finance decided to publish a somewhat watered-down version of his piece after all, in the seventh volume of the chronicle. However, the public has waited in vain since then for the actual appearance of this ominous seventh volume, which is announced each year in the publisher's catalogue. According to the publisher and Küster's son, the federal Ministry of Finance has not yet made available the funds needed to produce the volume. Küster's piece has meanwhile been published by a newspaper in Israel, where it was widely discussed.[1]

A historian might have written this book with less passion. Not without reason did Constantin Goschler, a historian at the respected Munich Institute for Contemporary History—something like the Vatican Council of German historical writing—accuse me, in a book on reparations that appeared four years after mine, of writing in the style "of a Western." The narrative of the power struggles, haggling, and intrigues surrounding the reparations laws and reparations practice does read like a mystery novel. I was carried along by this excitement in my research. This was also connected with the fact that the book came into being during a renewed public debate on reparations. I was dealing with both history and current politics.

Shortly after the book appeared, the Berlin House of Deputies adopted a hardship-fund arrangement for the "forgotten victims." Other states, such as North Rhine–Westphalia, followed Berlin's example.

On the contemporary political stage, I was dealing, not only with defenders of reparations in the government camp, but also with members of the West German "antifascist" left, who saw reparations as a hypocritical act with which Germany was attempting to pay off its guilt for Nazi crimes. For them, the reparations program was a capitalist creation, as the wealthier among the victims received more reparations, while the poor received only a pittance, and marginal groups like Gypsies nothing at all.

Through complicated personal contacts, I had met the head of a state reparations office—a young lawyer who was also critical of past decision-making practices by his office and who fought for more generous restitution for Gypsies. He had allowed me secretly to study files in his office.

At a political event, I watched people from the "antifascist" camp stage a tribunal against official reparations policy, targeting as its representative the same head of office who had provided me with access to the records. He was called upon to publicly criticize his office's past decisions, for which he was not responsible; naturally, he could not do so. I was chilled by the self-righteousness with which this well-meaning man was treated by these "smart-alecky young Germans" (as Walter Schwarz called them). Thus I found myself in the midst of a tussle over how and by whom the history of reparations should be recorded for coming generations.

The head of a state reparations office wrote me a long letter in which he agreed that I had revealed important new facts, such as acknowledging Küster's role for the first time, but said that I had "mercilessly" painted far too grim an overall picture, giving the impression that most reparations workers were members of a "criminal organization" whose purpose was to deflect victims' claims. He told me I had made factual errors in the chapter on Philipp Auerbach, as Auerbach's conviction had not been entirely unjust. I had personally encountered this office head at panel discussions; like the above-mentioned head of another state reparations office who was my "secret helper," he was a civil servant of the postwar generation who had tried to do the best he could for the victims within the limits of possibility—although naturally he could not make up for the failings of the 1960s and 1970s.

At one of the numerous events connected with the book, a representative of the Union of Sinti and Roma handed me a document containing a directive by Küster from the early 1950s, when he was still head of the Baden-Württemberg reparations office. The directive called for restrictive handling of reparations claims by Gypsies. From my conversations with Küster, I knew that he had also advocated excluding communists from the Federal Restitution Law. Küster was far ahead of his time, but he was also a product of his times. Only those who view history through the lens of the present alone can condemn him for this.

Today, ten years later, I would probably write the book with somewhat greater detachment from current political events. Nevertheless, I stand by the statements in the book. I would like to add only that I have not wished, then or now, to join in the chorus of those who believe that the reparations program was a failure overall. Despite all its shortcomings, all its small-mindedness, and all the injustice that accompanied it, it was probably the best that could have been achieved under the existing political circumstances. And given this, it was an enormous achievement by its political proponents and the many upright civil servants, legal advisors, and doctors who put their energies into gaining justice for the victims. Reparations were among the crucial building blocks for the reconstruction of democracy in Germany, establishing legal and moral standards that cannot be reversed today. The reparations program set the stage for a change in consciousness and for a transformation, beginning in the late 1970s, in the way German society dealt with the Nazi past. And, last but not least, it documented the crimes, in recorded victims' statements and through numerous witnesses, for future generations.

Preface to the German Edition

Reparations: I heard the word for the first time in the mid 1960s in grade school, when a classmate voiced outrage at the idea that Germany was being "milked like a cow" by Israel. Once again citizens of one of the wealthiest nations on earth despite, or as a result of, losing the war, Germans felt that they were being fleeced. They saw reparations—and still do—not as obligatory restitution for stolen property but as the squandering of their own money on others.

In 1945, the Master Race, beaten by aerial warfare, flight, and expulsion, and faced with the wreckage of its dreams of power, wanted nothing to do with the survivors of the concentration camps. The reparations issue was ghettoized, as it were, and the few people dealing with it were socially isolated. The sudden public interest in it that was reawakened forty years after the end of the war came too late. Reparations offices still exist, it is true; proceedings continue, and pensions will be paid out even after the year 2000. Nevertheless, reparations are no longer an issue in day-to-day politics; they are a matter of history.

Entering the offices of the United Restitution Organization (URO), the largest legal aid organization for victims of persecution, headquartered in Frankfurt, is like entering a museum. The organization is administered by a small group of elderly lawyers, who have long since earned a peaceful retirement. The fact that these émigré German Jews, now in their eighties and nineties, who returned after 1945 to carry out a task few Germans wanted any part of, are devoting their last years to the remaining reparations proceedings speaks for itself. Now, as in the past, there is almost no one familiar enough with the complicated area of reparations law to replace them.

For some time now, these old men have been plagued by hordes of young historians eager for access to the historical "treasures" buried in their file cabinets. On the one hand, they are happy about this, grateful for the interest shown by these young people; on the other, there is something shameful about the way in which they are squeezed to the limits of their endurance, flooded with written inquiries and interviews with

which they can barely cope. One has the impression that such historians—some of whom are no longer young outsiders—are exploiting these
witnesses to history. Reparations authorities and some of the judiciary
share the blame for this situation; it should actually be their job to open
their archives to historians and make their personnel available for questioning. Instead, they maintain an anxious secrecy. Some have even begun to destroy their files.

At a national conference on 14–15 May 1985, the reparations offices
responded to growing public interest by adopting restrictive guidelines
on access to files in order to prevent individual officials or receptive
employees from granting interested parties access to them, which had
occasionally occurred in the past. In line with the decision of 15 May
1985, the Berlin Department of Internal Affairs, in charge of the Berlin
reparations office, responded to my request for access as follows:

The majority of states have expressed the view that access to the files without
previous agreement by the parties to the proceedings or other persons whose
individual rights might be affected is not possible . . . Because the quantity of files
here (some 210,000 individual files), the non-updated address lists and the small
staff of the reparations office in Berlin make it completely impossible, as a general
rule, to procure the agreement of parties to the proceedings, I am unfortunately
unable to assist your research in the present legal situation.[1]

The state pension office in North Rhine–Westphalia also refused to
allow access, referring to the enormous number of files.[2] I then requested
access to a more manageable group of twenty selected files, supplying file
numbers and all other necessary data (they could have been located in a
matter of minutes), but I again received a letter of refusal, with the explanation that the administrative costs would be prohibitive.[3] When I finally went personally to the state pension office in Düsseldorf with a
written power of attorney from a victim of persecution, a group of star-
tled officials surrounded me as though I were a dangerous intruder and
demanded to know what I was planning to do with the files. When at last
I reached the office of the director, he examined my power of attorney
over and over and then confirmed to his reluctant assistant that I did indeed have a power of attorney, he could do nothing about it, and they
would have to allow me to see the files. The files arrived in only three
minutes, and I was allowed to study them, in the presence of a supervisor.

Strangely enough, during an earlier research project on Jewish doctors
in Berlin, I had had no trouble obtaining the restitution files of the doctors involved if they were dead; if they were still living, I was given their
addresses so that I could write to them. For this project, funded by the
city's Department of Culture, an official directive had opened all the
doors. When I asked an employee of the reparations office about this
differing treatment, he explained that a recent publication on the former

Berlin public health officer Käte Frankenthal had criticized the Berlin reparations office.[4] The book's publisher had been given access to Käte Frankenthal's files at the Berlin reparations office, he said, and had drawn the wrong conclusions from it. People could not be permitted access to the files if they were going to criticize the office!

In my request for access to the files of various offices and courts, I had written, "We consider ourselves bound by data-protection laws ... naturally, we will guarantee anonymity to the people involved. The fact that the reparations proceedings were public should obviate any legal problems. We would be very grateful if you would support this important research project in the public interest by assisting in processing this request." The chief judge of the Düsseldorf trial court (*Landgericht*) acceded to my request, largely because of this passage. The chief judge of the Berlin trial court did not.

I am very grateful to the chief judge of the Düsseldorf trial court, Dr. Liermann, and the presiding judge of the Düsseldorf trial court, Dr. Jansen, for their receptiveness. They were the only representatives of any government agency who allowed me access to files. I had to procure the majority of the files through private sources, in which task I was aided, generously and unbureaucratically, by lawyers, some doctors, and the organizations of victims of persecution. S. Pierre Kaplan, a former medical expert for the German embassy in Paris, gave me his entire archive, complete with reparations evaluations, official correspondence, circular letters, and the like. The lawyers and staff of the United Restitution Organization in Frankfurt, Kurt May and Ulrich von Bubna, and the head of the Frankfurt headquarters of the Conference on Jewish Material Claims Against Germany, Ernst Katzenstein, provided me with material from their archives. Eberhard Fellmer, a Hamburg lawyer, permitted me access to the files of his former clients; Hans-Joachim Herberg likewise gave me access to the records of the Documentation Center for Health Problems Following Imprisonment and Persecution, in Cologne, of which he is the director; and Gerda Ahrens, Else Werner, and Stephan Romey provided access to the archives of the Vereinigung der Verfolgten des Nazi Regimes (Organization of Victims of the Nazi Regime, or VVN) in Hamburg. For the historical portion of the study, a former employee of the Berlin restitution office, Helene Jacobs, made her private papers available. I am also grateful to Anette Meyburg and Siegfried Büttner of the Federal Archives in Koblenz.

The following study is based on: (1) 195 files from the private archive of S. Pierre Kaplan, Paris; (2) 27 files of the Düsseldorf district court; (3) 27 files from the private archive of Attorney Eberhard Fellmer, Hamburg; (4) 15 files from the archives of the Organization of Victims of the Nazi Regime, Hamburg; (5) 89 files from the archives of the United Restitution Organization, Frankfurt; (6) 1 file from the archives of the URO,

Berlin; (7) 15 files from the archives of the Documentation Center for Health Problems Following Imprisonment and Persecution, Cologne; (8) the private papers of Helene Jacobs, Berlin; and (9) the reparations files of the federal Ministry of Finance in the Federal Archives, Koblenz.

In addition, thirty-nine eyewitnesses were interviewed—lawyers, judges, doctors from Germany and abroad, victims of persecution, members of victims' organizations, members of parliament, and officials of the reparations offices.

The study is part of a project at the Hamburg Institut für Sozialforschung on "Life Stories of Perpetrators Under National Socialism," which seeks to portray German intellectuals who profited from the Nazi system. Doctors were a significant pillar of the Nazi state; they helped draft and carry out the social and health policies of the Nazi program that ostracized and exterminated the inferior, the weak, and those of foreign race. Within the framework of this program, the system of medical examining and reporting expanded enormously. Sick people who were to be sterilized or exterminated were subjected to thorough medical evaluations by doctors. Using reparations as an example, this study investigates to what extent, after 1945, former victimizers sat in judgment on their own victims in the guise of politicians, officials, judges, and especially medical experts; the framework in which these encounters occurred; and their consequences. Because of the availability of sources, and for methodological reasons, the biographies of the participants were pushed somewhat into the background, while the fundamental characteristics of the victimizer-victim relationship came to the fore. This was supposed to be a study of a few medical experts, but in the course of the project, it became a historical investigation into the political, psychological, and medical aspects of reparations. Since those involved are far too readily separated in the common view into Nazis and non-Nazis (although the inadequacy of this black-and-white scheme of things becomes apparent upon closer examination), to the extent that sufficient data were available, short biographical sidebars introduce the persons important to this study. Wherever the information in these has been taken from generally accessible reference works, no source has been cited.

I would like in particular to thank Götz Aly, whose encouragement, advice, and criticism were indispensable; Jan Philipp Reemtsma, who funded the project and was very much involved in it substantively; Hans-Dieter Heilmann, whose thoughts and valuable source references contributed a great deal to the success of this study; Susanne Heim and Peter Chroust for important discussions and suggestions; Kurt May, Otto Küster, Ulrich von Bubna, Heinz Düx, Martin Hirsch, and Alice Stertzenbach, who familiarized me with reparations law; Ludger Hermanns, Wolf-Dieter Narr, Ulrich Schultz, Helmut Dahmer, and Kilian Stein for their knowledgeable advice and critical reading of the manuscript; and Heike Schoop, who edited the final version of the manuscript.

I received important references and information from Walther Ritter von Baeyer, Heidelberg; Jan Bastiaans, Leyden; Otto Bental, Berlin; Józef Bogusz, Cracow; Günter Hand, Düsseldorf; Otto Heinz Hurdelbrink, Berlin; Klaus Hoppe, Los Angeles; Heinrich Huebschmann, Heidelberg; Hans Keilson, Bussum; Robert Kempner, Frankfurt; Milton Kestenberg, Sands Point, N.Y.; Stanisław Kłodziński, Cracow; Ernst Kluge, Freiburg; Uschi Körber, Berlin; Christl Langenberger, Berlin; Joseph Lautmann, Berlin; Joachim Luwisch, Forest Hills, N.Y.; Wolfgang Meywald, Hamburg; Jakob Moneta, Frankfurt; Herrman Müller, Frankfurt; William G. Niederland, Englewood, N.J.; Karl Heinz Roth, Hamburg; Zdzisław Ryn, Cracow; Hilde Schramm, Berlin; Hermann Steinitz, Tel Aviv; Ulrich Venzlaff, Göttingen; and Ruth Warnecke, Berlin.

Abbreviations
and Acronyms

Akademie Bad Boll, *Opfer*	*Die Bundesrepublik Deutschland und die Opfer des Nationalsozialismus* (proceedings of the 1983 conference of the Evangelische Akademie in Bad Boll) (Bad Boll Protokolldienst 14 [1984])
AL	Alternative List, Berlin (West Berlin's version of the Green Party before unification)
AvS	Arbeitsgemeinschaft verfolgter Sozialdemokraten (Association of Persecuted Social Democrats)
B-Schaden	health damage
BA	Bundesarchiv (Federal Archive)
BDC	Berlin Document Center
BEG	Bundesentschädigungsgesetz (Federal Restitution Law)
BErgG	Bundesergänzungsgesetz (Federal Supplementary Law)
Bericht der Bundesregierung	10th German Bundestag, Drucksache 10/6287, 31 Oct. 1986, *Bericht der Bundesregierung über Wiedergutmachung und Entschädigung für nationalsozialistisches Unrecht sowie über die Lage der Sinti, Roma und verwandter Gruppen* (Federal Government Report on Reparations and Restitution for Nazi Injustice and on the Situation of Sinti, Rom, and Related Groups)
BGH	Bundesgerichtshof (the federal Supreme Court of Appeals, the country's highest appeals court, but not a constitutional court)

BHE	Bund der Heimatvertriebenen und Entrechteten (Association of Expellees and People Deprived of Rights, a party of postwar ethnic German expellees from eastern European countries)
Bizonia	the combined British and U.S. zones of occupation in Germany
Black Book	Landesregierung Baden-Württemberg, *Unterlagen zum Bundesentschädigungsgesetz* (Stuttgart, 1953)
BMF	Bundesministerium der Finanzen (the federal Finance Ministry)
BMF, Wiedergutmachung	*Die Wiedergutmachung nationalsozialistischen Unrechts durch die Bundesrepublik Deutschland,* ed. BMF in collaboration with Walter Schwarz, 6 vols. to date (Munich, 1974–87)
Bundesrat	German upper house of Parliament
Bundesstatistik	Statistischer Bericht Bundesstatistik über Anträge und Entschädigungsleistungen (statistical report, federal statistics on claims and reparations payments), internal, unofficial reparations office paper, in PA Jacobs
Bundestag	German lower house of Parliament
BVN	Bund der Verfolgten des Naziregimes (Federation of Victims of the Nazi Regime; organization close to the Christian Democratic Union)
BWGöD	"Gesetz zur Regelung der Wiedergutmachung für Angehörige des Öffentlichen Dienstes vom 11. Mai 1951" (Law to Settle Reparations for Members of the Public Service), in *Bundesentschädigungsgesetz* (Munich: Beck'sche Textausgaben, 1955)
CDU	Christian Democratic Union (one of postwar West Germany's and present-day Germany's two major parties)
Claims Conference	Conference on Jewish Material Claims Against Germany
CSU	Christian Social Union, the more conservative Bavarian arm of the CDU

DGSP	Deutsche Gesellschaft für soziale Psychiatrie (German Social Psychiatric Association)
DM	*Deutsche Mark*
DP	Deutsche Partei (German party)
DP	displaced person
DV-BEG	implementing legislation for the BEG
2 DV-BEG	2d BEG implementation law
DVP	Deutsche Volkspartei (German People's party)
EM	*Erwerbsminderung* (reduction in earning capacity)
expellees	ethnic Germans expelled from eastern European countries following the war
FDP	Free Democratic Party
Féaux de la Croix, *Werdegang*	*Der Werdegang der Entschädigungsrechts,* ed. Ernst Féaux de la Croix and Helmut Rumpf (Munich, 1985), vol. 3 of BMF, *Wiedergutmachung*
FIR	Féderation Internationale des Résistants
FRG	Federal Republic of Germany (West Germany)
GDR	German Democratic Republic (East Germany)
Grossmann, *Ehrenschuld*	Kurt R. Grossmann, *Die Ehrenschuld* (Frankfurt, a/M, 1967)
KPD	German Communist Party
Küster, *Erfahrungen*	Otto Küster, *Erfahrungen in der deutschen Wiedergutmachung* (Tübingen, 1967)
Küster, "Geste und Geist"	Otto Küster, "Wiedergutmachung: Sprache, Geste, Geist" (MS)
LG	Landgericht (district or trial court)
MdE	*Minderung der Erwerbsfähigkeit* (reduction in earning capacity)
O.M.G.U.S.	Office of Military Government, U.S. zone
PA	private archive
PA Jacobs	private archive of Helene Jacobs, Berlin

PA Kaplan   private archive of Dr. S. Pierre Kaplan, Paris

RzW   *Rechtsprechung zum Wiedergutmachungsrecht* (a
                     journal of reparations law)

Schwarz,   *Rückerstattung nach den Gesetzen der Alliierten*
Rückerstattung   *Mächte*, ed. Walter Schwarz (Munich, 1974), vol. 1
                     of BMF, *Wiedergutmachung*

SEW   West Berlin arm of the East German ruling party,
                     the SED

SPD   German Social Democratic party (one of postwar
                     West Germany's and present-day Germany's two
                     major parties)

URO   United Restitution Organization, a nonprofit legal
                     assistance organization headquartered in
                     Frankfurt

vMdE   *verfolgungsbedingte Minderung der*
                     Erwerbsfähigkeit (persecution-induced reduction
                     in earning capacity)

VVN   Vereinigung der Verfolgten des Naziregimes
                     (Organization of Victims of the Nazi Regime;
                     organization close to the Communist Party)

WEU   West European Union

ZSTAP   Zentrales Staatsarchiv der DDR in Potsdam (the
                     East German central state archives in Potsdam,
                     now part of BA)

Paying
for the
Past

Chapter 1

Introduction

In April 1957, a textile dealer and a high school teacher seated near each other in a restaurant in Offenburg started discussing the Third Reich and the most recent desecrations of Jewish cemeteries. The teacher saw no problem with either of these; on the contrary, he declared that "far too few Jews were gassed." The textile dealer thereupon revealed that he was Jewish, and that his lower jaw had been bashed in in a concentration camp. Then they probably forgot to gas him, said the teacher, and besides, he was proud that he and his men had "broken hundreds of Jews' necks with a shovel" during the war. He assured the Jewish textile dealer that he "would throw him into a concentration camp even today," and would "also gas" his wife; as far as he was concerned, their two children would be permitted to live.

The textile dealer complained to the high school principal and to the state Ministry of Education about these attacks and threats, at first without result. An effort was made to mollify him by informing him that the teacher had toned down his statement, explaining that he had meant *only* Russians and not "Jews" when he spoke of killing hundreds of people with a shovel, but the man waited in vain for an apology. On the contrary, he was sued for slander after calling the teacher a "butcher" during a subsequent encounter. When *Spiegel* magazine ran a story on the case, it received numerous letters to the editor sympathizing with the teacher. A minister wrote in to express understanding of the hostility created by "the current legal inequality" between Jews and Aryans; the former were receiving "reparations in excess of the injustice suffered." The affair eventually reached the reparations committee of the Bundestag [the lower chamber of the German parliament], and three-quarters of a year later, the teacher was suspended.[1]

Nearly thirty years later, a representative of the Jewish victims of persecution, the retired Berlin attorney Walter Schwarz, faced members of Germany's postwar generation in Berlin's House of Deputies. The Berlin Alternative List (AL), at the time the Berlin version of West Germany's Green Party, had proposed legislation to recognize forgotten victims of Nazism who had never received compensation: Gypsies, victims of forced sterilization, homosexuals, so-called "aliens to the community" (the antisocial), and communists. Schwarz, invited by the Christian Democrats as an expert witness on the existing restitution legislation, much of which he had helped to write, was to take a position on the AL motion. He described the restitution provisions as a great success and a historically unprecedented achievement, of which the Federal Republic could be proud. His words elicited a storm of protest.[2]

In November 1983, at a conference of the Evangelische Akademie (Protestant Academy) in Bad Boll, a physician from Hamburg, Karl Heinz Roth, demanded the repeal of the Federal Restitution Law, saying its procedures were demeaning to the victims.[3] Following the conference, Walter Schwarz complained to the press that for nearly four decades, restitution had been conducted in a political ghetto, and that the active public interest so desperately necessary in the past was suddenly emerging among "smart-alecky" young Germans, who were focusing exclusively on marginal aspects of reparations. The charge that the victims were being demeaned, he said, was an attack on the honor of those Germans who had shouldered the "most thankless task of the postwar period" with their work on reparations.[4]

The conflict between Schwarz and those "smart-alecky young Germans" touched a sore spot in the relationship between Jews and Germans.[5] While the young people spoke passionately of the neglected minorities among the victims, they made no reference to the Jews, the largest and hardest-hit group; and when they did speak of them, it was only indirectly, as the "professors systematically privileged" (planvoll privilegierte Professoren) by the restitution laws[6]—that is, Jewish academics and civil servants under the Weimar Republic, who received comparatively high compensation. From this point of view, Russian and Polish prisoners of war and slave laborers were "intensively abused groups"[7]—apparently more intensively abused than the Jews. Such claims created a reverse hierarchy of victims, fanning resentment by suggesting that the Jews once again had too much money.

Invidious distinctions among the victims, something politicians had hoped for from the start, were also fostered in another way; with similar intentions, superficial historical analyses were put forward suggesting that the exclusion of minority victims was the only significant feature of restitution policy (aside from the familiar argument that reparations laws were capitalist and a whitewash perpetrated by former Nazis).[8] Conversely, in the press and at the hearing in the Berlin House of Deputies, Walter Schwarz characterized the victims who had gone uncompensated as "marginal groups,"[9] "dregs," whom "the legislators would not have thought of" and "who were not capable of speaking up." He questioned whether victims of forced sterilization could be counted as victims of persecution, since eugenics laws had also existed in other countries.[10]

The main spokespersons for Jewish victims' organizations considered the question of reparations over and done with, and at first they kept out of these more recent debates. That has meanwhile changed; at the opening of a 1987 exhibit in Berlin on the Nazis' euthanasia killings, Heinz Galinski, the then-chairman of the Berlin Jewish Community, stated that the Jews, as the main victims of persecution, considered it their duty to support other groups that had been unfairly treated or completely overlooked in the restitution process, including victims of forced sterilization.[11]

It is almost impossible for young people today to picture the hostile climate and the political opposition confronting those who fought in the 1950s to pass reparations legislation. The battles waged by the representatives of Jewish organizations and a handful of reparations advocates against a civil service laced with former Nazis, the fact that they had to squeeze out of this civil service any legal change in favor of the victims and that reparations represented a hard-won compromise between victims and perpetrators—all this is brushed aside by those smart-alecky German critics. Such a one-sided understanding of history ascribes an exaggerated degree of success to former Nazis in blocking successful reparations and suggests that the perpetrators won in the end, while branding as failures the victims' representatives and advocates who worked so hard on such inhospitable terrain in the 1950s and 1960s.

During the 1950s in Germany, victims encountered their persecutors at every turn. For the former, this was a nightmare; for the latter, a living accusation, an unpleasant irritant. Almost unavoidably, such encounters took place where they should never have occurred: in the offices of restitution agencies and physicians, and in courtrooms. The German people did not like the victims, and they certainly did not like paying for them. Reparations were a burdensome duty imposed by the victors. In 1952, the Allies, the state of Israel, and the Conference on Jewish Material Claims Against Germany, representing millions of murdered and victimized Jews, forced the Federal Republic through international treaties to pay reparations. In the country itself, only a tiny minority of lawyers, civil servants, and politicians favored such financial atonement, to the extent that it was possible—the lonely few, they called themselves, who saw reparations as a serious moral obligation and attempted to influence the laws accordingly. The first, historical, section of this book, on the origins and substance of the reparations laws, focuses on them. The "lonely few" included Walter Schwarz, Kurt May, Otto Küster, Franz Böhm, Adolf Arndt, and Martin Hirsch.

Walter Schwarz (1906–1987) fled from the Nazis to Palestine in 1938. His father was murdered in the Theresienstadt·concentration camp. Schwarz returned to Germany in 1950 and opened a legal practice in Berlin in 1952, specializing in reparations law; his work on individual cases and his publications effected significant improvement in Allied and German restitution laws. In 1957, he took on the editorship of the journal *Rechtsprechung zum Wiedergutmachungsrecht* (Administration of Reparations Law), which until then had consisted merely of a collection of legal opinions printed as a supplement to the *Neue Juristische Wochenzeitung,* Germany's main legal publication.[12] He transformed it into a critical forum for lawyers, judges, and officials involved in reparations.[13] He first approached the federal government in 1963 with a proposal for a comprehensive study of reparations law.[14] In addition to this work, which appeared as *Die Wiedergutmachung nationalsozialistischen Unrechts durch die Bundesrepublik Deutschland* (The Reparation of National Socialist Injustices by the Federal Republic of Germany), he also wrote the first volume of *Rückerstattung nach den Gesetzen der Alliierten Mächte* (Restitution Under the Laws of the Allied Powers) in 1974.[15] The idea for this compilation, which has now grown to six volumes of varying quality, was almost killed by the "leaden indifference" of the Social Democratic–Liberal coalition government of the time.[16] Despite all the setbacks on the reparations front, however, Schwarz never lost faith in postwar Germany's democratic renewal. Even during the war, as an RAF officer interrogating captured German soldiers, he was surprised that he "could feel no hatred toward the accomplices of the exterminators."[17] Schwarz sought compromise rather than confrontation with the government. He was like an understanding creditor, who did not "correspond to the mythical image of the unyielding and permanently unsatisfied man," but rather felt "that this time the Germans have accomplished a task of restitution that deserves recognition, even gratitude, from those to whom it was owed."[18] Pushing through reparations was the chief work of Walter Schwarz's life.

Kurt May (1896–1992) was a lawyer in Jena who lost his position in 1933 as the result of racial persecution. He emigrated to Palestine, where he made his living as a self-employed salesman. In 1948, he helped found the United Restitution Organization (URO); In 1986, at the age of ninety-one, he was still running its German headquarters in Frankfurt. Without self-promotion, May created a documentary archive on the persecution of Jews in Hungary, Italy, North Africa, and Romania; on the confiscation of Jewish possessions in Holland, France, Belgium, and Luxembourg; on the Polish Jews persecuted throughout the German Reich in 1938; and on the racial persecution of German Gypsies, which he was one of the first to document (in the early 1960s). URO archives include the most recent legal decisions on reparations and have served as a source of information for many lawyers, judges, and agencies. May's documentation helped many victims of persecution to pursue their cases successfully—people who on their own would not have had the evidence to submit with their applications for restitution.[19]

Otto Küster (1907–1989) deserves pride of place on the "debtor" side. This feisty Swabian Protestant never claimed to be a victim, although he was removed from his judgeship in autumn 1933 in part because of his "rejection of Nazi leadership."[20] Küster was one of the few Germans who viewed the consequences of Germany's policies from 1933 to 1945 as necessitating an uncompromising purification and made it their historical duty to "reestablish abused law and democracy in Germany." Küster became the symbol of the "conscientious debtor," fighting the general indifference to Nazi crimes and the sluggish handling of reparations with the extraordinary courage of his convictions.[21] In October 1945, the liberal prime minister of Württemberg, Reinhold Maier, put him in charge of legislation and education in a state Ministry of Justice again headed—as it had been until 1933—by Josef Beyerle. On 1 March 1947, he was also appointed commissioner for reparations of the state of Baden-Württemberg. With a rank similar to that of an undersecretary, he had the independent status of an elected official; he was neither a civil servant nor bound to any political party, a very unusual administrative position in Germany.[22] In 1952, he served as deputy German negotiator, along with the Frankfurt law professor and Christian Democratic Union (CDU) deputy Franz Böhm, at the talks in the Hague with Israel and the Conference on Jewish Material Claims Against Germany. The Allied restitution law of 1947, the 1949 restitution law in the U.S. occupation zone, and the Bundesrat draft of a federal restitution law all bear the marks of his influence. The Federal Republic had no advocate of reestablishing justice more competent and committed than Otto Küster. The fact that it ultimately had no use for him does not speak very well of it. In addition to his official position, Küster was active in the *Freiburger Rundbrief* Group, an organization of Catholics and Protestants working for reconciliation between Germans and Jews.[23] He never presented himself as a resistance fighter; rather, he admitted that the progressive deprivation of rights and expulsion of Jews under the Third Reich had affected him and others "like a narcotic," and that he had "closed his eyes to the possibility of an Auschwitz."[24]

Franz Böhm (1895–1977) served as an officer in World War I and worked from 1925 to 1933 in the "Cartel" division of the Reich Economics Ministry. He received his postdoctoral degree from the University of Freiburg in 1933 and taught law at the University of Jena from 1936 on. Böhm published on fair trade laws and the role of the state in keeping order in a free-market economy. In 1938, he was subjected to disciplinary proceedings for his criticism of the Nazis' racial policies, and he was sent into temporary retirement in 1940. In 1942, as a "lecturer at the University of Jena," he published a study entitled *Der Wettbewerb als Instrument staatlicher Wirtschaftslenkung* (Competition as an Instrument of State Control of the Economy) in the series issued by the Nazi Academy for German Law. This monograph would later form the basis for Ludwig Erhard's economic policies.

After 1945, Böhm became minister of education in the postwar government of Hesse; in 1946, he was named to the chair in Civil Trade and Economic Law at the

University of Frankfurt. During the Cold War, Böhm advocated a hard line toward Eastern Europe and the Soviet Union. He responded to a 1957 memorandum by German scientists on the dangers of the atomic bomb by claiming that the totalitarian Soviet Union posed a greater danger than the bomb, and demanded nuclear arms for the Bundeswehr. In 1952, the federal government appointed him to head the German delegation to the reparations negotiations in the Hague. From 1952 to 1965, he served as a CDU representative in the Bundestag; in the third and fourth sessions of the Bundestag, he was deputy chairman of the reparations committee. Böhm was a relentless critic of nascent anti-Semitism and nationalism and of the lack of serious interest in reparations on the part of Germans and their representatives in government and the civil service. He published a number of books on reparations, as well as a two-volume work entitled *Judentum—Schicksal, Wesen und Gegenwart* (Judaism—Its Fate, Its Essence, and Its Present), and received the Leo Baeck Prize, in addition to various German awards. Along with Ludwig Erhard, Böhm is considered a father of the social market economy, for which he was honored in a commemorative address by Frankfurt's mayor Walter Wallmann in 1985.[25]

Adolf Arndt (1904–1974) was a judge in Berlin from 1930 until 1933, when he lost his position for racial reasons. He was able to continue working as a lawyer, however, defending such prominent union leaders as Wilhelm Leuschner and Theodor Leipart. During the last two years of World War II, he was forced into service as a munitions transporter in France by the Organisation Todt. In 1945, he was made a division head in the Hesse Ministry of Justice, where he helped draft the Allied restitution law and the compensation law in the U.S. occupation zone. In 1949, he was elected to the first German Bundestag; as Kurt Schumacher's closest associate, he became top legal expert of the Social Democratic Party (SPD). Arndt strenuously opposed rearmament and the reintroduction of the death penalty and played a key role in drafting the SPD's 1959 declaration of principles, the Godesberg Program. In 1963, he temporarily resigned his seat to serve for a year as commissioner of arts and sciences under Mayor Willy Brandt in Berlin. In the 1965 debate on the statute of limitations for Nazi crimes, Arndt at first opposed extension of the limit, believing that state power could not be expanded retroactively. In the end, however, he advocated continued punishment of Nazi crimes, on condition that the statute of limitations be eliminated for all murders. Arndt withdrew from public life in 1969.[26]

Martin Hirsch (1913–1992) was a member of the socialist schoolchildren's and socialist students' unions before 1933. After earning his diploma in law in 1939, he took a position as legal counsel in the paper industry in Berlin. From 1941 to 1945, he served on the Eastern Front. After the end of the war, he worked as a lawyer in Marktredwitz in northern Bavaria, where he represented many victims of persecution; he was also an SPD city councillor, and was elected to the Bavarian state parliament in 1954 and the Bundestag in 1961.

In this capacity, he chaired the Reparations Commission during the fourth legislative period and played a major role in the creation of the Federal Restitution Law (BEG) Final Law of 1965 (discussed below). In 1981, he was appointed to the advisory board of the Reparations Disposition Fund, administered by the federal Ministry of Finance, part of the hardship fund for non-Jewish victims of persecution.

In the Bundestag, Hirsch worked not only on reparations but also on penal reform, the federal emergency laws, and liberalization of the penalties against demonstrations. In 1968, during the SPD-CDU Grand Coalition, he was one of the authors of a very controversial proposal to introduce preventive detention for potential serial offenders. From 1971 to 1981, Hirsch sat on the Bundesvervassungsgericht (Federal Constitutional Court).

Politicians and lawyers committed to reparations constituted a tiny minority of Germans, their only allies being a small group of intellectuals, journalists, and church people in Germany whose thinking coincided with public opinion in the United States, and who were supported, and sometimes even pressured, by the U.S. government. The coalition of reparations advocates crossed party lines, as did that of its opponents; neither fitted a neat right-left pattern, although the majority of the opponents were found in the Christian Democratic Union / Christian Social Union (CDU/CSU) sister parties and the Free Democratic Party (FDP). The staunchest allies of the opponents of reparations were the federal Ministry of Finance, the office in charge of reparations legislation, and the German people, the great majority of whom felt no sympathy for victims of Nazism. The Bundestag's debates on reparations and its legislation did not at all reflect the opinion of the voters; the Bundestag was far ahead of them, functioning as the conscience of a nation that had none. The entire history of reparations must be seen in light of these political relationships.

Each of the men profiled above fought in his own way for just reparations; nevertheless, they by no means always shared the same opinions. While Walter Schwarz—especially after becoming co-editor of the history of reparations for the Ministry of Finance—advocated a more pro-government attitude, Küster was from the outset an abrasive, uncompromising, and very outspoken critic. At the abovementioned conference at Bad Boll, their substantive differences became evident. Küster had charged that some victims of persecution were getting too much and some too little, that the Jews' spokesmen had almost all received good pensions for damage to their careers, and "to the extent that their hearts do not beat in sympathy with their fellow sufferers who have not done as well," they would feel they were being ungrateful "if they did not praise our reparations."[27] Hirsch criticized the federal Finance Ministry work co-edited by Walter Schwarz as an official history authored entirely by the bureaucracy.[28] Schwarz did not attend the Bad Boll conference, in part because of Hirsch's presence.

The opponents of reparations used less public methods. Because anti-Semitism was a political taboo in the Federal Republic, they hid behind economic arguments and pursued their goals behind the scenes. The primary and most important spokesperson for this group was Chancellor Konrad Adenauer's first finance minister, Fritz Schäffer. The prime minister of Baden-Württemberg, Gebhard Müller, and the Bavarian minister of justice, Josef Müller, held views similar to Schäffer's.

Fritz Schäffer (1888–1967) was a Bavarian People's Party deputy in the Bavarian state parliament in the 1920s. In 1922, before Hitler's Beer Hall Putsch, he had already made anti-Semitic speeches and expressed support for the Nazi ideology. In 1931, he became an undersecretary and Bavarian minister of finance. In national politics, he supported Field Marshal Paul von Hindenburg's reelection as president in 1930, and the Center Party government of Chancellor Heinrich Brüning (1930–32). In 1933, he joined the Bavarian cabinet in opposing the Nazis' seizure of power and resigned. He then worked in Munich as a lawyer. Schäffer was imprisoned in Dachau from August to October 1944 in connection with the attempted assassination of Hitler. After 1945, the Americans appointed him first prime minister of Bavaria, but when his anti-Semitic past became known and his government was found to be riddled with former Nazis, they relieved him of his post after only a few months. The U.S. military government accused him of being a Nazi sympathizer and backer during his entire political career and of obstructing the denazification process. He was cleared of these charges in a denazification proceeding that he himself initiated in 1947. In 1949, he became minister of finance in Adenauer's first cabinet, continuing in that position until 1957. He was considered the most powerful man in Bonn next to the chancellor. He became minister of justice in Adenauer's third cabinet, and in 1961 withdrew from political life. As minister of finance, he acquired the reputation of being a pedantic, petty bean counter, a miserly politician who was accused of hoarding large amounts of money. He viewed himself as the guarantor of a strengthened German currency and resisted any claims on the German state, especially reparations claims. Schäffer personally opposed Otto Küster in many reparations negotiations.[29]

Gebhard Müller (1900–1990) served in World War I and studied Catholic theology, economics, and law. Before 1933, he was in charge of tax and administrative matters for the Diocesan Administrative Council in Rottenburg and chairman of the Catholic Center Party there. Under the Third Reich, he sat as a judge on various Württemberg regional courts and spent some time as a soldier. After 1945, Müller was assigned by the French military government to rebuild the judicial system in Württemberg-Hohenzollern, and in 1948, he advanced to become governor of the state. In October 1953, a year after the state of Baden-Württemberg was formed out of the American-occupied states of North Baden and North Württemberg and French-occupied South Baden and South Württemberg–Hohenzollern, Müller replaced Reinhold Maier, who had until then headed the ruling coalition government of Free Democrats (FDP), SPD, and BHE (the small party of ethnic Germans expelled from eastern European territories).

One of his first official acts was to dismiss State Commissioner for Reparations Otto Küster, who was accused, in a campaign launched by Müller, of being too generous with reparations. Another of his first official acts, on 23 July 1954, was to pardon the psychiatrist Arthur Schreck, the former director of the Rastatt mental hospital, who had been convicted of the euthanasia murders of some 15,000 Rastatt patients, and Ludwig Sprauer, the former senior medical officer in Baden, who had been responsible for euthanasia in Baden.[30] In 1958, Gebhard Müller became chief justice of the Federal Constitutional Court, which he remained until his retirement in 1971.

Josef Müller (1898–1979) served in World War I and studied law and economics. Until 1933, he worked as a lawyer in Munich and was active in the Bavarian People's Party. Under the Third Reich, he worked as a legal and economic advisor to the Catholic Church and had ties to the Vatican's secretary of state, Cardinal Pacelli, later Pope Pius XII. During the war he was active in Admiral Wilhelm Canaris's military intelligence. He maintained contact with the planners of the 20 July 1944 attempt on Hitler's life and acted as their envoy in Rome. In 1944, he was arrested but was acquitted of high treason by the Reich Military Court in Berlin. Nevertheless, he was held in the Gestapo prison on Prinz Albrecht Strasse in Berlin and then in Buchenwald, Flossenbürg, and Dachau, from which he was liberated in 1945. After 1945, he became state chairman of the CSU in Bavaria, which he had helped found. In 1947, he took the positions of deputy prime minister and minister of justice in the CSU state government under state Prime Minister Hans Ehard. In 1951, he had Philipp Auerbach, head of the Bavarian state reparations office, arrested and tried. Because of his dubious role in the "Auerbach Affair," Müller was forced to resign as minister of justice in 1952. In 1960, he ran unsuccessfully for mayor of Munich against Jochen Vogel of the SPD. This ended his political career. In 1966, he was awarded Germany's highest honor, the Grosses Bundesverdienstkreuz mit Stern. In its obituary for Josef Müller, also known as "Sepp the Ox," the *Süddeutsche Zeitung* newspaper wrote, "This colorful, cunning, jovial, convivial and hard-drinking man . . . was a good democrat."

Along with the individuals mentioned, the organizations of victims of persecution also played a crucial role in the history of reparations. The largest and most influential was the Conference on Jewish Material Claims Against Germany, generally known for short as the Claims Conference. This was a federation of fifty-two Jewish organizations in Western countries, formed in New York on 26 October 1951 at the instigation of the Israeli foreign minister, Moshe Sharett, to act as the overall representative of Jews living outside of Israel who had reparations claims against Germany.[31] The conference had its own office in Bonn, and its chairman, Nahum Goldmann, functioned rather like the ambassador of a sovereign state. This status derived from the Hague reparations negotiations in 1952, at which the Claims Conference represented the "nation" of Jewish refugees and survivors all over the world, on an equal footing with Israel. One of Goldmann's closest associates was Ernst Katzenstein.

Ernst Katzenstein (1898–1989), who was a lawyer in Hamlin under the Weimar Republic, was forced to emigrate to Palestine in 1934 after losing his legal practice. In 1936, he moved to London, but he subsequently returned to Palestine and opened a legal practice in Jerusalem. He returned to Germany in 1949 as the chief officer of the Jewish Restitution Successor Organization (JRSO), a New York organization assigned by the restitution laws in the U.S. occupation zone to act in place of the German treasury as legal heir to unclaimed Jewish property. In 1956, Katzenstein became director of the German office of the Claims Conference in Frankfurt. As Nahum Goldmann's close associate, he played a key role in the deliberations on the Federal Restitution Law (BEG) of 1956 and the BEG Final Law of 1965.[32]

In the Hague Protocol Number 1, the Claims Conference entered into an agreement with the Federal Republic on the guidelines for German reparations legislation. No other group of victims occupied a comparable position and could contractually commit the Federal Republic to reparations payments. Through the respected German-language emigrant newspaper *Aufbau* in New York,[33] as well as through its connections with politicians and government circles in the United States, the Claims Conference carried on effective public relations and reparations politics, exerting international influence on German legislation and official practice. The State of Israel was also an influential advocate for Jewish victims of persecution.

Equally important was the United Restitution Organization. Formed in 1949 in London by the Council of Jews from Germany, the URO maintains offices in Germany, Israel, and various other countries. The members of the Claims Conference and the URO were mainly German lawyers who had emigrated during the Third Reich and were very familiar with German administrative practices and the legal system. At times, the URO had more than 1,000 members, and it represented some 300,000 clients from the time reparations began to be paid; each client made, on average, three to five different restitution claims.[34] The URO represented in particular those victims of persecution who could not afford a lawyer. The Frankfurt headquarters collected the latest administrative guidelines, court decisions, and medical opinions; the URO lawyers were among the best-informed, most knowledgeable reparations lawyers around. The URO joined the Claims Conference in registering protests to government representatives and members of parliament when an office or a claims assessor repeatedly made serious errors. The Berlin URO, for example, succeeded in having a judge whose decisions had been openly anti-Semitic removed from the reparations panel of the Berlin court.[35]

Other victims' groups sometimes resented the Jewish victims' effective promotion of their own interests. In 1985, at a hearing on reparations held by the Greens in Bonn, a representative of the VVN, or Vereinigung der Verfolgten des Naziregimes (Organization of Victims of the Nazi Regime), an association composed primarily of members of the communist resistance, claimed that the Jews had worked things out with the former Nazis much too quickly after the war, at the expense of the other victims.[36] In fact, however, the URO brought many test cases against restrictive agency decisions, from which other victim groups also profited, and the research undertaken by Kurt May, head of the URO headquarters in Frankfurt,[37] increased the documentation of the "facts of persecution" that had to be proven to the agencies in charge of reparations.

The URO was a unique institution; along with Otto Küster, Walter Schwarz, and several others, it managed to do for reparations what the German legal system failed to do—maintain constant debate on and scholarly examination of all legal issues relating to compensation and restitution. No German law professors have made reparations the focus of their research and teaching,[38] and the courts' restitution panels did not train any legal interns.[39] The lawyers, judges, and administrative law experts involved in reparations operated in a type of ghetto; the legal profession as a whole remained completely uninvolved.[40] The URO financed the only journal dealing with this shunned topic, *Rechtsprechung zur Wiedergutmachung.*[41]

Victims of political persecution founded the VVN immediately after the end of the war. In its early years, this was an organization for all victims of persecution; it included communists, social democrats, Christian democrats, liberals, and victims of religious and racial persecution. In March 1947, at an interzonal conference of victims of persecution, an all-German VVN council was formed. With the start of the Cold War, the VVN split. On 6 May 1948, the SPD steering committee declared membership in the VVN to be incompatible with membership in the SPD and founded its own organization, still in existence—the Arbeitsgemeinschaft verfolgter Sozialdemokraten (Association of Persecuted Social Democrats). This was followed, on 10 February 1950, by the creation of the Bund der Verfolgten des Naziregimes (Federation of Victims of the Nazi Regime), associated with the CDU and also still in existence.[42] On 19 September 1950, the federal government decreed that members of the VVN could not become civil servants. On 1 August 1951, the Hamburg VVN was banned by the police, its offices searched, and its files—mainly on reparations proceedings—confiscated. A few days later, the central office of the VVN in Frankfurt was closed by the police. Following the outlawing of the German Communist Party in 1956, the VVN was declared a communist front and its members were kept under surveillance by the police and judicial authorities. Not until 1967 did the Federal Administrative Court lift the ban on the VVN.[43]

The split among victims' organizations in Germany considerably weakened their influence on reparations practice and legislation, while making it easier for Adenauer's right-wing coalition to exclude former resistance members and persecution victims from the Federal Republic's political life. The Association of Persecuted Social Democrats was able to exert some influence on reparations policies, as its members were represented in the Bundestag and on the Bundestag's reparations commission.

In the 1950s and 1960s, communists were fighting a losing battle both within the various victims' groups and in their dealings with government agencies. If they did not comply with the demand that they cease political activity, their applications for reparations were rejected under § 6 of the Federal Restitution Law. Even if they held their peace, they were still subjected to much more of a runaround than other victims. Often, their concentration camp and jail terms were not recognized as political persecution, but instead classified as legal punishment for criminal activity.[44] In the context of the virulent anticommunism created by the Cold War, the stream of refugees from East Germany, and the building of the Berlin Wall, they had no advocates. It is true that members of the left wing of the SPD, like the Bundestag member Adolf Arndt, argued during deliberations on the first draft of the 1953 federal restitution law against legally excluding "opponents of the free democratic order from reparations"; however, they failed to get their view across.[45] The SPD, which as a whole criticized the way restitution was being handled in the Bundestag, maintained a firm policy of separation from communists.

Joachim Lipschitz, Berlin's SPD commissioner of internal affairs, and the Berlin reparations office also proceeded with great harshness against actual or suspected communists. Lipschitz had himself been a victim of the Nazis and enjoyed an almost legendary reputation among Jewish, Social Democratic, and Christian persecutees for his passionate support of reparations. He also deserves credit for the fact that—except for its treatment of communists—in the 1950s and 1960s, the Berlin reparations office was the most generous and least bureaucratic agency of its type.

Joachim Lipschitz (1918–1961), the son of a Jewish doctor, belonged before 1933 to the Jungbanner Schwarz-Rot-Gold, the youth arm of the SPD's paramilitary forces. From 1936 to 1938, he worked as a salesman's apprentice. In 1939, Lipschitz was drafted into the Labor and Defense Service, from which he was discharged in 1942 after losing his left arm. In 1944, he went into hiding to avoid deportation. After the war, he became a deputy factory manager and district councilman in Berlin's Lichtenberg district. In 1948, Lipschitz was dismissed by the Soviet military government for political reasons; moving to West Berlin, he became district treasurer and deputy district mayor of Neukölln, and later a member of the city parliament for the SPD. From 1955 until his death at forty-three, Lipschitz was Berlin's commissioner for internal affairs and was strongly committed to reparations. He often intervened directly with the reparations office to cut through red tape for victims with grievances. For a time he was also chairman of the Bundesrat reparations commission.

Thirty years later, in the spring of 1986, during a hearing at which victims' organizations were to testify in Berlin's House of Deputies on creating a hardship fund for forgotten victims of Nazism, a decision by the established parties to exclude the VVN was prevented only at the last minute by the personal intervention of the Alternative List deputy Hilde Schramm. As a result, former communist victims for the first time had the opportunity to describe to a parliamentary committee the decades of humiliating discrimination against them by agencies and courts. "To this day, we feel accused," they said.[46] With a few exceptions, other groups of persecutees not included under the restitution law, such as the "antisocial," the forcibly sterilized,[47] and homosexuals, have never dared to abandon their anonymity and isolation and publicly demand their rights, fearing this would subject them to further discrimination.[48] Until the creation of the "Central Council of the Sinti and Roma" in 1979, Gypsies had no representatives whatsoever.

Since efforts have increased in recent years to examine Nazism more thoroughly, the political and scholarly public has focused more and more on surviving victims. Resistance fighters, Jews, communists, Gypsies, homosexuals, and the forcibly sterilized, forced to live in isolation in Germany for years and often still faced with discrimination, began to find themselves in the spotlight forty years after the end of the war. The Evangelische Akademie at Bad Boll organized two conferences; the Green Party and, in 1985 and 1987, the Bundestag's internal affairs committee both held hearings on the forgotten victims and their lack of, or only partial, compensation. The Greens introduced legislation in the Bundestag and some state parliaments aimed at helping those who had not received reparations to attain, if not justice—that would be impossible—then at least a measure of recognition. Eventually, West Berlin and the state of North Rhine–Westphalia passed special laws to compensate the "forgotten victims."[49]

The shrinking minority of combative old men involved in reparations and the representatives of some associations of persecutees view the actions of the "sixty-eighters" with skepticism. They wonder why these children of Nazi perpetrators, politicized by the Vietnam War, the threat of nuclear war, and environmental pollution, have suddenly discovered the victims. The social discrimination these victims suffered in the 1950s and 1960s cannot be undone. There can be no compensation for mishandled compensation. For most, the political and legal debates are over for good.

Some of the victims of persecution who brought suit as late as the second half of the 1960s because their claims of impaired health had been rejected previously were evaluated by the professors of medicine who were at the same time calling the police to clear auditoriums occupied by rebellious students. Little was known then about the role these professors had played in the Third Reich, and their activity as evaluators of medical claims took place out of the public eye.

The advocates of a proactive reparations policy had attempted in vain to arouse interest in the public and among politicians. Eventually, they recognized that, under the existing political conditions and in a nation where the overwhelming majority had supported Nazism, nothing more could be accomplished; they felt lucky to have achieved as much as they had. Those who had fallen through the legal cracks and been denied justice by doctors, officials, and the courts placed their hopes in the Green–Alternative List legislative initiative and were effusively grateful to its initiators.

One can understand the combination of professed concern, lip service, and cold-blooded indifference exhibited by politicians on this issue only in the context of the history of reparations and postwar German history as a whole. In 1951, Konrad Adenauer admitted Germany's guilt in the Bundestag and promised generous reparations, while at the same time his finance minister was haggling with Jewish politicians over every penny and harvesting praise from the "generation of German veterans" in the right-wing newspaper *National und Soldatenzeitung* as the guarantor of their interests. And two years later, a representative of Adenauer's own party, Franz-Josef Strauss, would torpedo ratification of the Luxembourg Reparations Treaty with the state of Israel and the Claims Conference.[50] The "foul climate of creeping anti-Semitism" that SPD deputy Arndt blamed in 1954 for the sluggish pace of reparations legislation has not disappeared from Germany even today.

The multivolume compendium on reparations published between 1974 and 1987 by the federal Ministry of Finance, *Die Wiedergutmachung nationalsozialistischen Unrechts durch die Bundesrepublik Deutschland*, pays tribute to the "unique" historical accomplishment of reconciliation and reparations by the Federal Republic but suppresses any mention of the pusillanimous attitude that accompanied this accomplishment—except in the first volume, written by Walter Schwarz, *Rückerstattung nach den Gesetzen der Alliierten Mächte*.

The six volumes, also known as the "Blue Books," contain a wealth of interesting material, but they gloss over a great deal and promote a clear political agenda by not permitting certain groups and persons any say at all. The federal Ministry of Finance censored contributions by people who had played a major role in bringing about reparations yet had not hesitated to criticize the deficiencies and distortions of the whole program; thus they deleted an afterword by Otto Küster,[51] a critical section by Martin Hirsch,[52] and an essay by Hermann Steinitz, a medical expert in Israel.[53] Küster's afterword contained harsh criticism of the decisions reached by the Federal Supreme Court; he argued that the court should have interpreted federal restitution law in a spirit supportive of reparations rather than restricting it through hair-splitting. Sometimes the issues involved were as simple as this: if, for example, the minimum prerequisite for a claim was a year's concentration camp imprisonment, should deportation to Auschwitz in a cattle car (in the course of which many prisoners died) be counted? Or should widows from Middle Eastern countries, where civil weddings were possible, but Jewish couples almost always had only so-called rabbinical weddings, be recognized as widows under the Federal Restitution Law?

Thanks to the efforts of Walter Schwarz, Bonn ultimately decided to publish Küster's manuscript after all. At first, the editors deleted the following sentence from Hermann Steinitz's section in the chapter on "German Medical Officers and Officially Designated Experts": "I have read expert assessments that almost recall the atmosphere of the Nazi period." But even without this sentence, the manuscript, otherwise cautious in its criticisms, was unacceptable to the ministry.

In an introduction to the first volume of the series, published in 1974, Helmut Schmidt, at the time federal finance minister, wrote, "The federal Ministry of Finance felt it important to open the floor to authors from various fields and professions who had differing interests . . . The opinions of the authors may not always coincide with those of this office."[54] But this intention did not survive the 1982 change in government from an SPD-FDP coalition to one between the CDU/CSU and the FDP. Except for the lawyer Walter Schwarz, the only voices to be heard in the six volumes were those of ministry officials, leading staffers of the reparations offices, and individual judges. Not one representative of the legislature, and not a single plaintiff's lawyer or representative of a victims' organization, was permitted to present a "differing interest" from that of the executive. The federal Ministry of Finance had something to hide. It attempted to infuse its version of the history of reparations into a multivolume monument, intended for generations to come, when no one would be around who remembered the facts.

The section on the history of the Federal Restitution Law was written by one of the highest officials in the ministry, the retired deputy secretary Ernst Féaux de la Croix. His accounts, some 309 printed pages, appeared in 1985 in volume 3, entitled *Der Werdegang des Entschädigungs-*

rechts (The Development of Reparations Law).[55] In Adenauer's first cabinet, Féaux de la Croix served under Finance Minister Schäffer in Section VI of the ministry, which handled reparations as well as the areas of international financial relations, liquidation of the war, and legal matters. In Adenauer's second cabinet, this section was subdivided into Subsection V/A for banking and international finance, and Subsection V/B for reparations, liquidation of the war, and legal matters. Féaux de la Croix rose to become head of Subsection V/B, and in Adenauer's third cabinet was made section head, with his responsibilities expanded to include defense expenditures within NATO and the West European Union.

This administrative coupling of rearmament and reparations indicates how little the latter were viewed as separate, morally indispensable obligations—and how much they had become a mechanism for improving the climate within the new alliances, as well as for creating new friend-foe constructs. Thus the preferential treatment shown to Jewish victims of persecution in Israel and the United States, as opposed to Polish and Soviet forced laborers and camp inmates, also formed part of Germany's NATO strategy. In all those years, the reparations section remained a small subdivision of this department, sparsely staffed.

Féaux de la Croix was heavily involved in all stages of the creation of the restitution laws. His account is revealing; it documents, unmistakably and shockingly, the credo of the Bonn government bureaucracy on the question of reparations. In this official 1985 publication, he spontaneously employs such Nazi expressions as "world Jewry," the "Jewish press," "Jewry" (*Judenschaft*), and Jews who "manipulate world opinion." He writes that reparations were often described as the price "for American Jewry's allowing its president to accept the Federal Republic as a partner in the community of Western nations" and, in the same breath, that reparations were considered the prerequisite "for the willingness of Jews throughout the world to accept the German economy and its products as participants in world trade." While acknowledging that such absolute statements, often originating in clearly anti-Semitic tendencies, were undoubtedly exaggerated, he adds that they undeniably "contained a kernel of truth."[56] Numerous passages indicate what Féaux de la Croix considered this to be:

To this day it cannot be determined what role the reparations problem played in the Allies' deliberations on an occupation statute. The one thing that is certain is that Jewry attempted in every conceivable way to make provision for reparations in any future occupation statute.[57]

The later attitude of the major Allies to the Jewish demand for reparations—especially that of the Soviet Union—permits us instead to surmise that the Allies were skeptical, if not disapproving, of Jewish reparations claims. But Jewry would not let go.[58]

To write that Jews "would not let go," used "every conceivable method," was not enough for Féaux de la Croix. He asserted that "World Jewry," directed from its "headquarters," guided Adenauer's hand as he wrote; the "Jewish press" defamed German negotiators as Nazis and blackmailed the Germans with bomb threats and mass demonstrations:

Three basic Jewish conditions became clear: acknowledgement of the responsibility of the German people for Nazi crimes, a declaration of willingness to make material reparations, and a German invitation to Israel and world Jewry to begin talks. After Adenauer's acceptance of these points in principle, the content of a declaration to be made by Adenauer was determined in lengthy discussions— once again with constant supervision from Jerusalem and the headquarters of the Jewish associations.[59]

The Jewish press also attacked the head of the German delegation at the London Debt Conference, Hermann J. Abs, and the chancellor. They accused Abs in the most aggressive fashion, including humiliating personal defamation of Abs as an alleged Nazi banker, of having attempted and of still attempting to torpedo the German-Jewish special negotiations.[60]

The significance of this constant drumbeat to the discussions also had to be seen against the backdrop of a mass rally organized in March 1952 in Tel Aviv, at which, besides a renewed rejection of any talks with Germany, an oath of revenge for the murder of six million Jews was taken.[61]

Féaux de la Croix presumed that "extremist Jewish groups" were behind a letter bomb mailed to the German delegation at the negotiations with Israel in the Hague.[62] In his eyes, the Germans had become victims of the Jews.

The man who published such things in 1985 at the federal government's behest, and who influenced the history of reparations for three decades as its *éminence grise*, had been thoroughly trained in "racial terminology."

Ernst Féaux de la Croix (1906–1995) was an economist with a doctorate in law who began working in the international law department of the Reich Ministry of Justice in 1934. There he was responsible, among other things, for the legal status of foreigners—the gradations of discrimination in the treatment of foreign peoples (*Fremdvölkischer*). During the war years, he oversaw the international legal disposition of divorces between Germans and Poles, Hungarians, or Serbs who had become stateless through annexations in eastern Europe, and was responsible for resolving the question of how to inform the Vichy regime in legally correct fashion of the deaths of French prisoners in Dachau.[63] Féaux de la Croix also belonged to the Committee on International Law of the Academy for German Law, headed by the future governor-general of occupied Poland, Hans Frank; in June 1938, he co-authored a memorandum on "Race, *Volk*, Nation, and Territory in the Formation of

Concepts and Words" for its "Subcommittee on Terminological Matters." He and his colleagues from the academy defined here who was and was not German: "Germans are all those Aryans who belong to Germandom and thus to the German national community . . . People of foreign race cannot belong to the German people, even if they possess Reich citizenship and are exclusively German-speaking." The memorandum went into detail on "mixed peoples" in the border regions of the Reich, such as Silesians, Poles, Alsatians, Czechs, Danes, and so on, as well as the German minorities in the bordering countries (such as the Sudeten Germans and Danubian Swabians): "Here the expressions 'minority' and 'minority laws' have frequently been used in the past. These expressions derived from an outmoded, alien liberal parliamentary conceptual framework in which numerical proportions were determinative. Therefore, the expression 'minority' must be replaced by 'national group.' " The territorial distribution of the German people and bordering peoples is also clarified through explanation of the concepts "country of origin," "motherland," "fatherland," and "homeland."[64] This memorandum laid the conceptual and legal groundwork for subsequent occupation and nationality policies. Féaux de la Croix simultaneously served as judge on a court in Berlin, where he ruled on the treatment under international law of ships seized or confiscated in the harbors of occupied countries. During the final months of the war, when collaborators from liberated countries sought protection and shelter in Germany, he dealt for the Reich Ministry of Justice with issues involving the resettlement of former foreign heads of state, governments, and population groups in Germany.[65] After 1945, he first worked as a tax consultant and then, in 1949, was appointed specialist in the federal Ministry of Finance for the financial settlement of war debts.[66]

In the 1950s and 1960s, it was not remarkable for a former Nazi official to be placed in charge of reparations in the federal Ministry of Finance. In those years, former Nazis could be found everywhere in the Bonn government bureaucracy. The fact that it was Ernst Féaux de la Croix who became the top German reparations official rather than, for example, Otto Küster or Franz Böhm, who were considered for a time for the position of federal commissioner for reparations, reflects this state of affairs. But when the German government allowed Féaux de la Croix to write its official history forty years after the end of the war, while censoring Küster; when it allowed a Nazi official who blustered about "world Jewry" to whitewash the history of reparations, then it was time for us to start reconstructing that history for ourselves. The government's publication of its multivolume official history of reparations provided one of the main incentives for the writing of this book.

Chapter 2

History

The Regional Forerunners of the Federal Restitution Law

Reparations is an umbrella term covering restitution of stolen property, compensation for damage to health, professional harm, and so on. The first reparations law—Law Number 59 on Restitution of Property Stolen in the Course of the "Aryanization of the Economy"—was adopted by the U.S. military government in Germany on 10 November 1947.[1] It dealt with the individual restitution of real estate, factories, and securities by German "Aryanizers" who had enriched themselves by buying up Jewish property sold cheaply under pressure. The law had been drafted by German lawyers such as Otto Küster, Adolf Arndt, and Walther Roemer,[2] but after some discussion, it was adopted as an Allied law, not a German one.[3] Küster, the Württemberg state commissioner for reparations, expressed his disappointment at a press conference on 11 November 1947, after the announcement of the law, saying: "It will require desperate efforts if the German people are nevertheless to see restitution as a necessary legal act and not simply a consequence of the lost war."[4]

Some purchasers of Jewish property had agreed on trusteeship arrangements until law once again reigned. After the war, all of them now insisted that they had been "honest Aryanizers." They joined together in a "Union for Honest Restitution," founded by the mayor of Baden-Baden, Ernst Schlapper, and inveighed against the Allied restitution law in their monthly publication, *Die Restitution*.[5] These former Aryanizers did not succeed in changing the law, but they later succeeded in obtaining restitution as victims of reparations under the provisions of the Reparations Harm Law of 12 February 1969.[6] The Union for Honest Restitution exercised a significant influence on the ranks of the CDU/CSU, the Bavarian party, and the FDP. Their accomplices in the Bundestag and the press constantly managed to throw sand in the works of later restitution legislation as well, mobilizing latent hostility to the Jews. Particularly damaging ammunition was provided by a lawyer who had placed before the authorities a theft of valuable paintings from a Hungarian castle.

Supposedly, he had bribed former SS men to swear to the theft and con-cluded a settlement of 34 million DM with the responsible ministerial officials in Bonn. The lawyer, Hans Deutsch, was convicted of fraud. Another lawyer collected pensions for thousands of "dead souls," whose existence he proved by bribing employees of Israeli residency registration offices. The Israeli police—not German officials—uncovered this fraud. Such scandals, and the contingency fees of reparations lawyers, were, as Küster remarked sarcastically, all the average German and many politi-cians knew about reparations.[7]

All in all, restitution of stolen property was accomplished to the gen-eral satisfaction of all who had been robbed.[8] By the mid 1950s, most claims had been resolved.[9] Under the Allied Restitution Law of 1947, property obtained by private purchasers (Aryanizers), as well as property still in public possession, had been returned to the former owners or financial restitution had been made. The Federal Restitution Law of 1957 governed all remaining monetary claims against the German Reich and other legal arms of the public trust.[10] Thus former property owners were the first to receive relatively generous reparations, in the form of restitu-tion; in contrast, the mass of poorer persecutees, who had lost relatives, along with their health, freedom, and economic prospects, could make no claims based on the restitution laws. They had to wait for reparations under later compensation laws, and had far greater difficulties in assert-ing their claims. This conformed to capitalist, and probably also bureau-cratic, logic, which had an easier time with land and business registries than with personal, nonmaterial values such as physical and psychologi-cal health.

On 26 April 1949, the Council of States in the U.S. Occupied Zone adopted the first standardized state restitution law.[11] In the main, it was written by the state commissioner for reparations in Württemberg, Otto Küster, and was considered a model law that set standards for future state and national laws. The ministerial section heads Arndt and Roemer also worked on the law, as they had on the Allied restitution law. The initia-tive had been Küster's; he feared that reparations would not receive pref-erential treatment, but would be dealt with in last place, after Reich debt questions and the problem of war damages.

The law defined fundamental concepts for the first time—what con-stituted persecution, who was to be considered persecuted, what harms were suffered, and so on.[12] And—a decisive step forward compared with former reparations practice—it included the "displaced persons" (DPs) from eastern Europe freed from the concentration camps, who had not lived in the old German Reich and had up to this point had no claim to reparations, and who were now waiting in DP camps to return to their former homelands or emigrate to new ones. The law also made no excep-tions based on the political views of a persecutee. Such exceptions, a violation of international law, first appeared in the Berlin Restitution Law of 1951 and the Federal Supplementary Law of 1953.

In the transitional treaty of 26 February 1952, which repealed the occupational statute and granted the Federal Republic sovereignty, the Western Allies demanded that a uniform federal arrangement for reparations be adopted as soon as possible. Part IV of this treaty provided for "(1) effective and accelerated negotiation, decision, and fulfillment of restitution claims with no discrimination against groups or classes of persecutees, (2) a procedural and evidentiary arrangement for restitution that takes account of the difficulties of proof resulting from persecution—loss of documents, disappearance of witnesses, (3) creation of opportunities for reopening claims made under older legal arrangements when newer, more favorable restitution laws are adopted, and (4) appropriation of funds to satisfy restitution claims."[13] We must measure the reparations laws and practice of the following years against these standards.

The Allies set these conditions for achieving sovereignty because in its three-year existence, the German federal government had made no moves, aside from Chancellor Konrad Adenauer's declaration of intention in the Bundestag on 27 September 1951, toward creating a uniform national restitution law. On the contrary, Finance Minister Fritz Schäffer hoped that the state laws could remain in force, and that this would be cheaper for the federal government than a national law.[14]

On the other hand, one could not accuse the federal government of a lack of initiative when, on 11 May 1951, the Bundestag adopted a law on the reintegration of former members of the Nazi party into the civil service under Article 131 of the German constitution. On the same day, it also passed a law on reparations for members of the civil service (abbreviated as BWGöD),[15] under which bureaucrats dismissed under Hitler received restitution through a uniform national law. This restitution was far more generous than that for nonofficials under the later Federal Restitution Law (for example, under BWGöD, there are no deadlines). At the same time, former Nazis returned to their positions or had their pension entitlements restored. This regulation under Article 131 of the constitution sanctioned what was anyway already in full swing following the fiasco of denazification; in 1949, of 49,121 civil servants in Bavaria, 14,443 were former Nazi party members, while only 265 former political persecutees and 92 victims of racial persecution had been brought into the civil service since 1945.[16] Following the establishment of the Federal Republic, more former "party comrades" worked in the Foreign Office than had under Joachim von Ribbentrop, Hitler's foreign minister.[17] In the Berlin health care system, all positions were closed to civil service–level nursing personnel in city clinics until all the "131s"—the former Nazis being reintegrated—had jobs. On the other hand, the "unimplicated," that is, opponents of Nazism who had been persecuted, were at a disadvantage in employment.[18] Franz Böhm later admitted that it was embarrassing that the "131" Law had been adopted before the restitution law.[19]

The Luxembourg Treaty with Israel and the Claims Conference

A half million Jews fled to Palestine during the period of the Third Reich and after the liberation of the concentration camps. The state of Israel, established in 1948, demanded payments from West and East Germany in order to enable these refugees to build new lives. East Germany refused to pay. In November 1949, Adenauer offered Israel goods worth 10 million DM to help build up the country, an offer the Israelis indignantly rejected as a pittance. In a declaration of principles in December 1949, the World Jewish Congress demanded German acknowledgement of moral and political responsibility for Nazi crimes, material reparations, efforts to combat anti-Semitism, reeducation of German young people, and investigation of Nazi tendencies in the West German government apparatus.[20] After assumption of unofficial contacts between the Federal Republic and Israel through mediators, Chancellor Adenauer declared at a solemn session of the Bundestag on 27 September 1951:

The Federal Government considers it urgently necessary that the churches and the state educational authorities do everything in their purview to ensure that the spirit of human and religious tolerance find not merely formal acceptance among the entire German people, especially German youth, but that it become reality in their psychological attitude and practical actions . . . So that this educational work is not disrupted and domestic peace in the Federal Republic is guaranteed, the Federal Government has resolved to combat, through relentless criminal prosecution, those circles that continue to incite anti-Semitism . . . The Federal Government, and with it the great majority of the German people, are aware of the immeasurable suffering inflicted upon the Jews in Germany and in the occupied regions during the Nazi period. The overwhelming majority of the German people abhorred the crimes committed against the Jews and were not involved in them. There were many among the German people during the Nazi period who, despite danger to themselves, showed a willingness to help their Jewish fellow citizens for religious reasons, reasons of conscience, [or] shame at the dishonor to the German name. However, unspeakable crimes were committed in the name of the German people, which create a duty of moral and material reparations . . . Initial steps have been taken in this area. But much remains to be done. The Federal Government will ensure rapid adoption of reparations legislation and its just implementation . . . With regard to the extent of reparations . . . we must take account of the limits set on German ability to pay by the bitter necessity of caring for countless victims of war and the refugees and expellees [from eastern Europe].[21]

The content of this declaration had been the subject of laborious wrangling at the secret negotiations. The Israelis had demanded a passage on German collective guilt, while the German government wanted future reparations payments to be limited by the planned rearmament. Both demands were ultimately abandoned.[22]

Two months after this declaration by Adenauer, another secret meeting took place in London between Adenauer and Nahum Goldmann, president of the World Jewish Congress and the Claims Conference. At this meeting, Adenauer agreed to make the 4 billion DM demanded by Israel the basis for the talks.[23] Official negotiations between Israel, the Claims Conference, and the Federal Republic of Germany began on 21 March 1952 in the Hague, at the former headquarters of the Reich commissioner in the occupied Netherlands, Arthur Seyss-Inquart. The Israeli delegation was headed by Dr. Giora Josephsthal and Dr. Felix Shinnar; the Claims Conference delegation was led by Moses A. Leavitt, vice president of the American Joint Distribution Committee. The German delegation was headed by Franz Böhm and his deputy, Otto Küster. Shinnar and Küster discovered during the talks that they had gone to the same school in Stuttgart; Josephsthal had been born in Nuremberg. The Germans had purposely chosen two people who, as a result of their clearly antifascist views and involvement in reparations, possessed the necessary moral integrity and respect abroad.[24] Küster's appointment was the result of a suggestion by Goldmann.[25] Adenauer had first sounded out the Israelis on how they felt about this appointment. They let him know that they were not prepared to accept anyone but the persons named, which gave Küster and Böhm a relatively strong position behind the scenes in Bonn.[26]

Israel demanded payment of 4.2 billion DM as reconstruction assistance from the Federal Republic; the Claims Conference demanded 500 million DM for stolen Jewish property for which no surviving heirs could be found in the former occupied countries and a binding promise that a unified federal restitution law along the lines of the law in the U.S. zone, going beyond the state laws, would be adopted in the near future. However, it quickly became clear that the German delegation had been sent to the Hague without a concrete offer. Böhm and Küster were expected to start with mere talk. Hermann Josef Abs, Adenauer's financial advisor, and Finance Minister Schäffer were not prepared to make any concrete promises before the amount and payment method of Germany's total debt to the former enemy powers had been negotiated at the upcoming London Debt Conference. Abs wanted to deal with the payments to Israel as part of a comprehensive agreement to be reached in London, and he was therefore fundamentally opposed to any separate negotiations with Israel. He threatened Adenauer with his resignation as leader of the German delegation to the London Debt Conference should such separate negotiations take place, saying that "restoration of creditworthiness abroad" would be endangered if Germany paid the amount demanded by Israel and thus fell behind in payment of its remaining postwar debts.[27]

At this threat, Adenauer assured Abs that the German delegation in the Hague would in no way obligate itself or make any promises, and that the Israeli claims would only be dealt with in the context of an overall settlement of foreign debts.[28] Schäffer emphasized that he was fundamentally opposed to the negotiations in the Hague, because it would be impossible to "fulfill the highly charged expectations of world Jewry."[29] These delaying tactics on the part of Abs, Schäffer, and Adenauer were also based on the upcoming conclusion of a transitional treaty with the Allies, which already contained the Federal Republic's agreement to reparations. The country's duty to the "community of free peoples" appeared to have been fulfilled, and special obligations to Israel were no longer as urgent as they had seemed. Israel, calculated Abs, would be satisfied with far smaller payments because of its precarious financial situation.[30] Adenauer and Abs had in mind, for example, the donation of a hospital.

In a dramatic cabinet meeting, also attended by Abs, on 5 April 1952, Böhm and Küster attempted to convince Adenauer that it was at least necessary to acknowledge to the Israelis that they had incurred integration costs of 3 billion DM. Böhm had calculated these with the help of experts at the Ministry for Expellees, based on a sum of $3,000 per refugee. On the meeting, Küster noted in his diary: "It began slack and bad; Adenauer interrupts Böhm, we can spare ourselves the figures, the Jews cheat us after all; Abs does not let me finish, I must, encouraged by [Undersecretary Walter] Hallstein, literally demand to be heard out." Abs felt it was a great mistake in negotiating tactics to name any amount at all to the Israelis, and he again threatened to resign immediately as head of the London delegation. Adenauer ultimately agreed to Böhm's and Küster's proposal. This was preceded by the intervention of the U.S. high commissioner, John McCloy, who had indicated to the chancellor the day before that he should see to a satisfactory completion of negotiations.[31]

On 7 April, Böhm and Küster told the Israelis that they would recommend that the German government pay 3 billion DM, but could make no firm promises as yet. On the same day, a report by an assistant secretary in the chancellor's office, Herbert Blankenhorn, appeared in the newspaper *Frankfurter Allgemeine Zeitung* claiming that Böhm and Küster had exceeded their authority with this declaration. The Israelis became suspicious at this German double game and demanded in an ultimatum that the precise amount of the promised payments, payment dates, and modalities be provided. At this ultimatum, Abs, together with officials of the Finance Ministry and in coordination with Adenauer, dictated a new statement to the German delegation, saying the desired information could not be provided until a month after the London Debt Conference on 19 May 1952. At that, Israel indignantly broke off negotiations on 9 April 1952.[32] The foreign press recalled that Abs had been a Nazi banker.[33]

With the breakdown of talks, the federal government found itself in an embarrassing position. Adenauer had placed great hopes in the talks with Israel. Even if sacrifices had to be made, they would "very soon be very worthwhile from a political perspective," because of the "powerful Jewish influence in the United States" and the upcoming presidential elections there.[34] In the Bonn ministries, efforts were made to repair the damage. An interministerial working group was to determine further strategy. However, Finance Minister Schäffer intervened with his colleagues, asking them not to involve any gentlemen who aimed to "please."[35]

On 30 April 1952, Franz Böhm repeated to the press his delegation's view that a payment of 3 billion DM to Israel was reasonable. Schäffer thereupon summoned Böhm and Küster on 7 May and informed them that they were not authorized to make such an offer. He said such a sum could be raised neither from the federal budget nor through internal German capital markets. Böhm and Küster responded that they considered themselves covered by Adenauer's and the Foreign Office's declaration of principles, and that the German delegation in the Hague had to take a high moral stand and could not be responsible for a solution that was too limited and ungenerous. However, Schäffer demanded that they discuss each step with him beforehand and inform the other ministries of his reservations. At this point, Küster blew up; he said he was not interested in the views of a minister, and that he certainly was not going to play Schäffer's messenger to the other ministries. A bitter exchange ensued, at the end of which Schäffer threw Küster out of his office. In the minutes of this discussion, Schäffer's assistant added that Minister Schäffer had made not one statement that "could in any way be judged as expressing dislike of Jewry, that is, as an anti-Semitic statement."[36] Küster resigned as deputy head of the delegation.

The incident in Schäffer's office was not, however, the climax of the power struggle in Bonn. With the breakdown of negotiations, Abs appeared to have achieved his goal of waiting for the outcome of the London Debt Conference. Talks resumed there on 19 May 1952, and the same day Abs offered the Israeli delegation a preliminary payment of 100 million DM a year for the next four years and later determination of the final amount. The Israelis took this suggestion as an insult. Goldmann accused Abs of an "inadequate style of horse-trading."[37]

The backdrop to the amount proposed by Abs, in consultation with Adenauer and behind Böhm's back, was the fact that Israel was experiencing great financial pressure and England had refused it a loan. Now that the Israelis were up to their necks in difficulties, Abs believed, they would be satisfied with a pittance. Böhm had found out about Abs' new plans by 15 May 1952. At this point he was no longer willing to participate in this undignified game. After consulting with Küster, he offered

Adenauer his resignation on 17 May.[38] On 20 May 1952, Küster made his resignation public, explaining in a radio address:

Minister Schäffer has . . . resorted to the crudest forms to make it clear to me that I am, in his eyes, no more than an overly tiresome supplicant . . . I have come to the conclusion that the German people must know the spirit with which the decision was made in Bonn to leave the injustice of the Hitler period unexpiated and pass it on to our sons and grandsons . . . We were always told: Whatever we transfer, we can raise it. Raise means raise in a budgetary sense, in the sense that the necessary revenue is available in the budget of the Federal Republic. In the Hague we were almost embarrassed that the transfer issue [by this, Küster meant the form in which German payments to Israel would be made—in hard currency or in the form of goods] had from the beginning reduced the annual German payment so far that it was impossible to speak of a serious effort by the German people. But now, to our consternation, it appears that the critical factors in the federal government were not prepared, and had at no time been prepared, to structure their financial policies in such a way that even the most modest annual sum would remain in the budget for reparations. Didn't they have at least 100 million in a yearly budget of 20 billion? No. Impossible. A tax increase for this reason would be politically intolerable. The same for a domestic German bond issue. If the Jews wanted anything, they would have to finance it themselves through foreign credit. With this they wanted to send us back to the Hague . . . I appeal to the German people, I appeal above all to the young, guiltless heirs of Hitler's curse, to say no, to cry out that the way things are happening in Bonn at this time is not the way they wish to be governed in this truly fundamental question of our national honor.[39]

In a letter to a staff member of the Berlin reparations office, Helene Jacobs, Küster explained more precisely what he meant by the "spirit in Bonn." He said the spirit he had encountered in Bonn was essentially an extension of the spirit that had made possible the evils of the Nazi regime—one that went far beyond "mere spiritual barrenness . . . into positive evil." In his view, in the rare cases in which this spirit—which otherwise always evaded capture—could be caught, it was necessary to pin it down as firmly as possible. Despite everything that had happened, he said, an endless amount could be achieved if one could discern even the faintest sign of goodwill or desire for justice among the Germans. This basic prerequisite was lacking as long as people like Schäffer could speak for Germany in its capacity as reparations debtor. Coming from him, said Küster, the suggestion that the Jews finance their reparations themselves had been an absurd provocation.[40]

Helene Jacobs (1906–1993) began working in 1924 in the office of a Jewish patent lawyer in Berlin; after qualifying for university entry at the gifted level, she studied mathematics and natural sciences in 1930–31. In 1933, she was forced to break off her studies, as she refused to conform to Nazi rules. She helped out in her lawyer's office until it was closed and he was forced to emigrate in 1938. Jacobs helped persecuted Jews go into hiding by procuring documents, shelter, and food.

As a result, in 1943 she was arrested by the Gestapo and sentenced to two and a half years' imprisonment. From 1949 to 1952, she worked in the Berlin reparations offices, and eventually, until 1971, in the Berlin Restitution Office. In public speeches, she fought for generous, nonbureaucratic reparations. In 1963, because of her vehement concern for the interests of the applicants, the heads of the office transferred her—ostensibly due to "errors"—to the less significant department for hardship cases.[41]

Years later, Küster recalled: "During a break in the talks, Böhm said to me, you can always tell an anti-Semite because they begin by saying, 'I'm not an anti-Semite.' At the meeting that followed, Schäffer really did begin speaking with the sentence, 'I'm not an anti-Semite.' "[42] In a justificatory response to Küster's radio address, Schäffer said on the radio on 23 May 1952 that he had received thousands of letters that, although not at all anti-Semitic in content, complained about the tax burden for the German people because of Israel's demands, but "any respectable man who thinks with his heart and all his faith of the need and the burdens on the German people, and who is the spokesman and representative of the German people in its need and its burdens in the face of the entire world, must, if he acts uprightly and honestly, take into account that he will be stamped an anti-Semite in these political jungle wars." To Küster's demand for an "honorable German expiatory payment to the 'House of the Murdered,'" instead of the Federal Republic's haggling and delaying tactics, Schäffer replied, "It has never happened in diplomatic history that a member of a delegation believes he does not need to receive the instructions of the government that sent him, but can instead instruct the government. It has never happened that a member of a delegation believes he is not the spokesman of the homeland that sent him but the spokesman for the treaty partner."[43]

Küster's resignation was viewed in the foreign press and among persecutees with alarm, and he was greatly respected for his unyielding attitude. Schäffer, on the other hand, had mobilized German national sensitivities with his nationalist overtones. The national soul was relieved that someone had finally told off the Jews. In a typical letter, a jewelry dealer from Schwäbisch-Gmünd wrote to thank Schäffer for his "valiant answer to Herr Küster," saying that the Jews themselves were responsible for the harsh fate they had suffered during the Hitler period, for the "world Jewish press" had spread "propaganda against Germany and orgies of hate against the German people" even before the war. Jewish influence on radio had brought discrimination against the German people "to the boiling point," and was thus responsible for the fate of the ten million ethnic German expellees from the east. In their name, he protested against any payment obligation to Israel.[44] Another letter writer, a woman, asked the minister finally "to speak plainly on the Jewish question"; people were waiting silently for a man like him, who could sweep away "the cobwebs of the postwar period with a firm hand."[45]

Meanwhile, however, Shäffer had long since begun preparing a different attack on the negotiations with Israel. In a decree of 25 March 1952, he instructed the tax authorities to estimate the "currency violations committed by Jews" since 1945 and the "reduced revenue from customs and consumer taxes" caused by Jews since the currency reform. On 12 May 1952, using figures from the tax authorities, a Dr. Gurski of Section V of the ministry wrote up a confidential report in which he determined that "the Jews . . . have caused total damages of 10 billion DM."[46] With this survey, Schäffer hoped to prove that "the Jews" had already underhandedly obtained their own reconstruction assistance in their shady dealings in the DP camps in Germany. His own staff members, among them *Ministerialrat* Friedrich Kuschnitzky of the reparations office, had to reason with him and remind him, in an internal memo, that this "official measure directed against Jews" could cause enormous political damage.[47] The results of the survey were never used or publicly released. Making visible efforts to free himself from the taint of anti-Semitism after this unsuccessful approach, Schäffer asked the Foreign Office to send Kuschnitzky to the Hague talks as a representative of the Finance Ministry, expressly emphasizing that he was a "full Jew" (*Volljude*)—a Nazi phrase familiar from the Nuremberg racial laws.[48]

Schäffer and Abs were unable to tip the scales in their favor. Adenauer was at a complete loss once Böhm, too, had resigned. His ministers, on the other hand, were indignant at Böhm's attitude that he was convinced of the collective guilt of the German people. Transport Minister Seebohm accused Böhm of behaving irresponsibly and contrary to his duties, and emphasized that reparations obligations to the Jews ended when they endangered the task of "securing our people, and thus Europe, against a further advance of Bolshevik-Asiatic tendencies." On 19 May 1952, while Abs was making his 100 million DM offer to the Israelis in London, Böhm succeeded—in a passionate private conversation—in persuading Adenauer to abandon Abs' views. Arguing that agreement with Israel had overwhelming significance for Germany's relationship with the rest of the Western world, especially the United States, and that failure of the talks would have very serious political and economic repercussions, Adenauer was also able to overcome Schäffer's opposition in the cabinet in a meeting on 17 June 1952.[49]

Böhm thereupon contacted Goldmann, who stated his willingness to resume negotiations based on the amount of 3 billion DM offered by Böhm. The situation had been saved.[50] The negotiations continued from 28 June 1952 until the end of August, with the details worked out in a treaty. However, controversies arose again and again within the German delegation. Schäffer attempted until the very last minute to torpedo the agreements from behind the scenes. On 4 July, his agent in the German delegation at the Hague, Assistant Secretary Bernhard Wolff, told him that the delegation leaders were "rarely able to agree on a decisive 'no' to the wishes of the opposing side."[51]

Bernhard Wolff (1886–1970), a lawyer, was an officer in World War I and an official in the Prussian Ministry of the Interior from 1921 to 1933, where he ultimately rose to the rank of section chief; there, in the office of the Aliens' Police, he was responsible for the eastern European Jews who had immigrated to Germany, and is said to have behaved fairly and humanely toward them. In 1933, he was transferred by the Nazis, becoming a judge on the Prussian supreme administrative court. From 1941 to 1945, he was *Ministerialrat* in the Reich Ministry of Justice and simultaneously a judge on a court in Berlin, and shortly before the end of the war, he became head of the Office of International Law. In 1946, he became general officer in the joint German Finance Council. From 1947 to 1949, he was head of the legal department of the finance administration of Bizonia (the combined English and U.S. zones). From 1949 to 1953, he was an assistant secretary in the federal Finance Ministry and head of the department responsible for reparations, Department VI. His successors were Assistant Secretary von Spindler and finally Assistant Secretary Ernst Féaux de la Croix, with whom Wolff had already worked in the Reich Ministry of Justice.[52]

Following a personal conversation with Goldmann on 10 July 1952, Schäffer told the president of the directorate of the Bank Deutscher Länder that the Israelis would make more and more demands the more they sensed the Germans giving in. He was referring to a value-securing clause the Israeli representatives wanted included as insurance against a possible decline in the value of the German currency.[53] In a cabinet meeting on 11 July, Schäffer rebuked Böhm for being too soft.[54] Assistant Secretary Wolff let Böhm know that the Finance Ministry rejected almost all demands going beyond the original German offer, such as the value-securing clause, reduction in the payment period, and the Claims Conference's global demand for 500 million DM.[55] He said the federal government could risk a separate breakdown in the negotiations with the Claims Conference because it had already made a good impression upon world public opinion with its offer of 3 billion DM to Israel. There was no need to worry about political or economic problems for the Federal Republic or boycotts on the part of "Jewish financial circles" in the United States.[56] Conversely, the Foreign Office, represented by Undersecretary Hallstein, believed payment of 500 million to the Claims Conference was necessary "for the psychological resolution of the problem in the eyes of the world." Adenauer agreed, pointing out "the great economic power of Jewry in the world."[57]

As it became increasingly clear that Schäffer would be unable to get his reservations accepted, he approached Adenauer personally. In addition, he attempted, together with the parliamentary deputy Franz-Josef Strauss, to mobilize the CSU deputies in the Bundestag against the treaty with Israel. But Adenauer intervened, writing the minister, who was visiting a health spa at the time, that apparently his "nerves were not yet in the best shape."[58]

Finally, on 10 November 1952, Adenauer, Goldmann, and the Israeli foreign minister, Moshe Sharett, signed an agreement in Luxembourg on payment of 3.5 billion DM (3 billion to Israel and 500 million to the Claims Conference). At the same time, the so-called Hague Protocol was adopted, requiring the Federal Republic significantly to expand the existing state-by-state restitution rules in a federal restitution law to be adopted later.

Influential circles that disliked the Luxembourg Treaty attempted to prevent its ratification in the Bundestag by inciting anti-Semitism and defensiveness in the German population. Among the initiators of this campaign were the former "Aryanizers" of the "Union for Honest Restitution."[59] They were supported by sectors of the German business community greatly interested in Arab oil and expanding Arab markets. So as not to appear openly as opponents of the treaty and expose themselves to accusations of anti-Semitism, they at first launched their campaign with the help of the Arab countries. These had so far neither protested the negotiations in the Hague nor raised any objections to British and U.S. shipments to Israel, which had been going on for years.[60] But they had no interest in seeing Israel strengthened. After the treaty was signed, they complained to German representatives abroad, and on 13 September 1952, the Council of the Arab League decided to break off all economic relations with the Federal Republic.[61] According to the newspaper *Welt am Sonntag*, this occurred with the connivance of German experts who had fled to the Arab countries, especially Egypt, after the war because of their Nazi pasts, and who enjoyed great influence there. Specifically named were former SS Brigade Leader Oskar Dirlewanger, SS *Obersturmbannführer* Adolf Eichmann, SS *Standartenführer* Eugen Dollmann, the former German ambassador in Madrid, and Eberhard von Stohrer, formerly head of the overseas arm of the Nazi party in Cairo.[62]

Finally, on 15 December 1952, during a private trip to Damascus, Hjalmar Schacht, the former Reich economics minister and Reichsbank president, released a press statement in which he claimed that Germany was being crippled by the foreign occupation and that the Federal Republic had not been free in its decision to sign the reparations treaty with Israel. In answer, Franz Böhm wrote in the *Frankfurter Rundschau* that the truth could be determined if one assumed that Schacht had made his statement in the name of a functioning "shadow government" that was attempting to pursue a foreign policy diametrically opposed to the official one and was convinced it held actual, if not legitimate, power. In the name of an imaginary supporting segment of the German public, Schacht had encouraged the Arab boycott and, between the lines, promised non-ratification of the reparations treaty with Israel as a foreign policy program. Schacht's Damascus declaration was the first foreign policy test of strength by the old and new German adversaries of the Federal Republic, Böhm continued.

Once already—it is just now the twentieth anniversary—Herr Schacht let loose the same dark forces on his Fatherland. Back then, he offered the future Führer of the Third Reich the alliance of the Harzburg Front. Back then, the site of Schacht's announcement was the Kaiserhof Hotel in Berlin, headquarters of Adolf Hitler, who hankered after the office of chancellor. Anyone who has not yet forgotten everything will still recall that it was possible to admire Herr Schacht on the weekly news in December 1932 when, leaving the Kaiserhof with his long arm raised in the Hitler salute, he accepted the ovation of the masses assembled in the square. Back then, the slogan was "Germany awake! Down with the Jews!"[63]

A month after Schacht's statement, the CSU Bundestag deputy Franz-Josef Strauss wrote in *Chemische Industrie*, a publication of the German chemical industry:

In preparing the Israel treaty, the chancellor was badly advised by his diplomatic associates and placed in an extraordinarily difficult position . . . We must be aware that we obtain important imports of oil and cotton from the Arab states. Given the rapid economic developments in these countries, we can only guess at the significance they will quickly gain for our exports, especially for construction, steel, the engineering and electronics industries, the chemical and optical industries . . . It is no exaggeration to assume that in the course of the next five years, in the Arab countries alone, we would develop export opportunities of from 5 to 6 billion DM, which are now at stake.[64]

On the other side, prominent personalities from the Catholic and Protestant churches and the universities spoke in favor of ratification of the treaty, among them the publisher of the "Freiburg Circular Letter to Promote Friendship Between the Old and New People of God," Dr. Gertrud Luckner, a devout Catholic who had helped Berlin Jews and was imprisoned in Ravensbrück concentration camp; she was joined by Eugen Kogon, Helmut Gollwitzer of the University of Bonn, Deacon Herrmann Maas of Heidelberg, Professor Franz Büchner of Freiburg University, and many others.[65] Prominent Social Democrats such as Carlo Schmid and Adolf Arndt spoke in a similar vein. On 18 March 1953, the treaty was put to a vote in the Bundestag. All the SPD deputies voted to ratify the treaty. Eighty-six deputies of the governing coalition, consisting of the CDU/CSU, FDP, and DP, voted against it or abstained. The thirteen KPD deputies who were present also voted against it. Their spokesman explained that shipments of goods and payments to Israel were primarily aimed at building Israel into a military base for the United States in the Middle East, that the German and U.S. arms industries would be the main beneficiaries, and that individual persecutees would never see a penny of the 3 billion DM.[66] Adenauer was thus only able to get the treaty passed with the votes of the opposition, against significant resistance in his own coalition.

The Luxembourg Treaty must first of all be attributed to consistent and—given what they had to put up with—patient negotiating by the Jewish representatives. In addition, it was also the result of Küster's and Böhm's decency and Adenauer's tactical ability; he did a masterly job of neutralizing opposition to the treaty. Apparently, one element of Adenauer's policy was to bind a largely Nazified, completely undemocratic nation to his policies through the use of representatives like Schäffer. Public opinion could revel in Schäffer's "resolute" attitude toward the Jews and give its anti-Semitism free rein without creating an obstacle to Adenauer's policy of opening to the West and introducing American-style democracy.

The government's official report on the Hague negotiations, included in *Der Werdegang der Entschädigungsrechts*, the 1985 "Blue Book" volume edited by Féaux de la Croix and Helmut Rumpf, presented the situation as though the Germans had been coerced and tricked by the Israelis and the Claims Conference. In addition to bombings by supposed extremist Jewish groups and mass demonstrations in Tel Aviv, Féaux de la Croix claimed, it was above all the "clever interplay of all forces on the Jewish side" that, by soberly exploiting "all signs of division on the German side" had decided the outcome of the talks in their favor. "The direction and division of labor among the various Jewish institutions and the personalities working in them functioned with astonishing precision. Coordination of all measures and steps simply went off without a hitch." The coordinator, Nahum Goldmann, "one of the greatest figures in world Jewry," was responsible for the "exhaustion of German strength." Especially in the Hague Protocol No. 1, which established rules for future restitution laws, the German delegation had unfortunately "accepted a strategy that opened the door to unlimited expansion." Féaux de la Croix thought that the federal government should have employed more clever tactics; for example, Adenauer should have "signaled" to the Western powers that the Federal Republic had "alternatives other than unconditional submission to the West," since the Western powers had at the time been dependent on West Germany's future contribution to NATO. By playing this card, he believed, the Germans could have resisted the demands of Israel and the Claims Conference, which might have brought protests from the "entire Jewish world," but would not have prevented conclusion of the transitional treaty with the Allies that gave the federal government its sovereignty.[67]

The Auerbach Affair

On 27 January 1951, in a surprise raid applauded by the right-wing press, the Bavarian police occupied the headquarters of the state reparations office in Munich and began to examine some 175,000 reparations files for forgery and fraud. The search had been authorized by the Bavarian minister of justice, Dr. Josef Müller, a sworn enemy of the head of the reparations office, Philipp Auerbach. Auerbach was Jewish and a survivor of Auschwitz.

The police took over Auerbach's offices for ten weeks and behaved in a manner that led even the official in charge of them, Finance Minister Rudolf Zorn, to protest. Processing of reparations applications slowed almost to a standstill and payments to victims had to be suspended. Justice Minister Müller informed the press that evidence had been found of payments of 1.3 million DM in reparations money on the basis of counterfeit documents, and an investigation was begun against Auerbach, who was taken into custody on grounds of "danger of flight and suppression of evidence" and "suspicion of embezzlement" at the beginning of March. Shortly thereafter, however, the chief prosecutor in charge of the investigation, a Dr. Hartmann, was forced to admit that there was "no reason to suspect criminal involvement by Auerbach" or "embezzlement in the sense of misappropriation of government funds." Nevertheless, Auerbach remained in custody.

What had led up to this? The Bavarian reparations office processed applications from more than a hundred thousand so-called displaced persons from the large Bavarian DP camps. Refugee assistance organizations supplied the DPs with goods, particularly cigarettes and coffee, which some sold on the black market, quickly becoming wealthy on the proceeds. Auerbach feared that this might spark popular anti-Semitism and was therefore interested in having them emigrate as soon as possible.[68] During his four years in office, he succeeded in assisting 80,000 out of a potential 126,000 DPs to emigrate. However, to do so he had to overcome considerable difficulties; at the time, the Bavarian state did not pay the full amount for reparations claims of more than $600. It paid a first installment in cash and a second in the form of compensation checks (Feststellungsbescheiden) not redeemable until 1 January 1954. But in order to emigrate, the DPs urgently needed money, so they sold these promissory notes to a consortium of respected Bavarian banks at from 30 to 50 percent of their face value. Other former camp inmates generally mediated such sales, earning a commission of from 1 to 3 percent.

Over the years, the banks had bought up promissory notes worth roughly $2 million. In 1950, the Bavarian state prime minister, Hans Ehard, granted them express permission to continue these semi-legal financial transactions. There was apparently a secret agreement between the banks and the Finance Ministry under which the ministry was willing to redeem the checks in 1952 at from 60 to 65 percent of their nominal value. For the banks, this meant a profit of 50 percent or more. Auerbach was aware of this deal, which was common knowledge among the authorities, and took no action against it, as he saw no other chance to help emigrating DPs acquire funds.

However, in December 1950, Auerbach lodged a complaint about the fact that in some Bavarian communities, residency permits were being counterfeited for money—permits that affirmed that the bearer had lived there on 1 January 1947. Without such a permit, a DP could not receive reparations under the law. In the process, it was found that even a police station in Munich had been counterfeiting residency permits. Officials in other mayoral and state government offices who were interested in getting rid of the DPs rapidly through emigration had also been involved in the business.

But Auerbach's complaint was unsuccessful; instead, Justice Minister Müller attempted to pin the counterfeits on Auerbach. However, the search of Auerbach's offices turned up no incriminating material. On the contrary, the coup appeared to backfire against its initiators, and Auerbach threatened to tell what he knew about Müller's and his assistants' involvement in the scheme with the DPs. At that, at Müller's behest, the aforementioned investigation into fraud was initiated; the legal press office at the Munich State Supreme Court announced that Auerbach had kept state reparations funds for 111 nonexistent DPs. It turned out that the 111 DPs actually existed, but were the responsibility of the Baden-Württemberg reparations office; that office's head, Otto Küster, promptly confirmed that he had properly transferred money to the Bavarian office for payment to the DPs. On 4 April 1951, Baden-Württemberg's state prime minister, Reinhold Maier, also officially refuted the accusations against Auerbach before the state parliament.

Shortly thereafter, yet another charge dissolved into thin air. Because the state of Bavaria had never supplied the reparations office with a sufficient budget, Auerbach had acquired the funds necessary for reparations payments by means of unusual transactions—for example, state-guaranteed loans secured by Nazi property. At the end of April 1951, an undersecretary in the Bavarian Finance Ministry, Richard Ringelmann, announced that an extraordinary audit by the Main Bavarian Accounting Office of the period from autumn 1945 to June 1950 had revealed that Auerbach had behaved "entirely correctly" in the provision of loans. The prosecutor investigated for seventeen months.

Auerbach had become ill in jail, but an application for his release on medical grounds was rejected at the behest of Justice Minister Müller. Chief district court judge Josef Mulzer, a former member of Müller's law office who had been a member of the Supreme Military Court under the

Third Reich, was extraordinarily appointed by the justice minister to preside over the four-month main trial before the Munich trial court. One of the assessors at the trial was a former SA member, and the prosecutor was a former member of the Nazi party. A psychiatric expert—also a former Nazi party member—appointed by the court to examine Auerbach's mental state described him as a "pseudological psychopath and fantasizer," "egocentric, undisciplined, still in puberty, impulsive, self-pitying, hysterical," but not as possessing diminished capacity. Nothing remained of the indictment except that Auerbach had wrongly claimed the title of doctor and had acquired the funds for reparations payments in marginally legal, brilliant and unorthodox ways. It could not be proved that he had personally enriched himself. Although the indictment had essentially fallen apart, Auerbach was sentenced to two and a half years' imprisonment and a fine.

Auerbach took his own life in prison. In a farewell letter on 14 August 1952, he wrote: "They have done me an injustice. I never personally enriched myself and can no longer bear this degrading judgment." During the trial, Justice Minister Müller was forced to resign when his involvement in the "Auerbach Affair" came to light. In addition, it became known that he had belonged to the SD [Sicherheitsdienst; the security arm of the SS, commanded until 1942 by Reinhard Heydrich] in the Third Reich.

The majority of representatives of the Jewish communities in Germany had distanced themselves from Auerbach before his arrest, inasmuch as they apparently feared he might harm the image of the persecutees if he remained in office. However, the Axis Victims' League, an interest group for persecutees founded in 1943 by American Jews, had backed him and formed a Committee for Fair Play for Auerbach.[69] All eyewitnesses confirm that Auerbach was not an easy person. He had weaknesses—the "manners of a prima donna," a "preference for rank and title," and a "yearning for publicity."

The "Auerbach Affair" made waves. Germans saw it as confirmation of their diffuse sense that the Jews were doing crooked business with reparations; they felt it showed what could happen if persecutees were allowed to administer their own compensation. Some called for excluding the DPs from reparations altogether.

During his term in office as an administrative official in the British Zone of Occupation, Auerbach had made public the Nazi past of the future federal minister of the interior, Robert Lehr. This had cost Auerbach his position. In several radio addresses, he had called for the death penalty for Oswald Pohl, Otto Ohlendorf, and other war criminals convicted at Nuremberg in 1948 (Ohlendorf, a high-level Gestapo leader, was hanged in 1951). He called them men "smeared to the elbows with blood." As head of the Munich office, he attempted many times to initiate a unified national compensation law. The fact that the bosses of the Bavarian justice system succeeded in pinning the label of swindler on him would have serious consequences for reparations. Under Auerbach's successor, Dr. Franz Zdralek, the police maintained an investigative office with the right to inspect all the office's files.[70] Using the Auerbach case as justification, inspection offices were set up in numerous other state reparations offices to inspect the correctness of each staffer's decisions.[71]

Küster's Neutralization

In the opinion of the official government chronicle on German reparations, the "Blue Books," it was not a "ministerial official in Bonn [who] was the primary exponent of German reparations work, but rather Baden-Württemberg's commissioner of reparations, Otto Küster."[72] Following Auerbach's arrest, Küster took on the leadership of the conference of top reparations offices. He hoped to turn it into a conference like the Permanent Conference of Ministers of Education, which had become established in the field of education and culture.

Yet Küster was not a centralist. Originally, he had argued against a federal reparations law, instead advocating expansion and improvement of state laws on the basis of the relatively generous law in the U.S. zone of occupation, which he himself had drafted. When it became clear following the Hague negotiations that a unified federal law was in the offing, he took the initiative there as well. While the federal Finance Ministry at first did nothing, in early April 1952, Küster brought the first draft of a federal restitution law before the Bundesrat's Special Committee on Reparations. According to the government chronicle, he completed this work in "an astonishingly short time, with outstanding knowledge and masterly formulation."[73]

Féaux de la Croix's description barely conceals the opposition that rained down on Küster: "The federal Ministry of Finance began to realize from around the beginning of 1952 that it was not possible to continue the attitude prevailing thus far of federal government inactivity in the area of reparations . . . The pressure of world public opinion, inspired and at the same time directed by the large, mainly Jewish organizations of persecutees, became greater and greater."[74]

In late autumn 1952, a second, rewritten draft by Küster was finally available, the so-called "November version" of the Bundesrat bill, which was to be adopted by a plenary session of the Bundesrat on 19 December 1952. The federal Finance Ministry claimed that this draft did not conform to the obligations taken on in the transitional treaty and the Hague Protocols. The only truth in this was the fact that the Bundesrat bill did not include the DPs in the Federal Restitution Law, as provided for in the Hague Protocol, but instead would have adopted a new law for them. On essential points, however, the Bundesrat bill actually went beyond the standards agreed upon in the international agreement. Thus, for example, it provided for restitution even for victims of SA and Nazi terror during the preliminary phase of the Third Reich, between 14 September 1930 and 29 January 1933. Furthermore, the maximum amount of reparations for harm to professional advancement (harm to livelihood) would be raised from 25,000 DM, damage to livelihood suffered under private employment contracts would be compensated, and residency requirements and deadlines would be eased, which would considerably increase the number of people eligible for restitution.[75] (For average annual wages and salaries in the FRG, 1950–82, see Appendix B, table 9.)

The federal Ministry of Finance purposely prepared its own bill, with which it hoped to topple Küster's Bundesrat draft. Schäffer hurriedly gathered his officials and, at the end of November 1952, sent them, under the leadership of Assistant Secretary Wolff, to a conference in Siegburg at which they cobbled together a proposal from Küster's bill, the restitution law in the U.S. zone, a draft by the SPD deputies in parliament, the provisions of the Hague Protocol, and those of the transitional treaty. Playing on the idea that this draft was a supplement to the law in the U.S. zone, they called it the "Federal Supplementary Law."[76]

At the crucial Bundesrat session of 19 December 1952 at which Küster's bill was to be adopted, the Finance Ministry distributed figures showing that this bill would cost taxpayers half a million DM more than the draft being written by the Ministry of Finance.[77] With this preparation, Schäffer's undersecretary, Alfred Hartmann, was able to postpone a decision on Küster's bill at the 19 December 1952 meeting, arguing that it contravened international agreements and that they should wait for the Finance Ministry to complete its own draft law. In a close (5 to 4) vote, the Bundesrat agreed to a postponement.[78]

Alfred Hartmann (1894–1967), lawyer, senior executive officer in the Reich Ministry of Finance from 1925 to 1935, then head of the Tax Office. After the war ended, he joined the staff of the Bavarian Ministry of Finance. From 1947 to 1949, Hartmann was director of financial administration for Bizonia, and from 1949 to 1959 he was undersecretary in the federal Ministry of Finance. In 1955, Hartmann became a lecturer and honorary professor of financial policy at the University of Cologne. He was on the boards of directors of numerous mining companies and was chairman of the board of several energy firms.

At another session on 20 February 1953, the plenary voted, over Baden-Württemberg's objections, to adopt 41 alterations that further limited Küster's intended expansion of payments. Bremen's commissioner for labor, Gerhard van Heukelum (SPD), the head of the Bundesrat Special Committee on Reparations, pushed through the changes.

Gerhard van Heukelum (1890–1969) was manager of the Metal Workers' Association from 1920 to 1924 and a member of the Bremen civic assembly (SPD) from 1927 to 1933. He was imprisoned several times in the ensuing years; in 1945, he became mayor of Bremerhaven, and he served as commissioner for labor in Bremen from 1948 to 1959.

Küster and the Baden-Württemberg minister of justice, Viktor Renner (SPD), found themselves isolated; in vain they beseeched the state representatives not to decide purely on the basis of fiscal considerations. Küster's bill, the so-called "November version" of the Bundesrat bill, had been changed beyond recognition; an attempt to persuade the Bundestag to adopt the original version failed.[79]

Viktor Renner (1899–1969), a lawyer, joined the SPD under the Weimar Republic and served as a trial court judge in Tübingen; in 1946, he became undersecretary and minister of the interior in the provisional government of South Württemberg–Hohenzollern. In 1952, he was appointed justice minister in the Baden-Württemberg state government under Reinhold Maier. In 1953, Renner resigned in protest against Maier's agreement to plans for a European defense community within the scope of the European Community treaties. He became minister of the interior again in 1956 and remained in that position until the end of the Grand Coalition in Baden-Württemberg in 1960. The same year, he refused to accept Germany's highest decoration, the *Grosses Bundesverdienstkreuz mit Stern*, explaining that Germans of his generation should not wear medals.

After his success, Schäffer attempted to postpone adoption of a federal law until the following legislative session.[80] His colleague, Justice Minister Thomas Dehler, made it clear to him that it would be impossible to "get around" rapid adoption.[81] With the help of the CSU deputies Franz-Josef Strauss and Wilhelm Laforet, Schäffer succeeded in delaying a discussion of the Bundesrat bill (still not acceptable to Schäffer even in its mutilated form) and of an SPD bill, planned for 27 March 1953 in the Committee for the Legal System and Constitutional Law, until the governing parties' bill was completed. Committee member Otto-Heinrich Greve (SPD) protested that the federal Ministry of Finance was apparently striving to delay reparations until the last persecutee was dead.[82]

In June 1953, however, Schäffer suddenly changed tactics. Observers abroad expected the first Bundestag to pass a federal restitution law, and the Bundesrat was urging rapid adoption of its own bill, since the governing parties' bill desired by the Ministry of Finance provided for a very unfavorable distribution of expenses between the federal government and the states. Schäffer was very glad that the SPD deputies had not offered their own bill and that, in order to ensure that some law was passed, they would accept the executive branch's draft without change. In this altered situation, Schäffer thought it opportune to pass the governing parties' bill immediately and thus force the Bundesrat, under pressure of time, to abandon its financial reservations. If the Bundesrat called for a mediation committee between the two houses, the responsibility for failure to adopt the law could be "palmed off" onto it. Also, he felt the next Bundestag could not be expected to adopt the governing parties' bill unchanged, but that it would considerably expand it.[83]

Thus the executive branch drummed its bill through the various levels of parliament at an unprecedented tempo—one month, counting from the first reading on 24 June 1953. Should anyone still want to change any of the text, the governing parties threatened to withhold consent to the law under Article 113 of the constitution and allow the whole thing to collapse. After a rapid compromise in the mediation committee on distribution of funding between the federal and state governments, the so-called Federal Supplementary Law was passed on 29 July by the Bundestag and went into force on 1 October 1953.

Under this enormous time pressure, the Bundesrat—including Küster, against his will—and the SPD parliamentary deputies ratified the law, although with the stipulation that the newly elected Bundestag immediately amend it.[84] Küster and the justice minister of Baden-Württemberg, Viktor Renner, proposed that the Bundesrat and Bundestag adopt the law jointly on the site of the Bergen-Belsen concentration camp. The proposal was rejected.[85] The SPD Bundestag deputy Adolf Arndt described the law as so bad, both legally and morally, that it once again made one ashamed to be German.[86]

The law was in some ways an improvement over the earlier state laws. Thus refugees from the eastern European "expulsion territories" (the eastern European territories from which ethnic Germans had been expelled after the war) were eligible for restitution; for the first time, reparations claims for damages to professional and economic advancement were provided for persecutees in the states of North Rhine–Westphalia, Lower Saxony, and Schleswig-Holstein (in the British occupation zone); and a unified court system was created, with the federal Supreme Court of Appeals elevated to the status of Supreme Restitution Court. However, the law also had serious flaws. Overall, it achieved less than the restitution law in the U.S. occupation zone or the principles agreed upon in the Hague Protocols.

1. The persecutees had to prove they had been targeted by "officially approved measures" (§ 1, para. 3). This was difficult in individual cases, as Nazi measures were directed against all Jews, political opponents, and the like. People who had voluntarily abandoned their careers in Germany and left the country, after seeing others like themselves ruined and driven

to death, also received nothing. Similarly, the surviving relatives of the thousands who had committed suicide received nothing unless they could show that this death had been "officially approved." "Official approval" was not automatically assumed even in the case of Jews who chose suicide in the face of impending deportation; it could be assumed only if they killed themselves during deportation. Furthermore, people who had been privately employed received nothing if they had been fired by a prejudiced employer, but the firing was done without official assistance.

2. Persecutees who were not civil servants received only a one-time payment of 25,000 DM for harm to their careers. Thus the loss of a promising position in Germany, abandoned in favor of uncertainty and sometimes permanent social dislocation in a foreign country, was paid off for life with the equivalent of the amount earned by a senior ministerial official in a year.

3. For purposes of calculating their pensions and capital restitution, all persecutees were placed in one of four categories of civil servant, depending on social status before persecution began (junior, middle-level, upper-level, and senior). Küster had pointed out that categorizing persecutees by civil servant class had not worked in the restitution law of the U.S. zone, as most of the persecutees would have fallen into the lowest category of civil servant. He proposed uniform pensions, with supplements depending on the last-known or probable income. This would have put the highest income group at a disadvantage, but would overall have been a more just and socially conscious solution.[87]

An additional flaw in comparison with the "November" draft by the Bundesrat was the requirement that damage to health be eligible for restitution where it caused a reduction in earning capacity of at least 30 percent, rather than the earlier 20 percent reduction (the Federal Restitution Law of 1956 would later set a threshold of 25 percent).[88]

In addition, the law contained a wealth of restrictions and clauses, the function of which Otto Küster described as follows in June 1953 in a speech to the Society for Christian-Jewish Cooperation in Frankfurt:

It categorizes and equates, guarantees percentages of percentages, distinguishes between mandatory, possible, discretionary, and hardship entitlements, invents maximum amounts for every year of persecution as well as for the total claim, and for several claims by one person in total, and for claims by several people somehow joined, in total; it sorts heirs and censors wills, grants claims only if other legal claims are not made simultaneously; it snips and cuts with scissors brandished, and one senses that the legislature is only really satisfied when it arrives at the immense section on hardship compensation, in which everything which it had previously cut, dismembered, and forgotten is mildly cleansed with philanthropic gestures . . . All the parties behave as though this were an act of generosity, as in the countless distribution and benefits laws, with the compensation provisions for expellees at their head—oriented toward need or even neediness, toward all sorts of entitlements, and toward a comparison with what others are "getting" . . . The elementary functions of law appear to be dying off.

In this case, Küster believed, it was necessary to refer to Aristotle's two types of justice. One was distributive justice, which is not conceived of as being pitted against legal claims; it equips and provides, giving not for reasons, but for purposes. On the other side was "reconstructing, restorative justice, which straightens out law that has been bent, thrown to the ground, trampled on." According to Aristotle, it was the latter and not the former that formed the foundation of a people and a state.[89] Küster outlined a basic conflict that would continue to run through the entire chapter of reparations: the state again and again attempted to declare reparations payments the equivalent of public benefits or assistance to the disadvantaged, part of a broad-based social safety net, while the persecutees and their lawyers rightly insisted on defining them as clear-cut legal claims, or compensation.

Under pressure of events, Küster, as already mentioned, had voted for the Federal Supplementary Law in summer 1953. Only half a year later, he saw his negative predictions confirmed and regretted his vote in hindsight. In a speech to the Society for Christian-Jewish Cooperation in Freiburg on 3 December 1953, he again compared the law to the Bundesrat draft he had introduced (the November version):

The second clause of section 2 was cobbled together by coloring the Bundesrat version like a child with a drawing. The Bundesrat said, " 'political' includes beliefs that led those who held them to act, despite personal danger, against senseless sacrifice or ostracization by the enemy." Now it says, "persecution for political beliefs is equivalent to persecution based on the fact that the persecutee, because of a decision of conscience, and despite personal danger, actively worked against abuse of human dignity or against the extermination of human beings that could not be justified morally by the war." At every point where it deviated from the prototype, the addition of words can only act to allow frightened civil servants to develop nonobjective excuses for rejection. It will mean, for example, that a persecutee may actively have risked his life, but only because his superior or another respected person persuaded him [to do so]; thus there may have been a "decision of conscience," but not his own decision of conscience . . . Or a superior knew of his employee's actions and encouraged and made possible the action involved through silent toleration; he may also have been executed for this; but there was no active participation, as required by the law.[90]

Küster knew the perils of a single false word in the text of a law. He predicted that a reluctant bureaucracy would use such words against the persecuted, and he pointed out the two-facedness of Germany's treatment of its past:

For reparations, Bonn lacked manpower to the point of deficiency. For other things, meanwhile, they were able to mobilize impressive forces with an industry that put the bees to shame. On the first two pages of the Federal Government Bulletin of 22 October, its Commission to Regulate the Issue of War Decorations presented a report on how Hitler medals are to be worn in future. Any person seeking to serve his people in reparations work and receiving almost no assistance who reads this product of German seriousness, German zeal, and German industry will have difficulty freeing himself of his feelings of fury. Thus it remains unlikely that, during the lifetime of the persecutees, we shall have a reparations law that satisfies the most elementary demands of justice. But it is as good as certain that a tank destruction medal will soon once again decorate the breast of a German soldier, awarded for the—undoubtedly courageous—destruction of the last obstacle standing between a town in the east and the horrors following in the footsteps of German soldiers.

Küster openly called on all "judges and administrators, writers, organization representatives and lawyers" to "grant this law [the Federal Supplementary Law] no more respect than its content and origins deserve, and in this extreme case to obey the ideal of justice more than the human creation." To this incitement to resistance to state authority, he added a sharp polemic against Schäffer's ministry:

The federal government's officers, none of whom has ever made a law or handled such a reparations case, have precipitously completed a draft law, which they were not assigned to do until the Bundesrat had already finished its own bill. They then subjected the Bundesrat bill to an inflation of words and restriction of thoughts. They questioned several state officials on their work; these explained that they were unable immediately to appreciate the new wordings, most of which seemed unnecessary and opaque to them. In fact, it is the nature of legislation that someone who understands an issue can formulate the right words in ten minutes but requires ten hours to show why a text by someone else who does not understand the issue is wrong.[91]

Küster had his speech copied and sent to all the reparations offices. In February 1954, Schäffer got hold of it and immediately sent a letter to the justice minister of Baden-Württemberg, Dr. Wolfgang Haussmann, urging him to take action against Küster and saying that the speech defamed officials of the federal Ministry of Finance and incited those working in reparations to disobey the law. In the future, he said, he could no longer ask his officers to sit at the same negotiating table with Herr Küster, and that the government of Baden-Württemberg should send a different representative to Bonn for all future reparations talks.[92]

In October 1953, the old Baden-Württemberg coalition government of the SPD, FDP/DVP, and BHE under Reinhold Maier had dissolved. The new state prime minister was Dr. Gebhard Müller of the CDU, a sworn enemy of Küster's. After the Luxembourg Treaty with Israel, he whispered among internal CDU circles in South Württemberg that Küster had stabbed Adenauer and Schäffer in the back, betrayed the Federal Republic to the Jews and cost it many billions of marks, and that he was wasting Baden-Württemberg's tax revenues on the Jews. Müller said that if he ever came to power in Stuttgart, he would restore order.[93]

In fact, the first measure taken by the Müller cabinet was to require Finance Ministry approval of any enactments by Küster's office. The three-year-old Auerbach affair was dredged up to justify this. In addition, Müller demanded that Küster become a civil servant,[94] because, according to Müller, his position as an independent agent meant it was not even possible to initiate disciplinary proceedings against him. Müller made it clear to Küster that one principle of his policies was to take Baden-Württemberg out of the forefront of reparations. He struck from the draft inaugural speech the passage, "The government will continue reparations work with the same resoluteness it has shown thus far." Finally, another informer was found in Küster's office to claim that he had favored all sorts of people, given millions to persecuted DPs and collaborated with the head of the Bavarian restitution office, Phillip Auerbach. As if this were not enough, an "investigator" was found in the person of a retired state court president, Dr. Teufel, "a worthy reactionary from the idyllic Mardi Gras town of Rottweil," in Küster's words. Teufel investigated without keeping any records and, without first interrogating Küster, presented the financial committee with a report on Küster's transgressions.[95] Küster, as expected, refused to accept either dependence on the Finance Ministry or civil servant status.

On 30 June 1954, the state government revoked Küster's position as representative as of the end of the year. On 1 July 1954, at the height of this vendetta against him, and a day after he was relieved of his position, Küster made a speech to his colleagues in which he provided a point-by-point refutation of the charges by Prime Minister Müller. He also wrote a personal letter to his friend and fellow fighter Franz Böhm in which he aired his fury at the campaign being waged against him. He named the people behind it by name; about the new ministers in Stuttgart, he wrote, "Being dependent on this man [Finance Minister Karl Frank] would be an impossibility. Frank was lord mayor of Ludwigsburg until the end of the Third Reich; it was only with the help of the DVP manager and the current justice minister, Haussmann—a man made up only of tactics—that he was classed as less culpable and ultimately, at a second trial, issued a clean bill of health in the denazification procedure as a fellow traveler." Through a journalist, this letter ended up in the hands of Prime Minister Gebhard Müller, who used it as an excuse to fire Küster immediately on 4 August 1954 for insulting state government ministers. With the votes of the SPD deputies, the state parliament approved Küster's immediate removal. The spokesman of the SPD deputies, Dr. Alex Möller, declared that Küster was sadly mistaken if he thought he could "get his own way." Only the former justice minister and SPD deputy Viktor Renner defended Küster.[96]

The associations of former persecutees, the *Freiberger Rundbrief,* important commentators in the domestic and foreign press, and, on the radio, Böhm and Arndt in particular protested Küster's removal. The Social Democrats Renner and Möller managed to ensure that Küster had access, at least after the fact, to Teufel's report. The state parliament's Standing Committee then energetically took up the case, giving Küster an opportunity to present his side. Based on this, the committee, headed by a Tübingen professor by the name of Erbe (FDP), determined that the accusations against Küster were without exception ridiculous, and required the state government to clear his name and offer him an accrued pension. Küster had never denied the state government's formal right to fire him, as he had, at his own wish, operated only on the basis of his legal mandate.[97]

Küster's neutralization had been arranged by Schäffer's federal Ministry of Finance, along with an association of former Nazis, "Aryanizers," and so on, of whom Küster had made enemies at the Hague negotiations. In 1986, Küster said: "My father-in-law, a pastor, had already warned me in 1945 against getting involved in reparations; he said it could become a suicide mission. During the Hague negotiations, Böhm and I received threatening letters telling us that the lampposts from which we would hang had already been picked out. One letter to us contained explosives."[98]

In the official government version of the history of reparations, Féaux de la Croix mentions Küster's firing only in passing and says nothing about the background to it. He also conceals the crucial role played by the Finance Ministry in ignoring Küster's draft and in the development of the Federal Supplementary Law.[99]

Through his key role in the Hague negotiations with Israel and the development of the Allied Restitution Law and the reparations law in the U.S. occupation zone, Küster set standards for reparations that placed moral responsibility and "restorative justice" above the argument of limited financial means. In any case, the economic argument lost its force with the beginning of the German "Economic Miracle," and the federal Ministry of Finance changed its tack in the Federal Supplementary Law of 1953. Perhaps Küster would have succeeded in pushing his version of a federal restitution law through the Bundestag from his strong, independent position in the Stuttgart leadership and the Bundesrat. By removing him from the Stuttgart office and eliminating him from all further discussions concerning revisions to the law, the officials of the Finance Ministry retained the upper hand. The Federal Restitution Law of 1956 bore their stamp; it was an improved Federal Supplementary Law.

Küster's removal showed that Adenauer's restoration policies had disempowered not only the left-wing spectrum, ranging from Social Democrats to opponents of rearmament to communists, but even the more centrist opposition. It would be worth investigating to what extent the elimination of people like Küster set the tone, not only for reparations policy, but also for rebuilding the German administration in general.[100] The fact that the government consciously sacrificed the efforts of an involved expert during the period of the restoration under Adenauer throws a different light on the argument, often made today, that reparations were completely virgin territory and mistakes unavoidable. Küster very clearly analyzed the deficiencies and problems of the Finance Ministry draft from the start, and alternatives were always on the table; but the Bonn bureaucracy did not want a better law.

Debates on the Spirit of Reparations

In practice, the Federal Supplementary Law had exactly the effect Küster had predicted; it gave offices and courts excuse after excuse to reject or delay reparations claims. In April 1954, the Claims Conference concluded that the law had appreciably limited implementation of state regulations, to the detriment of the victims.[101] At the end of May, an SPD deputy, Herbert Hauffe, complained in the Bundestag that the frequency of decisions issued by state authorities had been twice as high before the law went into effect.[102] He accused Finance Minister Schäffer of failing to issue the necessary implementing regulations, thus blocking processing of applications. The deputy quoted from an exchange of letters between the ministry and a 74-year-old applicant who wanted to know when his application would finally be processed: " 'The regulations . . . have not yet been issued,' was the response, 'I suggest that you inquire from time to time of your reparations office as to the status of legislation.' "[103] Schäffer attempted to blame the Bundesrat for the delay and promised immediate attention to the matter. Four months later, SPD deputy Adolf Arndt accused Schäffer of failing to keep his promise, as not all regulations had yet been issued. The speaker of the Bundestag, Senator Gerhard van Heukelum of Bremen, denied any Bundesrat responsibility and blamed the situation on the small number of employees working on the issue at the Finance Ministry. An SPD deputy stated that "the federal government obviously does not want reparations to proceed."[104]

SPD deputies again and again compared these delaying tactics with the speed and generosity with which former Nazis were accommodated—the lord mayor of Dortmund, Dr. Pagenkopf, a former SA *Obersturmbannführer*, for example, who had received a retroactive payment of 42,000 DM; or a chief prosecutor of the Nazi People's Court, who had been receiving a pension of 1,300 DM a month for years, while the widow of a resistance fighter convicted by the same court had to make do with only 250 DM;[105] or the former members of the Condor Legion, for whom the period during which they had bombarded Spanish cities counted twice for purposes of their pensions.[106] Volunteers who had fought in the International Brigades against Franco, in contrast, did not begin receiving restitution from a hardship fund until 1981.[107]

Deputies quoted Baden-Württemberg's SPD state parliamentary deputy Alex Möller, who told of various complaints he had received: German authorities had demanded the affidavits of two witnesses to confirm the imprisonment, at age seven, of a girl, now seventeen, who was the only member of her family to have survived Auschwitz and had a prisoner number tatooed on her arm to prove it. A man who had been held in protective custody for some time was required to produce the names of the prison guards. A former police official in northern Baden had claimed restitution of 2,000 DM for the loss of his library; the court demanded a list of all 900 books, with titles, year of purchase, and purchase price, as well as receipts from the bookstores.[108] SPD deputy Arndt quoted from a decision by judges on the Berlin Supreme Court—Dr. Göbel, Dr. Schumann, and Herr Naumann—as follows: "The plaintiff admits that she was not personally the object of violent Nazi measures, and that she could easily have separated from her husband [the man was Jewish, commented Arndt]. She nevertheless followed him underground. Thus her life in hiding was based on a voluntary decision and was not caused by a Nazi measure aimed at her."[109]

Arndt also quoted a decision by the former Rottweil trial court president Dr. Teufel in the case of a Lieutenant Frauendiener, who died while trying, after the unsuccessful attempt on Hitler's life on 20 July 1944, to bring the wives and children of the executed conspirators to safety. Dr. Teufel now found that his survivors had no claim to reparations, as Frauendiener's mission had not been an act of resistance, and he had not died for political reasons; it was "merely a case of rescuing uninvolved women and children."[110] Survivors of a music critic named Schmidt, murdered on 30 June 1934, were denied continued payment of the pension granted them by the Nazis, as Schmidt, because of a confusion of names, "was only accidentally" killed, and thus was not a persecutee.[111] Arndt's conclusion:

In no other areas of law are the administration and courts so narrow-minded, sometimes heartless, so petty, or do they act in such a hairsplitting and quibbling fashion . . . Thus a task whose generous fulfillment should move an entire people has fallen to the ink blotters and pen pushers, and we must be informed by a liberal British newspaper, which cannot generally be accused of being anti-German, that Germans tend to see the survivors of National Socialism, and especially Jews, as a burdensome nuisance. This is the foul climate of creeping anti-Semitism.[112]

Numerous deputies from the ranks of the CDU and FDP agreed with Arndt and stressed that the cases mentioned were not exceptions but the norm.[113] "Because the laws give wide scope for discretion, we can see whether the spirit of reparations really exists where the law is applied," an FDP deputy, Dr. Hans Reif, said in a later debate. "I believe this is the bitterest disappointment that can be experienced by a parliament that has shown good faith—when hundreds of thousands of letters now tell us how unenthusiastically, inconsiderately, sometimes even spitefully, those people are treated whom we in the Christian Occident should treat with love."[114]

Hans Reif (1899–1974), an economist, was a member of the Reich Committee for Commerce, Industry, and Small Business and the Reich Committee for Middle-Sized Business of the German Democratic Party in the Weimar era. He was fired in 1933 for political reasons; during the war he had contact with the resistance group around Carl Goerdeler and Leuschner. After 1945, Reif was a co-founder of the Liberal Democratic party in Leipzig, then of the FDP in West Berlin. He later became a professor at the College of Politics at the Free University in Berlin. Reif was a member of the first and second German Bundestags.

It is noteworthy that the opponents of reparations from the CDU and FDP were silent during all these debates. They had nothing to gain in a public debate. The indignation of concerned deputies such as Adolf Arndt, Otto-Heinrich Greve, and Franz Böhm—it was, incidentally, always the same few reparations experts who spoke out—began to seem like tilting at windmills.

Otto-Heinrich Greve (1908–1968), doctor of law, was a member of the German Democratic party and the Reichsbanner Schwarz-Rot-Gold, the SPD's paramilitary force, prior to 1933; he was forced out of the judiciary in 1938 for political reasons. After 1946, Greve worked as an attorney in Hamburg, particularly on reparations matters. He was a co-founder of the FDP in Lower Saxony, but left in 1948 to join the SPD. From 1948 to 1949, he was a member of the Parliamentary Council. Greve was a member of the German Bundestag from 1949 to 1961, and headed the Reparations Committee from 1957 to 1958. He was forced to give up this post owing to accusations of conflict of interest because of his legal work. Greve was already calling for recognition of the Sudetenland as part of Czechoslovakia in 1956, for which he was sharply criticized even in his own party.

Half a dozen deputies were powerless against a bureaucracy of "hairsplitters" and "quibblers" subject to no direct control by the parliament. The only thing they could do was constantly to denounce the moral reprehensibility of this "spirit" of reparations. A question asked by FDP deputy Reif after the submission of a proposal for a new Federal Supplementary Law manifested this powerlessness: "Despite all our precision and clarity, do we have a guarantee that bad faith, reluctance and unconcern will not wreck what our good intentions hoped to achieve here?"[115] Arndt's attempt to introduce the following passage into the new reparations law is in the same spirit: "This law is to be interpreted and applied generously, so that its implementation carries out reparations to the maximum degree as a moral task and legal debt."[116]

How were they legally to obligate a narrow-minded bureaucracy and judiciary to be "generous?" To what extent was generosity legally definable and recoverable? Because of these difficulties of definition, the highest court in reparations matters, the federal Supreme Court of Appeals, felt it necessary to add this admonitory sentence to its decision of 12 November 1954: "The goal and purpose of reparations and compensation legislation is to compensate for wrongs done, as soon and as far as possible. An interpretation of the law that is possible and accords with this goal is preferable to any other interpretation that makes reparations more difficult or impossible."[117]

The petty and sluggish processing of claims frequently was as bad as a rejection for older survivors. On 17 September 1954, *Aufbau* magazine in New York warned its readers, "Every day elderly people eligible for reparations are dying before having seen even a penny of their reparations."[118] The SPD deputy Hermann Runge informed the Bundestag that 15,000 people over seventy-five years of age who were eligible for reparations lived in New York alone. Responding to a claim, German authorities informed a seventy-eight-year-old man that, at the time, only claims by people over eighty were being processed, and his would have to wait.[119]

Hermann Runge (1902–?), was a metalworker who became a member of the SPD and the Metalworkers' Association in 1919. After 1933, he was involved in illegal party work in what is now North Rhine–Westphalia. Runge was arrested by the Gestapo in 1935, convicted by the People's Court, and imprisoned until 1945. After the war he became SPD party secretary in Moers and Düsseldorf; he was a member of the Parliamentary Council in 1948–49 and a member of the first and second German Bundestags.

In his official historiography of reparations, Féaux de la Croix quotes not a single passage from these historic Bundestag debates. He mentions only the debate of 23 February 1955, in connection with which he accuses the deputies of undignified criticism of judges, suggesting a comparison with Nazi terror:

The debate is remarkable because it was whipped up into unusual passion and lack of objectivity. Quotes torn from their context and unconfirmable at the time, from supposed or actual erroneous decisions by reparations courts—decisions that coexisted with thousands of "good" ones, which of course were not mentioned—provoked criticism of judges (calls for prosecution of judges), reminiscent, in highly undignified fashion, of a terrible practice that had been eliminated. Such condemnation—or was it even supposed to be intimidation?—of reparations authorities and courts, combined with the attempt at personal disparagement of those who thought differently—they could only be "131," which was merely a hidden label for "Nazi"—was unfortunately a pseudoargument employed by many, even in parliament.[120]

In early 1956, shortly before the new version of the Federal Supplementary Law was adopted, Kurt R. Grossman took an informational trip lasting several weeks through the Federal Republic at the behest of the Jewish Agency for Palestine in order to investigate the state of reparations in the bureaucracy and public opinion on the issue of reparations. His conclusion was depressing; he found that reparations had been reduced to legal pedantry lacking feeling or reason, that the small number of reparations advocates, represented by men like Böhm, Küster, and Arndt, was disappearing, and that the victims of persecution living in the Federal Republic—some 300,000 in number—had no political influence. Claims were being processed at a "snail's pace," the behavior of state bureaucracies was confused, nonuniform, and contradictory, and their staffs were far too small. No one wanted to work in reparations, found Grossman; some qualified administrative bureaucrats were going into the private sector, others to the new Defense Ministry. Thus personnel fluctuation was very high, and gaps were generally filled by ethnic German refugees from the East, most of whom were former Nazis with no concern for the problems of the victims. The Auerbach affair continued to haunt reparations; thus the view was widespread within the bureaucracy that around a third of the claimants were liars. The justice minister of Baden-Württemberg, Wolfgang Haussmann, had recently spoken publicly of "pension hunters." Given this desolate situation, said Grossman, Jewish organizations were called upon to exercise influence on the German political climate through foreign media, for the press and "public opinion" in Germany responded only to pressure from abroad.[121]

The Federal Restitution Law of 1956

In summer 1954, a working group in the Ministry of Finance, composed of bureaucrats within the ministry, others from the state governments, and some Bundestag deputies, took on the task of reforming the Federal Restitution Law. Küster (then still in office) had vainly suggested in a petition to the Bundesrat that the Ministry of Finance should not lead in drafting the reform, but that a working commission supplemented by independent figures should do so instead. Although he was the state representative and actually destined for the commission because of his factual knowledge, Küster was not included in the working group—he had been declared persona non grata by Schäffer.[122]

The group's discussions took about a year. At first, Schäffer attempted to change some of the provisions of the draft, with the aim of reducing the total financial expenditure to be expected, but he was unsuccessful.[123] Representatives of the Claims Conference were also in constant contact with the members of the working group.[124] After the Bundesrat had also unsuccessfully attempted to limit the obligations contained in the reform, the Federal Restitution Law (Bundesentschädigungsgesetz, or BEG) was finally adopted on 29 June 1956.

The main improvements over the Federal Supplementary Law were that residence and deadline requirements were extended to everyone who had arrived in the Federal Republic by 31 December 1952 (the previous date had been 1 January 1947), and to all emigrants from Germany to other countries who had lived within the borders of the German Reich of 1937 (this included all emigrants from the territory of what became East Germany and the former German territories belonging to Poland). For health damage, pension entitlements began not with a 30 percent reduction of earning capacity, but with 25 percent. The upper limit for payments for damage to property and assets was raised to 75,000 DM, and for damage to professional and economic advancement, it was raised from 25,000 to 40,000 DM.[125]

Like the Federal Supplementary Law of 1953, the BEG was introduced with an oft-quoted preamble intended to honor resistance fighters and victims:

Recognizing the fact that an injustice was done to persons persecuted because of political opposition to National Socialism or for reasons of race, religion or world-view under the National Socialist tyranny; that the resistance to National Socialist tyranny, for reasons of conviction or religion or conscience, was a service to the German people and state; and that democratic, religious, and economic organizations were also wrongfully harmed by National Socialist tyranny, the Bundestag has passed the following law.[126]

Küster said this preamble spoke for itself. It showed, he said, "how, with a faint heart" and "gingerly," a duty had been fulfilled, and that, "a hundred months after the end of the criminal state," the Bonn legislature could not bring itself to do more than say that an "injustice had been done" to the millions of victims.[127]

Under the Federal Restitution Law of 1956, those entitled to compensation included people who had been persecuted "on the grounds of political opposition, race, religion, or worldview" (§ 1). Under the new law, "fact situations indicating harm" included: (1) harm to life, (2) harm to body and health, (3) harm to freedom, (4) harm to possessions, (5) harm to property, (6) harm through payment of special taxes, fines, and costs, (7) harm to career advancement, and (8) harm to economic advancement.[128]

Harm to life meant harm to the survivors through death of the breadwinner, for whom a pension was paid.[129] Harm to body and health meant that the victim was "not insignificantly" harmed in body or health and that a "causal connection" between the harm and the persecution "probably" existed. Compensation for this included medical care, pensions, capital restitution, retraining assistance and, if the victim died from the effects of persecution, support of the survivors. Compensation over and above medical care was granted only if the earning capacity of the person involved was reduced by at least 25 percent by the illness resulting from persecution.

The category "harm to freedom" included all types of imprisonment, concentration camps, ghettos, life under prisonlike conditions in hiding, wearing the Jewish star, and so forth. For each month of deprivation of freedom, the victim received the normal lump sum payment for false imprisonment, 150 DM. This amount, already low at the time, remains unchanged to this day.

Harm to possessions included furnishings, libraries, and other possessions lost through plundering or emigration. Property damage included losses through boycotts and liquidation (generally of Jewish businesses), loss during transfer of Reichsmark sums abroad, and costs of emigration. Harm through special taxes meant the discriminatory taxation of Jews by the German Reich, for example the "Reich flight tax" on emigration, taxes to the German Gold Discount Bank to obtain export permits, or the "Jewish property tax" (imposed on German Jews for the murder in Paris in 1938 of a German diplomat, Ernst vom Rath, by a Jew, Herschel Grynspan). The seventh type of harm—harm to career advancement—described any restrictions suffered by victims in practicing their professions, such as revocation of admission to legal practice, layoffs from the civil service (to the extent that the BWGöD had not already provided substantial reparations) or a private business, reduced income, prevention or interruption of education or training, and loss of contributions to life insurance.[130]

For harm to career, the persecutee could choose between capital restitution (one-time payment of a fairly large sum) or a continuing pension, but not for harm to health. Pensions were paid out based on the amount normally granted to civil servants. To assess this, each former persecutee was placed in one of the four civil services classes, depending on position before the start of persecution—junior, middle-level, upper-level, or senior civil servant. All current income was taken into account when calculating pensions for health damage, but not for harm to career. These regulations promoted the formation of underprivileged and privileged classes of victims.

The details of the regulations were extremely complicated, impossible for laypeople to untangle and even something of a hieroglyphic for lawyers. The 1956 law did represent an appreciable improvement over the Federal Supplementary Law, but many of the deficiencies and gaps in that law were retained. A whole range of victims of whom the public had only recently become aware continued to be disadvantaged. However, it would give a wrong impression to focus on them without acknowledging that, after passage of the BEG, it was finally possible to begin processing hundreds of thousands of claims. Harm to freedom, career, and property were dealt with fairly rapidly. The work developed a certain routine; reparations payments flowed, easing the plight of many who had been forced to wait more than ten years for compensation.

A year after the law was passed, Küster acknowledged with cautious optimism that progress had been made in reparations and that the Federal Republic had now embarked on the path to "restored justice." He also said that "the general attitude of the bureaucracy and those whose lead they had to follow had become more lively . . . The stalling bureaucrat is no longer the leading type; the earlier complaint of a senior reparations official that his job was that of a professional liar is a thing of the past." And the stubborn attitude of the German people had changed—"although silently." It was not only in the bureaucracy that the children of the former persecutors "made reparation from the heart."[131]

Because of foreign and domestic political alignments, continuing social ostracism, a lack of representatives, and a shortage of publicity, the following groups were excluded from the BEG payments or were only partially compensated: (1) all those who had been persecuted outside of Germany by German killing squads, who, because they had remained in their native countries, did not fulfill the law's residency requirements, (2) forced laborers, (3) victims of forced sterilization, (4) the "antisocial," (5) communists, (6) Gypsies (Sinti and Rom), and (7) homosexuals.

1. The first category included French, Belgian, Dutch, Danish, Norwegian, Greek, Polish, Czech, Hungarian, Romanian, and Russian Jews, members of national resistance movements in those countries, and Poles and Russians, especially Russian POWs, who were considered subhuman and thus also became victims of the Nazi extermination program. Persecutees from Western countries received a modest lump-sum compensation on the basis of interstate treaties; persecutees from eastern Europe only received compensation if they had emigrated to Western countries before the deadline date.[132]

2. Forced laborers were compensated under the BEG if they were considered victims of racial, political, or religious persecution, and if they met the residency and deadline requirements of the BEG. Most foreign slave laborers did not meet these requirements. Their claims were rejected with reference to the London Debt Agreement of 1952, as theirs were seen as reparations claims connected with World War II, for which no final arrangement had yet been made. With the support of the Claims Conference, some slave laborers sued the German weapons producers,

but only a few companies agreed to pay compensation to their former slaves.[133]

3. The demand by the forcibly sterilized that they be included in the BEG was rejected by the Bundestag reparations committee between 1961 and 1965 on the basis of expert hearings. The experts who testified happened to be some of the Third Reich's prominent racial hygienists, such as Professor Hans Nachtsheim of the Max Planck Institute for Comparative Hereditary Biology and Pathology, and Professor Werner Villinger, professor of psychiatry at the University of Marburg, who had been an assessor at the Supreme Court of Genetic Health in Hamm and Breslau in the 1930s, and in 1940 became a consultant to the Nazi euthanasia murder program. In its final report of 21 November 1965, the reparations committee explained that victims of forced sterilization were not entitled to compensation because the Law to Prevent Genetically Defective Offspring of 1933 did not contravene the principles of the rule of law, and no illegal or negligent decisions had been made by the courts of genetic health.[134]

4. The "antisocial"—who were thrown into workhouses after 1933 and concentration camps after 1938, following many major campaigns against the so-called "work-shy," prostitutes, vagabonds, and beggars—were denied compensation by the courts. This was rationalized with the claim that although putting them in concentration camps had been illegal, it had not occurred "on the grounds of § 1 of the BEG"—that is, on the grounds of race, religion, or political convictions.[135]

5. A special situation developed for communists and people who, during the Adenauer era, were situated to the political left of the SPD and fought against rearmament and the policy of integration with the West. Under § 6, para. 1, no. 2, of the BEG, they could be denied compensation as enemies of the "free democratic order."[136] An example of this was the philosopher and philologist Rudolf Schottlaender, who had survived the Third Reich in a "privileged mixed marriage" and was recognized as a racial persecutee in 1950 after adoption of the first Berlin reparations law. In 1949, he lost his position as professor of philosophy at the Technical College in Dresden (in the Soviet zone) because of political nonconformity, and then worked as a secondary school teacher in West Berlin. In the 1950s, he was involved in initiatives—begun by the future German president Gustav Heinemann, among others—against West German rearmament and the production of nuclear weapons. Because, in the course of this involvement, he made contact with East German representatives and worked toward overcoming the confrontation between the blocs, he lost his teaching position in June 1959. Right after this, and before a disciplinary action pending against him had even been completed, Berlin's SPD minister for internal affairs, Joachim Lipschitz, rescinded his persecutee status, explaining that he was a "supporter of a totalitarian

regime." Schottlaender had never been a member of any party. The Berlin district court overturned the administrative decision in 1962.[137]

The Constitutional Court made the exclusionary paragraph more precise, interpreting it to mean that only people who had "actively" fought the "free democratic basic order" even after the Communist party was banned in 1956 were ineligible for compensation.[138] This meant that a communist who was now willing to hold his tongue would receive reparations as a sort of political hush money. This § 6, which continues in force to this day, was a malicious idea. After all, communists had made great sacrifices; many of them had spent years—sometimes even all twelve years of the Nazi regime—in prisons, prison camps, and concentration camps, surviving brutal interrogations and torture.

6. The Sinti and Rom (Gypsies), who were racially persecuted and thus unambiguously among those entitled to reparations under the BEG, were stamped as criminals by some members of the judiciary. In a decree on 8 December 1938, Heinrich Himmler had said, "The experience we have had so far in combating the Gypsy plague, and the knowledge gained from racial biology, show it to be necessary to address regulation of the Gypsy question on the basis of the nature of the race."[139] Starting in May 1940, Gypsies were deported to collection camps in occupied Poland (the Generalgouvernement); on 16 December 1942, Auschwitz was declared to be the central camp for Gypsies. On 26 February 1944, all the inmates of the Gypsy camp at Auschwitz were murdered in the gas chambers.

Despite this fact, the Supreme Court, in a decision of 7 January 1956, concluded that racial persecution had begun only in 1943—that is, with the deportation of the Gypsies to Auschwitz. For the period before this, it was the court's opinion that "despite the appearance of racial-ideology points of view, it was not race as such that formed the grounds for the measures taken, but the Gypsies' antisocial characteristics, which had given reason even earlier to subject members of this people to special restrictions. There is . . . reference not only to knowledge based in racial ideology, but also to experience in the fight against the Gypsy plague . . . Preventing Gypsies from nomadism is not specific to racial policy, but has also been a common preventive police measure." It could be assumed, said the court, that the measures against Gypsies in 1939 and 1940 were begun "in general in order to prevent the possibility of spying."

This judgment, which quite literally employs the language of the SS, would have raised a storm of protest had it been aimed at the Jews. But the Gypsies could not mobilize any supportive public opinion. It was largely due to Kurt May of the URO and a judge of the Frankfurt appeals court, Franz Calvelli-Adorno, who had documented the racial persecution of Gypsies in the journal *Rechtssprechung zum Wiedergutmachungsrecht* and had sharply criticized the judgment, that the Supreme Court revised its opinion on 8 December 1963 to acknowledge that racial policy was one factor in the May 1940 resettlement of Gypsies. Under the Federal Restitution Final Law of 1965, Sinti whose claims had been rejected could apply again. However, many had been intimidated by the earlier judgment or had become resigned and failed to take advantage of this.[140]

7. For fear of renewed prosecution, homosexuals did not dare go public until after the criminal law reform of 1969. Suits by several homosexuals in the 1950s for liberalization of § 175 of the Criminal Code (outlawing homosexuality), which had been tightened by the Nazis in 1935, and for reparations in this connection were rejected.[141]

A further snag for many persecutees was § 6, para. 1, no. 4, of the BEG, which stated that those sentenced to more than three years' imprisonment after 8 May 1945 were not entitled to compensation.[142] The enormous material poverty suffered by persecutees who, because of psychological or physical infirmity or because they were criminals prior to their imprisonment in concentration camps, could not find a place in the working world, often became a catalyst for criminal behavior. The criminological and political exclusionary grounds not only disadvantaged certain victims, however; they were above all an expression of the arrogance of the German state, which, having just functioned as a mass murderer, now felt it could judge who was worthy or unworthy of reparations. An example is illustrative:

Frau G., member of a Sinti family, lived in Berlin with her six siblings. During Kristallnacht, at the age of 18, she was beaten with an iron lawn chair and suffered a double skull fracture. In June 1941, she was taken into "protective custody" by the Gestapo. During this custody, she was badly abused and lost the sight in her right eye. In November 1941, she was deported to Ravensbrück concentration camp, where she was starved and forced to perform hard labor. She was beaten on the back with a stick and shot in the left leg. The scars are still visible today and cause her pain.

In January 1945, she was transferred to a subsidiary of Buchenwald concentration camp, where she performed heavy labor in a munitions factory. At liberation in April 1945, she was unable to walk out of the camp. Four of her six siblings were murdered in concentration camps. She lived with her two remaining sisters. They had a difficult time making a living. As small businesspeople, they had no health insurance; thus Frau G. was forced to pay doctors' bills and the cost of medication for her sister, who had developed cancer. Out of ignorance and fear of government institutions, she never tried to take advantage of government assistance.

In this hopeless situation, Frau G. committed several thefts. Because of sentencing requirements for recidivism, she was sentenced to several prison terms in 1957. The trial court in F. then combined the various terms into one term of three and a half years' imprisonment. When she made a claim for reparations under the BEG, it was denied under § 6, para. 1, no. 4.[143]

Under § 7 of the law, anyone who "purposely or negligently provides incorrect or misleading information" about harms suffered is also not entitled to reparations. The offices and courts applied this paragraph even to minor misinformation. Because many victims could no longer remember dates and times, and few documents remained available, they became entangled in contradictions. If officials were able to find contradictions through inquiries to the International Search Service in Arolsen, where all the concentration camp files (including prisoner files, etc.) were collected, they would refuse reparations. The American lawyer Milton Kestenberg called § 7 "punitive."[144]

§§ 6 and 7 each included a subsection 3 under which pensions and benefits already paid out could be demanded back if it was later discovered that the beneficiary had actively fought against the free democratic basic order or had made contradictory statements. This provision of the BEG was far stricter than state laws, for example, Berlin's 1951 law, which also provided for exclusion of "persons who, as supporters of a totalitarian system, fought against the democratic form of state," but required no repayment of already paid capital restitution or pensions.[145]

One of the major hardships of the BEG was its deadlines for exclusion. First, under the new law, published on 29 June 1956 in the *Bundesgesetzblatt*, the federal legal bulletin, all applications had to be submitted by 1 October 1957.[146] Considering the fact that the persecutees were scattered all over the world, the difficulty many had with the bureaucratic red tape involved in an application, and how difficult and problematic it was for them to decide to ask for anything from the Germans, this fifteen-month deadline appears unacceptable.

Later the deadline was extended for an additional six months, to 1 April 1958.[147] The financial compensation law for ethnic German expellees from eastern Europe, on the other hand, had no deadlines. The deadline for restitution was intended to limit the numbers of applicants—certainly not only for financial reasons, but also to lay to rest once and for all the need to deal with the victims of Nazi crimes. Because of missed deadlines, thousands of applicants were left with nothing.

A large number of persecutees never applied for reparations. A study by the Munich psychiatrist Paul Matussek found that the main motivation for not making a claim was fear of having to face the painful memory of the concentration camps once again during the reparations procedure. Some of the victims were not happy about taking money, inasmuch as that merely allowed the Germans to avoid the whole issue of guilt. The procedure itself meant trusting and depending on the former persecutor for approval of a pension.[148]

Closing the Book on Reparations

In an address on 10 November 1965, Chancellor Ludwig Erhard declared that the postwar period was over. Two years earlier, he had refused requests that he lift the statute of limitations on Nazi crimes and reform the Federal Restitution Law: "We have no sympathy with efforts to derive a German original sin for all time from past barbarism and to conserve it as a political tool."[149]

By 1958, two years after the adoption of the BEG, demands for its improvement had already begun. They were addressed to the Bundestag reparations committee,[150] formed in 1957, which received complaints from around the world about the law's problems and injustices.[151] Yet hardly had the authorities begun to process applications under the new law when Finance Minister Schäffer again began complaining of the "mounting costs" imposed on taxpayers by reparations: "The effects of the reparations laws adopted unanimously by the Bundestag were probably not given full consideration by the deputies. It will probably turn out that within the next four to five years, we shall have spent, not 7 to 8 billion DM, as originally expected, but at least 16 to 18 billion."[152] Schäffer and his allies leaked reports to the press claiming that reparations payments would necessarily lead to devaluation of the mark. These attacks alarmed the Claims Conference, and the German ambassador in Washington had to reassure it that "a reduction or stoppage of payments to those entitled to reparations is not under consideration in the slightest."

In an interview with the New York immigrant newspaper *Aufbau*, Schäffer tried to justify his views, saying he was only concerned with the lawyers' high contingency fees. Thus he claimed that the Israeli government had sent a letter to lawyers demanding that, in reparations matters, they settle for a fee that might "in no case exceed the maximum of 20 percent."[153] Lawyers, especially foreign lawyers specializing in reparations, were indeed sometimes demanding horrendous fees—15 to 20 percent of the reparations won in a successful suit, and as much as 30 percent in some cases. The URO lawyers took contingency fees of from 6 to 10 percent from many clients, while German lawyers generally held to Germany's official fee schedule for lawyers.[154] But whether and to what extent some lawyers lined their pockets out of reparations, or generally merely charged justified fees, is beside the point; the excessive fees were never a burden on the German budget, but only on the persecutees, who were forced by the complicated bureaucratic procedure and restrictive official decision-making to hire lawyers to make their applications or appeal for their rights.

In December 1957, Schäffer spread more bad news at an event sponsored by the Lower Bavarian CSU in Plattling. Now he said that reparations payments had gone up not to between 16 and 17 billion DM, but to between 27 and 29 billion, because "no evidence, but only credibility, is required for actual harm." No office, he claimed, dared to do anything about this "for fear of accusations of anti-Jewishness."[155] In a letter to the editor of *Die Welt*, Probst Grüber answered Schäffer, saying that the old Nazi spirit was not dead, and that those who subscribed to it had now joined forces. Schäffer's statements, he said, were dangerously geared to reawakening slumbering hostilities and to leading the "aroused popular spirit" in a very specific direction.[156]

It did not go unremarked among officials in the reparations offices that the highest state representative for reparations, the finance minister, believed that reparations payments were causing imminent inflation, and that no one dared to speak out against the Jews. Pettiness, harassing evidentiary requirements, and distrust on the part of the reparations authorities were thus maliciously encouraged and legitimized. In fact, after Schäffer's speech in Plattling, representatives of the URO found a significant increase in rejections of reparations applications.[157] As the next step in his campaign, Schäffer's friends maneuvered the Rhineland-Palatinate CDU deputy Jakob Diel onto the Bundestag reparations committee. Although he lacked even the most basic understanding of the issues, Diel immediately became extremely active.

Jakob Diel (1886–1970), a Catholic born in Burg Leyen, near Bingen, was a farmer and winegrower. He was a soldier in World War I and received the Iron Cross, 2d class. From 1921 to 1933, he was a member of the Prussian state parliament, and in 1945 he co-founded the Rhineland-Palatinate CDU. Diel later became a member of the Rhineland-Palatinate state parliament and was for a time its president. He was a member of the German Bundestag in the third electoral period.

With the help of the chief of the Rhineland-Palatinate's criminal investigation department, Georg Heuser, who—as would become known only later—had led mass shootings of Jews as commander of an SS *Einsatzgruppe* on the Eastern Front,[158] Diel illegally obtained the files of clients of the SPD's Otto-Heinrich Greve, the committee head, who was also an active reparations lawyer. From these files, Diel copied bills from Greve's law firm that recorded contingency fees of 15 percent; he openly distributed these among the Bundestag deputies, along with the names of the clients and a pamphlet opposing reparations,[159] which declared:

The SPD has presented a bill to extend the registration deadline yet again, in order—as we know—to further increase the billions in payments. Apparently, for certain law firms, not "all" corners of our globe have yet been mobilized . . . When we speak of lawyers, this is a quite specific group. The chief, more or less, is our colleague Dr. Greve. Therefore, in the documents reproduced in the appendix, I quote not just anybody, but our colleague Dr. Greve in person and his law firm . . .

In the case example, the subject is a Frau Rachel Levy, formerly of Frankfurt [the names of the clients have been changed], who emigrated from Frankfurt to Tel Aviv and then emigrated back to her money in Frankfurt. She wanted to have her son Isaac educated in Frankfurt, for which she intended to use the money and the pensions . . . [there followed the bills from Greve's law firm, in which up to 15 percent of the reparations amounts were charged as contingency fees]. The criticism made in some places against our friend Minister Schäffer is in inverse proportion to the opinion of our nation. We are grateful to him for revealing the problem as it is, so publicly and with such frankness . . . I believe that in 1945–46, large numbers of people were treated as big Nazis, whereas in reality the latter were just as few, perhaps even fewer, than the number of the "protected" that the Third Reich supposedly wished to destroy from within. The "denazification procedures" have mitigated a great deal, but have not eliminated [the problem]. Here, too, an unfinished "reparations remainder" remains . . . But what does it amount to vis-à-vis those who have no genuine claim at all? The communists, the antisocial, and criminals? . . . Quite spontaneously, a trial court president told of having to promise notoriously "unworthy" people enormous sums on the basis of the provisions of the law, at the expense of the state and the taxpayer.[160]

This pamphlet combined all the favorite popular clichés: the Jews were after money; they came back to Germany especially for that reason and even wanted their children to study there. The SPD was in cahoots with them and made money off it. It was the victims of denazification who actually deserved reparations, not the supposed resistance fighters, communists, antisocial elements, criminals, foreigners, and the notoriously unworthy.

SPD deputy Arndt attempted to sue Diel for his statements and was sued by Diel in return for maintaining that Diel had written a letter to Chancellor Adenauer in 1952 saying not enough Jews had been killed. Both trials ended indecisively. Diel, said the court, had "merely" informed the chancellor that many Germans were of this opinion.[161]

Diel's disparaging comments touched a nerve: lawyers' contingency fees, a favorite subject of opponents of reparations. In fact, the 15 percent Greve took from his clients *was* excessive; besides, contingency fees were not permissible under German law. However, representation on a contingency basis was largely tolerated among lawyers, for example, for persecutees living abroad who could not pay in advance.

More serious than Greve's high fees, however, was the fact that he had profitably combined his position as head of the committee with his legal practice. Greve, who had gained prominence in the Bundestag debates on the BEG as a harsh critic of the Finance Ministry and the reparations authorities, could no longer be kept in office by the SPD and was forced to resign as head of the reparations committee in February 1958.

Greve's successor as head of the committee, the SPD deputy Alfred Frenzel, also had to resign. In autumn 1960, shortly before he had planned to introduce a bill to reform the BEG, he was arrested as a Czech spy.

Alfred Frenzel (1899–1968), a baker and glass worker, was born in a small Bohemian village and grew up an orphan in impoverished circumstances. In 1930, he was fired from his job as branch manager of a consumer organization for falsifying records. He avoided expulsion from the Communist party by quitting and joined the SPD. In 1938, after the German occupation of Czechoslovakia, he emigrated to England, where during the war, he managed an RAF officer's mess. He began his political career with the SPD in Bavaria in 1946. In 1953, he was elected to the Bundestag; in 1957, he became a member of the defense committee, and in February 1958, he was made head of the reparations committee. When episodes in his dubious past came to light shortly before the 1953 Bundestag elections, Frenzel took an oath in court, because of which the Czech secret service was able to blackmail him into spying for them. For four years, beginning in 1956, he betrayed military secrets to Czechoslovakia as a member of the defense committee. At the end of October 1960, he was arrested upon leaving the parliament building in Bonn, and in 1961, he was sentenced by the Supreme Court of Appeals to fifteen years' imprisonment for treason. In 1966, he was pardoned by President Heinrich Lübke and traded to Czechoslovakia for Western spies arrested in East Germany. He died there two years later.

The two forced resignations nourished Finance Ministry hopes that no further attempts to reform the law would be made for the present.[162] These hopes, however, were not sustained by Frenzel's successors as head of the reparations committee, Gerhard Jahn and Martin Hirsch. They turned the committee into a mouthpiece for demands that the BEG be reformed, something that was in any case unavoidable, because, after the BEG went into effect on 1 October 1953, many Jews from eastern Europe who had been persecuted by the Nazis emigrated to Western countries. Many of them did not fulfill the conditions for applications under the law, and some solution had to be found for them. (For simplicity's sake, they will be called "late emigrants"; officially they were known as "persecutees from the areas of expulsion" or "post-fifty-three-ers").

Gerhard Jahn (1927–) was conscripted into the Luftwaffe as a helper toward the end of the war. Beginning in 1950, Jahn made a career in the SPD in Marburg, where he studied law until 1956. He was elected to the Bundestag in 1957 and was head of the reparations committee from 1960 to 1961. He served as federal minister of justice in the Social Democratic/Liberal coalition from 1969 to 1974 and became president of the German Tenants' Association in 1979.

In addition, the law contained the unjust provision that widows of persecutees who died after 1 October 1953 had a claim to survivors' benefits, while those whose husbands had died before that date got nothing. Furthermore, it had meanwhile become clear that considerable problems arose in processing claims for disability compensation, as the doctors consulted were frequently unwilling to recognize illnesses resulting from persecution to be such according to the standards of international medical knowledge.[163] Victims with serious health damage had to fight in court for years to secure compensation. The main demands for legal reform from persecutees' organizations were:

1. Full inclusion of late emigrants in the BEG.
2. Survivors' benefits for widows of those who had died before 1 October 1953.
3. After at least five months of concentration camp, ghetto, other imprisonment or life in hiding under conditions similar to imprisonment, an *assumption* that, if disability was present causing a 25 percent reduction in earning capacity, this health damage was caused by persecution (for simplicity's sake, this was termed the "concentration camp assumption").[164]
4. Elimination of all exclusionary deadlines from the BEG.
5. Reconsideration of all claims that, under the new legal interpretation, had been unjustly rejected.

In the period between 1961 and 1965, the same games that had been played out while the Supplementary Law was being debated were repeated. Federal Finance Ministers Heinz Starke and Rolf Dahlgrün (FDP) opposed the demands, referring to "boundless" cost increases. The Finance Ministry formed a working group to draft a government reform proposal. Officials of various ministries and state agencies were included in the working group, but no Bundestag deputies or persecutee organizations. After two years, the working group presented a bill that went to the Bundestag for debate on 21 October 1963. The bill provided for a hardship fund for late emigrants containing only 600 million marks, guaranteed a concentration camp assumption only after at least one year of concentration camp, and, while it allowed survivors' benefits for people who had died before 1 October 1953, called for no change in deadlines.[165]

On 14 November 1963, at the first reading of the bill, Finance Minister Dahlgrün told the Bundestag that the late emigrants could not be fully included in the BEG, as this would be too expensive; a general easing of the burden of proof had to be rejected, as it would mean that "nothing concrete at all would have to be proven," which would "cause abuse"— abuse about whose "highly undesirable consequences one can only urgently warn." He insisted that deadlines for latest possible submission of claims had to be retained for financial and administrative reasons: "Every limitation based on fact situations, every deadline, every standard in general must necessarily draw a clear line between the eligible and ineligible, and may thus lead to hardship in individual cases."[166]

The basis of Dahlgrün's statement was an exposé by his deputy secretary, Féaux de la Croix, entitled "Finance Policy Aspects of Final Reparations Legislation," in which he claimed that the persecutee organizations' demands for an expansion of the restitution law could exceed the 4.5 billion DM estimated by the federal government by 15 to 20 billion DM. He also expressed the view that there were no legal grounds for reparations; the German Reich, he said, had gone bankrupt, and thus could not fulfill all its debts and responsibilities. All obligations had been discharged by the treaty with Israel and the Federal Restitution Law of 1956.[167] Accordingly, Dahlgrün declared to the Bundestag that the Federal Republic had no general liability for damages caused by the Third Reich, as the two were not identical.[168] The Finance Minister advocated this view at a time when the Federal Republic was otherwise everywhere presenting itself as the sole legal successor to the German Reich.

The committee chair, Martin Hirsch, responded: "I would not feel comfortable in a country that attempted to avoid its responsibilities with tricks, like a 'crooked' bankrupt debtor . . . I would like to be proud to call myself German again. As long as we have this material debt and are not willing to pay, as is right, I cannot be proud." He said the current law embodied not only hardships but also real gaps and errors: "Those who experienced worse things are disadvantaged."[169]

After a detailed acknowledgement of all the legislative achievements to date and praise for the "faithful" and "conscientious" staffs of the reparations offices, Franz Böhm argued that reparations had to be fulfilled "to the limits of the payment capacity" of the Federal Republic. He implored the deputies and the government, "We must not flag in our earnestness about reparations. No feeling must arise that we must now discharge a burdensome duty; we must proceed, until the last decision, with great seriousness. And no feeling must arise that might have a paralyzing effect on reparations authorities, government auditors, or reparations evaluations."[170]

Hirsch's appeal to a sort of reparations patriotism and Böhm's call to stay the course could not conceal the fact that the general feeling and the balance of power in the Bundestag boded ill for a reform of the restitution law. Chancellor Erhard's government address of 18 October 1963 took a different tone than Adenauer's earlier admissions of responsibility. And in his tried and true fashion, former finance minister Schäffer spoke up yet again, this time in the *Deutsche National- und Soldatenzeitung* newspaper, in an interview by its chief editor, Gerhard Frey:

Frey: They want more and more.
Schäffer: The mistake was in not clearly delineating from the beginning the limits that could not be crossed. The more we pay, the more we have to listen to.
Frey: Why didn't you make the limits clear at the time?
Schäffer: I tried, but I was unsuccessful in the cabinet. Now we're paying the

price. Eighteen years have passed since the end of World War II, and after all this time, I see new reparations as absurd; what are we still repairing?

Frey: Do you see any end to the payments?

Schäffer: To be honest, no. The German efforts have been based on attempts to keep the others happy.

In a concluding commentary, Frey wrote that the "German war generation" would "not forget" the minister's attitude.[171]

The chief editor of the *Deutsche Zeitung*, Hans Hellwig, wrote that proposals for reform of the BEG bordered "on the fantastic," adding that more thoughtful members of the population were increasingly turning away from "businesslike dealing with the past . . . in disgust." After all, German soldiers had not gone to war and prison voluntarily, but "today they must pay enormous taxes for all sorts of things, making reparations payments that often have no causal connection to German misdeeds."[172]

Die Zeit felt that the demands of the persecutee organizations would lead to an enormous number of new trials and proceedings: "In the still-closed world of the persecuted, especially the emigrants, it's buzzing like a beehive. New desires are being awakened." Increasing the sum, for example, for interference with education for "the peculiar people, the Gypsies" was completely out of place, as Gypsies placed no value on education and thus did not need to be compensated for lost educational opportunities. Instead of "perpetuating" reparations, *Die Zeit* believed, they should finally be brought to an end, so that a "new chapter unburdened by the past" could begin.[173]

People hoped to dispose of the burden of the past, not only by bringing reparations to an end, but also through the statute of limitations on Nazi crimes. The beginning of the statute-of-limitations debate in the Bundestag fell in the midst of discussions of the BEG Final Law. In November 1964, the federal government decided not to extend the statute of limitations for murder and genocide beyond 1965. This decision created such a public stir at home and abroad that, after several Bundestag debates, the statute of limitations was extended to 1969. Some advocates of a general elimination of the statute of limitations had Germany's reputation in mind; they feared "uncontrollable foreign-policy reactions" should Nazi murders lapse under the statute. For this reason, in May 1968, a CDU deputy, Kurt Birrenbach, held exploratory discussions at the United Nations in New York, as the UN planned to adopt a resolution establishing that genocide and war crimes could not be subject to statutes of limitations. The Federal Republic wanted to forestall the UN decision at all cost. On 10 July 1969, the Bundestag decided to eliminate the statute of limitations for genocide. The driving forces behind this decision were the justice minister of the Grand Coalition, Gustav Heinemann (SPD), and the minister of the interior, Ernst Benda (CDU).[174]

What was achieved for the statute-of-limitations issue following a change in political climate toward the end of the 1960s could not be achieved in the reparations debate of 1964–65. Chairman Hirsch, his deputy Böhm, and a minority of deputies were unable, in the debate on the government proposal for reform of the BEG, to enact a bill that would have contained most of the demands of the persecutees' organizations. In May 1964, the committee held a hearing of experts and victims' organizations. Earlier, the Finance Ministry had already arranged for a separate hearing with representatives of victims' organizations, in which the differences between their demands and those of the Claims Conference came to light. While the Claims Conference placed particular emphasis on inclusion of the late emigrants, the German associations were more concerned with the other demands listed above.[175] Küster also gave evidence as an expert, and demanded with particular urgency the elimination of deadlines.[176] But the Finance Ministry, represented by Hermann Zorn, made sure that the government bill passed rapidly through the committee, with only a few improvements (such as an increase in the hardship fund from 600 to 700 million DM).

Hermann Zorn (1924–) entered government service in Bavaria as a lawyer in the early 1950s. In 1954, he moved to the federal Ministry of Finance, where he worked with the reparations officer Georg Blessin. He participated in the debates on the BEG in 1956 and became the most influential man in the ministry's reparations office because of his outstanding knowledge. The government draft of the BEG Final Law of November 1963 bears the marks of his influence. In 1968, Zorn rose from being a senior official in the Finance Ministry to become a judge on the Supreme Court of Appeals. Zorn was one of the few experts in reparations law, an area largely avoided by the legal profession; until his retirement, he was the most influential person on the Supreme Court of Appeals' reparations panel. After passage of the BEG, the Finance Ministry ensured itself of a lasting influence in the judiciary in the person of Zorn.

When it became clear that the government bill would be adopted, survivors of the concentration camps in New York organized a demonstration at which they once again demanded full inclusion of the late emigrants in the law. The head of the Claims Conference, Nahum Goldmann, met with Chancellor Erhard and made it clear that he was not about to accept increasing the hardship fund for late emigrants to 700 million DM as a solution. He warned Erhard of further dissonance abroad. Twenty-four hours before the planned adoption of the law, at the very last minute—and after Adenauer himself had stepped in behind the scenes—the Bundestag's president, Eugen Gerstenmaier, worked out a compromise between the "pro-expansion" minority on the reparations committee and the Finance Ministry. It provided for an increase in the hardship fund to 1.2 billion DM and certain additional improvements to the tune of 500–600 million DM.[177] Additional reparations benefits were brought up to 4.5 billion DM from the original government proposal of 3 billion. On 26 May 1965, this compromise passed the Bundestag. Goldmann expressed satisfaction with the outcome and, despite considerable opposition within his own ranks, declared that the Claims Conference would make no further demands for improvement of the law, and that the work of reparations had come to an end as far as the Claims Conference was concerned.[178]

The significant changes in the law included: (1) a hardship fund for late emigrants of 1.2 billion DM; (2) survivors' benefits for widows of people who had died before 1 October 1953; (3) an assumption that, after one year in a concentration camp, any health problems leading to a 25 percent reduction in earning capacity were caused by persecution; (4) an increase in the pension for harm to career and benefits for loss of educational opportunity from 5,000 to 10,000 marks; and (5) bringing cases of harm to career and health that had already been closed into line with the new regulations.

The heads of agencies and organizations had reached agreement. The deputies of the governing coalition had insisted, when enacting the law, that it was a "final law," so it was officially entitled the BEG Final Law.[179] But once again, large groups of persecutees had been left with nothing, and substantial demands by persecutee organizations had gone unmet:

1. Neither ghettos, other forms of imprisonment, nor survival in hiding fell under the "concentration camp assumption," and the required period of imprisonment in concentration camps was one year rather than five months.

2. Not only did the old BEG deadlines remain unchanged; even for the new BEG Final Law provisions, an extremely narrow applications deadline of one year was set. The law was published in the German legal bulletin on 18 September 1965, and the deadline was 30 September 1966. However, the persecutees and their lawyers throughout the world would have a difficult time submitting well-documented applications within a year. After widespread protests, a further six-month "grace period" for substantiation of applications was granted, until 31 March 1967. But this substantiation deadline was only of use to those who were able to make a preliminary application by 30 September 1966. "Anyone desiring reparations must not only explain what happened to him, but must also know which of the endless facts of his life, and the lives of those from whom he derives his rights, justify a restitution claim and which do not," Walter Schwarz wrote in *Aufbau*. He or she had to know about the earlier rejec-

tion of an application, knowledge that could not be expected "of anyone unfamiliar with law." Thus the elimination of deadlines was "the only fitting solution."[180] A final deadline of 31 December 1969 was set for applications for restoration of the previous status of late emigrants, and for health problems that appeared later, in addition to already existing disability.

3. Correction of reparations claims that had been unjustly rejected in their entirety, as required by Article IV of the BEG Final Law, was subverted by reparations offices, and to some extent the courts, in the case of disability by a requirement that "prevailing medical opinion" in Germany (foreign medical opinion was expressly not the standard) on the illness in the particular case had to have changed. All that was necessary to reject an application for correction was the laconic affidavit of a medical official that the prevailing medical opinion had not changed. Countless victims of persecution who had never received disability pensions because of the restrictive decisions of the 1950s and 1960s once again failed to secure their rights. This was not necessarily the result of bad faith; so narrow an interpretation of Article IV simply saved work. The case was closed with a few sentences, and the proceedings did not have to start over from the beginning. Although the Supreme Court of Appeals put an end to this arbitrary behavior in 1968, claims for correction under Article IV that had already been rejected could not be reopened. This only became possible after a constitutional complaint by Küster in 1969. The Constitutional Court held that earlier incorrect decisions could be corrected through a second proceeding—that is, a completely new proceeding with new affidavits, and so on.[181]

4. The problem of late emigrants was not satisfactorily solved by increasing the hardship fund to 1.2 billion DM. For many of them, the BEG Final Law reduced their claims compared with the BEG of 1956. Obstacles and traps were not eliminated, and new ones were created.

No pensions, only one-time subsidies, were paid from the hardship fund, the distribution of which was regulated by Article V of the BEG Final Law. Formerly persecuted late emigrants who could take advantage of this fund included those who did not meet any of the conditions of the BEG. In contrast, late emigrants who had come to the West between 1953 and 1965 ("post-fifty-three-ers") had always been able to make claims under certain conditions. These people, if they were considered expellees under § 1 of the Federal Expellees Law, were already eligible for restitution under § 68 of the Federal Supplementary Law of 1953 and § 150 of the BEG, even if they had not emigrated until after the law went into effect (that is, after 1 October 1953). After the Hungarian revolt of 1956, in particular, many Hungarian Jews emigrated to Western countries.

Polish, Czechoslovakian, and Romanian Jews who had applied for permission to emigrate soon after the war did not receive such permission until the end of the 1950s or later. Some had been asking the German authorities about their rights since the early 1950s. At first, they were turned away with the argument that they did not meet the residency requirements or possess expellee status. When they came to the West in the late 1950s and early 1960s—whether to Israel, Germany, or the United States—and made application again, they were turned down because the deadline for filing claims had passed. However, many could repair this "omission" by applying for restoration of previous status.

In contrast, Romanian Jews who had been victims of the murderous operations of the *Einsatzgruppen* and their Romanian accomplices in Bessarabia, Bukovina, and Transnistria received nothing, because according to a Supreme Court of Appeals decision of 2 July 1958, these actions were the responsibility, not of the German, but of the supposedly sovereign Romanian regime.[182] Only after the UN supplied documentation, based on its own research, proving that Germany was responsible for persecution of Jews in Romania did the association of top state reparations authorities decide in Bremen on 22–23 June 1960, ignoring the restrictive Supreme Court jurisprudence, that Romanian Jews were entitled to reparations.[183]

Three years later, however, in November 1963, when the government presented its proposal for a BEG Final Law, the late emigrants—including Romanian Jews—faced a new hurdle. Hermann Zorn, who had risen to become the most influential man in the Finance Ministry's reparations department, had a major influence on the law. Zorn had always been of the opinion that the deadline of 1 October 1953 had been forgotten in § 150 of the BEG, and that granting restitution to late-emigrated persecutees did not therefore reflect the true meaning of the law. Thus Zorn added this deadline to § 150 of the government proposal for a BEG Final Law (§ 150 para. 2 in the new version), with the consequence that all claims by persecutees who had emigrated after 1953 and filed applications for restitution were retroactively disallowed. In anticipation of imminent adoption of the government proposal, offices and courts had begun to reject pending claims under § 150 by the end of 1963. With the adoption of paragraph 2 of the new version of § 150 in the BEG Final Law, thousands lost their rights to restitution.[184]

Six years later, on 23 March 1971, the Constitutional Court held that this section violated Article 20 of the constitution and was null and void.[185] However, during those six years, lawyers had had to inform their clients that it made no sense to apply for restitution or continue pressing their claims in court. By the time the news that the Constitutional Court's 1971 decision again granted them the right to restitution had reached refugees scattered all over the world, many had already resigned themselves to the situation.[186]

Unfortunately, Hermann Zorn, who as an official of the Finance Ministry had been responsible for disallowing the late emigrants' claims, had meanwhile been named a judge on the federal Supreme Court of Appeals, in which capacity he now employed farfetched arguments in dismissing renewed claims by late emigrants following the Constitutional Court's 1971 decision. Again, thousands were unable to collect on their claims. Once the retroactive introduction of a deadline had proven unconstitutional, the Supreme Court of Appeals, with Zorn as judge, developed a new construct that allowed it to deny restitution to *Ostjuden* (eastern European Jews): personal responsibility for missed deadlines. Two examples may be given. Many Polish Jews who succeeded in escaping the advancing German troops in Russian-occupied eastern Poland were deported to Siberia by the Soviet authorities. In the period when applications could still be made on time (that is, before 1 April 1958), the authorities and courts categorically denied—as with the Romanian Jews—any German responsibility for these refugees in Russia or their survivors. This became known in those countries where the survivors had ended up, and their advisors discouraged them from applying for restitution. The deadline passed unobserved. However, in 1962, the Supreme Court of Appeals recognized the responsibility of the German authorities for these people's fate, since those authorities had certainly been gratified by their hardships in the Soviet Union. For nine years, these claims were processed and often acknowledged. But then, in 1971, the Supreme Court entered judgment against the widow of a refugee in Russia, arguing that she had not explained precisely enough when, how, where, and from whom she had heard in 1962 that she was in fact entitled to reparations, and from whom she had heard earlier, when she allowed the 1958 deadline to pass, that she was not entitled to reparations. Because of this omission, the court held that it could not overlook the lateness of her application.

A Jewish woman living in Canada who had fled the Germans and been deported to the Arctic by the Russians explained the lateness of her application by the fact that she had just read in a Jewish newspaper that health disabilities suffered in Russia would also be compensated. The Supreme Court of Appeals held that such unjustified imprecision could not be overlooked, as she had given neither the name nor the issue number of the Jewish newspaper in her application.[187]

Despite numerous defeats, Otto Küster fought tirelessly until his death against this Supreme Court of Appeals and its influential reparations judge, Zorn, the perpetuator of the petty, half-hearted reparations policies of the 1950s and 1960s. "There was not only a duty to make inquiry, there was a duty of speed, and a duty to explain and make credible why one had not inquired more thoroughly and earlier and had not been quicker in making application," Küster protested.

Such censure applied to the victims' procedural duties, which, if we were to believe the Supreme Court, they had failed to fulfill on a large scale, with the result that their legal claims have "lapsed." The Germany that speaks through this decision does not speak with the voice of a conscientious or even embarrassed debtor who is searching for his victims, scattered throughout the world, and never tires of flushing out even the most well-hidden victim and pleading with him to accept our reparations and thus appease his memory.[188]

Küster appealed these decisions to the Constitutional Court. His appeal was dismissed, so he took the case before the European Court of Justice in Strasbourg, which decided in 1989 that the issue was one of domestic law and violated no human rights, the court's area of jurisdiction.[189] At a conference of the Evangelische Akademie in Bad Boll in 1983, Küster declared publicly that the Supreme Court of Appeals judges had gotten lost in details and that their juridical decision-making on supposedly missed deadlines was "an eerie scene of extralegal, retroactively planted surrogates."[190] At this, Judge Zorn, who had also been invited to speak, left the conference, visibly affected and angered.[191]

A further complication of the legal situation for the victims from the areas of expulsion in eastern Europe was the formula, also introduced in § 150 of the BEG Final Law, that victims had claims if "they belonged to the German language and cultural sphere" (until then, the wording had been "expellees within the meaning of § 1 of the Federal Expellees Law"). This passage, intended to ease the conditions for restitution claims, nevertheless had its perils; German authorities and courts now had to investigate who did or did not fit within it. This led to grotesque proceedings. Because it was difficult to determine who had belonged to the German "cultural sphere," the Supreme Court of Appeals decided that "language used in personal life" was the criterion. However, it was impossible to tell from behind a German desk which language the applicant had spoken decades ago in Kovno, Bialystok, or Budapest. Therefore, they came up with the idea of language tests, which had to be taken before members of the German embassies or, in Israel, at the Finance Ministry. At one such test, one person wrote in his test booklet, "Never again saw my wife, my three sons, mother, and siblings. Everyone dead in Auschwitz. I ask myself how I manage to sit here and say I am part of the German cultural sphere."[192] In one case, the Supreme Court of Appeals stated that the claimant showed no "desire to feel German."[193]

This provision was based on the BEG's basic concept that only German persecutees, that is, only "German" Jews, should receive restitution. In his historical account, Féaux de la Croix fails to mention the extremely confused legal situation and the harassment in dealing with eastern European Jews. He gives the impression that the only issue for them at the time was the hardship fund in the Final Law. Zorn's move in introducing a deadline to § 150 and the fluctuations in and perils of the Supreme Court of Appeals' jurisprudence are not included in the federal government's official account. After all, Féaux de la Croix had been Zorn's boss at the Ministry of Finance.

Chapter 3

Damage to Body and Health

On 7 February 1960, some 200 mostly Polish Jews gathered in New York to form the Committee of Nazi Victims Deprived of Justice and Compensation by the German Medical Service. They adopted a protest resolution addressed to the West German consulate general in New York calling for an end to assessment of their reparations claims for health disabilities by "diagnoses at a distance by hostile medical bureaucrats." They further demanded that no doctor be allowed to make such determinations if he had belonged to a Nazi organization and therefore had an interest in "covering up the consequences of persecution as far as possible." They argued that only doctors thoroughly familiar with all phases of the persecutions should be employed by the German consulates as medical evaluators, and that they should possess "a humane and sympathetic ear for the sufferings of the persecuted." Furthermore, they asked that reparations authorities at last cease their constant demands for evidence of persecution that was impossible to obtain, witnesses to abuse, and medical documents from the period following liberation. Representatives of the Claims Conference and the URO were skeptical of the Committee of Nazi Victims. In the view of the New York consulate general, its members "could [not] even begin to be compared with the representatives of Jewry here or the German Jewish émigrés."[1]

Those raising their voices at this gathering were victims of persecution entitled to reparations who had been short-changed; pensions for harm to health were reparations for the "little people" who could claim no material losses, but only loss of health. The disability procedure—known in bureaucratic jargon as "B-harm," the second type of harm listed in the law—was the stepchild of reparations; compared with other types of harm, it was the most complicated to process, replete with traps and hurdles for the applicant. Health damage was the source of the greatest number of proceedings and the longest processing periods. Some proceedings were still before the courts thirty years after application had been made.

The legal basis supplied by § 28, para. 1, of the Federal Restitution Law is clear. It reads: "A persecutee has a claim to reparations if he suffered not insignificant harm to body or health. It is sufficient for there to be a probable connection between the original harm to the body or health and the persecution." What was "not insignificant"? What was "probable"? Those responsible for evaluating, examining, and deciding were doctors, bureaucrats, and judges who had lived through the Third Reich, if not as persecutors, then almost never as persecutees.

The legislature demanded a "probable connection"—that is, there had to be more evidence for than against such a connection. Administrators and doctors often demanded more. First, the applicant had to fill out a form on "harm to body and health" (see appendix A). He or she was required to describe the complaint; explain which persecution measures had "caused the harm," in his or her opinion, and "indicate proofs"; and list the doctors, hospitals, and sanatoria by which he or she had been treated. Finally, the applicant was expected to provide detailed information on his or her finances and personal life prior to the start of persecution.

Once the application was received, the reparations office commissioned a doctor in the persecutee's locality to submit an evaluation.[2] Months and even years could pass before a medical examination took place, and an equally long time before the evaluation was formulated, written, and submitted to the office.

The examiner had to determine all the patient's complaints, estimate the reduction in earning capacity caused by each separate complaint (*Minderung der Erwerbsfähigkeit*, or "MdE" in bureaucratic jargon— often unavoidable even in the following description), and then estimate the total reduction in earning capacity from all the complaints. In a second step, he was required to determine which complaints had been caused by persecution, and in a third step, in what way they had been caused by persecution—whether "in the sense of their origins," as a "substantial cause," or whether they were hereditary and therefore worsened "distinguishably" (that is, only partially) or in "direction-setting" fashion (that is, to their full extent). Finally, he had to estimate the "persecution-induced reduction in earning capacity" (*verfolgungsbedingte Minderung der Erwerbsfähigkeit*; in the jargon, "vMdE") for all complaints caused by persecution.

Few could comprehend this jargon, least of all the foreign evaluators, who were completely unaccustomed to thinking in such categories.[3] Reduction in earning capacity was expressed as a percentage, as was the norm in the German social security system. To determine which types of ailments caused what reduction in earning capacity, examining doctors commonly used tables created for the purpose. These tables estimated, for example, loss of an eye at 30 percent and loss of an arm at 50 percent.[4]

Under § 31, para. 1, of the Federal Restitution Law, reparations were paid only if the reduction in earning capacity caused by persecution was at least 25 percent. Under certain circumstances, a course of treatment could be allowed for lower percentages, but there was and is no claim to a pension. If a recognized complaint worsened, a "worsening claim" could be made under § 31, para. 1—that is, an increase in pension could be requested. A follow-up examination was required for this purpose. Follow-up examinations were prescribed under § 6 of the second set of BEG implementing regulations, and it sometimes happened that, on the basis of such a follow-up examination prescribed by the authorities, an improvement in the complaint was attested, and the pension was reduced or rescinded. The same could happen as a result of the examination that followed a course of treatment. Therefore, lawyers advised their clients against applying for courses of treatment.[5] Such reparations were almost inevitably directed against cure, and perhaps against a desire to cure or improve. Today, in general, no follow-up examinations are required.

Pensions were calculated according to a complicated scheme involving reduction of earning capacity in conjunction with the income of a comparable civil-service group. Depending upon his or her occupational and financial position before the beginning of persecution, the applicant was classed as matching a junior, middle-level, upper-level, or senior job. If classed in the middle-level group, for example, the disability pension for a fifty-eight-year-old victim of persecution with 50 percent reduction in earning capacity in 1961 was 243 DM a month.

If an obvious disability was present, such as loss of a leg because of frostbite in a concentration camp, it was relatively easy to establish the reduction in earning capacity. This was more difficult for chronic somatic, psychosomatic, and psychological illness as a long-term consequence of being in a concentration camp; that is, it was left to a large extent to the good or bad will of the individual doctor. The necessary separation of complaints into those resulting from persecution and those not resulting from persecution—expressed as a percentage reduction in earning capacity—led to absurd calculations. For example, a stomach ulcer was considered hereditary (that is, a predisposition toward this illness existed in the genetic makeup or constitution of the person involved). An ulcer that had appeared before persecution could have been worsened by years in a concentration camp or the stresses of uprooting and flight. In this case, there were two types of worsening, the "distinguishable" (abgrenzbar) and the "direction-setting" (richtunggebend). In the case of the so-called "distinguishable" worsenings, the complaint had worsened only partly as a result of persecution, and only part of the reduction in earning capacity calculated for this complaint was blamed on persecution. If the worsening was "direction-setting," however, the complaint had taken a completely different course because of the persecution, and the reduction in earning capacity could be ascribed entirely to persecution. A hereditary complaint might have been "constitutionally" present, but under the prescribed terminology, it could also be recognized as "substantially caused" by persecution if it had appeared for the first time during or after persecution; this meant that the complaint would be fully counted in the reduction in earning capacity.[6]

The linguistic labyrinths that doctors were forced to negotiate are evident in an order to the evaluators from the Düsseldorf district court:

In accordance with the most recent jurisprudence, it is requested that a "worsening" be spoken of only for a complaint that became openly manifest before persecution. If merely a predisposition existed before persecution, only the phrases "substantial" or "not substantial causation" of hereditary complaints should be used. A causation is significant if the persecution component at its origin can be estimated to have caused a quarter of the reduction in earning capacity through the respective complaint. If it is assumed that a complaint that was substantially caused by persecution, and is thus eligible for a full pension, would have emerged later to the same extent or an extent that can be precisely determined, at a time that can be precisely estimated, through harms independent of persecution in conjunction with the genetic predisposition, this overtaking causation must be established with a probability bordering on certainty. No grounds for a reduction in pension exist if the complaint was substantially caused by persecution at the moment it appeared, but, as a result of a special predisposition in the patient, it irregularly failed to abate, as long as it is not established that this predisposition would have become manifest even without persecution.[7]

Finally, the examiner had to investigate when and to what extent the reduction in earning capacity had begun (for example, from the appearance of the first symptoms of illness in the concentration camp), how the reduction had changed over the years, what it was at the deadline date of 1 November 1953, and what it was at the time of the examination; also whether the condition could be expected to worsen or improve and whether a follow-up examination was therefore necessary.

The majority of the persecutees lived abroad. The West German consulates there appointed local doctors as evaluators. If they were not German emigrants familiar with the peculiarities of the German insurance system, they frequently submitted reports that failed to meet the required standards—that is, they did not include the required precise case details, findings, and tricks of calculation. Often they estimated their clients' medical disabilities according to the standards of their countries, which were completely different from Germany's. Frequently, the doctors in the reparations offices responsible for reviewing these foreign reports rejected them and demanded a second report from another doctor, or simply recommended denying the application. In more generous administrations, such as the Berlin reparations office, however, foreign reports were recognized in case of doubt, sparing the persecutees much injustice.[8]

The reparations offices' reviewing doctors were generally medical officers from other areas of the public health service or physicians in private practice working for the administration on the side. Larger reparations offices, such as those in Berlin, North Rhine–Westphalia, Lower Saxony, and Bavaria, had their own medical services.[9] These doctors judged and checked the correctness of reports without ever seeing or examining the applicants. Yet they had a greater influence on the offices' decisions than the examining doctors. This led to considerable distortions to the disadvantage of the persecutees. Their organizations and lawyers justifiably accused the medical services and reviewers of deciding the majority of cases on the basis of financial considerations. Willibald Maier, former head of the medical service of the Bavarian reparations office, thought, however, that the medical services enjoyed an independent status similar to that of judge. In a contribution to volume 4 of the official chronicle of reparations, Maier wrote:

The accusations against the medical service generally involved procedural tactics, or they were made by interest groups for whom objective arguments apparently no longer played a role . . . A frequent allegation suggested that the medical services . . . always decided in the Treasury's favor in doubtful cases, as they had to make decisions for the state, whose servants they were. In fact, however, permanently employed doctors or those with civil servant status are in a good position to implement the law positively . . . They claim the same independence as judges . . . who are also paid by the state.

Maier also saw no problem with the practice of making medical decisions from behind a desk: "Assessment of causal connections is a scientific question, in the answering of which personal knowledge of the person involved is not necessary."[10] The former head of the Office of Reparations in Hamburg, Karl Weiss, also insisted that the medical services of the reparations offices were completely independent in their decision-making. Because it was "not called upon to make final decisions on claims," the medical service, according to Weiss, was a "third party independent of" the authorities and the persecutees, and was in an especially suitable position to choose medical evaluators.[11]

The medical service had close ties to the staff members who decided whether to approve the applications. They worked in the same buildings, in neighboring corridors and offices. A medical service was not independent; it was part of the office, choosing medical evaluators and reviewing the incoming reports for the office. Officially, the doctors commissioned by the office to examine applicants were also independent, and their reports were unbiased. But in reality, the offices sought out doctors who, in accordance with the interests of the public purse, would not be overly generous in their recommendations. This was especially true of the physicians commissioned by the domestic offices, but less so with physicians employed by West German consulates abroad.

In his encounters with the persecutees in his function as medical evaluator, the doctor was an arm of the German state. He was required to ensure "the right of the state, as a community of all its citizens, to protection from unjustified claims."[12] The doctor was not primarily an advocate for the persecutee; he could not, and was not allowed to, see in him or her a patient who might need his help. Doctors who too often issued evaluations in favor of persecutees were considered "unobjective" by the authorities and were no longer assigned examinations. For example, the New York doctor William G. Niederland censored himself by never certifying a reduction in earning capacity of more than 40 percent, even for severe psychological disturbances caused by persecution, as he would otherwise have had to reckon with automatic rejection by the German authorities.[13]

William G. Niederland (1904–1993) studied medicine in Würzburg. After qualifying in 1929, he became a medical assistant at the Beelitz sanitarium near Berlin. He held the post of public health officer for occupational diseases in Düsseldorf in 1930–32, and then became head of the Rheinburg Castle spa-sanitorium for internal and nervous diseases in Gailingen, Baden. In 1934, to escape racial persecution, Niederland emigrated via Switzerland to Italy, where he opened a private practice in Milan and joined an aid committee for refugees from Nazi Germany. In 1939, he fled to England and became ship's doctor on the British ship *Dardanus*. He landed in the Philippines in 1940, where for a short time he was assistant professor at the university in Manila. That same year, however, he emigrated to the United States and began a private psychiatric and psychoanalytic practice in New York. He was also a lecturer and consultant at various university hospitals, and from 1970 until he gained emeritus status in 1978, clinical professor of psychiatry at the State University of New York. Beginning in the mid 1950s, he was the examining doctor for the West German consulate general in New York. Niederland published widely on the long-term psychological effects of persecution and, together with Henry Krystal, described survivor syndrome and the phenomenon of survivors' guilt. In the course of his work as evaluator for reparations claims, he clashed with the medical councils of the German reparations offices, accusing them of being "rejection councils." Because of the psychological stress involved, he voluntarily gave up his mandate as evaluator in 1973, from then on submitting medical opinions only in exceptional cases. A complete collection of his examination reports can be found at the Leo Baeck Institute in New York.[14]

The only doctors who had a chance with the authorities were those perceived as "objective" because they submitted negative recommendations in a certain percentage of cases. The same was true of evaluators commissioned by the courts. In the case of benefits for war veterans, § 109 of the Social Welfare Court Law allowed the plaintiff to choose his own evaluator; the court was obliged to accept that choice, and in case of an affirmative judgment, the state was expected to pay his costs. But such a choice was not provided for in the Federal Restitution Law. The persecutee could commission a private evaluation, but he had to pay for it himself, and it was in any case seen as a "biased evaluation" and given little weight. In reparations procedures, only the court determined the doctor, and the decision to appoint either a "pro-approval" or a "pro-rejection" doctor more or less determined the final outcome.[15] Willibald Maier described the contradictory role of the evaluator as follows:

From his everyday practice, the doctor knows that as a rule, a patient . . . especially at the first consultation, feels a certain tension as a result of an understandable feeling of alienation. Even the treating doctor does not always find out the truth. Toward a medical evaluator commissioned by the authorities or the court, attitudes are burdened with even more reservations, since, in addition, the fulfillment of certain expectations rests on his decision . . . The [persecutees'] wounds are very deep, and they frequently make even the minimal amount of trust necessary for the doctor's report more difficult. The medical evaluator is only too easily subconsciously connected with the former persecutor.[16]

It was trying for persecutees to be examined and assessed by a doctor of a nation that had only recently been abusing and murdering others like them. The examining style of many German doctors and the tone of their reports triggered negative associations. The problem for doctors commissioned by West German consulates abroad was a different one. Many of them were German émigré doctors, themselves victims of persecution, whom the persecutees did not view primarily as representatives of the German state; but even these doctors, if they hoped to achieve anything, had to adapt to this system of approval and rejection, percentages and calculations. There were also German émigré doctors who felt so at home in the German system of evaluations that they acted with inner conviction against their own fellow persecutees.

Most of the evaluators, especially those abroad, were overworked. In the late 1950s, the commission of examining doctors in Paris, in consultation with the North Rhine–Westphalia Ministry of the Interior, agreed that 65 doctors would be sufficient to prepare 1,800 evaluations a month and deal with the existing backlog of 5,000 evaluations. However, it soon became clear that 180 doctors—almost three times as many— were needed to complete this huge amount of work. Experience proved that a doctor could prepare no more than 10 evaluations a month, in addition to his practice and clinical work. Because of the overload, the period of time between commissioning the doctor and completion of the evaluation could be up to two years. In 1966, German university clinics took an average of six months to a year to issue evaluations.[17]

In West Germany, few qualified doctors were available to assess persecutees. Few were interested in the subject of persecutee illness, which led to no clinical or scientific career; they were more likely to be concerned with the health problems of war victims, German prisoners of war, or returnees from Russia. (The same was true of administrators and lawyers active in reparations.) Thus officials and courts fell back on medical officers and practicing physicians who were mainly former Wehrmacht doctors, some of whom had been active members of the Nazi party or the SS. They were neither personally nor politically suited for such work and did not possess the requisite professional qualifications in this difficult area of medicine.

Another serious problem was obtaining documents on privations suffered as a result of persecution that had caused health problems, as well as documentation of consultations with doctors and stays in clinics during and after persecution. Evidence from the Nazi period was generally nonexistent, and documents on treatment and findings from the immediate postwar period were often no longer available. In the chaos of the postwar period, many hospitals in DP camps and refugee aid organizations had failed to maintain files. In the postwar years, too, many victims of persecution had frequently changed residences or emigrated. Those from eastern Europe found it particularly difficult to submit evidence of treatment and physicians' reports. Although the law required that this general evidentiary difficulty not be interpreted to the disadvantage of the persecutees, in practice bureaucrats and courts constantly demanded such evidence. One of the reasons for this was the fact that medical evaluators required so-called bridge symptoms to prove persecution-induced complaints. The persecutee had to submit reports proving that signs of the complaint had emerged immediately after the persecution and had lasted through the years until the time of the assessment examination.

This requirement by German examining doctors flew in the face of all scientific fact. In Denmark and France, extensive studies in the early 1950s had already established that many chronic psychological and somatic illnesses in persecutees appeared only after a symptom-free latency period lasting many years.[18]

This had also been known in the Federal Republic since the mid 1950s. Nevertheless, not until 1965 was the evidentiary difficulty experienced by persecutees taken into account in the so-called concentration camp assumption of § 31, para. 2, of the BEG Final Law, which provided that, in the case of persecutees who had spent at least a year in a concentration camp and suffered a loss in earning capacity of 25 percent or more, this loss in earning capacity would be assumed to have been caused by the persecution. In this case, the applicant and the assessing doctor were not required to bring further proof that the attested complaint had been caused by persecution; the tiresome assessment of the "portion" of the reduction in earning capacity "caused by persecution" was eliminated, as was the evidence of "bridge symptoms," and so on. But by the time the law was changed in this way, most health damage cases had already been decided.

Persecutees with health damage were disadvantaged in reparations, as the numbers show. According to the official statistics cited in table 5 (see appendix B for all tables), the rejection rate for health damage was relatively high and, as shown by the differences in approval rates, the arbitrariness of the process was particularly crass. One-third (32.4%) of the applications from abroad were rejected, as were nearly half of those from within the country (46.4%) (table 5, col. V). In 18.6 percent of the cases, the applications were resolved in other ways—often, that is, through the death of the applicant (table 5, col. VI). The figures describe the situation on 17 September 1965, the day the BEG Final Law was enacted.

At the First International Medico-Legal Symposium on Health Damage Following Imprisonment and Persecution in Cologne in 1967, the president of the state parliament of North Rhine–Westphalia, John van Nes Ziegler, presented figures on the situation as of 31 December 1960 and 31 December 1966. The figures are not separated into domestic and foreign applications. During both periods, applications were rejected in slightly over one third of all cases (37% and 36.1%) (table 1, col. IV). Ziegler mentioned a further instructive figure: somewhat fewer than one-third (29.5%, table 1, col. III) of the affirmatively decided claims to a disability pension by 31 December 1966 had to be decided in court. Thus there were a disproportionate number of court cases on health damage, a veritable avalanche of suits resulting from the problems mentioned above—the confused legal situation and the tendency of so many doctors to reject claims. The starting point of such a suit was generally the fact that a commissioned physician or one working for the reparations authorities had refused to recognize an applicant's disability as being the result of persecution. If we add the 83,000 official rejections that were later reversed upon appeal to a court (table 1, col. III) to the 159,000 rejections by 31 December 1966 (table 1, col. IV), we find that over half (55%) of all applications for reparations for health damage were originally rejected by the authorities!

Table 2 shows the rates of rejection of the various offices, which differed significantly. The Berlin reparations office confirmed its reputation for generosity and benevolence, especially in health damage cases. At 15 percent, it had the lowest rejection rate of all the offices. This should not be underestimated, especially in view of the fact that a third of all German Jews had lived in Berlin before the war. In North Rhine–Westphalia and Hamburg, applications were rejected at double the rate in Berlin; in Baden-Württemberg, at around four times the rate. How the authorities decided apparently depended on the quality of medical service and the choice of examining doctors, and these varied greatly among the different offices. Berlin, for example, made it a point to ensure that no former Nazis were among the members of the medical service and the examining doctors.[19] The Berlin reparations office maintained close ties with German émigré circles in New York; the heads of the Berlin reparations office often traveled to New York to give talks and wrote pieces for *Aufbau*. After Küster was relieved of his position as head of the Baden-Württemberg office, Berlin played something of a leading role in all areas of reparations. Decisions made by the Berlin office received international publicity. It was very well staffed and worked faster than the other offices.

For this reason, persecutees from the former Reich capital—mainly German Jews of the middle or upper classes—were privileged in reparations, while other German and eastern European Jews, who generally came from a poorer milieu, were worse-treated; the reparations offices of North Rhine–Westphalia, Bavaria, and Rhineland-Palatinate were mainly responsible for processing their applications. The office in Rhineland-Palatinate, which would have had to process some half-million applications, was so understaffed and badly managed that a huge number of applications remained unprocessed for years, until at last the duties of this disorganized and incompetent office were transferred to Berlin.[20]

It is striking that, as the first deadline in the BEG Final Law passed on 31 December 1966, around a fifth, 110,000 of 550,000 (table 1; and see also table 5, col. III), of all health damage applications remained unprocessed. Because of the evaluation procedure, processing lasted years at the bureaucratic level alone; if it went to trial, decades could pass before a case was decided. Schwarz reports that for property restitution, 95 percent of all cases were decided at the lowest levels.[21] But for compensation, especially for health damage, many persecutees had to go through the courts, even as far as the state and federal supreme courts.

As a result of all these obstacles to reparations proceedings, some people occasionally turned to corruption. Some examiners turned out positive evaluations in assembly-line fashion; they demanded horrendous fees from the authorities and, in the case of private evaluations, from the persecutees themselves. Like the lawyers who demanded excessive contingency fees, doctors smelled a profit in reparations. In Paris, some evaluations came out positive or negative depending on what the persecutees had to offer. Thus applicants who were unable to pay had to wash a doctor's car or weed his garden on a regular basis. This forced the Paris doctors to form a supervisory committee to discipline those among them who took bribes and, if it happened again, to relieve them of their positions as evaluators for the German embassy.[22] Of course, persecutees occasionally also approached doctors to show their appreciation of favorable reports. In 1960, the Berlin reparations office sent a form letter to doctors asking that they report such incidents to the office.[23]

These incidents, like the occasional cases of fraud in other areas of reparations and lawyers' excessive contingency fees, were a welcome subject for opponents of reparations and gave the authorities an excuse to create even tougher standards for examination of applications and evaluations. And yet they can also be seen as a legitimate response to the former persecutors' audacity in saddling victims with the requirement of proving their own persecution. Within certain limits, this highly individualized procedure, which turned those to whom Germany actually owed something into carefully inspected supplicants, almost created a right to cheat and corrupt.

Beginning in the early 1960s, the rocky road of reparations in health damage cases increasingly became the subject of public discussion, catalyzed by critical German doctors and lawyers. Dr. Georg Ott, a lawyer in Munich, speaking at the international medico-legal symposium in Düsseldorf in 1969, typically summarized the situation:

1. The precise description of persecution harms, determination of illnesses suffered during the period of persecution, and proof of medical treatment since 1945 generally make time-consuming preliminary investigations necessary.

2. Because examining doctors are overburdened, issuance of an official medical evaluation almost always takes six to seven months. If specialist evaluations are necessary, another eight to ten months generally pass.

3. Review of the evaluations by the reparations authorities' medical services requires another two to three months. This review leads not infrequently to further questions to the examining doctors, with new findings necessary.

4. The end of the medical investigation hardly means that the procedure is ready for decision. For the administrative official or legal expert now goes into action, determining, for example, that two to three years have passed since the initiation of the medical investigation and there is no evidence of the applicant's income or the amount of his social security pension during those years. [Such income was subtracted from the health disability pension, although not from the pension for professional harm.] Thus more months pass.

5. If the procedure goes to court, one must expect even longer duration. One often has to wait far too long even for a court date. If the plaintiff or defendant objects to the medical report, after further weeks, as a rule, an evidentiary decision is reached in which the examining doctor is asked to provide an advisory opinion on the objections. If this opinion is incomplete or unsatisfactory, a higher-level evaluation must be obtained. The medical examination begins all over again. If the evaluation and the higher-level evaluation deviate greatly from each other, a frequent further step is to obtain a so-called "dossier report" from a univer-

sity clinic. This takes the dossier off the judge's desk for another six to eight months. And still no end is in sight. For after the physicians, the judicial system again goes into action, determining that several years have passed since the suit was filed or appeal was made and that in this period the plaintiff's personal or financial situation . . . may have undergone a change that must still be clarified. The wheel begins to turn from the beginning.[24]

Prevailing Scholarly Medical Opinion in the Federal Republic

The German medical profession began to deal with illnesses among war victims and returning prisoners of war immediately after 1945. A well-functioning network of medical evaluators was rapidly set up to work with war victims, with those involved trading information and constantly increasing their knowledge at government-sponsored medical conferences. The former nutrition inspector for the SS Main Office for Economic Administration, Ernst-Günter Schenck, played a leading role in this area.[25]

In contrast, little interest was sparked by the illnesses of those who had survived concentration camps or escaped their tormentors through flight or life in hiding. Although hundreds of thousands of sick concentration camp prisoners lived in DP camps in the early years after 1945, especially in southern Germany, no German doctors published on this group's special health problems in the postwar years. This was partially because DPs almost always accepted treatment only from the Allies or formerly persecuted doctors, whose office hours became hopelessly overbooked. These doctors were not in a position to evaluate the results of their work scientifically.[26]

It was frequently claimed that the sufferings of German prisoners of war in the Soviet Union were very similar to those of concentration camp inmates, making a special study of this subject unnecessary. Willibald Maier made this argument in the Finance Ministry chronicle: "Medical evaluators in the Federal Republic had at their disposal numerous publications on observations of health disorders among returnees from eastern prisoner of war camps. Although this was often denied, not always for objective reasons, the working and living conditions in the eastern prisoner of war camps were quite comparable with the German concentration camps. However, the significant difference was often overlooked that, to put it crassly, there were no crematoria in the eastern prisoner of war camps."[27]

Numerous studies that have since become part of the public record pointed out the fundamental differences between prisoner of war camps and concentration camps. These did not only consist in the fact that "there were no crematoria," but also that the goal was not absolute extermination, genocide, or complete degradation. Many German doctors nevertheless failed to acknowledge the disorders suffered by concentration camp survivors as persecution-induced, because they did not observe the same complaints in "Russia returnees" who had supposedly been exposed to the same privations.

This issue was dealt with quite differently in countries formerly occupied by Germany: Norway, Denmark, France, Poland, the Netherlands, and Czechoslovakia. There, many doctors—mainly those who had themselves survived the German concentration camps or fought in national resistance movements—were interested in survivors' illnesses. The French psychiatrist René Targowla began to study the neuro-psychological consequences of deportations to German concentration camps in 1946, summarizing his results in the concept of the "deportees' asthenia" syndrome. His first studies were published in 1949 and 1950.[28] In 1946, too, his colleague Eugène Minkowski published a study of psychological disorders in adults, young people, and children who had survived the concentration camps.[29] In 1948, the French internists Charles Richet, Louis-François Fichez, Gilbert Dreyfus, and Henri Uzan called the attention of the French medical academy to the "dangerous long-term effects of the physiological misery" of the former deportees.[30] In 1947–48, the Danish neurologist Paul Thygesen studied the effects of starvation on Danish concentration camp victims.[31] All these authors presented their findings to the international public for the first time in 1954 at the International Social Medicine Conference on the Pathology of Former Deportees and Internees in Copenhagen. In 1955, the talks presented there were published in a German collection.[32] Yet in Germany, the results of this conference were all but ignored.

In a Swiss journal, the neurologist and Theresienstadt prisoner doctor V. A. Kral reported in English in 1947 and in German in 1949 on an epidemic of encephalitis-in-typhus in Theresienstadt concentration camp in the winter of 1943–44.[33] In 1951, he published his observations on psychological illness among prisoners in Theresienstadt in the *American Journal of Psychiatry*.[34] In 1947, the internist Alfred Wolff-Eisner, also a former prisoner doctor, published a report on deficiency diseases in Theresienstadt.[35] In 1948 and 1949, the American psychiatrist P. Friedman published the first reports on psychological disorders in concentration camp victims.[36]

The official government chronicle on reparations, after referring to a statement by Dietrich Bonhoeffer, remarks, "Otherwise nothing was heard on this problem in the German-speaking world, although many hundreds, and possibly even thousands, of former persecutees sought advice and assistance from German psychiatrists, and especially from German clinics."[37]

When the survivors of the concentration camps were liberated by Allied troops, help came too late for many. Approximately four of every ten prisoners died in the first few months following the end of the war from the effects of hunger, debilitation, tuberculosis, typhoid fever, and other camp diseases.[38] At the beginning, these were the most widespread illnesses among the survivors, along with chronic exhaustion and the syndrome of premature aging, which was thoroughly described by French authors.[39]

Once the victims had somewhat recovered physically in the clinics set up by the Allies and refugee organizations, many enjoyed a relatively complaint-free latency period of several years. During that time, they frequently attempted—too rapidly—to resume their place in normal life and professions. Lack of success in these areas, social isolation, the not infrequent failure of marriages, and the news of relatives' deaths (many sought their relatives for years, only to find out many years after 1945 that they had died in the camps) led to the collapse of a laboriously maintained mental and physical equilibrium. Severe, deep psychological disorders and chronic physical illnesses appeared that had not been observed in victims of World War I or previous wars.

Ever since a decision by the Reich Insurance Office (actually the highest court for health insurance matters) in 1926 on the "medical and legal significance of traumatic neuroses," no obligation has existed in Germany to provide a pension for neurosis resulting from accident; according to that ruling, the organism's ability to compensate after psychological trauma is practically unlimited, so no lasting loss of earning capacity through accident neurosis is possible. This decision was based partly on works by Karl Bonhoeffer and a monograph by Ewald Stier on accident neuroses.[40] Both had dealt with assessments of the so-called *Kriegszitterer* ("war shiverers"), as the shell-shocked were called, after World War I, concluding that their abnormal psychological reactions to the experience of war were an expression of "a desire for a pension," and that the neurosis would only be perpetuated if such a pension were granted. Thus the therapy for this "pension neurosis" consisted of not granting a pension. Apart from some restrictions, this decision continues in force to this day.

This "prevailing medical opinion" could not be applied automatically to the severe and lasting psychological disorders in concentration camp survivors. Under the influence of the concentration camps, Bonhoeffer himself in 1947 revised his earlier position, saying that "where there is an overabundance of artificially induced, physically tormenting procedures that degrade the personality," there is in fact a limit to an individual's psychological resilience.[41] However, in an advisory opinion written for the federal Ministry of Labor in 1960 on the assessment of neuroses from the perspective of social and beneficiary medicine, Friedrich Panse, director of the Düsseldorf Psychiatric Clinic, Gustav Störring, a professor at Kiel, and others continued to support the thesis that neurotic reactions to situations unique to war were "calculated, wishful reactions . . . that cannot be viewed as consequences of harm."[42] On persecution disorders, however, they added the reservation that such neurotic states should be distinguished from lasting reactions that "must be considered commensurate in view of the unusual magnitude of the harm suffered." Although the opinion granted harms resulting from persecution a special status and did not fundamentally rule out their recognition, many medical officials referred in their evaluations to the passages describing neuroses as "calculated, wishful reactions."

Friedrich Panse (1899–1973) worked in the 1920s under Karl Bonhoeffer in the psychiatric clinic of Berlin's Charité hospital. At the time, he published several works on "pension neurosis" in which he claimed that shell-shocked war veterans would become symptom-free if their pensions were cancelled. In the same breath, he protested against the "Social Democratic attack" on his scientifically grounded position. In the Third Reich, Panse was an assessor on the supreme courts of hereditary health in Berlin and Cologne. During the war, he served as consultant to the euthanasia operation in the Rhineland and also headed the Ensen reserve military hospital near Cologne. There he practiced the infamous electroshock therapy, or, as he called it, "energetic suggestive treatment of war neurotics with strong galvanic currents." After the war, Panse became director of the Psychiatric Clinic in Düsseldorf. In 1952, in what would today be called a catastrophic medicine study on the reactions of the German civilian population to the air raids in World War II, he wrote, "people . . . whose psychological (character) structure had always shown deficiencies, such as . . . the intellectually substandard, are by nature even less able to resist the pressure of drives, emotions and instincts in the turmoil of fear than in everyday life."[43]

In the years 1957–58, some works began to appear by outsiders to the professional world who cautiously attempted to revise the "prevailing medical opinion." In assessing persecutees under the Federal Restitution Law, experts such as Walther von Baeyer, a professor of psychiatry at Heidelberg, the psychiatrist Ernst Kluge of Mainz, Professor Kurt Kolle of Munich, Ulrich Venzlaff, chief physician at the Göttingen University Psychiatric Clinic, and the German émigré psychiatrist Hans Strauss of New York found completely new, severe illness profiles that had been ignored by the German psychiatric profession. These were colored neither by calculation nor by desires, nor did they fit any of the usual diagnostic schemes. The doctors gave these illnesses various names, such as "restitution neurosis" (von Baeyer), "uprooting depression" (Strauss), "complete rupture in the lifeline" (Kolle), and "experience-based personality change" (Venzlaff), all of which described the same complex of symptoms.[44] They succeeded in revising negative initial assessments by their colleagues, who had made their judgments based on the concept of "pension neurosis."

***

Walther Ritter von Baeyer (1904–1987) received his doctorate in 1928. His father, a so-called half-Jew, lost his position at Heidelberg University in 1933. After completing his medical studies, von Baeyer went to the German Research Center for Psychiatry in Munich, where he wrote a study on the "genealogy of psychopathic swindlers and liars" under Ernst Rüdin, the Third Reich's leading professor of hereditary biology and racial hygiene (he was a coauthor of the commentary on the Law to Prevent Genetically Defective Offspring). During World War II, von Baeyer was a consulting psychiatrist on the Eastern Front, assessing "war neurotics" for the wartime military courts. His reports had a significant influence on whether mitigating circumstances were found or death sentences meted out. From 1945 to 1955, he was director of the Psychiatric Clinic in Nuremberg, and until his retirement in 1972, he served as director of the Heidelberg University Psychiatric Clinic. There he wrote studies on the psychiatry of persecutees that brought him world renown and, from 1966 to 1971, the office of vice president of the World Psychiatric Association. Von Baeyer was a founding member of Expert Committee VIII, "Psychobiology," of the federal Ministry of the Interior's safety commission; the committee dealt with behavior during war and catastrophic occurrences. For this committee, von Baeyer produced a study on psychoses in persecutees, a revised version of his work from the perspective of catastrophic medicine.[45]

***

Ulrich Venzlaff (1921–) was a communications officer and noncommissioned medical officer during World War II. In 1948, he interned at the Göttingen University Psychiatric Clinic under Professor Gottfried Ewald. Ewald was one of the few psychiatrists to oppose euthanasia during the Third Reich, and he supported Venzlaff's unorthodox assessments of persecutees. In 1956, Venzlaff earned his professorial qualifications under Ewald, with a dissertation on "Psychoreactive Disturbances Following Events Eligible for Reparations." Between 1962 and 1965, he held a temporary guest professorship in the United States, connected with conferences in Detroit organized by Krystal and Niederland on "Massive Psychic Trauma." From 1969 until his retirement in 1986, Venzlaff headed the Lower Saxony State Hospital in Göttingen. His area of specialization was forensic psychiatry, in which he made a name for himself as an advocate of liberal corrections methods, opposing conservative experts on criminal psychiatry. One of the first improvements Venzlaff made at the state hospital was creation of an open ward for the mentally ill in corrections.[46]

***

One case that made history was that of a severely depressed persecutee assessed by Venzlaff in 1952 at the behest of the Bremen district court. Venzlaff, at the time still an intern at the University Psychiatric Clinic in Göttingen, attested to a persecution-induced neurosis. This plunged the reparations office into turmoil; in an advisory opinion, a forensic psychiatrist commissioned by the office wrote that, if this report were to become the norm, officials would face an avalanche of pension claims, and that it had to be stopped. The office then called upon the influential psychiatrist Ernst Kretschmer, the leading German expert at the time in the field of neurosis research, to produce an opposing evaluation. Kretschmer, who had neither seen nor examined the patient, wrote many pages of theoretical justification explaining why what should not be, could not be—there was no such thing as persecution-induced neurosis, as the organism's ability to compensate for severe psychic trauma was unlimited.

The court caused a sensation when it found for Venzlaff, the lowly intern, and rejected the professor's recommendation as unconvincing. In contravention of the prevailing legal view that only a court-sanctioned evaluation could be considered legally binding and serve as a model, the office nevertheless sent copies of the Kretschmer report as a model to all offices. Since then, it has haunted the literature as the Kretschmer Report of 24 October 1955. Kretschmer's views gained particular weight through their inclusion in a commentary on the law by Ammermüller-Wilden, *Gesundheitliche Schäden in der Wiedergutmachung* (Health Damage in Reparations). This commentary, which declared granting a pension for neurosis to be "scientifically untenable," decisively influenced jurisprudence in the 1950s. In the leaflets sent to domestic and foreign examining doctors by the reparations offices, the applicable passages from Ammermüller-Wilden were cited on the neurosis issue.[47]

Ernst Kretschmer (1888–1964), who studied under the Tübingen psychiatrist Robert Gaupp, headed a rehabilitation clinic for "war neurotics" following World War I. Kretschmer, who became famous for his doctrine that various types of constitutions correlate with certain psychological illnesses, was director of the University Psychiatric Clinic in Marburg from 1926 to 1946. Although he advocated compulsory sterilization of the "degenerate," especially the feeble-minded, his theories on the lack of identity between constitutional and racial types ran counter to Nazi views. According to Kretschmer, the high culture of Nordic races had always emerged as a result of mixing with other talented races. From 1946 until his retirement in 1959, he headed the Tübingen University Psychiatric Clinic.[48]

At a regional conference of the Association of Southwest German Neurologists and Psychiatrists in 1961 in Baden-Baden, von Baeyer and others opened their criticism of prevailing medical opinion to public debate for the first time.[49] This earned von Baeyer curt attacks from supporters of prevailing views, especially from Hermann Witter, professor of forensic psychiatry at the University of Hamburg-Saar.[50]

Outside of Germany, the omissions by German psychiatrists in assessing persecutees bred discontent, and a "covert feud" developed between German and American psychiatrists.[51] In Norway and Holland, further pathbreaking works were published in the late 1950s, such as those of the Oslo psychiatrist Leo Eitinger, a survivor of Auschwitz, and the Leyden psychiatrist Jan Bastiaans.[52] If German psychiatry hoped to regain its international reputation, it would have to renounce its customary verdict of "pension neurosis" in cases of reparations evaluations. The federal Supreme Court of Appeals took account of this, deciding in a judgment of 18 May 1960 involving a recommendation by the Munich University Psychiatric Clinic that a persecutee might also claim reparations for "psychiatric disorders shown to be adequately caused by persecutory measures."[53]

After this decision, some German university clinics fell into line with the new view, among them that of the orthodox psychiatrist Jörg Weitbrecht in Bonn[54] and the Hamburg clinic under Hans Bürger-Prinz.[55] Plaintiffs' chances of obtaining reparations for psychological damage at trial improved, although only if the judge supported the new medical view rather than naming someone like Hermann Witter as court-appointed expert. Medical evaluators at the lowest level continued to assess according to the older schemata. As late as 1963, Venzlaff complained of the "tactlessness and offensiveness" of "sentences mined from the diluvian strata of psychiatry" in many evaluations.[56] In his experience, little had changed in the style of examining doctors by 1969: "When I receive files to read, I find again and again an inexplicable distrust of foreign evaluations that can only be explained by a missionary arrogance."[57] In 1968, the Supreme Court of Appeals made it easier to recognize psychological disorders by eliminating the requirements of particularly severe persecution and "restructuring" of the personality in determining a causal connection.[58]

Outside of Germany, numerous conferences were held, after the first one in Copenhagen, on permanent health damage to persecutees—in Brussels in 1955, Moscow in 1957, Oslo in 1960, Lüttich, Paris, and the Hague in 1961, Brussels in 1962, Bucharest in 1964, and so on.[59] (See the complete list of conferences in appendix C.) Most of these conferences were initiated by the Fédération Internationale des Résistants (FIR), an association of former resistance fighters and persecutees from the western and eastern European countries occupied by the Germans, which West Germany considered "communist-infiltrated" and therefore suspect. The first conferences in the Federal Republic devoted exclusively to this subject were held in Cologne and Düsseldorf on the initiative of the Cologne internist Hans-Joachim Herberg and an official in the federal Ministry of Health, Helmut Paul. Specialists in many fields from inside and outside Germany took part, even from eastern European countries; they included Frantisek Blaha and Eliska Klimkowa-Deutschowa of Czechoslovakia. The medical services of the reparations offices sent no representatives. They considered Herberg and Paul tendentious because of their sharp criticism of the restrictive practices of the North Rhine–Westphalia reparations office.[60]

In contrast to its generous support of doctors educating themselves to treat war victims, the government was conspicuously restrained in its support of such measures when they involved reparations issues. In 1964, Herberg, Paul, and several others used private funds (including funds from the URO) to found a "Documentation Center for Health Damage Following Imprisonment and Persecution" in Cologne. Its goal was to make possible continuing education and exchange of information among doctors dealing with reparations, which had been neglected by the authorities. Venzlaff criticized the failure of the government authorities in this respect at a conference in Düsseldorf in 1969:

One has to ask why an institution founded through the private initiative and idealism of a few scientists and physicians, the Documentation Center for Health Damage Following Imprisonment and Persecution, is holding a conference that should have been held long ago, soon after the war, soon after the creation of the Federal Republic, at least after enactment of the Federal Restitution Law, with government funding and government support . . . One should also ask why, outside the country, in France, in Norway, in Denmark, in the United States, these problems of health disorders in former persecutees have been studied very seriously, with great intensity and the contribution of government funding, and state that this should have provided an incentive here for government authorities to subsidize something similar.[61]

His partner in the discussion, Ulrich Brost, a general practitioner and reparations evaluator from Berlin, agreed, adding that it was too late now, in 1969, to make up for these earlier omissions: "With considerable arrogance, we have so far taken lightly the findings of foreign scientists, especially the French, but also the Russians and Norwegians, because we didn't deal with them here; but we can't suddenly now promote and develop what we failed to do for twenty years and say that, after a series of experiments over the next twenty years, we shall decide what is or is not premature aging."[62]

Survivors' Syndrome

The earliest studies by French and Danish doctors concentrated on organic disorders suffered by former prisoners, which were of primary interest at the time; psychological symptoms were seen as the results of debilitation, premature aging, and organic brain damage from hunger, encephalitis in typhus, and the like. The Mainz psychiatrist Ernst Kluge also held the view that organic brain-related components played a major role in prisoners' psychopathological symptoms.[63] In most German studies starting in the late 1950s, however, the bases of such disorders were considered to be primarily psychological events. Thus von Baeyer developed his "existential-anthropological critique" of the prevailing view of psychological trauma into a complicated personal conceptual system, the "experience-reactive syndrome among persecutees," involving twenty-five diagnostic subgroups.[64] American authors such as Henry Krystal and William G. Niederland classified persecutees' symptoms according to psychoanalytical criteria, under the heading "survivors' syndrome."

I shall limit myself here to a summary overview of "survivors' syndrome" or "concentration camp syndrome," as described by Niederland, Krystal and Leo Eitinger:

1. Severe, often quite sudden agitation and anxiety attacks.

2. An unarticulated feeling of "being different" from those who did not experience the hell of concentration camps, ghettos, labor camps, and years of life in hiding.

3. Deep survivors' guilt—that is, feelings of guilt on the part of those who survived vis-à-vis their murdered relatives and comrades.

4. A sense of being psychologically overwhelmed and diminished, difficult to describe and expressed in depression, apathetic withdrawal, lack of contact, inability to experience enjoyment and happiness, and even complete rigidity and psychological numbness.

5. The symptom of the "living corpse"—shadowlike, fearful, depressed behavior resulting from constant confrontation with death.

6. Painful reliving of the horrors of the camps (abuse, observing the murder of family members)—known in the literature as hypermncsia [abnormally graphic memories] —and nightmares.

7. Tiredness, rapid exhaustion, problems with concentration and memory.

8. Sexual disorders.

9. Psychosomatic disorders such as heart problems, headaches, dizziness, sweating, stomach and intestinal disorders, and sleeplessness.

10. Psychotic states with delusions (the feeling of still being in the camp and being persecuted).[65]

The causes of these symptoms were the specific traumas of the ghettos and labor and concentration camps, such as complete rejection and annihilation of the personality, suppression of all aggressive and altruistic impulses, constant danger and confrontation with torture and death, the poisoning of human relationships, destruction of human community and security, hunger, cold and disease, and the murder of family members, sometimes before the survivor's very eyes. According to von Baeyer, life in hiding was an only marginally less serious trauma:

What happened in hiding must be reckoned one of the most difficult psychological strains imaginable: at the mercy of the families who hid them, in constant tension and fear of being discovered, crowded together in the closest of quarters in closets, shacks, animal stalls, cellars, attics, even holes in the ground and haystacks . . . vegetating in inactivity and passivity, often worn down by conflicts among one another and in relation to their "hosts," who also feared the worst; then often forced into risky flight and frequent change of hiding place—these hidden people, each on his own and in his own way, survived a martyrdom that was hardly easier than the concentration camps.[66]

According to the psychoanalytic theory of trauma, the symptoms described did not involve calculated or wishful reactions, hereditary character disorders, symptoms of psychopathy, or endogenous illness, as German psychological orthodoxy claimed. They were the consequences of cumulative trauma that tore away the protective shell of body and soul, catapulting the individual back to a primitive, early-childhood stage of conflict resolution.

In the concentration camps, it was not possible to deny the horrors being experienced. The prisoner closed himself off from his surroundings, falling into a state of apathy and indifference that, in its extreme form—the so-called *Muselmann* stage—generally led rapidly to death. He remained fixated on this trauma even after liberation, experiencing it over and over, as a repetition compulsion in daytime and nighttime dreams. However, this repetition often failed to alleviate the fear. The dreams were not wish-fulfillment dreams to overcome experiences; they were tormenting nightmares that persecuted survivors for decades with undiminished intensity.

The fury of the dreams was not decisive in itself; just as crucial were the emotions triggered in the survivor. Thus the torments suffered were believed by many to be their own fault. The murder of their parents was irrationally perceived as a fatal realization of early-childhood, Oedipal death wishes against a mother or father, giving rise to extreme feelings of guilt. This was one source of "survivor guilt."[67] Remembered scenes of cannibalism among prisoners, or the fact that one had survived through privilege or theft at the expense of other prisoners, also created feelings of guilt.[68]

For these connections, Polish studies on concentration camp syndrome are significant; they took a fundamentally different approach from American and German studies. These include studies by a group of Cracow physicians around Antoni Kępiński and Stanisław Kłodzinski. The majority were former prisoners in Auschwitz who set up a treatment and rehabilitation center for survivors after 1945. Their method was not psychoanalytic, nor did it follow the dictates of orthodox psychiatry. They emphasized that survivors' sufferings and their aftereffects could not be explained through conventional medical concepts. "It was necessary to abandon the stereotyping of psychiatric thinking," Kępiński observed.[69] They also believed that "analysis of subjective experiences and the statements of the individual patients were more important than psychiatric analysis."[70] The Polish authors' methods are descriptive, based on detailed discussions with former prisoners.

The Polish doctors, most of whom had themselves suffered persecution and imprisonment, were in a very different position from, for example, the German doctors. They were in constant close contact with their clients; as fellow sufferers, they were able to place themselves in the shoes of former prisoners, who felt no one could understand them if they had not themselves experienced the concentration camps.[71] Kępiński wrote on his relationship to former prisoners:

Psychiatric contact with these people proved easier than with those who had never in their lives reached the lowest point of human existence. That is, the psychiatrist seeks an answer to the question of what the person truly is—what is hidden under the mask of expressions, gestures and words . . . Those who have experienced the camps often ask themselves the question, what is this person in front of you really like—how would he have acted in the camps, what would have become of his dignity, his honesty, if he suddenly found himself "there." A common aversion to appearance and masks linked the psychiatrist with the former prisoner.[72]

The survivors reacted extremely sensitively to simulated feelings and the lack of understanding in their environment. Just as a friendly word from a fellow inmate could save one's life in the camps, now a false word could destroy all trust. Kępiński believed that the oft-mentioned criteria of "concentration camp syndrome" were insufficient to describe the condition of the survivors. About the fact that the complaints of former prisoners were normally handled by various specialists, he wrote:

In discussing causal connections, a sharp separation of psychological and physical factors seems wrong. The former were so firmly linked to the latter that separating them is artificial. Hunger, infectious disease (especially typhus and typhoid fever), head wounds, and so on, could lead to lasting damage to the central nervous system . . . Conversely, the constant inner tension that was part of camp life could trigger a premature sclerotic process or impair the organism's overall resistance. In such a case, a syndrome of expressly somatic phenomena resulted from psychological damage. Discussions of this kind have only theoretical significance. In practice, it is impossible to separate the various factors from one another.[73]

Kłodzinski proposed that former prisoners be viewed from a general rather than a specialized medical standpoint.[74] "The superiority of Polish research over that in other countries," claimed Kłodzinski, "lies in the fact that it is not linked to pension claims, which often distort the results."[75] He found it equally distorting to "subordinate the complexity of the phenomena to a statistical approach."[76]

Very informative studies were produced by Zenon Jagoda, Kłodzinski, and Jan Masłowski on "Behavioral Stereotypes Among Former Prisoners in the Auschwitz-Birkenau Concentration Camp." Optical, olfactory, and acoustic stimuli could awaken memories of the camps and provoke acute psychological crises:

> I cannot listen to German, although I mastered the language before the war to a sufficient degree. Now the German language reminds me of the baying of dogs, as that is the impression it made on me during my time in concentration camp, and I always compared the SS guards with a pack of mad dogs, snapping at everything and barking at their victims . . . I cannot stand words like *"Los, schnell, weitermachen!"* [Get going, quick, keep it up!].

Other prisoners felt revulsion at loud German tourists, or panicked at the sight of uniforms or striped outfits, which reminded them of prisoners' outfits, loud noises, dogs barking, steps, the wail of factory sirens, screams, the smell of smoke, almonds (Zyklon-B smelled of bitter almonds), or the smell of unwashed, sweating bodies and dirty, damp laundry.[77]

Niederland reported on a woman who had emigrated to the United States after spending six years in various concentration and labor camps. When fire broke out in her apartment building in 1952, she was seized with delusions and wanted to throw her children out the window to save them from the Nazis. It later became clear that the fire and smoke had reminded her of her parents' deaths in Auschwitz.[78]

At the First International Medico-Legal Symposium on Health Damage Following Imprisonment and Persecution, held in Cologne in 1967, the Heidelberg internist Wolfgang Jacob reported on a forty-two-year-old Jewish woman from France whom he had examined at the Heidelberg University Clinic after the officials responsible for reparations had required her to come to Germany. The woman had spent several years in Auschwitz, performing the most difficult forced labor and suffering indescribable degradation at the hands of the male guards. It was difficult for her to speak about this. She seemed to have adapted fairly well and reported only that it had been terrible in the camps, and that she neither could nor wanted to remember anything. To objectify her nervous disorder, Jacob ordered an endurance EKG [stress test]:

> As usual, the quite friendly technical assistant asked the patient—as she normally did—in an energetic tone to climb the stairs to the third floor *im Laufschritt* [at a run], if possible, and then to come back down to have another EKG taken. Because the patient hesitated on the bottom steps, the technical assistant repeated her request; now the patient, in panicky fear, climbed several landings, and then ended the examination with the remark that she couldn't! Shaking all over, she returned to the doctor and explained to him that, with such treatment, there was no way she could endure even one more examination, and she would like to be discharged without an evaluation and, as far as she was concerned, without a pension.[79]

"Im Laufschritt!" was a command frequently given by SS guards in the camps. These studies illustrate how traumatic the confrontation with German officials and doctors could be for persecutees, if the very sound of the German language or certain words could have such a devastating effect.

Trench Warfare Among Scientists

The revision of prevailing medical thought on the question of accident or pension neurosis by von Baeyer, Venzlaff, and others encountered stiff resistance from advocates of the old school of German psychiatry. A professor of forensic psychiatry and criminology at the University of Homburg/ Saar, Hermann Witter, became their spokesman, along with a student of his, Dr. Rainer Luthe. At the conference of the Association of Southwest German Neurologists and Psychiatrists in Baden-Baden in 1961, Witter responded to the views of von Baeyer and his assistants as follows:

Unfortunately, it is very difficult to separate the psychological and psychopathological issues from the moral issue of reparations and the legal issue of reparations applications that stand directly behind them; affective attitudes detract from our objectivity and make a value-free, scientific discussion of the realities almost impossible . . . The "prevailing view," with its principle of not paying compensation for psychoreactive disorders, was probably necessary for the entire nation [*Volksganze*, a term frequently used by Nazi eugenicists], as Kretschmer most recently emphasized, and it was also right and proper in the great majority of cases . . . Whether in practice, in which a vast number of cases must routinely be handled by an administration with limited personnel and financial capabilities in a limited time, it would even have been possible to provide individual consideration without bringing down the protective barrier against unjustified neurotic claims, seems more than doubtful. Ultimately, a "prevailing view" emerges in order to label the normal case quickly; this is necessary to deal with the situation in practice, and simplifications are unavoidable . . . Whether, and how, an experience-based psychological examination of victims of National Socialist persecution should be made the object of reparations payments is primarily a question of ethical, legal, political and perhaps also economic considerations—considerations lying completely outside of psychiatry.[80]

Von Baeyer replied indignantly to Witter that he had described "reported cases from the Baeyer clinic as artistic sketches with a very broad application of subjective interpretations." Witter, in turn, denied that he "doubted the honesty of his opponents in the discussion" or had committed a "stylistic rupture" (*Stilbruch*).[81]

Hermann Witter (1916–1991) studied medicine in Göttingen, Freiburg, and Munich, joined the Nazi party in 1936, became a member of the Nazi Doctors' Union (NSD-Ärztebund) and a storm trooper in the National Socialist Automobile Drivers'

Corps (NSKK). He passed his state examinations in 1940 and became a medical officer in the "East Mark" (Austria), first in Vienna and later in Gmünd and Oberpullendorf in the Lower Danube region. Following the war, Witter wrote his postdoctoral thesis in 1953 and became professor of forensic psychiatry and criminology at the University of Homburg/Saar in 1966. Witter was an exponent of repressive criminal psychiatry; he called for castration of sex offenders and argued against too generous an application of § 51 (diminished capacity). He called opposing experts at trials *Systemveränderer* ("system changers," a derogatory label for the rebellious students of the 1960s) who issued "untrue evaluations as favors." In 1969, he resigned as dean of the medical faculty in protest against "progressive politicization of research and teaching," saying "an anarchy" was spreading that stood for the "destruction of our free social order." In 1973, he attempted forcibly to subject Ulrike Meinhof of the Red Army Faction, who was then in custody, to a brain scan to examine a brain tumor operated on a year earlier.[82]

Luthe railed against Venzlaff's concept of "experience-based change in personality," which had found a "lasting echo" in restitution evaluations because, in his opinion, it was "theoretically convincing and a catchy model." However, he said the concept had an air of "naïve lack of psychological underpinnings," as Venzlaff claimed that "a structural change in personality" took place in the persecutees. But, said Luthe, returning to the theory of the unlimited resilience of the human psyche, such a thing did not exist, as an "intelligent person cannot become dumber through experience . . . , no stocky person becomes a leptosome through external occurrences, an extroverted person does not transform permanently into an introvert . . . Even the deepest shocks of experience—for example, falling in love—pass without leaving behind a change in nature or personality transformation."

After this comparison, Luthe went on to claim that the sufferings of persecution were something like a transcendental experience of self-discovery that lent meaning to life: "The repeated traumatizing experience of this extreme psychological position may have led such people to a state that we know in a different context as 'wise,' 'holy,' as the goal of Far Eastern contemplation rituals and of meaningful psychotherapy aimed at life fulfillment and not merely at symptoms."[83]

Visibly horrified, Venzlaff responded:

Whether the example of falling in love was particularly well chosen in a discussion of the psychopathology of concentration camp or imprisonment damage may be more a question of good taste than scientific comparability, . . . with such . . . speculations, a degree of fantastic lack of touch with reality has been reached that poses the question of whether it is possible to find an acceptable level of discussion. One might ask the author of such lines whether humility before the horrible fate of these people should in itself forbid us from trivializing their psychological problems with such intellectual games.[84]

However, in their practical activity, Luthe and Witter were far from out of touch with reality. When these doctors were called as expert witnesses in a trial, the persecutee could expect their evaluations to be against him. Still, in a later publication, Witter would revise the standpoint he had held in opposition to von Baeyer at Baden-Baden, stating that compensation claims for neurotic disorders should not be rejected "if extreme psychological pressure lasted not only for a short time, but for months and years."[85]

The conflict over recognition of psychological damage resulting from persecution, aired publicly for the first time at Baden-Baden in 1961, was fueled again upon publication, in 1963, of *Psychische Spätschäden nach politischer Verfolgung* [Long-Term Psychological Damage from Political Persecution], edited by Hans-Joachim Herberg and Helmut Paul, in which advocates of the "new scholarly medical view," among them von Baeyer, Venzlaff, and Kluge, took the floor. Venzlaff wrote:

We must not forget the constant rousing of memories, aggressions, and resentments caused by the restitution process—the endless difficulties of producing witness statements and documents on damage to property and education, proof of persecution as such, the dealing with medical disagreements on the backs of the persecutees, the slowness of the process and the sometimes insistent narrowmindedness of the restitution bureaucracy that led to new illnesses: one of our patients, for whom lasting physical and psychological persecution damage had been attested to in two detailed reports by foreign university psychiatrists, was examined a third time (!) by a German psychiatrist, as the authorities did not recognize the foreign evaluations. His evaluation in 1960 found the woman, who had spent three years in Auschwitz, to have a psychopathic personality with a tendency toward abnormal processing of experience and an inability to deal with life, as general medical experience showed that a normal person would have overcome this burden six months after liberation at the latest.[86]

In this volume, Paul reviewed, for the first time in Germany, the results reached by foreign colleagues on long-term psychological damage, especially those of the Fédération Internationale des Résistants (FIR), an organization condemned in the Federal Republic. He quoted criticisms of German reparations practices, among them the polemics of the Danish psychiatrist Henrik Hoffmeyer at FIR's Moscow conference in 1957, who said:

After the deportees have risked their health in conditions having no equal in history, they return to a society that attempts to calculate the material restitution they deserve with administrative pedantry. The sick are sent from doctor to doctor, their joints and reflexes, hearts and lungs are conscientiously examined, and in general nothing objectively abnormal is found. The results of these examinations are reviewed by a huge, impersonal administrative apparatus that considers itself capable of judging whether a person who has gone through such hell is an 8, 10, or 12 percent invalid. This pedantic examination of reparations rights, typical of the normal method of pension granting, completely denies the existence of a law of all or nothing in this area, and this method is what often gives the sick person the feeling that he is suspected of being a parasite on society.[87]

Josef Fitzek, Hans-Joachim Herberg, and the medical team of the Documentation Center for Health Damage Following Imprisonment and Persecution, founded shortly thereafter in Cologne, presented, for the first time in the Federal Republic, a critical assessment of the medical evaluations of a reparations office. They investigated the reporting practices of the state pension office of North Rhine–Westphalia, based on 544 procedures involving health damage claims, mainly by persecutees from Belgium and France. Of these applications, 199 were rejected by the authorities. The mistaken judgments upon which these rejections were based were caused, in the opinion of the Cologne documentation center, by very superficial case histories, insufficient diagnostic measures, lack of knowledge on the part of the examiners of the special field of health damage following persecution, ignorance of the literature and of the guidelines for medical evaluation in the field of public benefits, and issuance of unclear and vague diagnoses.[88]

The general criticism of the medical evaluation process in Herberg and Paul's *Psychische Spätschäden*, as well as the specific criticism of the evaluators attached to the North Rhine–Westphalia state pension office, made quite a splash. The first edition of the book was soon sold out.[89] It was presented to the public at a press conference by the North Rhine–Westphalia Chamber of Physicians on 2 December 1963 and subsequently discussed in all the media. The reparations offices were jolted into action. At a nationwide medical conference of the top reparations offices called especially for the purpose on 13 May 1964, the head of the medical service of the North Rhine–Westphalia state pension office, Helmuth Lotz, laid out the official response to Herberg and Paul:

It is disconcerting that press reports on the press conference by the North Rhine Chamber of Physicians give the impression that long-term psychological damage has just now, for the first time, been discovered and publicized by so-called specialists . . . The question of whether the book really imparts new scientific discoveries and convincingly proves the existence of long-term effects for which there were no bridges to the period of persecution must be answered in the negative . . . Venzlaff's attacks on the slowness of the reparations process and the sometimes insistent narrow-mindedness of the reparations bureaucracy that led to new illnesses are unfortunate . . . Kisker and Häfner (Heidelberg), incidentally, speak of the symptom-free interval in long-term psychological damage . . . Why, in one case, a clearly vegetative intestinal symptom is described as an anxiety neurosis, is just as unclear as, in another case, classification as 60 percent MdE for an applicant born in 1928 whose psychostatus indicates no lasting invalidity . . . Witter (Saar University Homburg) has already, in *Nervenarzt* 11 (1962) admired the "artistic design" of the Heidelberg medical evaluations, without always being convinced of the evidence of the statements . . . The knowledge upon which a determination of cerebral disorders is based is extremely narrow; according to Bastiaans (Amsterdam), it "often cannot be clearly proven with the psychiatric diagnostic means available"—so how can one recognize them? . . . "Through a particular form of neuroticization . . . which is stronger than in other patients who did not live under such influences." On this quite vague evidence, Bastiaans erects what is in Paul's opinion a "quite useful" conception . . . Hoffmeyer (Copenhagen) appeared at the Moscow conference in 1957 with polemics against the restitution laws and the "gigantic and impersonal administrative apparatus" . . . Paul finds this description so accurate that he quotes it verbatim. Here one could have expected from government medical officer Dr. Paul, an official of the Federal Health Ministry with experience in the field of benefits, at least an explanatory word, a word that might have betrayed greater insight into the enormous difficulties of the reparations laws than could be expected from a scientist of a small country that has never faced such tasks! . . . Among the Russians, for example, the influence of nationalist views also appears, which affects the publications of other East Bloc countries as well . . . Mende (Tübingen University Clinic) speaks of the danger of describing "all sorts of damaging events and stressful situations as extreme," and demands, for the sake of limitation, a clear case history, avoidance of tendentious judgments . . . as otherwise, in fact, there is danger of "standards becoming uncertain" (E. Kretschmer 1957) in the determination of psychogenous reactions, and ultimately the door would be open to a recognition of any and all subjective disorders (Dubitscher 1957) . . . If, finally, we attempt to obtain an overall impression of the book, what remains is only . . . the realization that our knowledge remains incomplete, and that Witter, undoubtedly correctly, distinguishes between "knowledge" and "judgment."[90]

The summary of the conference states that the broad rejection of the book explained in this speech was shared across the board by the other conference participants. They found it incomprehensible that the minister of health had written a foreword to Herberg and Paul's *Psychische Spätschäden*, lending the book a significance it was not thought to deserve. The conference recommended that copies of Lotz's speech be sent to the foreign examining doctors by way of the Foreign Office[91]—an obvious attempt to obviate any agreement on the part of official medical personnel, and even foreign doctors, with the criticisms voiced in *Psychische Spätschäden*. Particularly remarkable is the way in which Dr. Lotz spoke of his colleagues ("so-called specialists"), and in particular his defamation of the foreign examining doctors—the speakers at the FIR congress who were influenced by the "Russians" or by "nationalist views," and the Dane Henryk Hoffmeyer, who came from "a small country that [had] never faced such tasks."

Helmuth Lotz (1924–1982) joined the Nazi party in 1942, the year he graduated from high school in Mainz. His medical studies in Heidelberg were interrupted by military service until the end of the war; in 1950, he took his state examinations and received his doctorate. In 1959, Dr. Lotz succeeded the head of the medical service of the state pension office of North Rhine–Westphalia, Dr. Paul Didden, who was considered too self-aggrandizing and was suspected of taking passive bribes. Lotz remained in this position until 1969, when he moved to North Rhine–Westphalia's state Ministry of Labor.[92]

Lotz's address was published, in somewhat briefer and more moderate form, in the professional reparations journal *Rechtsprechung zur Wiedergutmachungsrecht (RzW)*.[93] The debate did not, however, remain in the realm of a "scientific difference of opinion." Lotz and the state pension authorities managed to ensure that the Cologne working group under Herberg and Paul received no further assignments as evaluators for offices or courts in reparations cases; thus they would no longer officially receive evaluations to read and criticize. The staff of the offices' medical service received instructions not to carry on any professional exchange with the Cologne working group or participate in any of its educational events or congresses.[94]

It was normal practice for the authorities to influence the choice of court-appointed evaluators. In the Rhineland, this was done by an "old boy network." Judges and officials knew each other, and a telephone call or brief exchange at a social gathering was all that was necessary. Among lawyers it was common knowledge that there was no point citing publications by the Cologne documentation center or calling upon its members as evaluators, since they had an "extremely bad reputation" as a result of the efforts of Lotz and his colleagues.[95] But even in cases in which the court appointed an examining doctor who recognized persecution damage, officials had a way out: before the worst could happen, they reached an out-of-court settlement with the applicant, so that the decisive expert vote was never cast and could not become part of a court decision; thus it could not create law or be published in *RzW*. This meant, in turn, that persecutees and lawyers could not rely on such evaluations or judgments as precedents.[96]

Elsewhere, too, doctors considered by the authorities to be too "pro-recognition" were excluded. In official legal documents from the authorities to the court, such attributes were specifically mentioned in order to discredit certain evaluations and their authors. Hamburg internist Wolfgang Meywald, who frequently wrote medical evaluations under the Hamburg special supplementary pension law (*Sonderhilfsrentengesetz*)[97] and in the early years of the Federal Restitution Law, lost his mandate as an examining doctor in reparations matters at the behest of the Hamburg state reparations office.[98] The same fate befell the Heidelberg internist Heinrich Huebschmann,[99] who wrote many evaluations during his tenure at a sanatorium for tuberculosis and heart and circulatory illnesses and published the results in a monograph.[100] Huebschmann dared, like

Kluge and Venzlaff, to become one of a very few West German doctors to appear at international FIR conventions.[101]

The Berlin psychiatrist Max Burger was forced out as an evaluator by pressure from the restitution authorities. Persecuted as a resistance fighter in the Third Reich, he earned a "bad" reputation among officials, courts, and professional colleagues with his vehement advocacy on behalf of victims of Nazism.[102] Even well-meaning judges no longer appointed him as expert, since this would have ensured that the authorities would appeal their rulings.[103]

This conflict over medical evaluators should not be viewed only in the context of foreign versus German doctors, or persecutee doctors versus former Nazi doctors. Fierce debates on the restitution issue took place even among doctors abroad who were originally from Germany. The most spectacular case involved Hans Strauss, a doctor who carried out reparations evaluations in New York. Professor Strauss, a neurologist and psychiatrist of the old school from the University of Frankfurt, who had lost his post in 1933 for racial reasons, was one of the first American authors to describe survivors' syndrome. In 1957, he published a path-breaking work on "uprooting depression" (Entwurzelungsdepression) meriting compensation. According to Strauss, it was necessary to distinguish hysterical reactions in which wish fulfillment (Begehrungsvorstellungen) played a role.

Strauss acted differently in practice than in theory, however. Despite the wording of his article, in his medical evaluations, even in cases of serious concentration camp neurosis, he with conspicuous frequency diagnosed "hysteria" or an adaptability disorder (Anpassungsstörung) in the postwar period unrelated to persecution. He revised his 1957 article in an address to the World Congress for Psychiatry in 1961; in the same vein, at a panel discussion with examining doctors and émigré lawyers in New York, he took the position that fewer than half of the persecutees who had been in concentration camps suffered from a neurosis meriting compensation. A certain degree of "autosuggestion" among older people, he said, could not be ignored. For this he was criticized sharply by Niederland. When Strauss insisted that he harbored no prejudice against persecutees and had no "obligation to Germany," since he himself was a persecutee, a colleague retorted that the lack of understanding many doctors from Germany exhibited toward persecutees was a manifestation of the chasm, still far from bridged, between German and eastern European Jews. In a justificatory article in Aufbau, Strauss referred expressly to Kretschmer—that is, to the prevailing medical opinion of leading German psychiatrists.

The views of a respected psychiatrist and examiner like Strauss, himself a persecutee, often served the German authorities as a basis for rejecting claims. Aufbau documented numerous instances in which former concentration camp prisoners' claims, denied on the basis of the standard Straussian diagnosis of "hysteria," had to be taken all the way to the federal Supreme Court to obtain justice. In 1963, five New York psychiatrists, among them Niederland and Eissler, signed a petition in which they subjected Strauss's recommendations to a thorough critique. In a letter to the FRG's consulate general in New York on 21 September 1974, seventeen claimants examined by Strauss protested that he was "hostile to Jewish refugees" and that they had felt "so rudely treated" during the examination that he seemed more like a "tormentor" in the concentration camps than a well-meaning medical expert.[104]

Hans Strauss (1898–1977) was a student of Karl Kleist's at the University Psychiatric Clinic in Frankfurt on Main. Having lost his position in 1933 for racial reasons, he emigrated to the United States, where he became a neuropsychiatrist at the Royal Hospital, Kirby-Manhattan Psychiatric Center, Dunlap-Manhattan Psychiatric Center, and Mount Sinai Hospital in New York. He conducted reparations examinations for the West German consulate general and was the examining doctor in numerous restitution cases. His specialties were electroencephalography, traumatic disorders of the brain and spinal cord, and epilepsy.

A critical study by Paul Matussek of faulty examination and evaluation practices by German officials and examiners was published in 1971, eight years after Herberg and Paul's *Psychische Spätschäden*, at a time when most of the health damage cases had already been closed. Although Matussek backed up the theories of the Cologne working group with a wealth of statistical material, his study had little impact, especially since the authorities no longer faced waves of new claims and procedures, as they had in the early 1960s.

Between 1958 and 1962, Matussek, head of the Max Planck Society's Research Center for Psychopathology and Psychotherapy in Munich, examined 245 former concentration camp prisoners, 177 of them living in Germany, 42 in Israel, and 26 in the United States. He chose them randomly from the registers of the Bavarian state restitution office in Munich. The examinations were not connected with evaluations or the granting or rejection of restitution payments. Some of the people included had not even made a restitution claim. The data were compiled from interviews with the people involved and an evaluation of their compensation dossiers.[105]

In 1961, Matussek had addressed the conference of the Association of Southwest German Neurologists and Psychiatrists in Baden-Baden on the goals of his study. He hoped, based on exact data and without the distorting effect of the evaluation process, to examine the applicability of prevailing psychiatric views to prisoner illnesses, and also to determine specific hardship factors in the concentration camps, the prisoners' various ways of reacting to them, and their correlation to later illness, as well as to examine the integration of the prisoners into postwar society. Referring to the main theme of the Baden-Baden congress, "Illness and Society," Matussek spoke of the uncomprehending and even hostile atmosphere encountered in Germany by former concentration camp prisoners: "Survivors are in a certain sense still in concentration camp. For in order to eliminate the pressures, mentioned here only briefly, [German] society would have to be different from what it actually is; that is, it would have to be willing to internalize the most horrible indictment in history."[106]

In his eventual book on the subject in 1971, *Die Konzentrationslagerhaft und ihre Folgen* (Concentration Camp Imprisonment and Its Consequences), Matussek toned down this criticism of German society considerably, however. There is something artificial about the study; it is the artificial product that emerges when one attempts to subject the complexities of camp experience and its consequences to a statistically abstracted schematization.[107] The prisoners' statements, the actual basis of the study, are presented only in brief, small-print excerpts, and immediately placed in specific categories. Thus, for example, Matussek finds a statistical correlation between the degree of difficulty of the work in the camps and the psychophysical syndrome (Matussek's term for concentration camp syndrome), as well as—according to a precise breakdown by individual psychological symptoms—a correlation between difficulty of labor and the symptom of "resignation and despair." According to Matussek, severity of abuse, length of time in the camps, and difficulty of conditions (extermination camps like Auschwitz, for example, compared with Theresienstadt) all played a less crucial causal role in forming psychological disorders than the difficulty of the labor.

He found a further determinant for dealing with concentration camp trauma in the personality of the prisoner; prisoners capable of social contact were better able to assert themselves, developed better relationships with guards, and thus managed to obtain easier work, while passive prisoners with interpersonal difficulties were consigned to less favorable conditions. He maintained that prisoners capable of social contact had had better relationships with their mothers in childhood, while those with disrupted maternal relationships developed a passive attitude, reacted passively to persecution, exhibited uncomradely behavior in the camps, were exposed to more severe hardships, and later had greater difficulty making their way in life than others.

"The frequency of bodily injuries, such as blows to the head, shows a highly significant correlation to factor 4—that is, the psychological syndrome of distrust," Matussek told the Second International Medico-Legal Symposium on Health Damage Following Imprisonment and Persecution in Düsseldorf in 1969.[108] Such correlations are doubtful, and were not confirmed by other authors. Leo Eitinger, for example, determined in his study of former Norwegian concentration camp inmates that nothing in the period prior to imprisonment was significant for the development of concentration camp syndrome. However, he found that the severity of abuse, and the severity of imprisonment in general, played a crucial role.[109] At the aforementioned symposium, Eitinger responded to Matussek's theories as follows:

Professor Matussek has said that his material showed him how the pre–concentration camp personality had an influence on work placement and on dealing with the concentration camp situation. I believe that this is only the case for certain population groups, and that we must be very cautious in generalizing from this assertion. I do not wish to go into detail, as I might become too emotional . . . [My] findings are not processed as nicely from a statistical point of view as Professor Matussek's, but I believe they are entirely tenable from the perspective of clinical medicine.[110]

Matussek's theories on the pre–concentration camp personality were also problematic insofar as they provided arguments to German doctors who attempted to blame psychological disorders on the conflicts and privations of early childhood and youth, rather than on persecution. Matussek's study raised the fundamental question of what scientific methods could be used in examining victims, especially in Germany. "Many of the subjects became extremely agitated while describing the period of imprisonment," Matussek himself noted. "Not infrequently, severe anxiety dreams occurred the night after the interview. However, this affective emotional reaction did not detract from the credibility of their description of their sufferings."[111] In other words, Matussek's examination retraumatized his subjects, and this permits us to question the acceptability of his entire study. Most of his findings could have been gleaned equally well from the extensive camp literature written by prisoners themselves, or from the reports of Polish prisoners in the publications of the Cracow physicians' group or the International Auschwitz Committee. Sufficient findings on the questions addressed by Matussek were also available in Norwegian, Danish, and French studies, as well as those of von Baeyer, Venzlaff, Kolle, and Kluge. Thus the question remains to what extent it was not primarily scientific interest—the concentration camp prisoner as an interesting object for psychiatric study—that made the difference to him.

Nevertheless, Matussek's study did reveal some instructive details on the weaknesses of the official evaluation process. The interviewers found descriptions of complaints in the prisoners' statements with a very different emphasis than what was supplied in the physicians' evaluations. Matussek's explanation was that the persecutees were subject, in their meetings with examining doctors, to "pressure to conform their symptoms"—that is, they mainly supplied the complaints they believed would be necessary for recognition of health damage. Thus, for example, physical complaints were overemphasized in the evaluations, while psychological complaints were concealed or not mentioned. In contrast, psychological symptoms were described to the interviewers far more frequently than physical complaints, especially feelings of isolation, mistrust, difficulty with personal contact, fear of people, feelings of hate, and delusions. It makes sense that persecutees would have felt hatred for German doctors but would have repressed it during official examinations so as not to put their pension claims at risk. Accordingly, 78.7 percent were dissatisfied with the amount of their pensions, while only 21.3 percent felt their pensions were suitable.

Matussek did not assess this as an expression of neurotic querulousness, but as the consequence of faulty evaluations, in which psychoreactive disorders were underestimated. He showed in detail that psychiatrists rarely diagnosed long-term, persecution-induced psychological disorders; when they did, they assessed them as meriting only a very low pension—that is, they found only the 25 percent reduction in earning capacity necessary for a minimum pension. General practitioners, in contrast, recognized health damage far more frequently and assessed it as meriting a higher pension. Internists and physicians from the medical offices classed such disorders lower than general practitioners, falling somewhere between them and the psychiatrists. Matussek's findings may indicate that general practitioners were more open-minded regarding the sufferings of the victims and more likely to judge the entire person, like the Polish doctors and authors.

Matussek classified rejections of physical disability by official examining doctors according to various time periods. Thus in the years 1945–50, more than 30 percent of all claims for physical disability were rejected. In 1951–54, the rejection rate sank to 17 percent, only to rise again in the years 1955–60 to almost 44 percent. Matussek explained this fluctuation by the fact that immediately after 1945, uncertainty was very great among the doctors, since only a few foreign studies of the aftereffects of concentration camp imprisonment existed. As pension claims grew more frequent and knowledge of the extreme hardships increased, the willingness to recognize health damage grew; after adoption of the Federal Restitution Law, however, it diminished significantly, since the long period of time between imprisonment and filing a claim led to more cautious handling of the question of persecution causation. (It must be remarked here that it was after 1955 that publications on *long-term* harm following a symptom-free interval were becoming more available in the German-speaking world, so that the willingness to recognize it should have been increasing.)

Long-term psychological effects are not included in these statistics, as they only began to be diagnosed at all to any significant degree after 1955. In all, in Matussek's study sample, psychological illness was diagnosed by doctors in only 38.9 percent of the cases after 1955. However, in his opinion, the actual presence of such illness was undoubtedly much more frequent. Apparently, it depended on the attitude of the doctor whether a psychological illness was diagnosed and a psychiatrist brought in.

In the psychiatric diagnoses themselves, Matussek found great vagueness and lack of clarity. Aside from the general underassessment of pensions for psychological illness, he also found it remarkable that organic changes to the brain (hirnorganische Veränderungen) were believed to merit higher pensions than experience-reactive changes. In his view, this suggested that the doctors had a "somatic concept." In this connection, Matussek also mentioned that von Baeyer's clinic in Heidelberg found only relatively low reductions in earning capacity for experience-reactive disorders—25–30 percent—while in Norway, Denmark, and Holland, significantly higher pension classifications were established. Twenty-eight percent of those questioned appealed the authorities' first pension decision; half of them achieved no change in their pension allowance, one-third obtained an increase, and 8.3 percent had their pensions reduced.[112] (See, for comparison, the statistics in appendix B, table 7.)

Matussek's study appeared too late to influence the prevailing medical evaluation practices. The BEG Final Law had long since been adopted, and the application deadline had passed. Mattusek had determined that length of time in concentration camps was not the determinative factor in health damage, and that significant harm could have resulted even from a short period of imprisonment. This could have served to support the demand by persecutees' organizations that the minimum length of time for the "concentration camp assumption" be reduced from a year to five months.

Chapter 4

Examiners
and Victims

The literature on the subject contains ample evidence of the prejudice harbored by many German medical evaluators toward persecutees, as well as the pitfalls and laboriousness of the entire procedure. Along with Herberg, Paul, von Baeyer, Venzlaff, Kluge, Matussek, and other German critics, American psychiatrists harshly attacked the practices of German authorities and doctors. "The patient should actually receive compensation for the agitation and degradation suffered in the course of the reparations procedure," the New York psychoanalyst Kurt Eissler observed in 1963.[1] His colleague Dr. William Niederland spoke of a "murder of the soul" committed against the victims by the medical experts.[2] This aspect, the retraumatization of the persecutees through the medical examination and evaluation process, is discussed here.

The literature contains few references to the relationship between examiners and victims; after all, most of it was written by examiners and from their point of view, even if they endeavored to present their findings honestly. The only attempt to analyze the behavior of examining doctors from a psychodynamic point of view was made by Klaus Hoppe, a psychoanalyst who had emigrated to the United States from Germany in the 1950s. He distinguished four categories of behavior by doctors: (1) total denial, (2) rationalization, (3) overidentification with the victim, and (4) controlled identification.

Doctors falling into the first category identified with the aggressor and warded off their own fears, shame, and guilt feelings, caused by confrontation with the misery of the victims, by denying and trivializing the sufferings of the latter. Those in the second category exhibited openhearted and well-meaning behavior, only to find no scientific connection between persecution and illness. This understanding lip service to suffering helped relieve their guilt feelings, and their "objective" conclusions guaranteed that they would be recognized by the German authorities and their German colleagues as reasonable, unbiased evaluators. The victims associated this type of doctor with the "kind SS officer" who had offered them a cigarette during interrogations.

Doctors in the third category bound the victims to them, thus satisfying their own narcissistic need for omnipotence. Because their recommendations were generally not accepted, they disappointed their patients' hopes. Behind their exaggerated sympathy with and pity for the survivors lay a hatred of the Nazis, who had destroyed their own hopes, and a self-reproach for not fulfilling those hopes.

The fourth category, controlled identification, included the ideal doctor, who did justice to the problems of the survivors by keeping his own judgments to himself and believing the—unbelievable—experiences of the survivors; by not closing himself off to the—unbearable—terror; by feeling sympathy, while at the same time critically observing himself and remaining aware of countertransference phenomena or his own defensive maneuvers.

As a rule, however, doctors oscillated between overidentification and denial. Hoppe acknowledged that he did not live up to the ideal type. The doctor's understanding of the patient's sufferings, he said, met its limits where it touched on the doctor's own unresolved problems.[3] Thus he described patients who made him feel guilty for having been a member of the Hitler Youth in the Third Reich.[4]

At the first world congress of psychoanalysts to be held on German soil since 1933, the 34th Congress of the International Psychoanalytic Association, which took place in Hamburg in late July 1985, William Niederland maintained that a majority of medical experts in German reparations procedures had been "former Nazis."[5] This statement is correct; however, the question is the way in which the "former Nazi" encountered the victim—whether he faced him as an understanding physician, or appeared in word, gesture, and judgment in the likeness of the persecutor. Some doctors were blessed with the "Gnade der späten Geburt," the good fortune of having been born after the fact, and some foreign examining doctors were no less "pro-rejection" than their German colleagues. What was important was whether the "former Nazi" was "repentant," with a bad conscience that drove him to try to compensate for the past, or whether he continued to aim his dislike of the weak and sick at the victims.[6] According to Hoppe, in encountering survivors, the doctor had to expect to be identified with the persecutor, and had to be able to master this transference situation.[7] If the doctor appeared to the victim as another persecutor, the victim's fears, latent since the persecution, would become reality, with possibly serious consequences. One false word would suffice, considering the extreme sensitivity of concentration camp survivors to anything that reminded them of the camps.[8]

Only the victims can provide information about what went on in the offices of the examining doctors, and they have little voice in the existing medical literature. Therefore, from the 369 dossiers on claims for health damage to which I had access, I have chosen those containing letters and statements from applicants that they sent to the authorities either directly or through their lawyers. An additional selection criterion was the greatest possible transparency of the relationship between examiner and victim, to the extent that the evaluation report reveals anything about the doctor's attitude toward the examinee. In the following, I analyze 14 representative case histories. Their stories stand for many similar ones—for the years of going through the courts, from doctor to doctor; for the debate over fundamental medical issues carried out on the backs of the victims; for the revival of the trauma of persecution through trials and examinations; for the pseudoscientific arguments made by many evaluators (for example, the frequently used term "hereditarily determined" [*anlagebedingt*]); for the fact that psychoanalytic arguments were chosen only if they were helpful in getting a claim rejected; and finally for the discriminatory treatment of persecutees from lower social classes, Gypsies, and women.

In the files, patients had been given pseudonyms, as is the norm for medical records. However, the doctors and officials, because they carried out official functions, are named. In reading hundreds of dossiers, some of the effort that went into this process communicated itself to me: the forced, repeated description of barely imaginable misery, the mountains of paper, of sober notices in German officialese, of dozens of evaluations, each twenty or thirty or more pages long, of legal documents, court rulings, most of them written in almost unbearably cold legal language, far removed from the reality. After reading several hundred pages of files on a person that have collected over the course of years or decades, one is moved to cry, "Stop! In God's name, just give him his 150-mark pension!" The staff of the offices and the examining doctors may also have felt this way at times, but their irritation was all too frequently directed against the claimants rather than at the process itself. The transformation of spontaneous human reactions such as horror and sympathy into aversion and distrust in the course of the reparations routine can be seen in a description by one of those involved: "Every doctor and every administrative employee, like every judge and lawyer, would at the beginning of his reparations work be deeply impressed by the persecutees' descriptions and would feel sympathy in the most literal sense, which had to be the actual precondition for any objective, correct evaluation. However, once this reparations employee has processed several hundred similar cases, this ability to sympathize and understand evidently diminishes and is replaced by a state of habituation and deadening, or even aversion at the constant repetition. The descriptions of the persecutees' experiences, all similar and sometimes even using the exact same words—they could hardly be different, given that the persecution experience was the same—inevitably, over time, lead the reparations employee to become critical and perhaps even believe that the reports had all been written according to the same model, or prepared en masse, with only the place and name changed."[9]

Basic Medical Issues

Frau E.—Gathering Evidence on a Fall from a Ladder in 1944

Frau E. was born on 2 February 1903 in Magdeburg. She attended the lyceum until the age of sixteen and then went to trade school. After obtaining her diploma, she worked in an office. On 1 July 1933, she lost her job because she was a Jew, and she emigrated to Barcelona in November of the same year. In 1934, she found out that her mother had died suddenly, but she could not go to Germany for the funeral. In 1935, she was involved in an automobile accident that left her with stiffening in the right hip joint.[10]

Following the outbreak of the Spanish Civil War, Frau E. emigrated to France, and after the German invasion, she was imprisoned in the southern French concentration camp at Gurs. The horrors of the camp and the deaths of many fellow prisoners threw her into deep depression. She succeeded in escaping Gurs in a state of complete debilitation. She was hospitalized for undernourishment and psychological disturbance, and eventually found shelter in a convent. A year later, Frau E. had to flee when deportations began. At first, she hid in the woods; later she was supplied with false papers by the nuns in a girls' boarding school and employed as a maid. In 1944, she fell from a ladder while picking cherries in the school garden and suffered a severe concussion. She refused to call a doctor for fear of discovery.

After liberation, she worked in Paris for the persecutee assistance organization OSE and found out that her father and her entire family had died in Theresienstadt and other concentration camps. After a short time, Frau E. had to give up her job for health reasons. In 1956, Frau E. made an application to the state pension office of North Rhine–Westphalia for damage to body and health. She suffered from depression and the effects of the concussion and the automobile accident. On 30 August 1956, she was examined by the evaluator commissioned by the German embassy in Paris, Dr. W. Brunswic. He found a stiffening in the right hip joint, as well as a chronic infectious process with joint disorders: MdE (reduction in earning capacity), 50 percent; persecution-induced portion, 30 percent. Although he recorded in the patient report that Frau E. had suffered a severe nervous shock in the camp in Gurs and "went very much downhill psychologically and physically," Dr. Brunswic noted the results of his examination, under the heading "psyche," as "not apparent." The supervising doctor at the state pension office, Professor Paul Trüb, agreed with the medical report.

Carl Ludwig Paul Trüb (1894–1981) served as a soldier in World War I. He studied medicine in Tübingen, Münster, and Bonn, took his state examinations in 1920, and received his medical degree in 1921. He became city medical officer in Duisburg in 1925, and district medical officer at Merzig, in the Saar, in 1927. In 1933, Trüb joined the Nazi party and became a member of the SS. After holding interim posts in Magdeburg and Arnsberg, Westphalia, he became medical officer to the office of the chief of police in Berlin in 1938. In 1940, he rose to become chief medical officer in the subsection for People's Health and Care under the governor of Vienna, where he was responsible, among other things, for the Department of Hereditary and Racial Maintenance, implementation of the Law to Prevent Genetically Defective Offspring, and the Department of Hospitals and Asylums. In this capacity, he was responsible for the transports of Austrian "lunatics" to the extermination facility at Hartheim/Linz. He finished the thesis required to become a professor in 1944. After 1945, he became medical officer to the head of the Cologne district, officer in charge of general hygiene and combating epidemics in the state Ministry of Labor, and chairman of the examining commission for medical teaching facilities in the Düsseldorf region. From 1952 until his retirement in 1959, he was chief government medical officer in Düsseldorf. He wrote over two hundred works on the problems of the public health system. Before the adoption of the Federal Restitution Law and creation of the medical service of the state pension office of North Rhine–Westphalia, Trüb was one of the primary evaluators of persecutees in North Rhine–Westphalia. In 1954, he wrote a manual on reparations evaluations. He was active as a supervisory physician to the authority until the 1960s. In January 1960, he was officially delegated by the state offices and the Foreign Office to choose and train examining doctors in Paris. In his publications and evaluations, he endeavored to promote fairness in the evaluation practice.[11]

Frau E.'s application remained on the authorities' desks for four years. On 6 October 1960, Chief Medical Officer Hanns Bücken made a notation on it, all of ten lines, in which he objected that the hip joint stiffening was the result of the car accident in Barcelona. He said nothing at all about the other disabilities. Frau E. had not claimed in her application that the effects of the car accident were caused by persecution.

After first completing a banking apprenticeship, **Hanns Bücken** (1905–?) earned a high school diploma in 1930 and then went on to study medicine in Munich, Marburg, and Düsseldorf. In 1933, he joined the Nazi party; in 1935, he passed his state exams, and in 1938, he became a member of the Nazi Doctors' Union. He became local medical officer in Grevenbroich and, in 1943, medical officer to the government of Düsseldorf. After the war, he was a local medical officer in Neuss.[12]

Two more years passed until the state pension office issued a rejection on 5 April 1962, six years after the application. They claimed that only illnesses "due to fate" were present. On 10 July 1962, Frau E.'s lawyer appealed this decision to the Düsseldorf district court on the basis of a privately commissioned report by the Paris psychiatrist Dr. Joseph Fuswerk-Fursay, an internationally respected expert on the psychological consequences of concentration camp imprisonment and persecution. Fursay criticized the previous evaluations for not discussing Frau E.'s psychological problems. On his meeting with Frau E., he wrote, among other things:

She speaks without interruption, gets excited and becomes very irritable, with attacks of collapse and crying spasms. She is restless, anxious, starts at the slightest sound. At night she wakes with the feeling that someone is there; unjustified fear that she is still being persecuted. She is constantly hopeless and despondent, does not live like other people, she is aggressive and senselessly rebels against everything. She is aware of the failure of her life, she even thought she could keep herself going on Sundays with her work like an automaton. She is fearful, has heart pains, apprehension, and the feeling that her heart is being twisted in her body. She is afraid of dying, has fainting spells. She is constantly tired, exhausted, the tiredness cripples her. There is no doubt that she can only keep her job because well-meaning people are accommodating her. Contact with the world is hard for her; she lives alone, all the more so as she was unable to start a family, since her fiancé went overseas in 1939 and never came back, which makes her disappointment and grief even worse. Her sleep is quite insufficient, not refreshing, with sleepless nights, nightmares, restlessness, images of dead people leaving their graves to dance, and she is always among them. She remains completely fixated on the unfortunate epoch; every thought association returns her to it, even the difficulties she has had with the German authorities agitate her and strengthen her feeling of still being the victim. She is still obsessed with the horrible thoughts and ideas of the 15,000 Jews who were brought from the Lower Palatinate to Gurs camp, of corpses, the half-dead, twisted women, and so on.

The medical officer to the state pension office, Dr. Lotte Herrlich, responded in an advisory opinion on 3 September 1962 that the doctor, Brunswic, had presented no neuropsychasthenic complaints in his first report, nor had he objectified any in his examination findings. Although Frau E. had already offered a slew of documents on medical treatments during the occupation and after 1945, Herrlich demanded "proof of treatment that shows when, where, and how long and with whom she underwent medical treatment . . . The patient documents from the University Hospital in Barcelona must also be obtained." Frau E.'s lawyer answered the medical officer, "The plaintiff is neither able, nor does she wish, to obtain further medical files at her own expense."

Three months later, on 19 December 1962, Frau E. suffered a stroke, causing paralysis to the right side of her body and a slight speech impediment. This turned the attention of the doctor who would in future deal with Frau E. to the skull trauma she had suffered falling off a ladder in 1944, which might be connected with the stroke.

Because of the differing opinions of the evaluators, the Düsseldorf district court summoned all the doctors to a hearing on 30 April 1963, at which all repeated their findings orally or in writing. The court suggested another examination in a German clinic. However, Henri Jacobs, a doctor in Paris, certified that Frau E. was unable to travel, as the very suggestion of a trip to Germany triggered strong reactions of fear and agitation in her and there was danger of another stroke if she undertook such a journey. Dr. S. Pierre Kaplan in Paris was thereupon appointed by the court to conduct the examination; he examined Frau E. thoroughly on 15 December 1964 and 7 January 1965.

Vilna-born **Siegesmund Pierre Kaplan** (1904–1989) was relieved of his position as intern at Moabit Hospital in Berlin in 1933 during the police raids on Jewish doctors. He went to Paris and survived the German occupation of France in hiding, under a false name. He cared for injured partisans as a member of the French resistance. After the war, he ran a large internal medicine practice in Paris, specializing in cardiology and endocrinology. As the evaluator commissioned by the German embassy, he issued numerous reports on persecutees for the German reparations offices.[13]

A neurologist, Dr. C. Schaub, also thoroughly examined Frau E. and discovered in her electroencephalogram an abnormality on the left side. In summary, the doctors found in Frau E. an illness profile that mixed "postcommotional encephalopathy appearing after skull trauma" and an "acquired, chronified psychasthenic state" with a persecution-induced reduction in earning capacity of 45 percent. They judged Frau E.'s other complaints, joint pains and digestive disorders, to be non-persecution-induced. A year later, their evaluation had not yet reached the court. At the end of March 1966, Frau E. wrote to Kaplan:

I have just been informed that your report has still not reached the German authorities, despite your promise at the beginning of March. My refusal to go to Aachen so as not to place myself in the hands of German doctors, who would have tormented me unnecessarily, did not solve the problem. It has now been fifteen months since I was examined by you and your colleague—also tormented, but with a certain amount of consideration. Above all, you gave me hope of success, which I had already given up.

Finally, on 1 May 1966, three years after the appeal, the report reached the judge's desk, and the process could continue. After another half year, the medical officer of the state pension office responded to Kaplan's report with the objection that nothing had been said of a fall from a ladder in Frau E.'s previous information or previous evaluations. "Thus this fact situation presents a question of assessment of evidence, as such a serious incident could hardly have been forgotten." It was claimed, in addition, that Frau E. had lived in constant fear of being discovered and arrested during her stay at the girls' boarding school, to which the officer argued: "How picking fruit can be consistent with the fear of being discovered and arrested remains incomprehensible." On the medical consequences of the fall, he objected that posttraumatic epilepsy only appeared after brain injury in exceptional circumstances, in some 1 percent of all cases, and then only with close temporal proximity between the accident and the beginning of the attacks—that, he argued, was the opinion of all relevant literature. He concluded that "the differential diagnostic separation of a traumatic epilepsy," of which no one had spoken until then, was "urgently necessary." "A directed examination at a specialized clinic should be undertaken at a German university clinic. This should be assigned to Prof. Panse (director of the psychiatric clinic of the University of Düsseldorf)."

Frau E.'s laywer refused to accept Dr. Panse as the examiner, "for reasons having to do with the person of the expert" (see box on Friedrich Panse in chapter 3 above). In its judgment of 16 January 1967, the District Court accepted the Kaplan-Schaub recommendation and recognized a persecution-induced MdE of 45 percent for Frau E.; this meant capital restitution for the period from 1941 (beginning of persecution) to 1953 of 11,241 DM, a retroactive pension payment from 1953 to 1966 of 9,363 DM, and a monthly pension of 92 DM starting 1 February 1967. In its ruling, the court emphasized that the differential diagnostic separation of a traumatic epilepsy demanded by the medical officer of the state pension office would be senseless, as the entire illness profile could not be sorted out through differential diagnosis. A neurological and psychiatric syndrome was present in the plaintiff that was caused by persecution, and it did not matter in individual detail whether she had suffered a traumatic epilepsy or not.

Nevertheless, the state pension office appealed the judgment of the district court, because there had been no separation of neurological and psychiatric illnesses. The Düsseldorf appeals court thereupon proposed a settlement including only a 25 percent reduction in earning capacity. The reviewing doctor for the state pension office, Dr. Hans-Joachim Jentsch, was the first official examiner to permit a hint of sympathy to show through, in his recommendation on 20 September 1967: "It is a matter of not-insignificant persecution with credible losses, especially in the neuropsychological area. The plaintiff . . . went through a great deal." He suggested that she accept the appeals court settlement, with the formula "psychasthenic persecution syndrome, total MdE: 70 percent, persecution-induced: 25 percent." Frau E. rejected this proposed settlement, which would have meant only the minimum pension, as little more than alms. In her opinion, it was based on the officials' and doctors' doubts as to her credibility. The appeals court thereupon demanded completely new proof-taking on the question of whether the fall from the ladder was an employment-related accident or if she had picked the cherries from the tree on her own. The nuns with whom Frau E. had found refuge were sought out and examined by a French court. One of the nuns was so old that she could not appear before the court; she had to present a doctor's certificate that she was unable to travel. The appeals court, in its evidentiary decision on 10 January 1968, stated:

The head of the school . . . or an employee familiar with conditions in 1944, will be examined on the following questions:

1. Did the plaintiff . . . suffer a fall from a ladder while picking cherries in 1944 that caused a concussion? Was she treated, and if so, by what doctor? What type of injuries did she have?

2. Was picking cherries among the duties the plaintiff was expected to perform as part of her job as housemaid?

Frau E. herself visited her former rescuers in the convent. In a letter to her lawyer, she told him about this and gave free rein to her feelings about the entire process:

I was welcomed with great cordiality . . . When I finally decided to indicate the reason for my visit, an indescribable shame overcame me, shame that it had become necessary for me to ask the nuns to whom I owed my life for something again, and that I had to admit that the court had "doubts" . . . It was really a work-related accident that could not be reported and evaluated because of the situation at the time. How could I, as a German Jew, have sought unpaid work in a French convent if the terrible persecutions of Jews had not occurred . . . On 2 May 1959, I sent a detailed letter to Chancellor Konrad Adenauer. . . . Among other things, I said, "I firmly believed that the voluntary reparations would be carried out with humane sympathy and goodness. Instead, they demand from me not only the most detailed descriptions of the inhuman treatment suffered; one must seek in one's memories, rummage, to bring these torments alive again and swear to them. But once they have been sworn to, eyewitnesses must confirm the torments described. Is such treatment humane? *I do not want to beg for the reparations offered,* and I would like people to believe me when I give evidence under oath!!!" A cool answer from the secretary in the chancellor's office [Globke] on 6 May 1959 stated: "The Chancellor cannot, under his constitutional authority, influence the processing of reparations applications or accelerate a reparations procedure."

Now you will understand why the eyewitness was not examined [Frau E. meant an eyewitness who was also in the boarding school in 1944, and who lived in Cologne]. It is also clear why the expertise of the doctor appointed by the court, Dr. Kaplan, was rejected, because it probably was in my favor . . . It is a spiral without an end.

The fact that judges and high state officials can fight with such low weapons for many, many years against an aging woman surpasses my understanding and makes me completely doubt the existence of German justice. And that not a single person of the many who had in their hands my undoubtedly very marked up dossier wanted to end this terrible game permits many conclusions. After all, I have neither attacked nor even besmirched a particular person, nor committed a crime against the state. I have merely opposed a system that does not value human dignity very highly.

Did none of the judges ever realize that I really suffered a great deal, that the years 1945–49, which are so important in reparations, when I was still young enough to enjoy my life a little after all the terrible years, were blessed with pain and that I spent my free time on my bed? But they are probably not men, but machines set from the start to say "no."

The hearing of the nuns before the French court revealed that Frau E. had picked the cherries as a favor. However, Frau E.'s lawyer interpreted this, given conditions at the time, as a necessary favor: "Plaintiff naturally gave every possible voluntary assistance, for only in that way could she show her appreciation, to a certain degree, for being taken into the convent, which meant her life had been saved from the persecutions. Within this context, she had performed activities that a housemaid hired under normal circumstances and a normal contract would have considered impositions and refused."

Another year passed with the examination of the French nuns. Then the court once more appointed a private neurologist to issue a report based on the dossier. This doctor, Dr. Franz Josef Gierath of Hennef, basically confirmed the results of the examination by his Paris colleagues Kaplan and Schaub, and also assessed persecution-induced MdE at 45 percent. He believed Frau E. suffered primarily from depression. "After this life story, connected with frequent forced change of location, personal insecurity, social descent, and the death of her father in a concentration camp, an assumption of persecution-induced uprooting depression is justified." Further, he contradicted the professionally incompetent objections by the medical officer of the state pension office on the diagnosis of traumatic epilepsy: "The free interval of four years between the fall from the ladder and the first attacks does not—contrary to the view of the state pension office—mean there is no connection, as 42 percent of first attacks of so-called late epilepsy are rather evenly distributed along the twenty years following the accident."

Gierath further argued that the symptoms of both illnesses—persecution-induced uprooting depression and epilepsy independent of persecution—to some extent overlapped; "but as Frau E. did not even mention the attacks to anyone before Dr. Kaplan, we may assume that they appeared very seldom and very briefly." He said that this also meant that the thus-conditioned "psychopathological symptoms, in the sense of an essential change," had remained significantly retarded "compared to the persecution-induced depressive symptoms." Furthermore, by then the various partial illnesses could no longer be separated out.

Thus at least one German doctor did attempt to end this "terrible game." But the state appeals court was not impressed by this convincing exposition. "The variety of the complexes of symptoms, even if they intersect, permits a diagnostic separation." As a result, a "determination of a reduction in earning capacity caused by each of the two complaints" was possible and necessary. On the nature of the fall from the ladder in 1944, the judge remarked:

The plaintiff's original claim that she was employed as a housemaid in the girls' boarding school was refuted by the evidence in the second lawsuit. Both nuns agreed in testifying that the plaintiff was not employed, but instead participated voluntarily in work that arose at the school . . . The plaintiff can be believed when she says she felt obligated to perform work at the school. But she could only be expected to do such work as could be reconciled with her physical disability. This did not include picking cherries. The plaintiff, to whom a wide variety of work was available, did not need to expose herself to this danger . . . If the plaintiff nevertheless performed work such as picking cherries . . . this was outside all responsible behavior.

Her suit was rejected; twenty-four years after the end of the war and thirteen years after she had made her claim, Frau E. was granted only a 25 percent reduction in earning capacity.

Herr F.—"If at all possible, put an end to this old man's claims."

Herr F. had run a law office in the Hungarian city of C. for thirty-five years; he was sixty-two years old when the German Wehrmacht occupied the country in March 1944. Along with the other Jewish residents of the city, he was dragged from his home and thrown into a provisional concentration camp in a brickyard outside the city. There,

In a naked state, I received blows from three henchmen for an hour with clubs and boot kicks to my back, arms, legs, and soles, until I fell unconscious; when I regained consciousness and tried to stand up, this bestial beating continued for another half hour. Then I was forced to dress, but my feet were so swollen that I was unable to insert them into my shoes. I had to carry them in my hands when I was forced to crawl into a doghouse, where I lay for another hour until I was taken back to the barn of the brickyard, where the bunk I had been assigned was located. Afterwards I immediately had blood in my urine and a high fever. I spent more than two weeks this way without being examined or treated by a doctor. On the contrary, because I was brought back on a stretcher to the room in which I had suffered the described barbaric physical abuse and was threatened with a repetition of the same, I received such a shock to my nerves that I had a heart spasm and was carried out half dead. Only later was it determined that I was ill with a kidney infection and pleurisy . . . At the beginning of July 1944, we were deported to Bergen-Belsen concentration camp, and through a special rescue operation we were able, in the second half of August 1944, to reach Switzerland.

In the following years, Herr F. needed constant medical attention for his heart condition, a colon infection, and chronic back, lower back, and joint pains. When the Federal Supplementary Law was passed in 1953, Herr F. was seventy-two. In 1954, he applied for a health damage pension. The examining doctor commissioned by the German embassy in Geneva, Dr. Robert Hubleur, examined Herr. F. in his office three years later, on 20 November 1957, at 9 A.M. On his experience in Hubleur's office, Herr F. later reported, "His unfriendly attitude toward me was expressed right at the start of the examination. Namely, as I spoke of the pains in my back, lower back, and legs, he got up from his seat with an apparently derisive gesture and said that he himself was plagued by pains that could be ascribed to arthritis, which appears in many people of advanced age, and yet this did not prevent him from practicing his profession."

In his evaluation, Hubleur characterized Herr F. as "a 77-year-old claimant who is in an enviable psychosomatic condition." Under the preprinted rubric, "Any psychologically abnormal reactions?" he noted, "The usual exaggerations," and further, "In summary, it can be said that in this 77-year-old gentleman, who suffers from the usual symptoms of age (arteriosclerosis and arthrosis), no lesions can be found that can be traced back to National Socialist persecution." In estimating the reduction in earning capacity for Herr F., he argued, "At the time of the persecution, Herr F. was sixty-three years old (May 1944). His reduction in earning capacity began with this. If the claimant had had the opportunity to work again, this reduction in earning capacity would not have lasted long." In other words, since in 1944 Herr F. was already not far from retirement age, there was no point in estimating the reduction in his earning capacity.

In this context, it must be explained that under the Restitution Law, it was not the actual handicap suffered by the persecutee in his or her profession that counted for a reduction in earning capacity, but general impairment as a result of the complaint. That is, a persecutee could be fully active in his or her profession, but still receive a pension for health damage—for example, for an anxiety neurosis. The pension was not conceived of primarily as a benefit, but as compensation for harms suffered. Of course, it was frequently also the case that the victims were really invalids and unable to work.

At the very end of the report on Herr F., under the rubric "other remarks," Hubleur wrote, "If at all possible, put an end to this old man's claims for complaints that still exist."[14]

Persecutees often got to read these reports through their lawyers. Herr F. was one of them. He commented, "Can someone appointed exclusively for their medical perceptions and conclusions take upon themselves the authority for such unheard-of opinions?" Furthermore, he pointed out that in his report, Hubleur never mentioned his detailed description of the abuse in the brickyard in May 1944. "Jewish residents of Geneva who already lived here before World War II are convinced that Dr. Hubleur was one of those Swiss who sympathized at the time with the National Socialist regime in Germany."

On the basis of Hubleur's report, the Hamburg reparations office rejected Herr F.'s claim. That was the beginning of an endless stream of red tape; the treadmill of trials, evaluations, and counterevaluations took its course. Professor Georges Bickel, a Swiss orthopedist, the chief examining doctor for the Hamburg district court, diagnosed Herr F. as having an infectious spinal condition, a so-called Bechterev syndrome, partly triggered by the severe abuse and resulting kidney infection in the concentration camp. He estimated a persecution-induced reduction in earning capacity of 40 percent. "The cause of the Bechterev illness is still unknown," the reparations office responded on 5 January 1965. "It is remarkable that during the war, under the harshest conditions at the front, no increase in the Bechterev illness was found, neither on the German nor even on the American side . . . Time spent under the most difficult conditions, along with beatings and kicks in the back, together with the undeniable psychological hardship of persecution, represent, however, only thinkable and possible, but under no circumstances probable causes, according to the above explanation." In conclusion, the office announced, "Professor Bickel's evaluation is rejected because it was not based on German assessment principles."

The office demanded another examination of Herr F., this time by a German orthopedist from Cologne. Herr F. opposed this renewed delay in the procedure. Finally, on 5 March 1965, the district court found in his favor without another examination. It accepted Bickel's evaluation, but assessed the reduction in earning capacity as somewhat lower—30 percent. Following this decision, Herr F.'s lawyer wrote him:

In the meantime, in your health damage case, I have spoken in depth again with the head of the procedure department [of the reparations office] in order to persuade him to refrain from appealing. Unfortunately, I was unable to make clear to the responsible official that in the present case, an appeal is impractical. I reminded him in vain of your advanced age. The office is of the opinion that assessing a Bechterev illness is a matter of basic principles for the office. The office intends to judge according to German medicine and not according to Swiss medical opinion.

In its appeal, the office brought in the as-yet-unused argument that Herr F. had mentioned only heart ailments in his original application in 1954, and mentioned the spinal complaint only after the examination by Dr. Hubleur three years later. Besides, no proof of treatment existed for this complaint before 1957. Finally, the office had the impression that the Swiss orthopedic expert, Bickel, was "not particularly knowledgeable" about the Bechterev illness.[15] On 27 October 1965, the Hamburg appeals court rejected the reparations office's appeal, and Herr F. received the health damage pension to which he was entitled.

Herr O.—Doctors Break Down Organs into Persecution-Induced and Non–Persecution-Induced Sections

Herr O. was born in Hamburg on 2 November 1914. He attended school there and began studying law at the University of Hamburg in 1934. As a Jew, he was expelled a year later and had to make a living as a salesman in different parts of Germany. After 9 November 1938, he and his family were deported to Poland in the so-called Zbaszyn Operation. When he returned to Hamburg in 1939 to prepare for emigration, he was arrested by the Gestapo. He was first imprisoned and then sent to the concentration camps Sachsenhausen, Dachau, and Buchenwald for five years, from 1940 to 1945. In autumn 1941, as part of a punishment operation in Dachau, he was hanged by the arms from a tree. He developed a phlegmon in both lower legs and a severe soft tissue infection, and also suffered from frostbite in both legs. This left behind considerable mutilation through scarring, as well as ulcers on both lower legs. Because of deprivation in the camps, he also contracted tuberculosis in both lungs. In 1956, a 40 percent reduction in earning capacity was certified for him, and he was granted a disability pension.

After the war, Herr O. emigrated to the United States via France and Israel. In 1965, he underwent a complicated vascular operation to treat clogged arteries in both legs. He applied for reimbursement of hospital costs, based on his right to medical treatment under the Federal Restitution Law. The reparations office in Hamburg rejected this application, arguing that only venous circulatory problems of the legs had been recognized as persecution-induced complaints, while the complaint for which he had undergone the operation was the result of constitutionally based arterial circulatory problems having nothing to do with his venous circulatory problems. He sued, lost, and appealed the decision. The Hanseatic appeals court found in his favor on 20 August 1971, ruling that the issue was not whether the operation was to treat a recognized persecution-induced complaint—especially as the first medical report, by a New York medical expert, Dr. Cronheim, in 1956 had already mentioned persecution-induced *arterial* circulatory problems. However, in a new evaluation in 1965, Cronheim had retreated from this assessment, classing O's arterial circulatory problems as constitutionally based.

In 1968, while the suit was still in progress, Herr O had to undergo a second vascular operation; in 1972, he suffered a heart attack that forced him to give up his job completely. He made a "worsening application" to the authorities. Because he happened to be in Israel at the time, he called upon the Tel Aviv internist Dr. Kurt Epstein to act as examiner. Dr. Epstein examined Herr O. in his office on 24 November 1974. According to the lawyer's record of his client's testimony, the following took place in Epstein's office:

Dr. Epstein asked the plaintiff how high his monthly pension was. Although the plaintiff wondered about the seemliness and purpose of the question, he responded with the truth. Dr. Epstein then said in condescending fashion: "Well, that's nice. Today the reparations offices and courts reject almost all applications, and no court in Germany would concoct a ruling like that of the Hamburg appeals court." The plaintiff felt deeply humiliated by Dr. Epstein's attitude, and burst into tears. In retrospect, the plaintiff is embarrassed and angry at himself for being too cowardly to tell Dr. Epstein what he thought of him and leave the office.

On page 3 of his report, Epstein referred to this incident. After describing Herr O.'s illnesses, he wrote: "All of this has undermined the applicant's resistance. Herr O., who during the years of persecution suffered endlessly, suddenly began crying like a small child during the examination, for no reason."

Based on his examination, Epstein concluded that no worsening of Herr O.'s persecution-induced disorder had occurred. The disease of the leg arteries and the heart attack were "age-related arteriosclerotic conditions in an extremely advanced stage, with no relationship to persecution." An endoradiogram of the leg arteries had been done in Israel in July 1974, indicating that the artificial bypass was again almost completely clogged. Epstein also mentioned this finding in his report, but drew no further conclusions from it, except that the total reduction in earning capacity (not the persecution-induced reduction) had risen from 60 to 80 percent. Based on Dr. Epstein's report, the reparations office on 28 August 1975 rejected Herr O.'s "worsening application." His lawyer brought suit, arguing that the Supreme Court, the highest German court of appeals, had already accepted the need for a hospital stay for the arterial disorder, and that therefore the office had to acknowledge the worsening and grant a higher pension for the same illness, which had led to a heart attack. Dr. Hagemann of the medical service of the reparations office responded, "If one followed the attorney's present arguments, the Supreme Court's mistaken assessment would be made still worse." The district court named Gotthard Schettler, professor of internal medicine at the University of Heidelberg, as primary examiner.

Gotthard Schettler (1917–1996) began studying medicine in Jena in 1937 and then volunteered for the Luftwaffe, which he left after being wounded. He joined the Nazi party and rose to become Gau student leader in the Thuringian Gau. Schettler continued his medical studies in Leipzig, Vienna, and Tübingen and received his medical degree in 1942. After the war, he studied under Hans Erhard Bock in the department of internal medicine at the Marburg University Clinic. In 1950, he qualified to become a professor with a dissertation on "Nutrition and

Cholesterol Metabolism," and in 1956, he became medical director of the medical clinic at Stuttgart–Bad Canstatt. In 1961, he took a chair at the medical polyclinic of the Berlin Free University, and in 1963, he was named to the chair for internal medicine at the Ludolf Krehl Clinic in Heidelberg. Schettler was one of the most influential figures in German medicine. He was chairman of numerous national and international professional associations. His areas of specialization were lipometabolic disorders and arteriosclerosis. Although Schettler advocated recognizing arteriosclerosis as a disorder suffered by returning prisoners of war, as a rule he rejected the same claims by victims of Nazism in his evaluations. As Schettler was considered the top expert in West Germany, his view of the arteriosclerosis issue had almost legal force in reparations evaluations. Most examining doctors followed Schettler and ignored differing foreign studies, such as one by the Czech pathologist Frantisek Blaha, who as a prisoner doctor at Dachau had found severe arteriosclerotic changes in young prisoners, which he published reports of after the war.[16]

Schettler had his chief physician, Dr. H. Mörl, issue an evaluation based on files, in which he determined that the arteriosclerosis, as the illness behind the arterial vascular disease in the legs and the heart attack, had nothing to do "with the recognized facts of persecution, and that "the recognized health damage had in no way worsened." Upon receipt of this report, Herr O. called his lawyer, and then wrote him, "I regret that I got so excited on the telephone, but I know that you understand that the unjust attitude of the Germans still greatly agitates me." In a decision on 17 July 1978, the Hamburg district court ruled against Herr O., saying, "The chamber followed the convincing statement of Prof. Schettler, one of the leading German physicians in the field of heart and circulatory disease."[17]

Herr O. appealed the decision, submitting a report by Professor Lawrence Friedman, a New York vascular specialist, who had thoroughly examined Herr O. Friedman suggested that the arteriosclerosis would have had "considerably fewer serious consequences" without the persecution. Dr. Hagemann of the medical service at the reparations office responded on 27 February 1979 that this was only a description of the course of the disease with various etiological considerations, and imparted no new facts. In addition, he claimed that the "non-persecution-induced diseases," such as the arterial circulatory disorder in the legs and the heart attack, had overtaken the "persecution-induced circulatory disorders" (namely the venous disorders) to such an extent that an "assessment of the overall presentation of the state of disease would instead result in a lowering of the persecution-induced reduction in earning capacity."

Another three years passed before the case came before the Hanseatic appeals court. Herr O.'s condition rapidly worsened, and he died at age seventy on 29 January 1982 of the consequences of his severe heart and vascular disease. His lawyer continued the suit in the name of his heirs.

The Supreme Court rejected the appeal, among other things because pensions were not hereditary and the plaintiff therefore had no claim to one, and because the death of Herr O. had made the issue of a hospital stay moot. No appeal of this judgment was allowed. Otto Küster, the lawyer, thereupon petitioned the federal Supreme Court to allow an appeal—with no success.

All three of these cases leave the impression that the authorities and some of the examining doctors were on the lookout for any details of the patients' biographies and medical histories that could possibly help construct grounds to reject their claims. They demanded medical reports from 1935 Spain, called for complicated evidentiary hearings on a 1944 fall from a ladder as though a murder were being investigated, and figuratively carved a person into pieces, searching every organ and every vein for non-persecution-induced portions. Dozens of doctors were called upon to consider the extent to which a persecution-induced depression could be distinguished from a supposedly non-persecution-induced skull trauma. One imagines all these doctors, judges, and officials surrounding the patients, dissecting knives at the ready, to examine every corner of their bodies for tissues that were or were not harmed in a way that would entitle them to pensions.

In a man whose legs were both mutilated during five years in concentration camps, doctors insisted on separating the arterial and venous blood vessels in the legs, whose diseases supposedly had nothing to do with each other, into persecution-induced and non-persecution-induced damage; and the court preferred to follow the German doctor, Schettler, rather than the American, Friedman, explaining simply that Schettler was the "leading" expert. Even in the case of an old man beaten half to death by the SS, German authorities wouldn't let a Swiss professor tell them their jobs. Instead, they fought his suit for over ten years, to the bitter end, supposedly in order to clear up a basic medical question. In fact, it probably had less to do with medical questions than with something quite different: "Bringing an end" to the claims and the "usual exaggerations." After all, these claimants couldn't possibly have had it worse than the soldiers "on the front lines."

Paradoxes in Freud's Name

Herr W.—"Social discrimination strengthens the ability to cope with life."

Herr W. was eleven years old in 1933. He was the only Jewish student at Hindenburg High School in Hamburg, ranking among the best in his class and popular with everyone. But everything changed overnight:

For no reason, students with whom I had gotten along well before the seizure of power now suddenly treated me with disdain, as if I were something inferior; they spat at and slapped me during recess, when the teachers weren't looking. I was threatened constantly and often beaten up . . . The students in my class waved the swastikas on their jackets and coats under my nose and threatened a "one-way ticket to Jerusalem." They often emptied my schoolbag onto the wet street and ripped up the books. My complaints to the teacher led nowhere. I recall one big, fat boy who threatened and slapped me for almost two years, usually during the long recess or before the first class hour. If I didn't come early enough, later I had to make twenty or more deep bows, to the laughter of all fellow students who were present, and call the big boy a "great lord." If I didn't say it well and loudly enough, I immediately got two slaps in the face. In this way I broke numerous pairs of glasses, and I never dared tell my parents the truth, as I got still more beatings from my stepfather for all the broken glasses. I was completely helpless, confused, intimidated, and abandoned. This was a deeply distressing experience— a bad dream—because before I had been popular with all my classmates, and probably with the teachers; and now, as an eleven- and twelve-year-old little boy, I did not understand where this hostility suddenly came from.

In October 1934, W. and his parents emigrated to Palestine. There he was unable to adapt to his new environment; he could not take the hot climate, and contracted dysentery and hepatitis. There was conflict at home, as his stepfather could not find work and there was never enough money. After a long search, W. finally found a position as a banker's apprentice at the age of twenty-five, but after five years he had to give up the job due to illness; after that he sat around the house "like an idiot." In 1957, having married in the meantime, he emigrated to America, on the advice of his doctor, because of the hot climate. There he again tried to work in a bank, where his Arab boss harassed him because he was a Jew. His wages were not enough to support his family, and he was forced to give up a second job for health reasons. He was soon deeply in debt. His constant illnesses—anxiety and tension, as well as chronic diarrhea re-sulting from the dysentery—strained his relationship with his wife and two children.

In 1965, he applied to the Hamburg reparations office, under the BEG Final Act, for delayed health damage. He was examined by various doc-tors, who found an enlarged liver and spleen as a result of dysentery and hepatitis, as well as a chronically inflamed colon, causing persecution-induced diminished earning capacity of 40 percent. A number of psychia-trists also examined him, including the New York psychiatrist Joachim Luwisch, who wrote in his report of 17 September 1971: "The patient is a 49-year-old married man with pedantic and obsessive tendencies, who was subjected to persecution in Germany at the highly sensitive age of 10–12 years and later suffered the consequences of emigration and an unfamiliar climate . . . Diagnosis: psychoneurosis with attacks of anxiety and tension . . . 25 percent persecution-induced reduction in earning capacity."

Joachim Luwisch (1905–) studied medicine in Erlangen, Freiburg, Munich, Vienna, and Cologne and interned in Berlin with the neurologist Professor Kurt Goldstein, among others, at Moabit Hospital. He was a member, along with Goldstein and the Gestalt psychologist Wolfgang Köhler, of a working group on the cerebral cortex. A victim of racial persecution, he emigrated to Abyssinia in 1934, where he opened a general practice. Because of the impending invasion by Mussolini's fascist troops, he fled to the British colony of Aden, then emigrated to the United States in 1941 by way of India and the Pacific Ocean. He became an intern on the neuropsychiatric wards of Goldwater Memorial Hospital and Bellevue Hospital in New York. In 1945, he became a specialist in neurology and psychiatry and consultant in neuropsychiatry at Goldwater Memorial Hospital as well as a lecturer at the New York University School of Medicine, and began building a private practice. In 1961, Luwisch began conducting examinations in reparations cases for the German consulate general in New York, and by 1987, he had examined over 6,000 victims of persecution. Until a few years ago, Luwisch continued to work as an expert examiner, while providing psychotherapeutic treatment to numerous survivors in his practice.[18]

On 21 December 1971, Dr. Günter Wellbrock, chief medical officer of the reparations office in Hamburg, offered his opinion of the case of Herr W.:

> The plaintiff did well in religion classes in school. The plaintiff first mentioned supposed direct and lasting mistreatment in a letter of December 1970 in Hamburg. Given the circumstances in Hamburg at the time, especially at Hindenburg High School in Hamburg-Hamm, these statements are absolutely unbelievable, especially as the plaintiff is a half-Jew. The fact that this mistreatment was first spoken of in a pension-granting proceeding also diminishes the credibility of the other information on his background. When the current examiner [Dr. Luwisch] says the plaintiff makes the impression of a man who obeys rules precisely, has something neurotically compulsive about him, exhibits a pedantic attitude and is easily hurt, these are typical indications of a primary disturbed personality structure.

Günter Wellbrock (1918–) entered labor service after earning his high school diploma. Wellbrock was an infantry volunteer in World War II, while simultaneously studying medicine in Hamburg; in 1945, he took his doctorate and state examinations. Later he became chief medical officer and examining doctor with the medical service of the Hamburg reparations office.[19]

Wellbrock demanded a "further psychiatric assessment based on the dossier." That is, he demanded that the report of the foreign psychiatrist be checked by a German psychiatrist. This was undertaken on 24 January

1973 by Dr. Christoph Jannasch, who ran a private psychiatric practice in Hamburg.

Christoph Jannasch (1925–) attended high school in Lübeck. In 1943, he was drafted into the Hermann Göring Division and served in Holland. Jannasch was a prisoner of war in U.S. and British prisons until 1947, after which he studied medicine in Mainz and Hamburg. He took his state examinations in 1954, earned a doctorate in 1955, and opened a psychiatric practice in Hamburg. He served as an evaluator for the office of reparations in Hamburg.[20]

Jannasch deduced from the previous reports that Herr W. had been traumatized, not by mistreatment as a boy of ten to twelve years of age, but as a small child, due to the separation of his parents, the loss of his biological father, and a troubled relationship with his stepfather:

Early childhood is decisive for the emergence of psychoneurotic disorders, not only in the primitive Freudian view. The first six years of life lay the crucial groundwork: during puberty there are psychodramatically exaggerated secondary formations: in the in-between years, gradually diminishing influences that may still be important are quite possible, but to a smaller extent, and they are clearly reduced by a stage starting at age ten. At the same time, it goes without saying that the force and penetrating effect of relatively late traumatization, or its longer duration—each unfolds a proportionate and complementary effect. Severe traumas in early childhood are very bad; lesser traumas later are not bad; in between, the dual scales of earliness and severity combine to create harmful influences.

To Herr W.'s statement to the American doctor that he had had a happy childhood, Jannasch responded, "Statements that his father made an effort to win the children's trust, or that they had lacked for nothing, or that nothing at all pointed to neglect are completely useless for understanding the relationship between father and son . . . and cannot be inflated into a significant positive overall assessment of childhood psychological relationships just because this is a case of the son of someone who was discriminated against unjustly, that is, a Jew."

Jannasch continued that if W.'s childhood had been happy, the discrimination at age ten should not have made any difference. On the contrary, it would have toughened him. Such social discrimination "does not lead to psychological harm; it is more likely to strengthen the ability to cope with life."[21] With zealous thoroughness, Jannasch reviewed all the possibilities:

If the "normal child" affected by the traumatization had, in all the listed developmental contexts, experienced only half of the optimum—that is, had been in pretty bad shape, but not absolutely bad—then temporary intimidation and slowly diminishing hurt could probably be expected. Even under these less positive conditions, discrimination such as that suffered by W. in school at ages eleven and twelve would not have engendered permanent deformations of the psychological structure. If this magnitude of social hardship or social discrimination—even under earlier personal developmental conditions that were half as good—could have brought such lasting psychological deformation, the percentage of psychological deviants in the population (of the cultured nations) would not be, as now estimated, 7 to 15 to 20 percent, but 90 percent or more.

But none of these less good, half as good, or not really bad conditions were present for W.; instead, "If the 'normal child' affected by the experience of persecution . . . in reality has long possessed an anxiety-neurotic structure, then naturally the harm must have a greater and more lasting effect, as it follows a channel already cut. But even then, *these* traumatizations, which are so brightly illuminated in the spotlight of the reparations question, would in no way have had decisive significance for the entire development of his life." To make a long story short: "The groundwork for an anxiety-neurotic structure, with all its consequences, is laid in the early years of life . . . Discrimination experienced in school or in the environment of the school at age eleven and twelve is thus not geared toward creating a direction-setting worsening of existing neurosis, or even a distinguishable worsening of the same."

In 1973, the reparations office rejected Herr W.'s application for compensation, and Herr W. sued before the Hamburg district court, represented by his lawyer. The court appointed Professor Hans Strauss of New York, a former professor of neurology and psychiatry at the University of Frankfurt, as chief evaluator. Herr W. was examined for the tenth time. What happened in Strauss's office on 16 and 27 March 1976 led Herr W.'s lawyer to attack the doctor for bias:

At the very first meeting, the doctor repeatedly interrupted the plaintiff, telling him that the plaintiff was to answer the doctor's questions with only a "yes" or a "no." The doctor's complete lack of understanding of the plaintiff's neurotic personality was also demonstrated by the fact that he soon began to argue with him, and yelled at him several times. The plaintiff had the impression that the doctor "himself needed psychological help." On the one hand, he told him that he believed everything he said without proof, while on the other he showed no understanding of explanations given by the plaintiff for his behavior and questioned the plaintiff's statements. The plaintiff ultimately had the feeling that it would be pointless to talk to the doctor any further because he clearly saw that, given the doctor's preconceived opinion, he was fighting a losing battle. The following incident was typical. The doctor asked the question, "Did your father work in Palestine in 1935?" The plaintiff answered, "No, he couldn't find any work." At that, the doctor snapped at him, "I didn't ask you that, just answer yes or no." The second session was equally stormy. As a Jew, Dr. Strauss was himself a member of a group persecuted by the National Socialists, but he probably experienced very little of this persecution personally, as he emigrated to America early on.

The Hamburg court referred to Strauss's report in rejecting Herr. W.'s suit on 21 July 1971. In his report, Strauss utilized Jannasch's argument that Herr W. had been psychologically damaged by an unfavorable family situation. In addition, he claimed the latest complaints merely involved problems adapting to his new home, the United States. Several passages in the report revealed something of the scenes that took place during the examination. After describing the abuse experienced by Herr W. at school, Strauss wrote: "At this point I would like to underline the fact that he wanted to describe many more details of the persecution aimed at him during this period. I explained to him that, in my opinion, this was not necessary to assess his case ... The applicant was extraordinarily verbose during the entire consultation; he tended to describe many details, and I often pointed out to him that certain specific things had no influence on the assessment of his case, and that we should leave them out."

Here he was in agreement with the medical service of the reparations office in Hamburg, which took the following stand on the accusations against Strauss on 9 November 1976: "Neither the insulting criticisms by the plaintiff's lawyer—the lawyer seems to insult any doctor who provides an unfavorable report—nor the lawyer's amateurish, to some extent nitpicking, statements provide the defendant with a reason to change the documents submitted up to now ... The plaintiff's lawyer has not grasped the fact that only the existing psychopathological findings have any significance for an objective assessment, not the patient's subjective explanations."

Herr W. appealed all the way to the Federal Supreme Court of Appeals, which rejected his claim in 1983. During the eighteen years of the case, Herr W. was examined by a total of seventeen doctors.

Herr S.—"Bland hypomanic depressive state with an abnormal primary personality"[22]

Herr S. was born in 1930 in Hamburg. In 1933, the family lost its livelihood, and in 1936, they emigrated to Denmark. They frequently changed quarters, forcing little S. to live with strangers on occasion. In 1943, his two elder brothers succeeded in fleeing to Sweden, but he and his mother, stepfather, and younger brother were caught trying to escape and brought to a Danish collection camp. S.'s mother tried to save him from deportation by telling the head of the camp that her son had been born out of wedlock in a relationship with an Aryan man. The camp head thereupon gave the 13-year-old boy the choice of joining his brothers in Sweden on his own or going to a concentration camp with his mother. S. did not want to lose his mother and decided to stay. The family was deported to Theresienstadt in a cattle car. They survived and returned to Denmark following liberation. After that, Herr S. complained constantly of stomach problems, back pains, attacks of gout, and skin rashes. In 1954, X rays found a stomach ulcer.

Herr S. studied education, music, and German and took his master's degree in 1959 in Denmark. Subsequently, he went to Italy, where he hoped to train as a singer and actor. Nothing came of this, however, because he became ill whenever he had to sing or perform. Herr S. then supported himself as a driver, translator, and tour guide. He felt uprooted and incapable of settling down, and began psychoanalysis. The analyst confirmed an anxiety neurosis accompanied by occasional depression. After years of therapy, Herr S. felt capable of beginning training as an opera director. He met a Danish woman, married, and was soon expecting a child. Because his wife wanted the child to be born in Denmark, they returned there in 1964; Herr S. broke off his training for that reason. He found work as a teacher, but his aim in life remained to become a director. The marriage did not go well, and he began suffering from depressions again.

Herr S. had already made a disability application to the reparations office in Hamburg in 1959 because of his stomach ulcer, general joint inflamations, and a back disorder. In 1962, in a settlement, he received a small pension. In the 1965 application, he also mentioned his psychological problems, which had first manifested themselves in Italy. He traveled from Denmark at various intervals for treatment by his analyst in Rome. Herr S. was first examined for the supplementary application nine years later, in 1974, by the Hamburg psychiatrist Dr. Wilhelm Liebermann.

Wilhelm Liebermann (1921–) took his high school diploma in Berlin in 1941. As a racial persecutee, he was forced to work in Berlin factories until early 1944. After the war, he studied medicine in Berlin and Erlangen, taking his state examinations in 1952. Liebermann then interned at the University Pediatric Clinic in Erlangen. After earning his doctorate in 1953, he opened a private practice in Hamburg, where he performed examinations for the Hamburg reparations office.[23]

Liebermann questioned Herr S. on his experiences in Theresienstadt and wrote in his report, "The period of imprisonment apparently was not a great hardship for the applicant, since, according to his own statement, he occupied a privileged position in the camp as a Danish refugee and orchestra member. He lived for nine months in a youth house with forty boys in a large room; in addition, he received a better ration card because he could play the trumpet."

In a letter to his lawyer on 4 February 1975, Herr S. described his statements to Liebermann very differently: "I told him truthfully that I was not myself physically beaten or tormented, and, as a Danish prisoner, was not sent to the gas chambers at Auschwitz. To that extent, I enjoyed a privileged position in comparison with the other prisoners, who died of typhus or hunger. I still dream about those other boys. I am one lone survivor, which can still fill me with fear; only three orchestra members survived. I witnessed mistreatment of other prisoners and feared beatings. The privileged rations consisted of an additional 20 grams of bread and quarter-liter of skim milk a week. Dr. Liebermann's report gives the impression that it must have been a quite pleasant vacation site. I envy people who were not persecuted in their childhood and youth."

He included in his letter a poem he had written at the age of sixteen, describing a dream he said he still had, thirty years later. The dream proved, he said, that he had not found Theresienstadt to be a vacation.

More

I stand in line
shivering with cold and hunger—
clutching the bowl tightly to me
—is anything else left?

it rains cold—
the gray coats are vague
—like spirits
mute and dull—
the cold steam of the kitchen
envelops us—
feet stamp—
rigid looks—
I stand in line
waiting—waiting—
but now a murmuring begins
—cries—screams—curses:
let's storm the shed
maybe there are still potato peels
or barley—
maybe there is something
we're starving—
the dogs keep it for themselves—
they give us nothing—
although they have—
they let us starve—
are full themselves—
come—let's storm—
we are hungry—

but suddenly I realize
that I'm standing here all alone screaming—
no one cries or curses
no one screams and wants to storm—
only dull disappointment in their eyes—
dry eyes—dead eyes—
and mute with bent head
the people disappear in the cold darkness—

hurry back, silent as spirits—
to the hopeless depths of hunger—

now—now it's moving forward
suddenly the spirits come alive—
each pushes forward—
pots fall rattling to the ground
the line moves—
eyes ask:
is anything left?
is anything left?
will anything be left when it's my turn?
—or—
nothing again today—
once again, disappointed and hungry
back home to the barracks—
I stand in line
and count the people in front of me—
twenty more before it's my turn—
—but it's moving forward
it won't be much longer now—
only ten more—
now eight—now six—
soon I'll get something to eat—
—soon—

but suddenly the people are quiet—
a mute restlessness steals through the line—
what's wrong?
—now it's closed!
nothing left—
nothing more—
—closed—
the crowd grows rigid and dies, turning to spirits again—

Liebermann dealt thoroughly with the question of whether Herr S.'s psychological disorders were caused by traumas in early childhood or by his experiences in the camp. Tellingly, Herr S.'s pension dossier contained excerpts from Hamburg police and court files from 1932 and 1933. Apparently the reparations office had requested these files from other offices. Liebermann quoted extensively from these files:

In a letter to the Hamburg trial court of 15 March 1933, the applicant's father declared that his wife cared neither for the house nor the children, neglected the children completely, and regularly stayed out every night until one or two in the morning, spending her time in coffeehouses or dance halls. He said the mother used welfare payments to buy beauty products and that she occasionally mistreated or tormented the children for no reason.

In a letter to the trial court of 15 March 1933, the applicant's mother explained that she had been threatened, cursed, and beaten by her husband for approximately the past half year. She said he had used the worst curses against her in the presence of the children.

According to an affidavit by the Hamburg police authorities on 1 November 1932, the applicant's family had been receiving public benefits since 1931, as well as Jewish welfare support.

From this, Liebermann concluded, "The information in the files indicates that Herr S.'s social and family circumstances were quite bad from 1930 to 1934." Thus an anxiety neurosis such as that attested to by the Italian psychoanalyst was out of the question: "It is rather a personality-based behavioral disorder that can, if anything, be connected only with disturbances in early childhood (parents' unfortunate marriage, bad social conditions) or is genetic, but certainly cannot be blamed on persecution." In the letter to his lawyer, Herr S. wrote, "Herr Liebermann is lying; my parents yelled at each other, but they didn't hit. It is also a product of Dr. Liebermann's imagination that they did not take care of the children; my mother is and always was a 'mother hen.'" Ultimately, Liebermann concluded, "According to his history and impressions, Herr S. is a person of above average intelligence with many interests, somewhat hyperthymic, maybe purposely not quite centered enough, with a sensitive, somewhat weak personality and a somewhat exaggerated sense of self-worth . . . Diagnosis: bland hypomanic depressive state with an abnormal primary personality."

In the abovementioned letter to his lawyer, Herr S. summarized his impression of the examination: "Dr. Liebermann presents it as if I were to blame for my symptoms." To Liebermann's claim that the marriage had destroyed his professional career, he responded, "It was not the marriage, but the psychological disturbances, that destroyed my career . . . Dr. Liebermann purposely sought arguments to make my rejection possible."

On the day he saw Liebermann, Herr S. was also examined by Dr. Armin Schütt, a Hamburg internist, who in his report basically repeated Liebermann's observations, adding that all Herr S.'s physical ailments were genetic.

Armin Schütt (1919–) received his high school diploma in 1937 and joined the Nazi party that same year. Schütt studied medicine in Hamburg, Leipzig, and Rostock, earning a doctorate in 1941. After the war, he specialized in internal medicine and became chief medical officer and an evaluator in social security cases, as well as evaluator for the Hamburg office of reparations. Because of his obviously biased attitude toward pension applicants in the social security system, the Hamburg trade unions demanded his dismissal as evaluator.[24]

On the basis of this evaluation, the reparations office rejected Herr S.'s application. He appealed the decision to the trial court and wanted to present the court with a detailed certification from his Italian psycho-analyst as evidence. Since the analyst did not blame his client's neurotic disorders solely on the experiences in the camp, but also on his mother's depressions—also persecution-induced—and a dysfunctional mother-son relationship, his lawyer advised against this, saying:

> This certification is so dangerous to the restitution proceedings that I would not recommend giving it to the court at the present time. Even if your mother's psychological state is seen as persecution-induced, your own state, based upon it, might well *not* be recognized as persecution-induced, because to that extent it would not be an immediate, but an indirect, harm (as defined by our jurispru-dence) . . . Judging from my experience, all later examiners will immediately drag the other causes (e.g., mother-son relationship) into the foreground.

The proceedings dragged on for another four years, until the office agreed on 7 May 1980 to settle and grant Herr S. a pension based on a 25 percent reduction in earning capacity under the BEG's § 31, para. 2 (the "concentration camp assumption")—402 DM a month. However, Herr S. was required to desist from any future restitution claims (such as, for example, a worsening application). In a letter to his lawyer, he protested: "For me, this is a basic question of justice. The office cannot rule out possible harm or worsening in the future, thus nullifying the law. I do not see the settlement as charity. The more the reparations office gives me, the happier the Germans should be that they can pay off some of their responsibility that way."

However, the office insisted on its clause, and Herr S. went along with it.

Frau B.—"One who does not remember his childhood in the concentration camps cannot have suffered from it."

From birth until the age of four, Frau B. was imprisoned in the Gypsy camps of Krychow and Siedlce, as well as the Warsaw Ghetto. Her father was murdered; she was separated from her mother, and the rest of the family was torn apart. As a small child, she knew only deathly fear and the privations of the camps.

After the war, at the age of thirteen, Frau B. first experienced severe attacks of fear. Whenever she saw a uniform, such as those of mail car-riers or police officers, she panicked and believed they had come to take her back to the camp. As an adult, she applied to the reparations office in Hamburg for restitution for a heart and nerve condition.[25]

The office's examining doctor determined that Frau B.'s heart ail-ment was a result of smoking and overweight, not of persecution. On 1 July 1974, the authorities rejected her claim. Through a lawyer, Frau B. brought suit on 25 September 1974 before the Hamburg court. Professor

Karl Peter Kisker of the psychiatric clinic of the Hanover Medical College was appointed to conduct the examination.

Karl Peter Kisker (1926–1997) earned a doctorate in medicine (1952) and another in philosophy (1955). He won his professorial qualifications in 1957. A student of Walther von Baeyer's in Heidelberg, he collaborated with him to publish a standard work on the psychiatry of persecutees. In 1966, Kisker became head of the Department of Clinical Psychiatry of Hanover Medical College. As a colleague of von Baeyer's and co-author of his book, Kisker enjoyed a good reputation among persecutees as an honest evaluator. In the reparations proceedings of the 1970s and 1980s, he was one of the few psychiatrists actually qualified and practicing in this area, and was thus frequently appointed to conduct examinations. However, in later years he began to advocate views running counter to his original attitudes and earlier publications. Thus he often described the psychological disorders of Gypsies and Jews who were persecuted as children as genetic disorders or the results of a temporary state of psycho-physical exhaustion in the initial postwar years. The New York lawyer Milton Kestenberg, co-founder of a research center on persecution of children, saw in Kisker's sudden change of heart and that of other young doctors an attempt to whitewash the generation of their fathers, with their Nazi past.[26]

Frau B. did not obey numerous requests that she be examined, as she was afraid of doctors, especially those connected with the authorities. Finally, she allowed Kisker to examine her on 2 May 1981. He diagnosed a temporary psycho-physical exhaustion syndrome during the early postwar years and an ongoing anxiety neurosis, involving claustrophobia, fear of the dark, fear of isolation and crises of cardiac neurosis, that could be traced to the trauma suffered as a small child in the camps, creating a reduction in earning capacity of 25 percent. Because Frau B. could not express herself very well, he felt it could be assumed that her actual complaints were probably worse than she admitted.

In a ruling on 1 July 1981, the office rejected Kisker's evaluation. The anxiety neurosis, they claimed, was not persecution-induced, inasmuch as it had manifested itself at the age of thirteen, and Frau B. could not even remember the period of her persecution. The court thereupon decided she should be reevaluated by the Heidelberg University psychiatric clinic. On 28 June 1984, Frau B. was examined there by the chief physician, Dr. Richard Avenarius, a student of von Baeyer's, who confirmed Kisker's findings. But in a supplementary psychological report, a trained psychologist named Henke found no evidence of psychological trauma on the basis of test results. (The tests used were the Hamburg-Wechsler intelligence test, the Standard Progressive Matrices, the Freiburg Personality Inventory, the Giessen test form S, the Rorschach test, and the Thematic Apperception test.) Henke reported that Frau B. had undergone the examination patiently, apparently accepting the frequent evaluations. Only occasionally and briefly did displeasure and rebelliousness appear. The Hamburg-Wechsler test and the Rorschach test, on which her language problems had a negative effect, confirmed the suspicion that she possessed a "simple intellectual makeup." Her lack of independence and feeling that she could not cope appeared, according to the Freiburg Personality Inventory and the Thematic Apperception test, to be more connected with her "given achievement limits" than to "some psychological trauma."

The reparations office based its ruling of 25 March 1985 on this passage in the psychological report, rejecting Avenarius's evaluation and repeating its own conclusion that the plaintiff had "no memory" of the period of persecution; her knowledge, the office said, came from relatives, who had frightened her as a child, telling her "with considerable exaggeration" about the period of persecution. Thus the harm arose from "the particularities of the Gypsy milieu" and the neurosis had taken actual form in the postwar period. The office demanded another supplementary evaluation from Avenarius, in which he was to explain more precisely "to what extent the anxiety-neurotic deviancy was caused by the persecution directed at the plaintiff in Poland, and from what point on this persecution influence led to a pensionable MdE." In his supplementary evaluation of 9 April 1985, Avenarius finally explained to the authorities that it was to be expected that a neurosis would not manifest itself until age thirteen. Puberty caused a reappearance of the disruptions of early childhood, a fact that was well known in developmental psychiatry and psychology. The proceedings were still pending in 1987.

The type of pseudo-psychology practiced in the examination of persecutees, as illustrated in these three cases, was challenged by the Israeli psychiatrist and psychoanalyst Hilel Klein, who wrote:

I am ashamed to read the evaluations by my psychiatric colleagues in Germany. They use psychoanalysis to conclude in one case: "This child was only two years old; how could he experience persecution!," while in another case maintaining, "The boy was already thirteen years old and had lived with his parents, so he had experienced the so-called warmth of the family nest." These paradoxes in the name of Freud and psychoanalysis are still perpetrated by reputable professors in Germany. I speak in fury, because I believe that many of my colleagues, with their obsessive tendencies, unconsciously identify with the aggressor.[27]

The Hamburg psychiatrist Christoph Jannasch and his colleague Wilhelm Liebermann transferred the persecution traumas experienced by Herr W. and Herr S. in their youth into early childhood, while in the case of Frau B., the authorities blamed her early-childhood camp traumas on the postwar period and the particularities of the Gypsy milieu. Concepts were twisted and turned to fit each case. It was argued, for example, that the claim that Herr W. had had a happy childhood could not be "blown up into a positive overall assessment" merely because he was "the son of someone who was discriminated against unjustly, that is, a Jew" (if one takes this wording at face value, there were apparently people who were justly persecuted), and that the cruelty of his incited classmates at the Hindenburg High School in Hamburg could be seen as a useful, harsh lesson in life for the eleven-year-old ("societal discrimination strengthens the ability to cope with life"), or that oppression could not have occurred because Herr W. was only a "half-Jew." In the case of Herr S., Liebermann even brought in the 1933 files of the Nazi authorities to prove that Herr S. had been traumatized by a shattered family life, not by his experiences in Theresienstadt.

Jannasch's language in his report on Herr W. is remarkable: "Psychodramatically exaggerated secondary formations," "severe traumas are very bad, lesser traumas are not bad, in between there are dual scales of earliness and severity," "traumatizations that are brightly illuminated in the spotlight of the reparations question . . . "

Jannasch's psychiatry seems to be a series of artificial constructions built on his own verbal inventions, reminiscent of Dr. Rainer Luthe's "tasteless games," while Liebermann, who diagnosed a "bland hypomanic depressive state with an abnormal primary personality" in Herr S., was more likely to use the general framework typical of psychiatry. What the evaluating doctors did to the victims was clearly expressed by Herr S.: "Dr. Liebermann presents it as though I were to blame for my symptoms."

Retraumatization

Herr R.—"Crises . . . that repeatedly force me to break off the examination"[28]

Herr R. was born in Poland in 1906 and attended a Jewish school until the age of seventeen; he then went to rabbinical school, while also training to become an accountant. In 1927, he married, and his wife bore three sons and a daughter in the following years. He worked in a bank and owned a fabric shop, which his wife ran. At the same time, he headed a religious girls' school and taught religion privately. Following the occupation of Poland by the German Army, R.'s village was turned into a ghetto and he was made to work in a nearby camp. When the ghetto was liquidated in 1943, he was forced to witness the shooting of three of his children (aged fifteen, twelve, and eight). He, his wife, and his eldest son were deported to a concentration camp, where he performed hard labor repairing airplanes at the Heinkel plant. There he suffered cold and hunger, was dressed only in paper, and was constantly mistreated and beaten over the head.

In 1944, R. was sent to Majdanek concentration camp. As the German troops retreated, he was transferred from camp to camp—including Auschwitz and Mauthausen—until he was finally liberated by the British in 1945 in Bergen-Belsen. His son was beaten to death there by a kapo shortly before liberation.

After liberation, Herr R. collapsed—he weighed only 35 kilograms—and a German prisoner doctor treated him with sleeping cures in the Bergen-Belsen hospital for five months. After his release he complained of sleeplessness, anxiety attacks, extreme irritability, and stomach pains. In 1947, he was diagnosed with a duodenal ulcer. He told the doctor who treated it that he had been impotent since concentration camp. His wife had also survived the deportations and was psychologically ill.

In 1946, Herr R. emigrated to France with his wife to find his brothers and sisters. Three brothers and two sisters had survived, but his father, four other brothers, and two sisters had been murdered. R. settled in Paris, where he taught in a Jewish children's home and a Jewish school. His ability to work was limited, however, and in 1960 he had to stop working altogether.

In 1956, he applied to the state pension authorities of North Rhine–Westphalia for a health damage pension. The doctor commissioned by the German embassy in Paris, Dr. H. Salomon, certified general weakness accompanied by premature aging, impotence, obesity, high blood pressure, rheumatism, a duodenal ulcer, and neurodystonia. He found an overall reduction in earning capacity of 75 percent, with a persecution-induced portion of 60 percent.

Two years after this initial examination, on 7 February 1959, the state pension authorities complained that the examination findings failed to explain the 75 percent reduction in earning capacity. Dr. Günter Hand of the medical service of the state pension office considered the duodenal ulcer and high blood pressure to be genetic disorders and found that the rheumatic complaints had not been objectified. Given the history of severe persecution, however, Hand thought it probable that persecution had contributed to the neurodystonia and duodenal ulcer, as well as the development of high blood pressure. He estimated a total reduction in earning capacity of 50 percent, with a persecution-induced portion of 40 percent.

Günter Hand (1919–) earned his high school diploma in 1938 and was subsequently conscripted into labor service. In 1941, while an officer on the Eastern Front, Hand was wounded. Starting in 1942, he studied medicine in Bonn, Göttingen, and Düsseldorf. From 1969 to 1982, he headed the medical service of the state pension authority of North Rhine–Westphalia.[29]

Herr R. appealed the ruling, demanding a higher classification. The Düsseldorf district court rejected his claim, and he appealed to the supreme court. On 27 July 1961, five years after the application had been made, the court appointed Dr. S. Pierre Kaplan of Paris as chief examiner. Kaplan examined Herr R. three times, in December 1961 and January and April 1962. In his evaluation, he wrote, "He seemed disturbed and broke into heavy sobbing several times while describing the events of his persecution, especially when describing the shooting of his children, and was difficult to calm down."

Dr. Kaplan therefore had him examined by a psychiatrist, Joseph Fuswerk-Fursay, who had to interrupt the examination several times when Herr R. broke down completely:

One sees a man whose psychological state has been badly affected; a horrified face, horrified eyes, strange and restless behavior. The patient is absent-minded, speaks very rudimentary French, is not aware of the severity of his condition and is surprised that he has been sent to a psychiatrist. Right after his first words, unable to control himself, he bursts into tears. He tried to take up some sort of work by giving Hebrew lessons, but could not continue, and since then has probably lived on public assistance. He feels an extreme weariness; he wakes up, but then lies down again immediately, unable to make any efforts. He is in a constant state of sadness, demoralized, is vegetating; his religious beliefs do not permit him to commit suicide, although he questions the purpose of his life—he asks what purpose is served by the efforts he is presently making, his place is with the dead. Gripped by fear, anxious and depressed, plagued by the feeling of a lump in his throat and attacks of choking, he consulted a cardiologist, thinking he had heart problems. He was subjected to experiments in the camps; traces of injections can still be found in the groin area, which left behind a sense of serious mutilation, especially since his sexual functions have died away. He has difficulty falling asleep and frequently wakes up at night. The minute he falls asleep, he sees his children before him and has terrible nightmares. He suffers from headaches, especially in the back of his head, as he cannot sleep on pillows. He has acoustic hallucinations and thinks he hears the sound of a speeding train. He complains of severe loss of memory; he remembers nothing, is unable to recall important dates in his life, loses the thread and ultimately ends up in a state of confusion in which he loses perception of place and time. He is completely fixated on the epoch of the war; his life ended there. He is tormented by thoughts and pictures of what he went through in the camps, of the cruelty, abuse and torture, of executions, of his wounds, whose scars remain clearly on his head, left arm, and legs. Above all, however, he is haunted by the thought that he passively witnessed the execution of his children and had to look on as they were thrown into already-dug ditches, along with other victims. All this provokes crises of complete collapse that repeatedly force me to break off the examination.

His conclusion was, "Severely marked neuropsychiatric syndrome in the deportee. He is a 100 percent invalid. I would estimate the persecution-induced reduction in earning capacity at 50 percent."

Based on Fuswerk-Fursay's report and his own examination, Dr. Kaplan assessed an overall reduction in earning capacity of 75 percent and a persecution-induced percentage of 60 percent.

The dossier does not indicate the ultimate decision.

Herr G.—"An acceptance without anger, ambition, or intentions"[30]

Herr G., who was born in 1902, grew up in a poor peasant family in East Prussia. By age sixteen, he had joined the agricultural workers' union. In the 1920s, he worked in various factories, an ironworks, a tobacco factory and a rice mill, becoming unemployed in 1930. He headed an oppositional union group in Hamburg-Eimsbüttel and was arrested for this activity in 1935 by the Gestapo and sent to Fuhlsbüttel concentration camp. There he was severely abused for ten days. Four weeks later, he was released, but he was arrested again three weeks later and sent back to Fuhlsbüttel for distributing illegal flyers. This time he was shackled to his bed at night with iron chains and kept in solitary confinement. His hands were also tied behind his back during the day. He was interrogated by the Gestapo three times a week; in an attempt to extract a confession and betrayal of the names of his union comrades, they beat and kicked him on the head, eyes, and ears and threatened to kill him and arrest his wife. Besides these tortures, he lived in constant fear for his wife and four-year-old daughter, who did not know where he was and from whom he received no news.

Herr G. was sentenced to three and a half years at hard labor, which he served in part at the Fuhlsbüttel prison and, after March 1937, at the Börgermoor and Aschendorfer concentration camps. There he was forced to perform heavy physical labor, dig ditches, and so on, and was exposed to the abuse of a foreman who drove him at a run with a fully loaded wheelbarrow until he collapsed. Once, when he had a high fever, he was driven out of the infirmary to work. All the prisoners were frequently sick because of bad nutrition and because the work on the moors, summer and winter, often involved standing in water in scanty clothing.

Upon his release from the moor camp in September 1938, Herr G. had lost a third of his body weight, and his health was ruined. During his years in prison, he had contracted tuberculosis, a chronically suppurating ripped eardrum, a corneal injury, and an injured disk. In the following years, he returned to work in a factory; in August 1944, he was conscripted into Punishment Battalion 999, used, among other things, for clearing-up work in Buchenwald concentration camp. After the war, Herr G. worked as a construction worker, again became involved in political activity, and for a long time served as works council head.

On 3 April 1967, Herr G. applied to the Hamburg reparations office for compensation for the injuries suffered during his imprisonment: the eye injury, heart, circulatory, and nerve conditions, and sciatica. In the course of the proceedings, he was examined by nine doctors. Dr. Armin Schütt, the Hamburg internist, reported on 3 November 1971 that, calculated purely on the basis of the numbers, Herr G. had lost 180 percent of his earning capacity as a result of his numerous complaints, but only 15 percent could be blamed on persecution; the remainder were, "with a probability verging on certainty, not caused by concentration camp." This wording is significant because it counters the "concentration camp assumption" in § 31, para. 2, of the BEG.[31]

In the explanation of his evaluation, Schütt included, among other things, the fact that Herr G. had had to perform heavy labor in concentration camps, but "also performed such labor many years after his imprisonment." In his assessment, Schütt also referred to a report by the psychiatrist Wilhelm Liebermann, who had examined Herr G. in his office on 29 May 1971. Liebermann admitted that Herr G. had "experienced severe persecution," and that because of this, he had to be accorded a "persecution-induced MdE of 25 percent due to experience-reactive psychological disturbance" for the period from his arrest in February 1935 to the end of 1939. However, he added,

certain manifestations of decline, such as greater difficulty in adjusting or slowing of the psychomotoric processes, could not be ignored and, given the patient's age and high blood pressure, must be seen as symptoms of a hypertonic-sclerotic vascular condition . . . Given when they occurred, the psychopathological findings and conditions described are not connected with Nazi persecutory measures, and apparently appeared only in recent years."

Diagnosis: "Beginnings of an organic process of brain deterioration and attacks of dizziness accompanying a hypertonic-sclerotic vascular condition . . . with a probability, verging on certainty, that they are the result of causes other than concentration camp.

Based on Liebermann's evaluation, the reparations office paid Herr G. capital restitution of 535 DM for the period from 1 February 1935 to 21 December 1939. In addition, he was granted a right to treatment for the experience-reactive psychological disturbances, as well as a 10 percent reduction in earning capacity for his eye injuries (left-eye corneal scars with scar pterygium and recurring conjunctivitis), but no pension. All other complaints were, according to the office's decision of 20 September 1972, "illness processes whose manifestation was predestined—that is, genetic and age-related."

Herr G. appealed this decision to the Hamburg district court. In a letter to the court on 26 July 1973, he once again described in detail the ongoing psychological consequences of his imprisonment:

For someone who did not himself experience it, it is hardly possible to describe the feelings of fear, reaching deep into oneself; the great despair and deep hopelessness; that is, the entire psychological burden in all its manifestations . . . Incidentally, it is not fun to talk about it, because everything one has experienced is stirred up again . . . At night, while sleeping, the fear and horror suddenly return; sometimes the terrible experiences he went through [in the letter, Herr G. speaks of himself in the third person as "the plaintiff"] come back in nightmares; the plaintiff frequently has the tormenting feeling that someone is standing behind him with a gun—bathed in sweat, he wakes in great pain . . . Sometimes strangely oppressive states overtake him, with thoughts and feelings difficult to describe, because they are unclear and confusing, a sort of apprehension is part of it—maybe deep inside it is something like despair or grief at what people are capable of doing to one another.

Subsequently, Herr G. was again examined by the internists, orthopedists, and ear and eye doctors of the Hamburg university clinic. None of them found a reduction in earning capacity that could be traced back to persecution and was significant enough to justify a pension. Herr G. tried in vain to have the court call on a psychosomatist, Dr. Hellmuth Freyberger, as evaluating doctor. Instead, he was sent to a psychiatrist, Dr. Christoph Jannasch, in Hamburg-Blankenese, who examined him on 8 July 1978 and concluded:

The worst suffering experienced during the period of persecution hardly indicates extraordinary abuse. G. experienced what was, under the circumstances, the usual general disparagement, degradation, and mistreatment, to which, as a particular permanent hardship, the combination of very heavy physical labor and entirely insufficient nutrition (in the moor camp) probably gave added weight. The details mentioned—that his arms were shackled behind his back and his limbs chained to the bed at night—in Fuhlsbüttel concentration camp during the initial months—or especially bad beatings with rifle butts in the labor camp must reasonably be considered more as marks and highlights of the general persecution. One would judge these incidents wrongly, or more precisely, one would not do justice to the accompanying situation of constant persecution, by ascribing to them an exceptional significance as individual traumatizations.

Dr. Jannasch addressed all of Herr G.'s complaints and conditions and revealed typical symptoms of survivors' syndrome not yet mentioned in any of the evaluations: general slowness, increased irritability with apparently unprovoked outbursts of anger at family members, chronic headaches, sleeplessness, anxiety dreams, and resignation. In addition, Dr. Jannasch referred to Herr G.'s numerous written statements, in which he described his experiences and occasionally quoted from the appropriate literature on health damage following concentration camp:

The citations from scientific literature in regard to the psychological effect of persecution attached to these statements fall into the abyss of subjective lack of balance, and ultimately, almost blindly, into argumentation for the purpose of being granted reparations, which then nourishes its passion in the accusation that doctors' assessments of psychological aftereffects are unjust, unfeeling and even discriminatory . . . The persecutees are even being punished by the doctors. I find these indignant—although never excessive—complaints by the plaintiff to be "distressing" . . . because an understanding of one's own individual fate is lost in the wake of an ultimately subordinate partial aspect, whose externality and limitedness are not automatically canceled out by the fact that they involve experiential content. A forced emphasis on psychological suffering for the very evident purpose of gaining acknowledgement of a pensionable harm burdens the writer and the reader by violating the intimacy of the personal zone of privacy. Finding a meaningful position in regard to one's own fate and suffering involves, after all, the innermost assessment of one's own person . . . it is, at bottom, a profession of belief that cannot be questioned, whose publication for others requires a "careful!," in order to become cognizant of its own existence in its sense of belonging to other people. It thus requires openness, dedication, sympathy, complete honesty, recollection of one's own problematic background, and above all a perception, or more precisely, an acceptance, without anger, ambition, or intentions, of the conditions applying to one's own person during the period of the experience. Only a quiet knowledge or willingness to learn, which sensitively takes in the historical background, as well as all possibilities of personal development, allows an understanding that provides a basis—although naturally not clear in all its details—for one's own or a stranger's cautious judgment of the life actually lived. Thoughtlessly tearing out parts from the overall context simply to achieve a purpose obscures such knowledge; and the luster, equally incautious, of the so complicated! context of science, presupposing so much experience and knowledge in the assessment, bedazzles instead of illuminating.

On Herr G.'s political activity, Jannasch commented, "Subjective assessment of his persecution apparently attains particular importance for G. to the extent that it has a close concrete and symbolic connection with the socially disadvantaged position from which he started in life and his fight for a more just system. This is also the root of G.'s argument as plaintiff, which so greatly oversteps the bounds of reality."

Schütt had used against Herr G. the fact that he had worked until retirement age and been politically active as works council head, maintaining that he had been fully able to work and thus could not be sick. Jannasch reached the same conclusion in his evaluation: no lasting damage. On 25 September 1979, a year after he was examined, Herr G. died, without ever obtaining justice.

The last two cases demonstrate, in particularly crass form, something that held true for every medical examination of this type: people were forced to recall their experiences, with destructive consequences for many. Frau E., quoted in the first case study, was at least able to implore the judge to "end this terrible game." Herr F., humiliated by Dr. Hubleur in Geneva; Herr S. of Denmark, also treated dismissively; and Herr G., a political persecutee, all at least still had the strength to send letters of complaint about their treatment. Herr R. was never able to do so. The hell he had lived through dominated his entire existence; each medical examination was one too many, each prolongation of the procedure became a torture. The reader must decided for him or herself why the reviewing doctor at the state pension office, Hand, reduced the recommended reduction in earning capacity from 60 percent to 40 percent, although he explicitly accepted the seriousness of the persecution, and thus purposely provoked a complicated legal dispute requiring further evaluations. Herr R. broke down even with the well-meaning doctors Kaplan and Fuswerk-Fursay, especially when speaking of the children murdered before his very eyes.

To Herr G.'s complaint about discriminatory and punitive treatment by the examiners, Jannasch responded that Herr G. should learn to take the path of "perception, or more precisely, an acceptance, without anger, ambition, or intentions." This reveals the message at the heart of reparations: the victims could receive restitution at the discretion of their former persecutors, but they were not to attempt to escape the role of victim by making demands or complaining; they were to accept their fates and keep silent.

Diagnoses of the Underclass

Frau M.—An "eccentric character"[32]

Frau M. was born in Russia in 1892. The third of nine children of a poor family, she was unable to attend school or learn a profession. She married a tailor when she was eighteen and had two children who died in infancy. In 1914, she and her husband emigrated to France, where she divorced him. She worked as a cleaning woman while raising her third child, a son, born in 1914. In 1941, following the occupation of Paris by the German Army, she was forced to wear the yellow star and lived in constant fear of deportation. Her son, the focus of her concern, was taken to Buchenwald concentration camp in 1941. She herself hid in cellars and attics once the raids began. Forced to change hiding places constantly, she had no ration card, was exposed to cold and damp, and feared for her son. He returned in 1945 with his health ruined. Her former husband had been killed by the Germans; her entire family in Russia was missing and presumed dead.

While living underground, Frau M. became ill with digestive problems alternating between constipation and diarrhea, sleep disorders, and anxiety attacks. After liberation, she often suffered from intestinal colic and was twice ill with hepatitis. Her nervous states, accompanied by sleep disorders, nightmares, headaches, heart problems, and dizzy spells, became progressively worse, so that she had to give up her work as a cleaning woman in 1955. From then on she lived in poverty, supported by Jewish welfare organizations. In 1959, she applied for a health damage pension and was examined by a doctor commissioned by the German embassy in Paris, Dr. Jacques-David Biezin. He diagnosed "character disturbances and neurovegetative symptoms," with a persecution-induced reduction in earning capacity of 25 percent. Apparently, he clashed with the patient during the examination: "Woman full of bitterness, extremely irritable, flares up at every question asked by the doctor." Frau M. refused to allow any additional examinations, especially psychiatric ones. Biezin reported that she only gave him the desired information after he had energetically rebuked her.

In a statement made on 16 June 1960, the medical officer at the North Rhine–Westphalia state pension office, Chief Medical Officer E. Nitschke, called Frau M.'s condition "an emotional illness with an eccentric character" that had already existed before the war and was only marginally worsened by persecution. He found a reduction in earning capacity of 15 percent at most—considerably beneath the pension threshold. On 19 September 1960, the office approved a course of treatment for her "eccentric character." Frau M. appealed to the Düsseldorf trial court and submitted a privately arranged evaluation written by a Paris psychiatrist, Dr. Eugene Minkowski—a man who had himself barely escaped deportation.

Eugène Minkowski (1885–1973) was born in St. Petersburg and as a student was active in the 1905 revolution against the czarist regime. He then studied medicine in Warsaw, earned his doctorate in Munich, worked for Eugen Bleuler in Zurich, and studied philosophy with Max Scheler. In 1915, he went to France as a military doctor. After World War I, he practiced psychiatry in France and was a leading European proponent of philosophically oriented, phenomenological psychiatry. From 1940 to 1944, he lived in hiding in occupied France. In 1946, in Basel, he gave one of the earliest lectures on psychological disorders following Nazi persecution. He served as evaluator in numerous reparations cases until his death.[33]

Minkowski's examination proceeded without a single incident. "The patient is a simple, correct woman whose statements are very reserved; she instills confidence. Although illiterate, as she never went to school in her fatherland, she is nevertheless open to everything, not at all mentally backward, so that one has no difficulty having a normal conversation with her." He estimated the reduction in earning capacity at 25 percent. On the other hand, Kaplan, the doctor appointed by the Düsseldorf court, to whose office Frau M. came on 2 November 1961 after several summonses, wrote:

It was extraordinarily difficult to take the patient history. The plaintiff was highly distrustful, irritable, could remember nothing, did not understand why an examination had to be repeated that had already taken place once. She stated that she would under no circumstances undergo further examinations. She absolutely did not understand the necessity for the formalities necessary for the report, did not want to show her identity card, and constantly asked questions herself, such as, "Why do you have to know what my parents died of? What does the question of my earlier illnesses have to do with the evaluation?"

Frau M. could only be persuaded to undergo an additional psychiatric examination and another, final examination after she had been informed several times that the evaluation had been sent back by the court because it was incomplete, and after her lawyer urged her to do so. On 1 December 1961, she visited the psychiatrist Fuswerk-Fursay, who reported:

She had vivid memories of her life in hiding, her fear for her son, the misery that returned during the examination and, in her words, would make her ill for the next few months. She remained in a constant state of sadness and discourage-ment, behaves bizarrely during the examination, laughs and cries for no reason. Everything causes her fear, especially people. She is indifferent to everything; she is aware of her condition and agrees that she is "not happy, even when she could be." Nausea "rises in her throat"; she complains that she sleeps badly, with night-mares, headaches, dizziness, and pains that travel through her whole body. She is irritable and lacks control of herself, even against her own will. Her psychological equilibrium is disturbed. Her relationships are difficult, even with her son; she leads a lonely life, is unable to work, and is among the economically disadvan-taged (she shows her benefits card from the city government).

Kaplan summarized the examination in the diagnosis: "Favorable cli-mate for development of a neurovegetative syndrome with manifesta-tions in the digestive tract and the cardiovascular system and formation of a chronic-reactive depressive state with anxiety-reactive manifes-tations and personality changes." Reduction in earning capacity was assessed at 25 percent. Regarding Nitschke's arguments, he wrote: "I assume that a personality change probably occurred even before the per-secutions. The experiences during the period of persecution, however, led to a considerable worsening in the psychological profile . . . However, a certain psychological primitivity appears to be present."

On 26 July 1963, Kaplan sent the report to the Düsseldorf court. The examining physician for the state pension office took another year and finally, on 13 July 1964, five years after the application had been made, offered Frau M. an out-of-court settlement for payment of the minimum pension, in accordance with Kaplan's evaluation.

Herr K.—Gypsy = Feebleminded[34]

Herr K. was born in Hamburg in 1938 and deported with his family to oc-cupied Poland in 1940, at the age of two. He was sent to the Gypsy camps at Belzec and Krychow. In 1941, the family managed to escape the camp, but they were arrested by the SS in Kattowitz in early 1943. Herr K. was separated from his parents and sent to the women's concentration camp at Ravensbrück with his sister, who was eighteen years older. There, his sister had to perform forced labor and became ill with typhoid fever. In April, both were transferred to Bergen-Belsen. There Herr K. fell ill with typhoid fever, typhus, diphtheria, and a lung infection. During food dis-tribution, an SS guard beat him unconscious with a metal soup ladle. His face was very swollen, and for a few days he was semi-conscious. When the camp was liberated by the British, he was in such terrible condition that he had to be treated for three months by British military doctors at the hospital there. His sister lost track of him during the last few months in the camp and only found him again in the hospital.

Upon returning to Hamburg, he found his mother, who had survived the concentration camp. His father and three of his siblings were dead. In school, Herr K. was teased and taunted for being a Gypsy child. He did not complete a school for the learning disabled, withdrew into his family, and lived from occasional jobs. He was afraid of large groups of people and enclosed spaces. His family told him that he sometimes cried out in his sleep; he occasionally suffered fainting spells and often talked of nothing but the camps.

In 1956, at eighteen, he applied in Hamburg for reparations for health damage. For reasons that are not clear, the proceedings lay dormant for eight years, until in 1964 the office demanded that he fill out an additional questionnaire regarding his application for "B harm" and provide all treatment information from family and hospital doctors. After a long search, he came up with two certificates; however, they contained no information relevant to his application. The health damage for which Herr K. claimed compensation included stomach problems following cerebral and stomach typhoid fever in the camps, headaches since the blows on the head by the SS guard, vomiting, dizziness, and rheumatism. On 8 September 1965, he was examined at the behest of the office by a psychiatrist and neurologist from Heidberg General Hospital, Dr. Thorwald Piepgras.

Thorwald Piepgras (1923–) served as a soldier on the Eastern Front from 1942 until the end of the war. He was a Soviet prisoner of war until 1947 and then studied medicine in Kiel, taking his state examinations and doctorate in 1952. Later he became a psychiatrist and neurologist at the Heidberg General Hospital in Hamburg and conducted medical examinations for the reparations office in Hamburg.[35]

In his patient report, Piepgras quoted Herr K.'s statements in part as follows: " 'I have headaches in the front of my forehead. I usually have them always. Always! I also have it with the heart. And with the stomach. And then the attacks.' He said he had such 'attacks' frequently. The first time it happened was three months ago. He said he always lay still when he had the attacks and did not cramp—his wife told him." Under the heading "Psychological Findings" he noted,

Herr K. willingly made contact and behaved trustingly. He spoke German without an accent, but his linguistic expressive ability was awkward and clumsy. The primary impression of lesser ability was confirmed by the experimental psychology intelligence test. Of the math problems, he was able to do only simple addition and subtraction with relative certainty. He could only do the most simple multiplication and division problems. A problem such as 21 divided by 3 was already too difficult. His school knowledge was very scanty; he had hardly any idea of geography. He also failed the pure comprehension problems . . . Nor could he explain sayings. To the saying, "Lies have short legs," he said, "One must not lie." . . . Assessment: in terms of psychiatric diagnosis, Herr K. is a barely differentiated personality with congenital feeblemindedness to an imbecilic degree . . . Herr K. does not possess an experience-reactive personality—as one often finds among victims of the National Socialist regime. An abnormal development of that kind requires a higher degree of personality differentiation than Herr K. possesses.

To determine his physical condition, Herr K. was examined on 21 July 1965 by the senior physician of the Heidberg General Hospital, Dr. Paul Bünger.

Paul Bünger (1920–) joined the Nazi party in 1938 and took his school-leaving diploma the same year, followed by labor and army service. He studied medicine in Hamburg, interrupted by combat duty. In 1945, he earned his doctorate under the Nazi genetic pathologist Professor Wilhelm Weitz. In 1955, he became senior physician, and in 1965, chief physician, of the nephrology department of the Heidberg General Hospital in Hamburg. His specialty was internal medicine, with a focus on nephrology. He was a member or chairman of various professional organizations and author of numerous monographs on nephrology and haemodialysis treatment.[36]

Bünger recorded his patient history in part as follows:

Questions on the illnesses claimed, such as stomach problems and rheumatism, were answered sketchily; no exact, targeted patient report is possible—probably because of K.'s mental inadequacy . . . Psychological impression: during the entire examination, K. made a very anxious impression; for example, he refused a gastroscopy and stomach biopsy, saying he "couldn't stand" such an examination. He was accompanied by his wife, who did not let him out of her sight. He would even have liked to have her present during questioning . . . Discussion: Based on the complaints indicated, it is improbable that a stomach illness is present. It can be assumed that the stomach problems are connected with the pill abuse that has gone on for six or seven years . . . In the area of internal medicine, there are no somatic illnesses present that could be considered caused by Nazi persecution.

Bünger did not ask why Herr K. was addicted to pills (he took two or three painkillers a day for his chronic headaches).

After these two evaluations, the reparations office denied Herr K.'s claims. He took the case to the Hamburg district court, which required him to undergo an examination at the University Psychiatric Clinic in

Hamburg-Eppendorf. Herr K. ignored three summonses to the examination, despite repeated reminders by his lawyer. He moved frequently and was difficult to reach. Finally, on 26 June 1970, the court dismissed the claim without a new evaluation, saying Herr K. had declined to be examined. After several attempts, Herr K.'s lawyer succeeded in having him come to his office for a personal talk. The lawyer reported on this conversation in his appeal to the state appeals court: "The plaintiff is completely psychologically inhibited and afraid of a medical examination. He suffers from the illusion that some harm could come to him through a medical examination." Herr K. had already told Bünger, the doctor, that he did not like to go to work and had protested vehemently against a gastroscopy. At a later opportunity, he revealed that he had been examined by a doctor in concentration camp and been beaten by him: "That is why he wants nothing to do with them."

Finally, after a long series of organizational obstacles, Herr K. allowed an examination, at the behest of the Hamburg appeals court, by the head of the Department of Children's and Youth Psychiatry at the Hamburg University Clinic, Professor Thea Schönfelder.

Thea Schönfelder (1925–) attended high school and medical school in Hamburg. She joined the Social Democratic party in 1946. Schönfelder earned her doctorate in 1951 and her professorial qualifications in 1966. At first she worked as senior physician, then—beginning in 1970—as a full professor in the Department of Children's and Youth Psychiatry of Hamburg University. She has published works on sex research, especially sex crimes.

In December 1973 and April 1974, Professor Schönfelder had Herr K. come in for three outpatient examinations. He came to trust her and told her his whole story, from beginning to end. Among other things, he said: "I am always afraid when there are a lot of people, I'm so nervous. I can't bear to see uniforms. We were beaten whenever they [i.e., the guards] were in the mood. The women were worse to us children than the men. I am often sad. I think about the past and brood over everything, especially the fact that I can't get anywhere. Nothing has any point." He added that he had also sometimes considered taking his life.

In her report, Professor Schönfelder reviewed the results of a Hamburg-Wechsler Intelligence Test, which showed an IQ of 76, in the "very low intelligence" range. "His range of knowledge, mathematical ability, verbal abstraction capability, intellectual agility, etc." were especially underdeveloped. In a twelve-page assessment, she explained that Herr K. had never experienced the "crucial trauma of separation from a close relationship," as his grown sister had taken his mother's place. Undoubtedly, he had lacked "means of educational advancement" in the camps:

However, in the case of Herr K., doubt arises here whether it was only or overwhelmingly the conditions in the camps that determined his subsequent development. The difficulty in judging lies, first of all, in the fact that Herr K., because of the particularities of his cultural background, could not make up the existing loss of positive learning experiences (in the intellectual, emotional, and social sectors) under more favorable social conditions following imprisonment, but instead continued to live in a marginal group as a Gypsy. The description of his own reaction in conjunction with his unsuccessful school career and his report of attempts at vocational integration during our conversations make it clear what experience-based reaction formations took place in Herr K. *after* the concentration camps, and how these strengthened over time under the influence of rejection by his environment. Such a mechanism, containing within itself the danger of personality abnormalization, is encountered in precisely such members of so-called marginal groups when, because of unfavorable conditions of socialization, they cannot sufficiently follow the usual scholastic (and extrascholastic) learning processes . . . The emergence of anxiety symptoms and rash, affectively conditioned reactions in the style of so-called "primitive reactions" are, in my view, indications that Herr K., because of his very limited intellectual abilities in some areas, does not have the ability to solve problems when they exceed the bounds of concrete experience and go beyond the relatively narrow horizon of his own circles.

On his psychosomatic complaints, such as headaches, she remarked, "In such a simply structured personality, which is also understandably under pressure to offer a purposely tendentious description, such a psychosomatic effect context cannot be proven." And on his drug abuse, "On this point, the evidence is not 'objective,' but obtainable only with the help of the examinee."

Schönfelder's doubts were strengthened by the fact that in his previous consultations with doctors, Herr K. had never spoken about his psychological problems. In summary, she diagnosed him as "abnormally experience-reactive on the basis of his lower intellectual abilities." However, she acknowledged a connection between his complaints and the persecution for the first year after liberation from concentration camp, 1946: "I assume that the persecution-independent causes had largely replaced the persecution-dependent causes in the course of a year after the end of imprisonment, so that the persecution-dependent ones made up less than a fourth of the total causes." All the doctors, incidentally, denied the existence of any lasting damage from the cerebral trauma caused by the SS guard or the typhus encephalitis probably suffered in concentration camp.

Herr K.'s lawyer managed to get a statement on Schönfelder's evaluation from the head of the Department of Psychosomatic Medicine of Hannover Medical College, Dr. Hellmuth Freyberger.

Hellmuth Freyberger (1923–) earned his doctorate in 1952 and became senior physician under A. Jores, internist and psychosomatic expert at the university clinic at Hamburg-Eppendorf. In 1975, he became director of the Department of Psychosomatic Medicine at Hannover Medical College. He conducted medical examinations in numerous reparations proceedings and published several studies on the psychopathology of victims of persecution and on psychosomatic factors in intensive care, dialysis, and transplants.

Freyberger considered Schönfelder's assessment to be regrettably wrong:

Herr K. apparently has difficulty with people around him (including doctors) in verbalizing complaints, biographical data, and substantive content sufficiently so that they can be understood and registered by examiners. Because of this, a wrong impression can emerge for the examiner. This occurs not infrequently among former persecutees who have suffered persecution as severe as that of Herr K. Psychological testing—especially projective procedures—would be necessary to sufficiently acknowledge and avoid this inhibited verbalization, which can give a "distorted" impression of the objective situation of the examinee.

However, in a later statement, Schönfelder found such further testing unnecessary.

Herr K. had been in a concentration camp for over a year. If a reduction in earning capacity had been found of at least 25 percent, the "concentration camp assumption" of § 31, para. 2, of the BEG would have applied to him. But Schönfelder had not provided a general degree of reduction in earning capacity; she had merely stated that the "persecution-dependent factors" for his reduction in earning capacity had been "replaced by the persecution-independent factors" by the end of 1946. Thus the appeals court had to ask her for clarification in regard to the "concentration camp assumption." It took another two years for the court to receive this clarification. In her statement of 5 July 1976, she estimated Herr K.'s overall reduction in earning capacity at 25–30 percent; however, with a "probability verging on certainty," his complaints did not have a "causal connection to the persecution measures suffered." Thus the concentration camp assumption was refuted.

In a response to the doctor's report, Herr K.'s lawyer asked Schönfelder how she could conclude with a probability verging on certainty that Herr K.'s psychological problems would have appeared even *without* persecution. She was then summoned as an expert to an oral hearing before the court and was questioned by the lawyer. She defended herself with the argument that Herr K. had earlier given no information on his psychological problems, but had only complained of them now: "I consider it possible that the plaintiff—to put it simply—is exaggerating."

In a decision of 9 February 1977, the appeals court denied Herr K.'s appeal, based on Schönfelder's evaluation and statements. That was the end of the proceedings. Herr K. received no pension for the psychological damage suffered as a child in the concentration camps.

Frau O.—"Gross demonstrative tendencies" and "psychogenous deviations"[37]

Frau O. was born in 1927 and deported at thirteen to the Gypsy camp at Belzec. She was left with a back problem as a result of abuse by a German guard. Her mother was murdered. The only thing she could remember in connection with her mother's death was that one morning she was all alone in the barracks; her siblings were all gone. She found out from a woman she knew that they were all supposed to have been deported on the same day. This woman then took her mother's place and took care of her.

In 1954, she applied to the Hamburg reparations office for a disability pension under Hamburg's Special Supplementary Pension Law. Her application was not processed. Eleven years later, in 1965, she applied again, this time for delayed health effects under the BEG Final Law. Specifically, she listed a heart condition, headaches, rheumatism, and kidney problems. Ten more years later, on 4 April 1975, she was examined at the behest of the office by Dr. Armin Schütt, the internal medicine expert. In his evaluation, he described her deportation to Poland as follows:

She was resettled in Poland with her family on 16 May 1940, primarily for racial reasons; there she was in the Belzec collection camp until December 1940, and then in various places. She was not allowed to return to Germany, but otherwise was supplied with an identity card, rations cards, and cards entitling her to housing, work and financial support. She gradually returned to Germany in June 1944. She came via Lübow, near Lüchow, in late 1944, arriving in Hamburg in May 1945.

Schütt then gave his assessment of Frau O.: "She says only that her nerves are bad and she is afraid. She says she always has to have people around her and doesn't like to be alone. Things go black before her eyes. Considering that the applicant is illiterate and never worked, these statements point to a tendency toward psychological breakdown, without there being any indications of a genuine vital disorder." He issued the diagnosis: "small stature, asthenia, premature aging, insufficient chewing ability, high BSR [blood sedimentation rate] and leucocyte count. It is unlikely that any of these ailments has any causal connection to Nazi persecution, with regard to either their origin or their worsening." Nor did a supplementary orthopedic examination find any persecution-induced back problem. The office thereupon denied Frau O.'s application. She appealed to the Hamburg district court, which appointed Professor Klaus Diebold, senior physician at the Heidelberg University Psychiatric Clinic, to conduct the examination.

Klaus Diebold (1933–) received his doctorate in 1961 and his professorial qualifications in 1971. In 1972, Diebold became senior physician at the Heidelberg University Psychiatric Clinic under von Baeyer's successor, Professor W. Janzarik. He specialized in biological psychiatry and psychiatric genetics.

On 13 and 14 November 1978 (in the meantime, the case had been delayed another three years), Frau O. was observed as an inpatient at the Heidelberg University Clinic. In his report, Diebold listed the following:

Gross demonstrative tendencies are present. In the sensitivity test, O. constantly reacted to contact with "no." In the finger-nose test, she consistently pointed past her nose, in the direction of her ear. In the tightrope walk, she also indicated psychogenous deviations. Other findings without abnormality . . . Psychological findings: On the day of her appointment, O. arrived punctually at the clinic. She was accompanied by her husband and youngest child. At first it was very difficult to make clear to O. that she had to remain in the clinic for purposes of the examination. She insisted on sleeping with her husband and child in the station wagon in which they drove from Hamburg. She was very unreasonable. Only after a long discussion did she agree to remain here with the child. The child was always present during the subsequent examination. The examination was very laborious and sluggish, as O. constantly gave very vague answers. She frequently answered simple, insignificant questions with "I don't know, I'm sorry." This expression was frequently repeated in stereotypical fashion. Here too, as in the neurological examination, gross demonstrative tendencies were unmistakable . . . A more accurate intelligence test is impossible, as O. can neither read nor write. She generally solved simple mathematical problems, which she should have mastered in daily life, only on the second try. Here, too, demonstrative tendencies probably play a role.[37]

Diebold summarized his conclusions thus: "She claims she cannot even remember her father and mother. Repeatedly expressed doubts about the accuracy of such statements did not impress O. in the least. She continued this grossly demonstrative behavior throughout the examination."

Diebold employed this wording [i.e., "grossly demonstrative behavior"] five times in his report—on every second page, as it were. "In fact, O. appears naturally small in stature and delicate, and somehow 'used up,' " he wrote. "This overall clinical impression, however, cannot be objectified. The plaintiff's nervous disorders correspond, in our opinion, most closely with the symptoms of 'neurasthenia,' . . . which causes a persecution-independent MdE of a maximum of 15 percent."

The Hamburg court denied the claim, based on Professor Diebold's report. The case dragged on another four years and went all the way to the federal Supreme Court of Appeals, without success. The lawyer tried in vain to bring the Dutch psychiatrist Jan Bastiaans into the case as chief evaluator. The reparations office also rejected his attempt to bring in a Professor Meyer of the Hamburg University Psychosomatic Clinic, claiming that a report by Professor Meyer had been unusable in another case: its wording had "been reminiscent of Courths-Mahler [a well-known German author of soap operas]."

Frau M., Herr K., and Frau O. were unable to express themselves verbally with a skill that would be helpful to a doctor. They did not like dealing with people in positions of authority and were distrustful of doctors, having had too many bad experiences with them. The doctors conducting the official examinations interpreted this unfavorably. They stigmatized the patients as "deviant characters," "congenitally feebleminded," "gross," "small of stature . . . somehow used up." And this stigma of stupidity and inferiority served as evidence that their complaints were not persecution-induced. Thus Piepgras felt that Herr K. could not have an experience-reactive personality disorder (Venzlaff's phrase, from which this was taken, was an "experience-reactive personality *change*") because Herr K.'s personality was too "undifferentiated." The German examiners thus gave particular weight to intelligence tests, although they were completely meaningless in determining a connection between persecution and illness.

The doctors' biases against the "undifferentiated" was especially apparent in Diebold, the Heidelberg psychiatrist. The way in which he spoke about Frau O. is reminiscent of the combination of curiosity and disgust with which psychiatric experts in the Third Reich described their victims of forced sterilization and euthanasia. Frau O. submitted to the examination, in part helpless, in part resisting, and Diebold found it incomprehensible and annoying that she wanted her child present during the examination, instinctively seeking protection from a family member. He mocked her saying "I'm sorry"; with annoyance, he recorded the fact that she consistently pointed to her ear in the finger-nose test and the badly performed tightrope walk as being "grossly demonstrative behavior" and "psychogenous deviations"—that is, as ill-mannered, theatrical, dissimulating behavior.

Schönfelder's method was more subtle. Possessing particular experience with marginal groups, she succeeded in winning Herr K.'s trust and questioning and examining him thoroughly. She expressed herself with greater refinement than the other doctors. Instead of "feebleminded," she used "of limited intelligence"; instead of negating persecution-related complaints with curt diagnoses such as "deviant character," she said in the case of Herr K., marked by "such a mechanism . . . among marginal groups, bearing within it the danger of personality abnormalization," that "experience-determined reaction formation [was present] mainly after the camp period." Where others spoke of "dramatization," "exaggeration," or "gross demonstrative behavior," she said, "His simply structured personality is, understandably, under pressure to offer a purposely tendentious portrayal." Dr. Schönfelder could "understand" Herr K. better than others. This ability and her digressions into scientific rhetoric would make a great impression on any nonexpert judge, and made it harder for the victims to figure out what was being done to them.

Assessments of Women

Frau N.—"Tender, vulnerable feminine delicacy"[38]

Frau N., born in 1920, was the only "half-Jew" in the Eppendorf Weg school in Hamburg. The new principal, an SS man installed in 1933, forced her to take part in religious instruction. There he told the children that the Jews had always persecuted Christians and had crucified Jesus on the cross. He also forced Frau N. to participate in the singing of the "Horst Wessel Lied" (a Nazi song) at morning assemblies. Because his persecution became worse and worse and she was completely isolated in the class, she sought out a sympathetic pastor and was baptized in 1934. This baptism also helped protect her Jewish mother, who was divorced from her Christian father.

After graduation, Frau N. found work in a Jewish firm in Hamburg. The family's material situation worsened in 1936, however, with the emigration of a wealthy uncle who had hitherto supported them, and had especially helped her sick grandfather. Now Frau N., a young girl, had to support the family. Because her mother was too fearful, she also had to take care of most official business at the city government's office of Jewish affairs.

Frau N. had her first migraine attack at fifteen and was unable to sleep nights. On 9 November 1938, the night of the Kristallnacht pogrom, she witnessed the destruction of the Jewish business in which she worked and the deportation of the owner. She ran home in panic, hid her grandfather with friends, and obtained pills to prevent him from falling into the hands of the Gestapo. Frau N. lived in constant fear for her relatives; good friends abandoned her, suddenly pretending not to know her. Her doctor sent her to a neurologist because of fainting spells accompanied by vision problems. When she noticed the SS uniform under his white coat, she broke down completely. Another doctor protected her from being forced to perform heavy labor in the armaments industry. In 1938, she began a clandestine relationship with an Aryan tenant, her future husband. The janitor's wife, a Nazi, found out about it and reported her and her tenant to the Gestapo for miscegenation [Rassenschande] and theft. In January 1943, she was sent to Fuhlsbüttel concentration camp for three months, where she caught tuberculosis from a fellow prisoner.

After her release, she was diagnosed with open tuberculosis, but was refused treatment at a lung sanatorium for racial reasons. At her release, she was forced to sign a separation agreement from her fiancé (the tenant); he had been conscripted into a work detail in Cracow, in the Generalgouvernement. As her illness kept her from working and she and her mother were bombed out in July 1943 (her grandfather died of cancer shortly before deportation), her fiancé brought her to Poland, got her false papers, and sent her to friends in the mountains to recuperate. In 1943, she had a miscarriage; in 1944, while fleeing west in a truck, she bore a daughter. Until liberation by the British, she lived in hiding on the Lüneburg Heath with her child, fiancé, and mother.

On 11 April 1958, the reparations office in Hamburg denied her application for reparations for bodily and health damage because, according to a report by an expert on pulmonary disease, a Dr. Huhn, she had only an old, already healed pulmonary tuberculosis that, according to a 1943 X ray, had already hardened and thus could not have appeared or worsened during the short period of imprisonment. An appeal to the Hamburg district court was unsuccessful. In November 1965, after enactment of the BEG Final Law, Frau N. applied through her lawyer for an adjustment proceeding, pointing to the fact that she suffered from the psychological consequences of twelve years of discrimination, temporary imprisonment, and life in hiding, and that she experienced severe migraines. The processing of her application was interrupted for a time when her former janitor's wife—the same one who had denounced her to the Gestapo in 1943, and who had been convicted, but soon after pardoned, for her work as an informer—denounced her once again, this time to the reparations office, claiming she had been imprisoned under the Nazis for a criminal offense. Frau N.'s lawyer was able to refute this libelous charge.

The first examining doctor in the new proceeding was the Hamburg psychiatrist Wilhelm Liebermann. Frau N. came to his office with her husband on 14 January 1972. Under the heading "Psyche" in the report on his findings, Liebermann explicitly referred to the matter of the former janitor's wife and informer:

He [her husband] appeared very self-confident and assertive and declared, with his wife's agreement, that she continued to suffer because of the Nazis, who unfortunately continued to hold leading positions in Germany. In this connection, he pointed out that the informer had only been sentenced to a brief penalty after 1945, but continued to receive her full pension. He said she had not changed her views, like most Nazis in Germany. In this connection, Frau N. mentioned the NPD [a right-wing nationalist party] and several other Nazis whom she said were doing very well, while the actual victims often had to live in poverty. It was quite difficult to point out the ridiculousness of these claims to the couple. Herr N. tried to circumvent the question of why they had not emigrated in 1945 or later by referring to his wife's lung disease and his own Aryan background. Frau N. was reduced to generalizations and could not ultimately refute the view that she was not doing badly in Germany, that even the most pessimistic observer could not say there was any danger of war, and that the Nazis and NDP members described by the couple hardly held positions of power in Germany.

In his report, Liebermann wrote, "Until 1943, Frau N. was exposed to the same general persecution as her half-Jewish fellow citizens in Germany ... Diagnosis: Vegetatively colored exhaustion syndrome in menopause in a sensitive, asthenic woman with a tendency toward migrainous headaches." For the period from her arrest on 7 January 1943 until the end of 1945, he confirmed a persecution-induced experience-reactive disorder with a reduction in earning capacity of 25 percent. In a supplementary internist's report, the head physician of the Heidberg General Hospital, Dr. Paul Bünger, confirmed the negative assessment of persecution-induced tuberculosis by Huhn, the preliminary evaluator.

Frau N. took the case to the Hamburg district court. More years passed, during which new evidence was demanded by the court, such as proof of treatment in the postwar period. According to the court, Frau N. had given contradictory statements and provided mistaken information on times and places of persecution. In addition, she had claimed to have been a *Geltungsjüdin* (one who counted as a Jew); that is, she had been raised as a Jew and therefore occupied a lower position in the eyes of the authorities than a *Mischling* (half-caste), class 1. In a brief, the reparations office contradicted Frau N. with reference to the Nuremberg racial laws: "The records suggest that, under § 5, para. 2, of the First Directive on the Reich Citizenship Law of 14 November 1935, which established the concept of the so-called *Geltungsjude*, the plaintiff was not a *Geltungsjüdin* and would not have been even had she not been baptized ... The defendant finds it necessary to discuss this issue, as the tendency of the plaintiff's presentation is clearly to dramatize the plaintiff's history of persecution."

In a personal hearing before the court on 13 September 1974, Frau N. declared, among other things, "After thirty-five years, I would like to be finished with these things at last." In a letter to her lawyer accompanying a detailed report on her experience of persecution, she wrote, "I ask for your understanding of the fact that I have delayed the issue so long, but memories of the past so weighed on me that I again had severe migraine attacks and could hardly sleep at night, and I simply could not find the strength to write up everything within a few days."

The Hamburg psychiatrist Christoph Jannasch was finally called in as the court-appointed evaluator. He examined Frau N. in his office on 15 May 1976—eleven years after she had applied for the adjustment proceeding. We are told the following about his meeting with Frau N.:

At first, she was not enthusiastic about the challenge of another examination. However, there soon developed a lively affective participation, even excitement and deviation, with complaints, more discouraged than angry, over the unending reparations proceedings, the ignorance of the people who were to judge her, and her almost complete lack of faith that they could grant her justice ... In the hurried current of affective burden, a quite lively acceleration, even so to speak a dizzying acceleration appeared; while then for longer periods the strength of the continuous stream diminished and a fundamentally increased exhaustibility or reduction in the basic vital tension became apparent . . . In Frau N.'s self-description, despite internal resistance, a will always asserted itself toward friendly (on occasion somewhat more than cooperative) adaptability and ultimately obliging affection and agreement. Preservation of a certain tender, vulnerable feminine delicacy came into play; however, at times it was inconsistent with the irritability arising from the increased exhaustibility of basic vitality—as well as a veiled defensive tendency, ultimately also present, against the treating party when he came too close, which mobilized fragments of distrust.

Dr. Jannasch, the doctor who so described himself, reached a final diagnosis of "chronic anxiety-neurotic integrational personality disorder with lasting limitation of ego strength and vitality, with increased infantile dependency on relational persons and a chronic low disorder value subdepressive exhaustion." He estimated Frau N.'s neurosis as persecution-induced, with a permanent 25 percent reduction in earning capacity, but emphasized that there had been no "experience-based personality change."

The office immediately seized upon this reservation, saying that the absence of an "experience-based personality change" meant no permanent persecution-induced neurosis. The office also maintained that Frau N.'s statements had been "confused and incorrect," and that she displayed "behavior showing a neurotic tendency." To clear up the question of the "experience-based personality change," the court asked the Heidelberg psychiatrist Walther von Baeyer for another consultation. Frau N. traveled to Heidelberg and underwent a third examination by a psychiatrist. The office's objections were successful. Von Baeyer confirmed a 10–15 percent persecution-induced reduction in earning capacity only for Frau N.'s migraines and found no experience-based personality change; she was "asthenically-leptosomatically disposed" and her "psychological-emotional disturbances seemed to be constitutionally determined." Apparently, however, the lawyer was able to moderate the office's position and persuade it to accept a symbolic settlement of 5,000 DM.

Frau A.—Loss of Value Following Forced Abortion[39]

Frau A., a Polish Jew born in 1907, was deported in 1941 to the Vilna Ghetto and later to the Riga-Kaiserwald, Stutthof, and Mühldorf concentration camps. She was thirty-four when a forced abortion was performed on her in the ghetto in her sixth month of pregnancy—without anesthetic or any hygienic precautions and with no aftercare. Since this operation, she had suffered from a chronic abdominal infection. Her first husband, a brother, and a sister died in the concentration camps. She herself became ill in the camps with typhoid fever and frostbite in both feet, and she was beaten on the head with rifle butts. Her deep desire for children was not fulfilled in her second marriage, after the war. She was unable to have children after the forced abortion and maltreatment. In 1960—she had meanwhile emigrated to Canada—she made a health damage application with the Rhineland-Palatinate restitution office in Mainz. The office's consulting doctor, Fritz Struwe, confirmed a state of psychological and physical exhaustion only from 1941 to 1946, with a reduction in earning capacity of 25 percent.

Fritz Struwe (1915–) completed school in 1936 in Bad Ems and then entered labor service for a year and a half. He joined the naval SA and studied medicine in Bonn, Freiburg, and Jena, taking his state examinations in 1941. Following the war, he served as public health officer and medical officer in Mainz, and also conducted examinations for the district reparations office there.[40]

Frau A. filed suit against this finding. In the course of the subsequent years, she was examined by numerous doctors, and her claim was rejected by the Koblenz court. Finally, she was examined on 5 July 1977 by a professor of psychiatry at Hannover Medical College, Dr. Karl-Peter Kisker, at the behest of the Koblenz appeals court. Kisker found "long-term, severe persecution stress," but added the caveat that Frau A. had, after all, married again, "showed sufficient professional continuity into advanced age," "achieved linguistic and sociocultural re-rooting in Canada to a great degree," and "had required no psychiatric assistance and experienced no other breakdowns for which she needed support." He diagnosed a "moderately pronounced psychoreactive disturbance," which had become linked, until the end of 1949, with psychological exhaustion symptoms: "MdE until 1949, 30 percent; since then, 10–15 percent." He classified Frau A.'s enduring depression as a "progredient psychological symptom of aging . . . with a probability bordering on certainty, it is not persecution-induced."

In contrast, the psychiatric evaluator in Canada had found an "experience-based personality change" in Frau A., with an MdE of 25 percent. He said she suffered from sleeplessness, tormenting nightmares, and severe headaches and was being treated with psychological drugs. In the Rorschach test, the doctor had found indications of a chronic-reactive depression. He said the fact that the previous evaluator had declared Frau A. to be psychologically normal could be explained because "psychological symptoms are often denied in people with eastern European educational backgrounds." In contrast, Kisker denied Frau A. a pension, based on a finding of only 10 to 15 percent reduction in earning capacity.

In a response to his opinion, her lawyer wrote that Kisker had not adhered to the "concentration camp assumption," which would apply to Frau A., as a 40 percent overall psychiatric reduction in earning capacity was present; in addition, he failed to acknowledge the trauma of forced abortion and consequent sterility as persecution-induced harm. Kisker answered in a supplementary evaluation: "It is certain that, from a medical point of view, the increase in MdE since 1965 may be traced to age-related psychological changes." On forced abortion: "However, nothing can be concluded, from such brutal stress details, on the degree of manifestation and the handicap value of a possible lasting impairment of a persecution-typical character." On sterility: "No doubt, the experience of loneliness intensifies with age because of childlessness. This normal psychological fact, however, is not at the same time necessarily a psychological disease of old age. Not even an attentive and sensitive reading of the shocking report by Frau A. on the details of the abortion and her later yearning to have a child permits any other assessment."

In order to settle the issue, Kisker called for an additional gynecological evaluation. On 12 September 1977, such an evaluation was issued on the basis of the files by the Mainz University Gynecological Clinic. Dr. Hans Schaudig, an intern, and his chief physician came to the unequivocal conclusion that Frau A.'s sterility was the result of the brutal forced abortion in the ghetto and was thus persecution-induced. In addition, "experience shows that delayed and permanent traumas in women who have become sterile due to persecution are especially severe, so that they can lead to a significant reduction in earning capacity."

In a further supplementary report on 6 December 1979, Kisker responded that although he himself had written the chapter on psychological damage in victims of forced sterilization in Walther von Baeyer and Heinz Häfner's *Psychiatrie der Verfolgten* (Psychiatry of Victims of Persecution), and although it was "both gynecological and psychological examination practice to equate the biological-psychological value loss connected with sterility with an MdE of 30 to 40 percent . . . such an MdE of 30–40 percent covers only the biological-psychological reduction in value that is conditioned by forced childlessness. This value loss, however, no longer comes into play beyond child-bearing age, that is, after menopause—that is, at age 55 at the latest." Professor Kisker conceded Frau A. a reduction in earning capacity of 60 percent from summer 1942 to the end of 1949, and then a reduction of 45 percent until age 55—that is, until 1962—and from then on a reduction of 10–15 percent, as in his preliminary evaluation. That is, from 1962 on, Frau A. was not entitled to a pension.

Frau J.—"No measurable reduction in earning capacity" through forced sterilization[41]

Frau F. was sentenced to forced sterilization on 2 May 1941, at the age of sixteen, by the Court of Genetic Health in Hamburg. In its ruling, based on an advisory opinion by the medical officer, Heinrich Maintz, the court said:

J. is significantly backward in psychological development. She traveled around with her parents in a Gypsy wagon, and the only place she lived for a longer period of time was Lüneburg. There she attended public school for several years, and then a school for backward children. Otherwise, she took part in schooling on their journeys wherever the family happened to be. J. has been known to the police for some time as a vagabond and dishonest. During examination by a doctor, clear intelligence disorders in the sense of congenital feeblemindedness were found in J. Despite attending school, she had learned neither reading nor writing. This was joined by severe disorders in the area of emotional life and strength of mind. The diagnosis is concretized by the extraordinarily severe genetic handicap in blood relations in the areas of intellect and character, which emerges from the genetic health files available . . . Congenital feeblemindedness is a great genetic threat. Experience shows that it is frequently passed on to offspring. Such a misfortune must be prevented through sterilization.

In June 1941, Frau J. was forcibly sterilized at the Wandsbek General Hospital. In 1942, she was taken to Ravensbrück concentration camp, and later to the Buchenwald subcamp of Altenburg. She was abused and forced to do hard labor.

Following liberation, she found the rest of her family in Bavaria. Her father had also spent years in concentration camp, and a sister and brother had died in Auschwitz. In 1950, she married; three years later, her husband divorced her because she could not have children. She constantly complained of abdominal pain and strong, irregular menstrual bleeding. A gynecological exam in 1951 found deformities in the uterus resulting from sterilization. She first made an application for reparations in 1950 under the Hamburg Special Supplementary Pension Law; on 21 February 1953, she was examined at the Hamburg University Psychiatric Clinic by Professor Hans Bürger-Prinz: "The fact that she feels possible slight abdominal pains with particular intensity may be conceded, given the existent tenderness of feeling and a strongly marked physical self-awareness perceptible in the examination, as she must have felt her sterilization to be an especial loss of her female wholeness. However, this does not create a reduction in earning capacity." This opinion made rejection certain.

Hans Bürger-Prinz (1897–1976) became director of the Friedrichsberg-Eilbecktal Psychiatric Clinic near Hamburg. He served as a lay judge on the Genetic Health Court in Hamburg. During the war he was a consulting psychiatrist in Military District Ten and among other things directed electroshock therapy for shell-shocked veterans. After the war, he was director of the University Psychiatric Clinic in Hamburg-Eppendorf.[42]

In 1963, Frau J. applied once again under the Federal Restitution Law. The reparations office refused, explaining that Frau J. had been sterilized not because of race, but due to "congenital feeblemindedness" under the Law to Prevent Genetically Defective Offspring, and that, based on prior examination reports, no measurable reduction in earning capacity had been found. On 10 June 1965, however, Frau J.'s lawyer managed to have the finding of the old Genetic Health Court nullified by a Hamburg lower court. It explained in its opinion that, according to an examination report by the University Psychiatric Clinic, no feeblemindedness was present, and that the claimant made a "clean, fresh impression" at the appointment.

After this decision, the reparations office solicited a report from an internist, Dr. S. John; he found that Frau J. had "no measurable reduction in earning capacity" as a result of sterilization and confinement in the concentration camps. Frau J. appealed and, at the behest of the court, was examined by, among others, Dr. Wulf Wunnenberg, a psychiatrist, who found three syndromes:

(1) the "gynecological syndrome," involving constant sharp and dragging abdominal pains, the psychological suffering effect of which, because of neurotic fixation, far outweighs the possible objectively grounded effects; (2) the "internist syndrome," involving subjectively felt circulatory disorders, reports of swelling of the extremities, kidney pain, and leukocytosis . . . ; (3) The "psychological syndrome," involving occasional anxiety-laced reminiscences of the concentration camp and sad despondence over the death of family, however without production of pathological symptoms.

Wulf Wunnenberg (1918–) took his high school degree in Hamburg in 1936, followed by labor service and voluntary service in the navy. In 1938, he began studying medicine in Munich, and in 1939 he was drafted into the navy; in 1940, he began frontline service on the Channel coast, but was given leave between tours to complete his medical studies. Wunnenberg earned his doctorate and took the state examinations in 1943. After the war, he opened a private psychiatric practice in Hamburg. He was chief physician at the general hospital in Hamburg-Ochsenzoll and conducted examinations for the Hamburg reparations office.[43]

Wunnenberg estimated a total reduction in earning capacity of 30 percent, of which, however, only 7.5 percent was classed as residual psychological damage (point 3) and persecution-induced. However, he acknowledged that 15 percent of the total MdE could be attributed to the gynecological syndrome, and that it remained to be clarified, gynecologically and legally, whether or not the sterility should be considered a persecution harm. Furthermore, he said the "concentration camp assumption" had to be seen as irrefutable.

The office objected to this view, and also felt no gynecological evaluation was necessary and that sterilization had not been "accepted into the definition of persecution." At the request of the court, Frau J. was then examined by a gynecologist named Dr. Franz, who found a "parametropathia spastica" (uterine adhesions), which, however, he said could not be seen as a consequence of sterilization, but as the result of endogenous and other exogenous causes: "Besides, Frau J. has been married in the meantime and enjoyed a fulfilled marriage with her husband for a long period of time. A relationship between the complaint and the absence of periods during the period of incarceration must also be denied. This phenomenon, known as 'emergency amenorrhoea,' generally subsides after the stressful situation has ended, without leaving any physical damage." Franz did not mention her childlessness and the divorce.

In addition, Frau J. was psychologically examined by Dr. Werner Lungwitz, a psychiatrist, who wrote, among other things, "Among the functional achievements of the brain, the ability to write is completely lacking," and one could, in regard to the gynecological complaints, "speak only of a fixated conversion reaction, which additionally in no way hindered the marriage, gainful employment, or the social integration visible in a cross-section of life," and "represented no measurable MdE."

Werner Lungwitz (1907–) took his high school diploma in Erfurt in 1928 and entered medical school in Jena. He passed his state examinations in 1933–34 and earned a doctorate in 1935. He joined the Nazi party in 1941. After the war, he practiced psychiatry in Hamburg and performed medical examinations for the Hamburg reparations office.[44]

In an opinion on the two evaluations, Frau J.'s lawyer suggested,

Especially among Gypsies, with their pronounced sense of family and appreciation of children, the loss of fertility must be rated especially highly. It is common knowledge that Gypsy women unable to bear children are viewed by their clans as second-class people . . . Even by analogy with legislation on state disability benefits, one cannot take the view that intrusions into the sexual sphere should not be compensated because no diminution in earning capacity can be proven. According to commentaries on benefits law, physical harm to the genital area in men is rated at 10–30 percent of MdE, depending on the case. This includes inability to conceive despite continued ability to engage in sexual intercourse. The same standard should be applied to women whose ability to bear children is lost. Above all, there is no reason to assess a woman who is a victim of racial persecution at a lower rate than one injured in war.

Upon application by the lawyer, the court again solicited an evaluation by Professor Hellmuth Freyberger of the Hamburg University Psychiatric Clinic's Department of Psychosomatic Medicine. Freyberger was the only one of all the doctors up to this point who allowed Frau J. to speak for herself in his report. On the sterilization, he quoted Frau J. as follows:

I don't know why: they got my files, but they didn't like me and everything happened; . . . frequently one can hear every sound at night, one becomes anxious and fearful; just as when I see many men in white coats, then I'm afraid; one saw too much in the camps; the things I experienced there I will never forget; I also have difficulty watching things on TV, anything that has to do with deportation, criminal stories, and concentration camp films . . . Everything I went through in concentration camp, I think about it in the evening, and what was done to me even after these terrible things and the sterilization, the divorce, and the child-lessness, this punishment was added; when I imagined how my siblings were killed in the camps, that affects me very much; if I had children, one would say one still had responsibilities. I don't like to talk to other people about it, I prefer to keep it to myself; only someone who lived through it can understand and offer sympathy.

On the basis of the patient report and psychological tests (TAT, Rorschach test, Hamburg-Wechsler intelligence test, Progressive Matrices by Ravon, Benton (visual retention test), Purdue punch board, Hamburger repression scale, Maudsley Medical Questionnaire [MMQ], Sate supplementary test, and Thematic Apperception test), Freyberger arrived at the following diagnosis: "(1) chronified depression (in the sense of an exhaustion depression), (2) infantile regressive traits with a need for contact, (3) feelings of inferiority in regard to subjective experience of the female role, (4) strong desire for children (as a result of failure due to sterilization)." He provided the following explanation, among others, on the subject of the consequences of forced sterilization:

Hartwig demonstrates the rapid sinking in the prospects for marriage among sterilized women. The literature indicates that those who were sterilized were frequently precisely those who were "simply structured" and frequently had not completed their education. It is precisely such people who are supposed to demonstrate a "fine and complex psychological reaction" that is supposed to be documented in their way of dealing with the forced sterilization. It is said to be noteworthy that it is these people—apart from some exceptions—who had difficulty verbalizing what infertility meant to them, the extent to which they were subjectively affected by it, and what influences it had on their external life. It is easy to see that similarities exist here with Frau J. Remarkably enough, her problems were demonstrated primarily in the results of the psychological tests and not in the explorations, within which verbalization is disproportionately more direct.

Freyberger assessed the reduction in earning capacity at 30 to 40 percent and claimed that, because of the obvious tendencies toward dissimulation, a more precise estimate was not possible. In contrast to all the other doctors, Freyberger determined that Frau J. was not exaggerating her problems, but rather understating them. The office, on the other hand, declared the inclusion of sterility as a persecution harm to be inadmissible. Freyberger was therefore called to testify again in court as an expert witness. He essentially repeated what he had said in his report.

The office ultimately settled with Frau J. on 15 July 1969 and paid a minimum monthly pension of 165 DM and a payment of back pension of 15,207 DM, on the basis of a persecution-induced reduction in earning capacity of 25 percent.

Apparently, women are beings possessed of an inherent "delicacy of perception" and a "strongly marked physical self-awareness"; yet their disabilities, when their bodies were maimed through the cruelty of the persecutor, were seemingly unmeasurable, and thus provided no entitlement to a pension. Their psychological reactions to forced sterilization or forced abortion that destroyed the uterus were trivialized, or it was offhandedly declared that because all older women lost their fertility in any case, there was no loss of value, or that loneliness in old age caused by childlessness was a "normal psychological state" (as Kisker claimed). In Frau J.'s case, the doctor considered her supposedly "fulfilled marriage" to be evidence that the forced sterilization had not disadvantaged her. Frau N.'s evaluator, Liebermann, blamed her problems on her "sensitive aesthenic" nature and menopause, rather than persecution: "exhaustion syndrome in menopause." He dismissed her indignation over the reparations process and the continuing influence of former Nazis as "ridiculous." His colleague Jannasch located a "hurried current of the affective burden," even a "dizzying acceleration." He managed to transform Frau N.'s resistance to the doctor into "obliging affection and agreement," in which she preserved her "tender, vulnerable feminine delicacy," although the "too closely approaching treating party" may have "mobilized fragments of distrust." Obviously, the files do not indicate whether these statements arose from the doctor's sexual fantasies or reflected what really went on in his office.

It is remarkable how little can be found in the literature on the specific consequences of concentration camp imprisonment and life in hiding for women. One exception is the contribution of the Munich gynecologist Gerd Karl Döring to Herberg and Paul's collection of essays on delayed psychological effects, *Psychische Spätschäden*.[45] Almost all women ceased menstruating in concentration camps. In Döring's estimation, this "camp amenorrhea" continued in some 5 percent of all cases even after liberation. Young women, in particular, were likely to experience permanent sterility or frequent miscarriages. D. Klebanow, too, reported frequent premature births and miscarriages, as well as deformities in children of female concentration camp prisoners, evidence of long-lasting damage to the gonads as a result of the imprisonment.[46] Döring wrote of the consequences of sterility for former concentration camp inmates:

These are often women whose children were murdered in the camps, and who were then also robbed of the possibility of ever becoming pregnant again. Especially those women on whom forced sterilization was performed tend toward severe psychological disturbances . . . Added to this is the fact that feelings of inadequacy due to unwanted sterility weigh more heavily on people who have a generally very positive attitude toward children, as tends to be the case among Jewish women in general.[47]

Aside from forced sterilization and abortion for racial reasons, which affected mainly Jewish women and non-Jewish Poles and Gypsies, X-ray castrations were performed on women in concentration camps, as well as the infamous experiments with injections of tissue-damaging formalin solutions into the uterus.[48] In general, children born in concentration camps were taken from their mothers immediately after birth and killed. Survivors report that prisoners killed their newborns themselves in order to save at least the mothers from the gas chambers. Life in hiding also meant privations, especially for women when they had to give birth in cellars, barns, and the like without midwives or medical assistance or the necessary hygiene.

Rape in the concentration camps is barely discussed to this day, and it was almost never mentioned in the evaluations. Women left it out of their reparations applications to prevent anyone finding out about it. They seldom admitted it to their lawyers.[49] Krystal and Niederland reported on eight women who spoke of rapes in a targeted questioning of a large group of patients. These women were among the most severely psychologically ill in the group.[50]

Relatively little has been written on the psychological consequences of forced sterilization, since women who had undergone forced sterilization only received reparations under the BEG if they could prove they had been so maimed for racial reasons, rather than for legal, supposedly medical reasons. Von Baeyer, Häfner, and Kisker reported on seven Gypsy and colored women (*Mischlinge*, or half-castes) who were victims of forced sterilization, nearly all of whom suffered from depression and frigidity. Like the other authors, Kisker called for assessing the psychological damage suffered through forced sterilization as a 25 percent reduction in earning capacity.[51] This makes his attitude in the case of Frau A. even more puzzling.

Chapter 5

Taking Stock

Reparations—The Final Act

With Chancellor Helmut Kohl's visit to Bitburg and President Richard von Weizsäcker's 1985 speech on the fortieth anniversary of the end of the war, Germany appeared to have achieved what Ludwig Erhard had hoped for in 1965: the end of the postwar period. Germans could finally "step out of the shadow of the Third Reich."[1]

Reparations were to have ended in 1965 with the BEG Final Law, and many Germans hoped that the victims would finally leave Germany in peace. But this desired peace was constantly disturbed by the persecutees' associations, although they were unable to achieve another revision of the law (to date, there have been over twenty revisions of the financial compensation law for ethnic German expellees from eastern Europe). In 1973, the Organization of Victims of the Nazi Regime (VVN) proposed a reform that included elimination of § 6, para. 1, no. 2 (providing for exclusion from the reparations program for "fighting against the free democratic basic order"), lifting of application deadlines, extension of the "concentration camp assumption" to all forms of imprisonment and life in hiding, eliminating the possibility of refuting the "concentration camp assumption," and reparations for forced sterilization.[2] The proposal was not considered by the Bundestag. A proposed reform by the German Society of Lawyers of § 150 of the BEG, which would—albeit insufficiently—have regulated the claims of persecutees from the same eastern European areas from which ethnic Germans were expelled after the war, was rejected by the Bundestag petition committee on 7 August 1974.[3]

In May 1974, Chancellor Helmut Schmidt stated, in response to demands for reform raised by persecutees' organizations, that legislation on the complex of issues involving German responsibility for the consequences of the war was to be considered closed; the federal government, he said, had so far paid out 220 billion marks because of this responsibility, but saw no possibility of "imposing further burdens on taxpayers." In late 1974, an SPD deputy, Rudolf Schöfberger, directed a question at the governing party based on a resolution passed by the Association of Bavarian Persecutee Organizations. It criticized the fact that people who had served the criminal Nazi regime to the very end were generously granted positions and pensions, while some victims of persecution or their survivors lived in the bitterest poverty; that the situation of many victims of Nazism with reparations claims was deplorable and scandalous; and that, in an act of unacceptable discrimination, a final law on reparations had been passed years earlier, while no such final law had been adopted for war veterans—instead, the laws with respect to them had been amended.

An undersecretary in the federal Ministry of Finance, Haehser, denied the allegations but promised to look into the possibility of limiting unavoidable hardships. In a report on all questions involving legislation on the consequences of the war, issued on 9 April 1976, the ministry determined that no further measures were necessary to compensate victims of Nazism. In regard to these various attempts to change things even after adoption of the Final Law, the federal Ministry of Finance calculated that "the activities of the associations lack the strength and backing they had enjoyed in earlier years."[4] The Claims Conference made yet another unsuccessful attempt on 19 October 1978, when it again approached the federal government asking for a reform of § 150 of the BEG.[5]

In the early 1980s, after a number of attempts on the part of the persecutees' organizations, the federal government finally agreed to create hardship funds. On 3 October 1980, a fund of 400 million DM was transferred to the Claims Conference, earmarked for Jewish victims of persecution who had emigrated to western countries after 1965 and did not fulfill the residency and deadline requirements of the BEG. This fund could disburse one-time assistance of up to 5,000 DM.[6] This was followed on 26 August 1981 by the establishment of a 100 million DM hardship fund for non-Jewish victims of persecution, of which 80 million DM was administered by the Cologne regional commissioner and 20 million by the Finance Ministry.[7] This fund disbursed one-time assistance payments of up to 5,000 DM, mainly to former fighters for Republican Spain, and after 1965 to victims of political persecution from East Germany and other eastern European countries, as well as Gypsies.

The 20 million DM fund administered by the Finance Ministry, known as the "reparations disposition fund," provided ongoing support to victims of persecution who had suffered extraordinarily severe harm (meaning a long period in a concentration camp) and were in serious need—that is, people who could not earn a living. Allocation of support from the 80 million DM fund was determined exclusively by the Cologne regional commissioner and handled very restrictively. The Finance Ministry, in contrast, controlled the disposition fund with the help of an advisory board, half of whose members were from persecutees' groups, appointed at the recommendation of the Bundestag. The board had no decision-making power, however; it could merely make recommendations. Since 1980, on the basis of an executive order, victims of forced sterilization may also receive a one-time payment of 5,000 DM.[8]

Many of the ongoing trials in reparations cases involve denial of survivors' pensions. Under BEG § 41, relatives of a victim of persecution have the right to survivors' pensions if the person involved died as a result of harm to body or health. Many of these survivors are widows or widowers who spent years caring for their sick spouses; they often have no incomes or pensions of their own, making them dependent on survivors' benefits. Most assumed that they would have no trouble receiving such a pension, and experienced a rude awakening when the pension was denied because, supposedly, no connection existed between the relative's death and the persecution-related harm. As with the determination of health damage in the living, the machinery of examination and evaluating once again had to be set in motion. The deceased was dissected, as it were, in file form; his or her various ailments were carefully broken down, classified, and commented upon, and an investigation was made into which one had caused death and whether it had been persecution-induced or non-persecution-induced. The following is a case in point.

Herr Z. spent six years in various concentration camps, starting at the age of sixteen. As a result of a blow from a gun butt to the back of his head and a subsequent mastoidectomy, he suffered from a right-handed facial palsy. After liberation from Buchenwald, he contracted typhus and typhoid fever and spent months in various Bavarian hospitals. In 1947, Herr Z. went to Poland to look for relatives. Only a sister and a cousin had survived the mass murder. In Poland, he had to be treated for the first time for heart problems and high blood pressure. In 1957, he emigrated to Israel and applied to the Bavarian state reparations office in Munich for reparations. In 1961, for the first time, he experienced attacks of cramping on his left side (Jackson attacks) as a result of the cranial trauma suffered in the concentration camp.

Following several rejections by a number of evaluators, the reparations office finally acknowledged an uprooting depression, posttraumatic attacks, and mid-range hardness of hearing in the right ear as persecution-induced, causing a reduction in earning capacity of 60–69 percent. Herr Z.'s high blood pressure and indications of coronary disease, the existence of which had already been established at the time, were not considered. In subsequent years, his health gradually worsened; during numerous stays at health spas, doctors measured extremely high blood pressure, and Herr Z. had to be hospitalized repeatedly for worsening left ventricular failure and attacks of cramping. In 1982, he was hospitalized in Berlin's Wenckebach Hospital for combined right and left ventricular failure and a lung inflammation. He suffered septic shock with paralytic ileus and was temporarily placed on a respirator in intensive care. In addition, chronic kidney failure and toxic liver damage were found, resulting from years of treatment with drugs for cramping attacks.

Herr Z. was discharged in improved condition; however, only two months later, he was admitted to St. Theresa Hospital in Bad Kissingen for increasing difficulty breathing due to heart failure. Three weeks later, he died there suddenly at fifty-nine. Doctors suspected a pulmonary embolism or heart attack.

The Bavarian reparations office denied an application by Herr Z.'s widow for a survivor's pension; according to Dr. W. Fiolka of the office's medical service, a connection between the persecution-induced ailments and the death was unlikely. Frau Z. brought suit in a Munich court and submitted reports by two internists and a neurologist, doctors who had treated Herr Z. for years and knew him well. They concluded that, given his history of severe persecution, the serious illnesses suffered by Herr Z. since the persecution, and the relatively high recognized reduction in earning capacity of 60–69 percent, a causal connection existed as required under the BEG. Under BEG § 41a, a right to a survivor's pension existed even without a connection between the death and the persecution, as long as a persecution-induced reduction in earning capacity of at least 70 percent was present. Thus, had Herr Z. been granted a single percentage point more of reduction in earning capacity during his lifetime, his widow would have been spared the entire dispute.

In contrast, in an evaluation on 26 February 1985, the court-appointed physician, Professor G. Riecker, director of the First Medical Clinic of the Grosshadern Clinic of Munich University, emphasized that Herr Z. had died of the effects of coronary disease based on high blood pressure. The first reference to this ailment, however, was found in documents after 1962; therefore, said the doctor, no close temporal connection between the beginning of the illness and the persecution had existed. Instead, he said, it was a case of the "fateful course" of a coronary disease, worsened by "persecution-independent risk factors" such as nicotine consumption, high blood pressure, and diabetes. This diagnosis was based on the fact that, according to one of the health spas he visited, Herr Z. sometimes smoked two cigarettes a day, and that he had been found to have mild diabetes three years before his death.

In a supplementary evaluation on 30 June 1986, Professor Riecker also denied a connection between the medication-induced liver ailment and the acute worsening of Herr Z.'s cardiac condition. The doctor also found it irrelevant that one of the medications prescribed for his cramping attacks had a damaging effect on the heart. Riecker, one of the leading

West German cardiologists, backed up his report with numerous allusions to the literature, including the controversial literature on the connections between persecution and arteriosclerosis; he gave preference to authors who found only a limited connection or none whatsoever. He then separated out Herr Z.'s "non-persecution-induced" cardiac ailment from the overall context of his complex of serious ailments and labeled it the sole cause of death.

Meanwhile, the widow's lawyer had gone to Poland and obtained an affidavit, which he submitted to the court, from the doctor who had treated Herr Z. after the war. It showed that Herr Z. had suffered from high blood pressure and stenocardiac ailments directly following the period of persecution. The court refused to wait for a further private evaluation by a respected Swiss internist and psychosomatics expert. At the time this book was written, Frau Z. had to appeal to a higher court, and no end to the case was in sight. Frau Z., who had cared for her husband for years and lived on his pension, now earned a living, at her advanced age, working in a hotel.[9]

In 1985, twenty years after adoption of the BEG Final Law, the Green Party in the Bundestag and in some state parliaments succeeded in bringing public attention to bear on the forgotten victims of Nazism who had never received reparations. On 7 November 1985, the Bundestag for the first time debated the situation of persecuted Gypsies and the continuing discrimination they faced.[10] However, even the mere consideration of a draft law, dated 17 October 1985, submitted by the Green Party on "Regulation of Suitable Support for all Victims of Nazi Persecution in the Period from 1933 to 1945" was postponed. The Central Council of Sinti and Rom (Gypsies) protested that this postponement represented a cynical hope that time would solve the problem.[11] Only the Berlin House of Deputies, at the urging of Berlin's Alternative List, actually created a hardship fund, on 26 June 1986, for those who had never received anything under existing laws; they also called on the Bundestag to expand the scope of the Federal Restitution Law.[12]

At a hearing of persecutees before the Bundestag Internal Affairs Committee on 24 June 1987, at which the spokeswoman of a newly founded Union of People Harmed by Euthanasia and Forced Sterilization had the opportunity to speak, representatives of the governing coalition expressed the customary shock. However, by the time concrete measures were discussed in the Internal Affairs Committee on 3 November 1987 and the Judiciary Committee on 13 January 1988, the shock had apparently worn off; most of the expansions of the law and the hardship fund arrangements that had been hoped for by persecutees' organizations were rejected.[13]

100 Billion DM by the Year 2000

Only fragmentary source material and statistics on reparations have been available until now. No comprehensive statistics were included in the federal Ministry of Finance's multivolume chronicle; they were supposed to appear in a planned seventh volume. Kurt R. Grossman's short history of reparations, published in 1967, contains some statistics, but they are incomplete and sometimes incorrect.[14] The data used in this chapter are based on official statistics from Helene Jacobs' private archive and the scanty figures contained in a federal government report of 31 October 1986.[15]

The tables in appendix B provide data mainly between the time the Federal Supplementary Law went into effect and the time the BEG Final Law took effect; that is, from 1 October 1953 to 17 September 1965. The majority of claims were processed between passage of the Federal Restitution Law and the date the Final Law went into force (from 1 July 1956 to 17 September 1965). The sluggish processing, described repeatedly above, under the Federal Supplementary Law of 1953 is shown in table 3. It indicates that only 20 percent of all claims were processed in the three years before adoption of the Federal Restitution Law.

Tables 3, 4, and 5 provide information on the number of *claims* made, classified by the different types of harm—harm to freedom, harm to life, harm to career advancement, harm to body and health, and so on. They give no information on numbers of claimants, as the same claimant frequently lodged claims for various types of harm.

Nearly three times as many claims were made from abroad as from within Germany (table 3, col. I). This is because Jews who fled Germany and the occupied countries during the Nazi period, or who emigrated after 1945, make up the majority of persecutees entitled to make claims. Only about half of the claims processed by 17 September 1965 were decided positively; one quarter were denied, and another quarter were "otherwise resolved" (table 3, cols. III–V). The latter formulation conceals the fact that many claimants died while their claims were being processed, without ever seeing a penny in reparations. It is noteworthy that claims by persecutees within Germany less frequently had a positive outcome for the persecutees (only 40.4%) and were more frequently denied (38.6%) than those of persecutees living abroad (54.6% confirmed and 22.9% denied).

Another 480,194 claims had been filed by the deadline in the Final Law (see table 4). Processing of 61.6 percent of these had been completed by the end of 1966; of these, 60.6 percent had been recognized, 14.3 percent denied, and 25.1 percent "otherwise resolved."

According to a federal government report of 31 October 1986, a total of 4,405,582 claims had been made by 1 January 1986, of which 4,403,833 had been taken care of and 1,749 were still pending. The federal government report gave no listing of the number of claims according to deadlines, nor did it provide information on other significant issues. We are not told how many claims under the BEG were decided positively and how many were denied, or how many had to be decided in court. Only the number of claims and the amount of payment is given; the number of those who received nothing or spent years in court is not.[16]

Unpublished federal statistics from 1965 demonstrate that the numbers of claims recognized and denied have been very different depending on type of harm; there is also a pronounced difference between foreign and domestic claims. Claims for health and property damage from abroad were recognized with comparative frequency, while similar claims from within the country were denied in the majority of cases (table 5, cols. IV and V). In almost half of all cases (46.4%), claims for health damage from inside Germany were denied, and only about a third (35%) were recognized, whereas half of those from abroad (49%) were recognized and a third (32.4%) denied.

For other types of harm, too, persecutees living in Germany were worse off than those living abroad (table 5, cols. IV and V). Thus for loss of assets, claims from abroad were recognized in 49.3 percent of all cases, but those from within the country in only 26.4 percent; for harm to freedom, 69.3 percent of all cases from abroad were recognized, but only 43.3 percent of those from within the country. Of the three main types of harm (freedom, career, and health damage), claims for health damage were treated the least generously; they were more seldom recognized and more frequently denied.

Disbursements for health damage made up the main share of reparations payments; by 17 September 1965, they constituted around a third of all payments under the BEG, or 6,105,933,000 DM. By 1 January 1986, payments for health damage had increased fivefold, rising to more than half of all payments (table 6, col. 1). Payments for health damage were high because, in comparison with the other types of harm, much more was paid out in ongoing pensions than in one-time capital restitution (cf. table 6, cols. 5 and 8). Most claims involved deprivation of freedom. However, much less was paid for these claims than for harm to health and career because of the extraordinarily low capital restitution of 150 DM per month of imprisonment.

While approximately twice as many claims for career damage from abroad were paid than from within Germany (table 6, cols. 3 and 4), payment in the form of capital restitution to persecutees from abroad was four times as high, and in the form of pensions, five times as high, as to claimants living in Germany (table 6, cols. 6 and 7, 9, and 10). Especially in the area of pensions for career damage, persecutees living abroad, including numerous émigré academics, were compensated at a markedly higher level. The fact that these people, who exercised a certain degree of influence on public opinion in Western countries, were so generously treated led to a degree of gratitude and goodwill toward West Germany. The spokespersons of Jewish organizations, according to Küster, were almost always recipients of these higher pensions for career damage, and "as long as their hearts did not beat for their comrades who did not do as well," they would have "thought themselves ungrateful if they did not praise our reparations."[17]

Not only were persecutees confronted with German bureaucrats to an extent far beyond what should have been reasonably asked of them; they were far too often forced to deal with the German judicial system. Of 2,841,621 cases closed by 17 September 1965 (table 3, col. II), 361,010, or 12.7 percent, were decided in court. The number is derived by adding the 308,853 cases decided by district courts, 49,701 by state appeals courts, and 2,456 by the federal Supreme Court of Appeals (table 7, col. III). If we consider that each persecutee, as a rule, made several claims (deprivation of freedom, health damage, harm to career, etc.), individual persecutees were forced into the courts far more frequently than the figure of 12.7 percent implies. A third of all appeals were dismissed by district courts; almost another third of all cases were settled, and only 10.3 percent of the cases (table 7, cols. IV, V, and VI) were decided in the claimant's favor. When the claimant appealed to a state appeals court (*Oberlandesgericht*; in Berlin, *Kammergericht*), again only 10.1 percent received judgments in their favor, 42.1 percent were dismissed, and 23 percent were settled. When, however, the state reparations authorities appealed a district court decision to the higher court because they considered it too favorable to the persecutee, the decision went in their favor in over a third of all cases (34.4%). This overwhelmingly pro-bureaucracy tendency in the courts was even more apparent in the federal Supreme Court of Appeals, which found in favor of claimants in only 31.9 percent of cases and dismissed their appeals in 51.5 percent of all cases, while deciding in favor of state restitution authorities on appeal in 61.6 percent and dismissing 28.3 percent of all cases (table 7, cols. IV, V, and VI).

In 1965, twelve years after passage of the first nationwide restitution law, the Federal Supplementary Law, 47,249 cases were still pending in district courts, 9,538 in state appeals courts and 341 in the federal Supreme Court of Appeals (table 7, col. II); this provides an indication of how protracted the proceedings were. As late as 1966, every eighth case before the civil law panel of the federal Supreme Court of Appeals was a reparations case.[18] In about 25 percent of the cases, the process ended in the district and state appeals courts with retraction of the appeal or "otherwise" (table 7, col. VII)—that is, not infrequently because of the death of the plaintiff.

In the first twenty years after the end of the war, the Federal Republic paid 28.676 billion DM for reparations (table 8). In the years 1964 and 1965, reparations payments made up 1.9 percent of all public budgetary expenditures. In the fiscal years 1948–57, the entire budgetary expenditure for matters arising out of the war was 196.65 billion DM, of which 6.4 billion DM, or 3.3 percent, was expended on reparations. In the years 1958–66, the total increased to 287.06 billion DM, of which 29.06 billion, or 10.1 percent, went to reparations. Following adoption of the Federal Supplementary Law, the share of reparations in the overall budget for matters arising out of the war tripled; in 1961, it reached a high of 17.1 percent, but it steadily diminished over the succeeding years.[19]

According to federal government estimates, 102.653 billion DM will have been paid out as reparations by the year 2000 (table 8). This considerable sum, emphasized by the government during the debate in the mid 1980s as evidence of the generosity of German payments, tells us nothing, however, about the process of restitution in individual cases.

Domestic Stability and Moral Redemption

On 6 January 1969, the lawyer for a professor of medicine who had fled to Palestine after 1933 wrote to the responsible reparations office: "I must point out here the political effect that a possible denial of the petition would have on medical circles in Israel and the world, especially as the cases known there, such as that of Professor H., have long since been decided in Bonn in his favor."[20] This lawyer knew how to exploit the political constellations.

Petitions and complaints from persecutees piled up at German consulates abroad, especially in the United States. Thus, for example, the German consulate general in Los Angeles urged "special consideration of emigrant groups of especially high intellectual standing," culture workers and academics, who had "a significant share in forming American public opinion on Germany." When the leading U.S. economics magazine *Business Week* directed an inquiry to the German government on the state of German reparations, telephones in Bonn rang off the hook.[21]

The Federal Republic did not pay reparations out of a sense of moral responsibility, but above all for political reasons. Germany's relations with Israel and the Claims Conference were of great significance to its foreign policy. They meshed with U.S. interests in Europe and the Middle East. The Western allies, especially the United States, desired an economically strong, rearmed Germany as a counterweight to the increased influence of the Soviet Union after the defeat of Hitler's Germany. While the Roosevelt administration and its advisors, who included many German emigrants, aimed at depriving the Nazi elite of power through the Nuremberg war crimes and follow-up trials, the hardliners around President Truman stopped denazification in its tracks. The planned proceedings against Deutsche Bank, the financial backbone of the German war machine, never happened.[22] Most of the Wehrmacht generals and state secretaries convicted at Nuremberg were pardoned. Former Nazi colleagues—Globke, Oberländer, Seebohm, and others—met again in the ministries in Bonn. The counterweight to this American-approved reinstallation of the Nazi elite by the Adenauer regime was reparations; the Federal Republic used reparations to buy itself Marshall Plan aid and integration into the Western alliance.

At the same time that talks preliminary to the Hague negotiations with Israel were taking place in 1951, Hitler's bureaucrats were being reintegrated into the civil service under Article 131 of the Basic Law, West Germany's postwar constitution. The World Jewish Congress's 1949 demand that Nazi tendencies in the West German government apparatus be investigated was not echoed in the 1952 Luxembourg Agreement.[23] *Aufbau*'s warning of a creeping renazification of the German bureaucracy went unheeded.[24] The persecutees paid the price: reduction of "denazification" to a farce, loss of power by many of the antifascists installed in key positions in government and society by the Allies in 1945, dismissal of trials against Nazi criminals or failure ever to hold them, pardons of convicted criminals, and the fact that emigrants who had returned to Germany left the country again, horrified and resigned. Reparations were linked, not only with the return of former Nazis to office, but also with the loss of any influence on political developments in Germany by persecutees and their advocates.

To achieve his rearmament aims, Adenauer needed to neutralize the pacifist opposition that brought hundreds of thousands onto the streets in the 1950s, and in which former resistance fighters of all types were involved. The cause of the ban on the Hamburg Organization of Victims of the Nazi Regime was its involvement in collecting signatures for the Stockholm Appeal (demanding prohibition of nuclear weapons) and its participation in a plebiscite against remilitarization in 1950–51.[25] Section 6 of the Federal Restitution Law should be seen in this context. Opponents of armaments and of Adenauer's Cold War politics were denounced as communist-controlled enemies of the democratic order. Former victims of persecution in Germany received reparations only on condition of political restraint—political hush money, as it were.

Reparations thus became not only an instrument of foreign policy but also a way of restabilizing the Federal Republic internally. In 1956, the year the Federal Restitution Law was adopted, the KPD (German Communist party) was outlawed and the first soldiers were drafted into the Bundeswehr. The anticommunist consensus that grew out of the Nazi concept of the Bolshevik enemy went so deep that even a man like Otto Küster failed to protest the clause in the BEG's § 6 that excluded communists from reparations entitlement.[26] Finance Minister Fritz Schäffer told

Aufbau that defense spending had to take precedence over reparations because of the "struggle against Bolshevism."[27]

This restoration affected not only actual and suspected communists; the Auerbach case in 1951 heralded a change in the way in which all victims would be handled. They had enjoyed privileges in the early postwar years, but the trial of Auerbach, who had been one of the DPs' most prominent representatives, was also a figurative trial of hundreds of thousands of DPs in camps in the U.S. zone of Germany. Because the persecutee associations had no further domestic power, owing to Germany's rehabilitation abroad, they could do nothing to prevent this; only the Claims Conference could, through a degree of foreign political pressure, at least insist on adherence to the laws and exercise some influence on the reforms of 1956 and 1965.

Israel received money through the Luxembourg Agreement, restitution of stolen capital to former owners was accomplished relatively rapidly, and the upper classes among the emigrants were granted relatively high compensatory pensions; but the "little people," the politically persecuted, the minorities without a lobby, were exposed to the unreserved spite, pettiness, and coldness of the bureaucracy. The absurd logic of judgments and official decisions, debated in the Bundestag with rare openness in 1954, brings to light this flip side of reparations. At the same time, top representatives of the state, such as the finance minister, spread the subliminal message throughout the population that the reparations program was nothing but a playground for clever lawyers and pension cheats. Ordinary Germans believed that persecutees lied, demanding reparations for harm they had never suffered.

In this atmosphere, German bureaucrats felt empowered to scour each reparations application like police detectives for errors and inconsistencies, and the applicants felt they were being forced to prove their innocence. In casting the German state in the role of the plaintiff and the persecutees in that of defendants or supplicants begging favors, the former Nazis in the government, administration, and judicial system ensured that reparations would not become an accusation directed against them. The reparations process brought to light politically harmful material on German officials, officers, doctors, block leaders, informers, and the like, and they had to avoid the possibility that the victims' reparations trials could become international accusatory forums.

Apart from the atmospheric aspect—the spirit of reparations—the restitution law and its implementing regulations were designed to make the lives of the claimants difficult. The law, with its wealth of clauses, grounds for exclusion, deadlines, and harassing demands, was structured to allow the state, while acting the part of the kind philanthropist, to cut and slash its benefits to the point of unrecognizability, ultimately leaving a complicated system of settlements, minimum pensions, and hardship funds. After what were often years of running the gauntlet between legal clauses, rules, doctors, and bureaucrats, many persecutees were so intimidated that they were willing to accept even the most minimal settlements.

The system of individual reparations was completely uneconomical. It cost the Federal Republic an enormous expenditure of personnel and administration for both the reparations offices and the judicial system, which had to deal with thousands of appeals. Would it not have been in the state's interest to pay lump sums to the persecutees' organizations, which could then have distributed the money among their members? The persecutee organizations and the German politicians and lawyers interested in reparations had drafted the system of individual reparations in the 1950s, when they had seen it as the only possibility of legally obligating the Federal Republic to pay reparations. In retrospect, lump sums would have been far less than the amounts actually paid out, and they might have been more justly distributed.

However, the existing system fitted in well with the state's interests, as it divided and isolated the victims. And by placing management and distribution of the funds in the hands of its own bureaucrats, judges, and doctors, it subjected the victims to a ritual of subservience, determined their entitlement to reparations according to its own whim and political opportunism, and forced them into the role of supplicants.

Nevertheless, it was the gratitude of these very victims that helped deaden the German conscience, against a background of self-pity, finger-pointing, and accusations. The victims permitted their former persecutors to be transformed relatively rapidly, and without any apparent disjunction, into their benefactors. Ernst Féaux de la Croix provided rare insight into this type of post-Nazi psychology when he wrote:

Would not any society sooner or later break down if it believed it could exist without honor and decency? Anyone who answers yes to this question must realize that the Hague Treaties brought the German people precisely that which is actually invaluable and of immeasurably great worth: the feeling of behaving decently. Wrongs were done among the German people; some are guilty, and many shared responsibility through their political failure and shortsightedness. Must not an *inwardly pure* [emphasis in original] person find it an unspeakable relief that, with the Hague Treaties, the victims receive at least material assistance from the German people? . . . We can thus justly speak of the morally self-redemptive significance of the Hague Treaties for the German people.[28]

The Machinery of Examining and Evaluating

For all types of harm, the procedural regulations, examination and decision methods of the evaluators, and the slow machinery of the judicial system, formed a complex and very effective system with which to deflect claims. These were most complicated, however, for health damage. The key positions in this system were occupied by doctors. Wrapped in the mantle of the helper and healer, they held a power that generally concealed their social function. For practical and clinical doctors, this mantle might have been justified, but in the role of the evaluator—be it as court-appointed medical expert or examining doctor for the health, pension, or accident insurance authorities, the war victims' benefits system, or the reparations offices—the physician functioned not as the patient's advocate, but as an extension of the state. The oft-emphasized relationship of trust between doctor and patient turned into mutual distrust. This conflict was greater in reparations, because the doctors who were supposed to investigate and judge restitution claims faced the persecutees as representatives of the very state that had only recently tormented, maimed, and plundered them. For this reason, many persecutees refused to subject themselves to reparations proceedings.

German embassy officials abroad had good reasons for appointing mainly Jewish émigré doctors from Germany, who had themselves suffered persecution and who understood the German insurance and medical evaluation system, as medical experts for the reparations examinations. It is understandable that some of the emigrants thus called upon were reluctant, aware of the contradictory role they would be playing. Asked by the German embassy in Paris whether he would make himself available to conduct examinations under the reparations laws, Dr. Kaplan at first answered: "What are you trying to repair? There is nothing to repair!"[29]

Some resolved the conflict by unreservedly taking the victims' side, which led to constant battles with the German authorities. Others resolved it by judging restrictively, in order not to be suspected of bias. Neither did the persecutees a service. The former soon had a reputation among reparations offices and courts that made their evaluations worthless; the "harsher" doctors were willingly accepted by the authorities, but failed to do justice to the victims. (Both attitudes, and the corresponding responses to their evaluations, could also be found among some doctors in Germany.)

The ideal evaluating doctor, to the authorities, was one with a balanced number of approvals and denials. In addition, he had to be familiar with the prescribed medical evaluation system, completely master the complicated game of subdivision and calculation of the reduction in earning capacity applicable to each separate ailment and the "persecution-induced portion," and be able to exploit the legal niceties of the reparations laws. His reports had to be watertight on the law and the insurance aspects if they were to carry weight with the authorities or courts. Few doctors fulfilled these requirements; reparations evaluation was a "science" all its own, not taught in colleges or clinical practice.

Moreover, the evaluators could not show any apparent identification with the victims' sufferings; they had to avoid any indication that would have allowed the authorities to consider them biased. That is, they had to remain "objective"—to be experts making "objective findings" rather than basing their findings too heavily on the claimants' "subjective information." Given the abyss of misery that doctors encountered in the former concentration camp prisoners, such an objective, purely observant attitude was difficult to uphold. But spontaneous reactions such as horror, indignation, or sympathy could not be reflected in the evaluations. The dimensions of cruelty and pain surpassed the doctors' own imaginings, and in the face of such dimensions, traditional norms of medical behavior, the normal range of medical concepts, were useless. The doctor had either to enter the victim's world, leaving the secure foundations of his own world behind, or he had to distance himself and coolly take account of the suffering and the crimes as possible etiological factors in a sickness—just as he did all the time with other findings, laboratory results, and the like.

After 1945, German doctors—apart from some exceptions—did not deal with survivors' ailments, ignoring the relevant foreign studies for nearly two decades. As examiners, they made it difficult for survivors to have their suffering acknowledged. The law played into their hands. It did not provide for free choice of doctor, and it demanded individual proof of connection to persecution, the breakdown of the person into his or her separate organs, and largely arbitrary estimates of a "vMdE," bringing with it the fateful, endless battle of the evaluators. The "concentration camp assumption," intended to end the absurd bureaucratic game of percentages-of-percentages once and for all, came too late and applied only to a limited class of people.

From the dossiers available and case studies in the literature, we can summarize the doctors' distancing and denial methods, utilized alternatively and in combination, as follows:

1. Sicknesses were generally hereditary or the result of age, largely independent of outside influences.

2. If an exogenous cause was a possibility, in case of doubt it was attributable to something other than persecution: a pathogenic family milieu, an unfavorable marginal group milieu, the hardships of the postwar years, and the like.

3. Victims generally exaggerated their ailments and the persecution they suffered; therefore, one could only rely on "objective findings" and not on their subjective information.

4. The victims had suffered no unusual privations, but only "general persecution" or the normal hardships of war.

5. Germans who were not persecuted went through just as much dur-

ing the war, both on the front lines and on the home front, but suffered no psychological damage. It could be no different for the persecutees.

6. "What doesn't kill us, makes us tougher"—people as a rule survive extreme hardship without lasting damage.

7. No one who experienced broad social reintegration after the war—through marriage, career, or group integration—could have suffered harm.

8. The "feebleminded," "unsophisticated," and "primitive" were ill because they were what they were, not because of persecution.

9. Women's ailments were generally an expression of feminine "delicacy" or their "hysterical" tendencies, or a symptom of menopause.

10. For political persecutees, the reparations claim was part of a political struggle against the social order of the Federal Republic.

It is a truism that heredity plays a role in all illnesses. Very few illnesses, however, allow the heredity factor to be identified and quantified. Thus *heredity* is a collective term for something about which very little is known. The fact that this concept was used so frequently in evaluations of persecutees is an expression of a tradition in which, since the late nineteenth century, and especially under the Nazis, comprehensive significance has been attached to hereditary factors in the emergence of disease.

The belief that claimants were generally exaggerating their ailments, so that only objective findings could be trusted, had a similar history, going back to the "pension neurotics" after World War I. In contrast, Walther von Baeyer and others emphasized that practically no actual "pension neurotics" could be found among the persecutees; they were much more likely to downplay or keep silent about their ailments in front of the doctors, in order to avoid reliving the trauma.[30] In traditional German psychiatry, in the words of the textbook author Gerhard Kloos, one is not dependent on "truthful information about subjective symptoms," since "as soon as [the patient] enters the examination room," he or she "is classified in one of the familiar categories."[31]

A particularly drastic example of how "objective findings" were made is shown by an exchange recorded in an examination room by the son of a persecutee; von Baeyer considered it typical enough to publish it in his standard work as a warning against "falsification of the medical expert's collection of experience":

Dr. X: "We have to make a diagnosis; we have no diagnosis."
Frau Y [nervously]: "Wasn't a diagnosis already made?"
Dr. X.: "The one by Dr. Z wasn't a diagnosis at all." [This sentence was repeated six times.]
Frau Y [confused]: "Wasn't I already examined by Dr. Z?"
Dr. X: "He didn't make any diagnosis. He didn't make any diagnosis. Why were you unhappy?"

Frau Y: "For many reasons. We had to leave, suddenly, from one day to the next."
Dr. X: "A lot of people had to do that."
Frau Y: [silent]
Dr. X: "So?"
Frau Y: "We had to flee."
Dr. X: "Did you have a passport?"
Frau Y: "Yes."
Dr. X: "Then you didn't flee, you emigrated normally."
Frau Y [confused]: "But we did flee."
Dr. X: "That wasn't fleeing. What else?"
Frau Y: "My son . . ."
Dr. X [interrupting]: "I'm talking about you, not about your son."
Frau Y [nervously]: "Then I don't remember . . ."
Dr. X: "Then why were you unhappy?"
Frau Y: "My best friend and her whole family . . ." [obviously does not want to say
  that they were murdered].
Dr. X: "I don't want to know what happened to other people, but to you. We're not
  concerned with the others."[32]

Reports by persecutees themselves clearly show that this way of "taking patient history," reminiscent of a police interrogation, was no rarity.[33] The trauma of such an encounter was intensified by the fact that victims were compelled to go from doctor to doctor; thus what the persecutee went through during the first examination was repeated dozens of times. Even if the evaluators who examined the victim had all been well-meaning and the evaluations had been rejected, or new ones demanded, only by the German authorities, retraumatization of the persecutees was an intrinsic part of the procedure. From a psychotherapeutic standpoint, forcing them to repeat their stories over and over to new, strange doctors was tantamount to what would be called malpractice in surgery or internal medicine. The Israeli psychiatrist Hilel Klein reported that some of his patients were so affected by this torture that they fell ill with acute psychosis upon receiving their first check from Germany.[34]

The goal of reparations for health damage should have been alleviation of the pain. Suitable pensions and treatments could accomplish this, but only for victims able to enjoy those payments in time—that is, those who were lucky enough to be recognized in the first go-round and thus avoid the trial and evaluation machinery. And this was also only the case for those who, after being granted a pension, did not then have to fight to receive treatment or, if their ailments worsened, a corresponding rise in pension. The law's aim of healing was perverted by the fact that doctor and hospital costs were covered only for treatment of persecution-induced illness and that, in doubtful cases, a new evaluation was necessary to determine whether such illness was the reason for the treatment. In addition, once a treatment was completed, there was danger that improved health would lead to a lowered pension, which prevented many from even applying for treatments.

The quintessence of reparations was not therapy and healing, but consisted instead of keeping the persecutees in the role of the suffering victim, placing them in pension categories, and measuring lasting harm. If they showed in any way that they could still enjoy and participate in life, this was held against them and reduced their pensions. To be worthy of reparations, a person had to be completely broken, practically unable to walk or stand erect. Hilel Klein termed this expectation that they remain "eternal victims," which he considered inherent in the restitution process, Hitler's retrospective triumph.[35] It must be asked why no fundamental restructuring was undertaken of a process that individualized and hierarchized the victims, hindered medical treatment, and made resocialization more difficult. An enormous government bureaucracy and, where the evaluators were concerned, a paragovernmental bureaucracy as well, turned reparations into a second persecution for many. Renewed suffering could have been prevented by granting a sufficient pension, based on a broad "assumption of persecution," and permitting free choice of examining doctors, or at least choice from a prescribed list. However, the German medical profession, which had been more nazified than almost any other profession, could not have been expected to treat those harmed by persecution with goodwill and helpfulness. Every type of restitution granted the victims was tantamount to an admission of guilt. In the confrontation with the victims—living accusations, witnesses to murder and torture—German doctors denied the crimes that had been committed. The way in which the doctors dealt with the victims as evaluators obviously served to deflect their own guilt.

Kurt Eissler believes that the origins of these doctors' hostility toward the victims lay in a general contempt for suffering handed down from heathen times. In his view, these feelings had been largely repressed and made taboo, as they contrasted crassly with ethical values inherited from the humanist tradition.[36] In the twelve years of the Third Reich, contempt for suffering and weakness was resurrected as a desirable attitude. This neither began abruptly in 1933 nor ended in 1945. The treatment of the surviving victims of Nazi terror demonstrated the state of the German medical profession. Medical professionals had helped create the social Darwinist, racist policies of the Nazi state toward those considered "inferior," and they had implemented or silently condoned mass sterilization and the euthanasia murders; they continued their battle against the "inferior" as restitution evaluators after 1945, with the help of a small-minded bureaucracy and on the basis of a halfhearted law.

However, the balance sheet was not entirely negative. A minority of German evaluating doctors did see the misery of the persecutees as a moral challenge and broke with the prevailing medical view, as well as with the unfortunate tradition that doctors existed above all to serve the state. This was a considerable achievement at a time when dealing with Nazism was much more of a societal taboo, especially in the medical profession, than it is today. The courage of the few, and the pressure of international experts, made inroads into the indifferent or hostile denial of the majority and forced a liberalization of jurisprudence. Even though few know even today about survivors' syndrome, and its significance for an alternative concept of illness has yet to be grasped, several conclusions may be drawn. After World War I, the German medical profession reacted to the social crisis resulting from the war with a rigorous policy against victims of war and social misery. The fight against "pension neurotics" was followed by policies that institutionalized, forcibly sterilized, and ultimately exterminated the weak and "useless." After World War II, however, an active minority of German doctors came to different conclusions. Their advocacy for the survivors of genocide opened up more hopeful prospects. Perhaps their reception could be the beginning of a new view of medicine as something to be conducted for the benefit of, rather than against, the weak—if this is conceivable in light of the current resurgence of social Darwinism.

Still, a 1982 study by von Baeyer and W. Binder, *Endomorphe Psychosen bei Verfolgten* (Endomorphic Psychoses in Persecutees), financed by the Ministry of the Interior, gives cause for skepticism. Von Baeyer is a founding member of the Eighth Psychobiological Committee of Experts of the Safety Commission of the Ministry of the Interior. This committee deals with the "psychophysical effects of catastrophes, the events of war, and other massive, extreme stress."[37] Von Baeyer sat on this committee with, among others, the former Nazi forensic and military defense psychiatrist Max Mikorey, a specialist in early diagnosis and prevention of panic.[38] In his study, made for the committee, von Baeyer analyzed his extensive patient files and evaluations of persecutees, looking at the extent to which a relationship existed between persecution trauma and later emergence of endogenous psychosis. Forty-four percent of the psychoses, the study found, were caused in part by persecution. In scientifically hedged language, von Baeyer and Binder informed their clients that psychosis could also be expected to emerge after "future extreme stress."[39] Shortly after completion of von Baeyer and Binder's study, the Federal Ministry of the Interior began stockpiling large stores of psychiatric drugs, such as Valium and haloperidol, to sedate those who might lose their nerve during future disasters (that is, war).[40] In the context of such disaster or war medicine, von Baeyer and Binder's 1982 study, although apparently neutral at first glance, takes on a different quality from the writings of the active minority of pro-reparations doctors in the 1950s and 1960s. Here the survival of the persecutees takes on the retrospective character of a large-scale scientific experiment. Even before the last reparations cases have been closed, the architects of future disasters are gathering data for operational plans to control psychological reactions among the public, using knowledge of the suffering that hundreds of thousands of survivors were forced to reveal to German authorities.

Making Good Again: Historical and Ethical Questions

Erich H. Loewy

A little while ago I was discussing the trials of some of the former members of the Stasi (the East German secret police) with a German friend and colleague of mine. The whole question of guilt and punishment naturally came up. My friend felt that digging out the truth about the Stasi outrages and bringing those guilty to a speedy, full, and public trial was of great importance for Germany, especially, he said, since Germany had never really come to terms with or fully acknowledged its involvement in the atrocities of the Nazi period. He felt that it was essential for a people to confront the evil committed and to assess the questions of involvement, guilt, and eventual rectification.

Christian Pross's book, published in Germany in 1988 as *Wiedergutmachung: Der Kleinkrieg Gegen die Opfer*, is a work that has ramifications far beyond recounting a shameful (indeed outrageous) episode of history. It is a work that inevitably raises not only historical but also profound social and ethical questions. The remaining historical questions concerning the issues Dr. Pross describes in Germany are only marginally questions of fact: the facts as related in Dr. Pross's book speak quite sufficiently and eloquently for themselves. The historical questions go beyond these facts. They ask, among other things, how people could have done better and why they didn't; whether and where such Nazi influence continues to prevail; and who, besides those named, were involved. They also ask how we can apply what we have learned to the future. Indeed, the future is upon us: the current concern in Germany with some of the outrages committed by the Stasi, the question of involvement and collusion from sometimes unexpected quarters, and the way such information will ultimately be dealt with hearkens back to the immediate post-Nazi period; recent events in the former Yugoslavia, and

Erich H. Loewy, M.D., is professor and Endowed Alumni Association Chair of Bioethics, as well as associate in the Department of Philosophy, at the University of California, Davis.

atrocities that continue to go largely unexamined and almost entirely unpunished, cry out to heaven. The historical questions, just like the ethical questions that arise from them, are however not purely questions one can relate to the German or to the Yugoslav experience. They go far beyond what happened in Germany or Yugoslavia.

The ethical questions are, of course, profound. Grappling with them raises a whole host of related issues, issues that are hardly confined to Germany and the Nazis' treatment of the Jews or Gypsies. Nor are the ethical questions strictly questions of the twentieth century, although the twentieth century has certainly seen some of the worst outrages in history. They are, however, ethical questions that, for many reasons, have been more explicitly and more urgently addressed in this century than ever before. The events provoking such questions are events involving all of us: all of us, in one way or another, have been party to them. Our being "party" to them may be as victims, as active or even as passive members of a society victimizing others, or simply as bystanders watching from afar. Our involvement, furthermore, may, at different times and in different places, be both as victim and as oppressor: aptly so, the prayer "let not the oppressed become the oppressor" is central to every Yom Kippur service. Its lesson, unfortunately, often remains unlearned, even by those praying.

It is not difficult to find the victims this century has produced. Some of them have been continued from other centuries (for victimization is a process as old as history): Native Americans, blacks in America, and women. Others are new victims created by the particular events of this particular century: Armenians in Turkey, victims of Stalinism, Japanese-Americans, Cambodians, Haitians, Palestinians, Central and South Americans, Kurds—there is almost no end! Still others have been recurrent victims; not only the Jews but blacks, Gypsies, and many others. Among the victims, the economic victims of a capitalist society (a society in which profit and individual enterprise have become the highest good) must also be counted.

The word *Wiedergutmachung* is not easy to translate: *rectification, reparation,* and *restitution* all fail to convey the flavor of the verb *Wiedergutmachen* ("to make good again"), which, among other things, and most important, implies a healing process. It is a healing process that, while it cannot eliminate the scars could, by reestablishing lost trust, go far in making these scars almost (but not quite) an unpleasant remembrance of things past. Such a healing process is necessary if societies that have historically harmed or disadvantaged groups within or outside their borders are to live internally and externally in peace, and, perhaps equally important, if they are to regain or maintain their own self-respect.

Wiedergutmachung is not quite restitution: returning wrongfully obtained property is restitution. But returning such property does not reestablish trust, does not truly heal. *Wiedergutmachen* goes beyond restitution. As a necessary condition of "making good again," *Wiedergutmachen* includes an element of restitution: one cannot "make good again" or heal without, where possible, giving back what one has wrongfully taken. But beyond this, to heal or to "make good again" recognizes that specific material goods taken and returned often cannot make up for the damage done. Giving back the material goods that were taken from them to people who have been imprisoned in concentration camps or have had their lives shattered can hardly be considered to be "making good again." Making good again must do all it can to show compassion for the victim, must show the victim that the individual or society has come to realize and now truly feels that "there but for the grace of God (or the accident of genetics) go I."

It is often said that money cannot rectify what was done. There is no question that this is true: one cannot compensate the murdered; one cannot compensate those whose physical and psychological existence was shattered or whose lives were uprooted and distorted. The truth of such a statement does not, however, mean that monetary compensation cannot at least help ameliorate the pain and suffering, nor that those who are responsible are not obligated to do their utmost to provide fair compensation. While monetary compensation hardly "rectifies" the situation and certainly does not heal, it nevertheless helps in both material and, perhaps of even greater importance in the long run, in symbolic ways. Trying to give just compensation permits those whose lives were seriously affected to at least (and that necessarily only to a limited extent) recoup their material losses. Furthermore, and most important, trying to give just compensation, when properly done, helps in the healing process. When those responsible for causing the damage (or those historically associated with causing it) are themselves willing to apply balm to the wounds they caused, healing will proceed more easily. Scars, often deep and disfiguring scars, will be left; but such scars will be firmer and better healed. It is here, especially, that German *Wiedergutmachung* has (probably irremediably) missed its opportunity: the story Dr. Pross relates is one of a forced and grudging process, a process engaged in, not to truly heal, but so that an "unpleasant problem" could once and for all be gotten out of the way. And just as is the case with the Japanese-American victims of incarceration in the United States during World War II, time and the death of the victims has served to make most (but not yet quite all) of the problem moot.

Fundamentally, restitution or rectification needs to be a worldwide issue if healing is to take place. It would be easy to see the problem as an isolated event: a merely and specifically historical problem that concerns the survivors (both the victims and those who were somehow involved in the victimizing) of the Nazi era while ignoring the wider lessons that this book can teach us. If these wider lessons are not recognized, internalized, and acted upon, then nations and societies that have committed flagrant injustices to their own or to weaker populations over whom they exerted control cannot expect to live in peace.

Survivors of the Nazi era on both sides (victims and perpetrators) are inevitably linked by a common history. It is necessarily, and on both sides, an uneasy linkage. The question of responsibility is often brought up here: after all, there were not only many Germans who looked with horror at these outrages (and some, even if but a few, who actively tried to oppose them) but also others who, while not opposing them, "took no part"; and there are today many more (indeed, the majority) who were either small children or not even born at the time. Responsibility needs to be defined before the question of restitution to the victims of Nazism by the present German state can be answered. It is not a unique question, one confined to the results of the Nazi era. Rather, questions of this sort need to be raised throughout the world: the question of affirmative action in the United States and in South Africa, the Palestinian question, Yugoslavia, and a multitude of other issues. In a broader sense, the same question appropriately needs to be asked when it comes to what exploiting nations owe those whom they have historically and devastatingly exploited.

To hold all Germans (either all Germans who lived during the Nazi period or who are alive today) personally responsible for the outrages that occurred during the Nazi era is obviously absurd. Persons who were not even born, persons who actively opposed the Nazis, persons who were appalled but who did nothing, and even those who simply closed their eyes and refused to see, cannot be thrown into the same historical pot with those who ordered, carried out, or actively condoned the evil.

There are several senses in which the word *responsibility* can be used. I may be causally responsible by having played a greater or lesser role in a causal chain. Responsibility, in this sense, may or may not be culpability. Being involved in a causal chain does not mean willing participation. I may be the driver of a car that skids or whose brakes fail and that, therefore, kills a child. My involvement in the causal chain is beyond doubt, but to hold me culpable under circumstances truly beyond my control is absurd. On the other hand, I may be driving a car and deliberately kill the child, or I may be driving recklessly, drunk, or knowingly with faulty brakes. In that case, I am causally responsible as well as (albeit perhaps to a variable degree) culpable.

To be responsible not only in the sense of causal responsibility but of culpability implies a possible alternative: something I could have done no matter how difficult the doing might have been to break the causal chain. When I could have done things differently or when I could have opposed an action, we can begin to speak of responsibility in the sense of culpability. In that sense, a three-year-old living in Nazi Germany can-not be thought "culpable"; an adult who knew what was going on (and most did) and who failed to in some way oppose it could, in some sense, be held culpable. Even here, matters are far from clear: culpability may or may not be different depending upon the degree of involvement or the proximity of the actor to the act. The person repairing the rails when he knows that, among other trains, the trains to Auschwitz roll over this track may, in the sense of being culpable, be co-responsible with the person who scheduled the trains and the one who operated the gas cham-bers: but while all bear some responsibility, assigning the same degree of guilt to all hardly seems fair. One could, perhaps, argue that part of the difference here is similar to the difference between freedom of action and freedom of will: it is the person who wills the action (in the original German Kantian sense of *Wille* as *Gesetzgebender Wille*, or law-giving will: the will that then determines the person's action) who could be argued to be the most culpable. Such a distinction hardly frees from personal guilt those who did not will the action but who more or less freely participated, but it does state that assigning guilt is hardly an easy matter. Inasmuch as persons knew what was going on and could have done otherwise than they did, they are in some sense implicated not only in acting but in willing such an action.

Responsibility as culpability may be active or passive. The person who knew about Auschwitz and who repaired the rails over which the trains to Auschwitz passed: the person who, knowing about Auschwitz, drew up the train schedule; and the person who operated the gas cham-bers, all were actively involved. To a different degree in each, they "willed the action." Others, who knew of Auschwitz or who at least knew of the rounding up of Jews, of concentration camps, and of the misery caused by the Nazi regime and who failed to protest even when they themselves were not directly involved in the causal chain, may (and in a different sense) be culpable. Here culpability is culpability for not interfering when interference was possible.

Germans who lived as adults in Nazi Germany and failed to in some way resist Nazi atrocities known to them (even if only by speaking out) inevitably made themselves a party to such atrocities, just as Americans who know about racism in America and who fail to speak out or to act make themselves a party to injustice. Germans living in Nazi Germany who actively spoke out took grave risks: they endangered life, limb, and freedom, as well as those of their families. Speaking out against racism in the United States may, at times, be risky: but it is not of the same order of risk as was speaking out in the Nazi state.

If we acknowledge that the Germans living after the war (or those living today) have a responsibility to rectify past historical evils, then the stories recounted in Dr. Pross's work speak eloquently that this responsibility has been largely evaded. It would appear that many government officials implicated in forging or carrying out Nazi policy were the very ones who played a major role in setting the policies that controlled rectification; likewise former Nazi physicians, some actively involved in causing the damage they were now to judge, played a major role in deciding who would and who would not be entitled to help. This resulted in a charade that, far from helping the healing process, rubbed salt into the wounds.

The atrocities committed in Germany by the Nazis were not committed out of context with Germany's history, social setting, and economic realities. Neither the claim that those living there for the most part "knew nothing about what was going on" nor the claim that all those living at the time "were guilty of participating" can be sustained. At the end of the war, the initial attempt to investigate, assign culpability, and digest the monstrous crimes committed was begun, but it was soon deflected by the fear of communism and the beginning and soon the escalation of the Cold War.

Forces similar to those that helped propel Hitler to power served to help hide much of the evil done and even to spirit some of the perpetrators into hiding. Just as Western capital helped build Nazism as a hedge against the perceived threat of communism, Western influence and at times direct intervention helped guide greater and lesser criminals into secure hiding. It is well known that U.S. authorities, in collusion with, at the very least, members of the Catholic church, if not indeed with the Vatican, and often working through safe houses set up in monasteries, actively participated in the escape of some of the more odious Nazis, sometimes through what came to be known as the "rat line" running from Germany via Austria and Italy and sometimes via Spain and Portugal. The ultimate destination was South America, especially Paraguay and Argentina. A number of such Nazis, men who had actively participated in, and some of whom had been responsible for, the barbarism of that era, were used as U.S. agents or, at times, worked for the U.S. scientific establishment. They were placed on U.S. payrolls and enjoyed U.S. protection.[1] A pervasive and often paranoid fear of communism, or of anything conceived as possibly not entirely hostile to communism, helped Hitler gain and initially consolidate power and later helped those guilty of some of the most heinous atrocities to escape. The story of Klaus Barbie, the "Butcher of Lyon," is not unique in this respect.[2]

In the Nazi period itself, the nations of the world largely stood idly by while Hitler persecuted and eventually exterminated Jews, Gypsies, and any other population group that he saw as opposing him. Despite lofty international pronouncements, little assistance was given to these persecuted people. The League of Nations through its High Commissioner for Refugees in 1934 announced that "governments had been induced to postpone or soften admission regulations . . . and some countries of potential permanent residence had been persuaded to lessen restrictions on immigration."[3] But this was pure window dressing: nothing substantial was ever accomplished. The Evian Conference, purportedly called to find a solution to the problem of Jewish refugees and attended by most Western nations, took place in 1938 as the curtain was ready to fall. It, too, not only failed to produce concrete results but, as an article in *Newsweek* stated, the case resulted in "most governments promptly slamming their doors against Jewish refugees."[4] Historically, the Evian Conference showed that: (1) the world was hardly unaware of the deplorable conditions in Nazi Germany and the threat hanging over the Jewish population, and (2) beyond pious platitudes, and although it could have done so, the world was not only quite unwilling to interfere but also quite unwilling to help.

Western nations used every excuse possible to refrain from accepting refugees (especially Jewish refugees) trying to escape. I personally remember consulates telling my family and friends that American "quotas were full," only to find out many years later that the U.S. quota had never been filled except for one year: in fact, from 1933 to 1942, only 45 percent of the quota was actually used. During this entire time, except for regular quota admissions with their families, the United States allowed only 240 children into the country, and those were charged to the quota. Individual consuls had the ultimate power of deciding who would receive visas. Many used their power to keep out as many refugees as they possibly could, or to drag their feet until those trying to enter vanished. Some consuls, unfortunately often in key consulates, were at the very least suspect of being antiforeign if not outright anti-Semitic. Many, many lives were lost because of this maximization of red tape.[5]

Those refugees from Nazi terror who were grudgingly allowed to enter the United States often found hostility and pervasive anti-Semitism rather than welcome: the term "refu-Jew" was coined and much used during this period. Pelley's Silver Shirts, members of the German American Bund, and the Coughlinite Christian Front movement were vocal and active throughout the United States. Persons dressed very similarly to storm troopers, wearing swastika armbands, railed in the streets against the Jewish threat and sometimes engaged in fights with passersby. Father Coughlin, the much-listened-to radio priest who was also the publisher of the rabidly anti-Semitic tabloid *Social Justice*, cleverly used economic fears to rouse latent anti-Semitism. In this he was supported by, among others, the Brooklyn Catholic diocese's weekly paper *Tablet*. The Protestant *Defender* magazine played essentially the same tune. Surveys as late as 1940 showed that one-third of Americans favored anti-Jewish legislation, one-third disapproved, and the rest were neutral. Despite extensive evidence to the contrary, some newspapers and some speeches by many members of Congress continued to warn of the alleged economic threat posed by allowing refugees to enter this country.[6]

I can state from personal experience (fortified by the pertinent literature on the subject) that arriving and living as a refugee in America was a not altogether pleasant experience. Escaping from the Nazis only to watch the rising tide of American Nazism, to be goaded by thugs with swastika armbands, or to read and hear the distorted railings of the right-wing press and radio was bad enough; to be avoided, if not indeed ostracized socially, was worse. It was not, however, merely social isolation. The government itself became suspect when, in 1939, the German ship *St. Louis*, carrying over nine hundred people, was not allowed to discharge passengers in the United States. Almost all of the *St. Louis*'s passengers were refugees from Nazi Germany, and 734 of them would have visas to the United States the moment the quota cleared a few months from then. The passengers on board the *St. Louis*, who were bound for Cuba, where they were to find intermediate sanctuary before being allowed into the United States, were refused entrance even though they held valid transit visas at departure. Despite the pleadings of the German captain, the United States refused to grant temporary asylum to these refugees so that they could subsequently legally enter the country.

Suspicion of the U.S. government's stance deepened when, during the war, the railroad spur into Auschwitz was never bombed and the traffic into the extermination camps was never effectively interfered with, even though the West controlled the air and what was going on was well known. Intervention would have been easy.[7]

When the United States became involved in the war, American citizens of Japanese origin were imprisoned in detention camps while their sons fought gloriously in the U.S. Army. American concentration camps were hardly the same as those of Nazi Germany: people were not beaten, starved to death, or exterminated. Nevertheless, what happened in Nazi Germany and what occurred at the same time in the United States are frighteningly similar. Japanese were imprisoned merely because of their racial heritage: being Japanese, they were suspected of being enemies of the state.

There are many parallels between Germany's experience with making restitution to its victims and the story of the Japanese incarcerated in the United States during World War II. The Japanese in the United States were either Issei or Nisei. Issei were the first generation, born in Japan, who, even when they had been in the United States for a decade, could not become citizens. Nisei were the second generation, born in the United States and citizens by virtue of birth. Most Japanese-Americans lived on the West Coast. The outbreak of the war brought with it a wave of anti-Japanese feeling in this country—not feeling against Japan but hatred of all Japanese on a racial basis. The Japanese suffered insult, assault, and indignity at the hands of the U.S. population. While this persecution was not carried to the extreme of anti-Jewish persecution in Germany, it was based on the same blind hatred of what was labeled as a different race. Newspapers and the airways carried a stream of racial attacks urging America to "herd 'em up, pack 'em off and give 'em the inside room in the badlands. Let 'em be punched, hurt, hungry and dead up against it." Government propaganda intimating sabotage at Pearl Harbor and suggesting that the Japanese in California were ready to sabotage the U.S. war effort did not help ease America's hysteria. Although the Japanese both in the continental United States and in Hawaii were repeatedly accused of disloyalty, sabotage, and spying, no proof of these charges was ever forthcoming; nor were weapons discovered in their homes or on their property except for those used in hunting, or dynamite used for routine earth moving for farming purposes. In the midst of this hysteria, the decision to intern not only the Issei but also their children (who had been born in the United States) swiftly followed.

It was not until 1988 that Congress, against considerable opposition, finally decided that perhaps some *Wiedergutmachung* was in order for the Japanese-Americans: a *Wiedergutmachen* that took the form of giving $20,000 and an apology to each internee left alive. Many internees, of course, had died in the intervening years. And even for those who were still alive, payment was delayed for a few years. Germany is not the only nation in which *Wiedergutmachung* was obfuscated and delayed![8]

Another historically persecuted group in the United States are African-Americans. Before, during, and for some time after the war, blacks in many areas of the United States lived under a restrictive system of near-apartheid. And elsewhere in this country, blacks were treated far from equally to whites. Educational opportunities and jobs were often not open to them and when open, were not open on an equal basis. Blacks could not live where they wanted and were discriminated against in a multitude of tacit and overt ways. During the war a black fighter squadron was finally established, largely to show that "Negroes" couldn't effectively serve in this capacity. Pilots not only served effectively but went on to form a squadron escorting bombers over Germany. They set a record of not losing a single one of their charges. Despite being highly decorated pilots (officers in one of the U.S. Army Air Corps's top fighter squadrons), they could not enter the Officers' Club when they were rotated back "home" to their base for rest: they were, after all, black![9] Although the U.S. armed forces were grudgingly integrated after the war, it was not until the 1960s that any real attempt was made to end overt segregation in civilian life throughout the nation. Today, while legal equality theoretically exists, ghettoization continues and opportunities for blacks remain relatively sparse. Affirmative action, an American attempt at *Wiedergutmachen*, was resisted (and resisted often quite successfully) with a tenacity that equals the German obfuscation of justice. Today it is being steadily dismantled.

Victimization and exploitation are hardly limited to political situations. In the United States today, as well as in the nations that have recently emerged from behind the Iron Curtain, the rate of poverty and homelessness is not only appalling but, at least in the United States, getting worse. This has created a large number of economic victims of a crassly market-oriented system that gives to the wealthy while increasingly denying the poor. It is a state of affairs in which the affluent have gained and maintained their affluence largely by first exploiting and then ignoring those who have been exploited. It is a state of affairs that also cries out for *Wiedergutmachung*, for restitution and for healing.

Neither are victimization and exploitation limited to nations victimizing population groups within their borders. Those of us who live in the more prosperous areas of the world, for example, do so, at least in part, at the expense of those who have been and continue to be exploited. Governments can only pursue policies and carry out programs with the tacit approval of the citizenry. While this holds particularly true in truly democratic societies, it is to a lesser extent (and especially in the long run) true even of dictatorships. No power structure can, over the long haul, pursue policies diametrically opposed to the general will without collapsing. The citizenry, while it need not actively embrace the government's policies, must either not oppose or not really care about them. Among others, it is this truth that underwrites historical guilt, be it in Germany, the United States, the Far East, or anywhere.

One suspects that the population of Germany (like the population of the United States when it comes to affirmative action or restitution for the illegally incarcerated Japanese of World War II) either did not care about or was basically hostile to *Wiedergutmachung*. Not caring, however, easily turns into active opposition when persons, justifiably or not, believe that they will have a price to pay. Many Americans are neutral about (or even pay lip service to) seeing justice done to their fellow citizens; when, however, "doing justice" might involve them in paying a price (be it a money price through increased taxes or a more personal price by giving special opportunities to the historically disadvantaged), their opinions quickly change. In order to be willing to pay a price, not only must one be convinced of the justice of a given course of action, but likewise one must be willing to acknowledge responsibility. This "responsibility" does not have to be culpability; it can be personal, communal, historical, or simply human: if community is to have any meaning, undoing a wrong and healing a wound is a human responsibility. One must, in other words, recognize, acknowledge, and then come to terms with one's own and one's community's history.

It is this that—at least when it comes to the issues that Dr. Pross has so carefully researched and written about—Germany and my native Austria have only lately begun to do. In Germany, this process, and the entire process of "coming to terms" with what has been done, is far more vigorously pursued than it is in Austria. The reasons for this are beyond the scope of this chapter, but they include the incredible fact that following the war, Austria was declared to be an occupied nation, a *victim* of the German Nazis!

In drawing analogies between Germany's guilt and the guilt of other nations, I am hardly relativizing or exculpating either the Nazis or the Germans. The action of the Nazis and the complicity of many Germans cry out to heaven, as does Western complicity with Nazi deeds. I am in no way attempting to justify these actions or to lessen the guilt of the Nazis or of those who went along. My robbing a store is not in any sense justified by my neighbor's holding up a bank. My obligation to try to "make good again" by returning what I made off with, as well as attempting to undo other damage I caused, is not lessened by my neighbor's evasion of this responsibility.

Germans living today have an obligation to "make good again" as far as this is still possible, and this process has lately been gaining momentum. Such a process does not end with material restitution: German attempts to remember the Holocaust by fitting memorials, days of remembrance, and other symbolic actions have gone far in advancing this process. The fact that Germany has advanced this process both materially and symbolically owes much to German historians, journalists, and many others, including the author of this book, who have appealed and continue to appeal to the German conscience. They have appealed successfully in part because they have appealed to a new generation. Germany since the end of World War II has had three distinctly different generations: (1) the generation of the perpetrators, those who, in one way or another, witnessed it—a generation one might call the generation of actors; (2) the generation of their children, a generation one might, with notable exceptions, as a whole classify as one of silence; and (3) the generation of *their* children, a generation one might look upon as that of inquiry. It is this generation on whose ready ears these appeals have fallen. But beyond the German experience, we all must confront the evil committed and the sad fact that each of us is capable of similar actions. We must come to terms with the question of our own national and personal involvement, guilt, and eventual rectification. And we must do what little we personally can do to advance the process of "making good again." Ultimately, the world's peace and prosperity depend upon this process.

Appendix A

Reparations Claim Form

Harm to Body or Health (§§ 28–42 BEG)

Preliminary Remarks!

You will accelerate the processing of your application if you fill out this form *exactly* and *completely* and return it as soon as possible to the restitution authorities.

I. Personal information on the persecutee who suffered harm to body and health:

Family name: .... First name: ....

date of birth: .... place of birth: ....

to (maiden name): .... married on: ....

divorced: .... widowed: ....

Current address: ....

Citizenship prior to persecution: .... today: ....

II. The harm to body and health:

1. What ailments do you ascribe to persecution measures?
   (Exact information on appearance of bodily harm and disruptions it caused to working ability.)

   ....

   ....

   ....

   ....

   ....

   ....

   ....

2. In your view, what special measures of persecution or what persecution-induced circumstances caused the harm? (Provide the time period and precise description of events, indicating evidence.)

....

....

....

....

....

....

....

....

3. a) When did the ailments named in 1 first appear?

Ailment: Time period:

....

....

....

....

....

b) How did the bodily harm become evident?

....

....

....

....

....

....

....

....

....

....

....

4. Are you under a doctor's treatment because of the bodily harm, or were you treated in a hospital (including infirmary or prison hospital)?

From-to	treated by whom or where (address)	ailment	type of treatment

5. What insurance carrier were you a member of?

Prior to persecution: ....

in: ....

During persecution: ....

in: ....

What insurance carrier are you currently a member of? ....

.... in: ....

6. Was an earlier application for treatment and pension made for the bodily harm named in number 1? ....

When and to what office? ....

....

7. What benefits have you received in the past for this bodily harm? ....

....

a) from what office? ....

b) how much? ....

c) what degree of reduction in earning capacity was found due to this bodily harm? ....

8. Have you been evaluated or cared for by a health office, another official office, or at the behest of a social insurance carrier?

In what time period? .... Where? ....

For what reason? ....

9. When, where and because of what illness did you undergo medical treatment or therapy at the expense of health insurance carriers, insurance carriers, agencies, or at your own expense?

....

....

....

10. What illnesses do you suffer from, or what bodily injuries or health damage exists that you do not attribute to persecution?

Description of illness, bodily injury or health damage	Starting when?	Address of doctor or hospital where treated	Address of insurance carrier
....	....	....	....
....	....	....	....
....	....	....	....
....	....	....	....

11. Was an application made for benefits under the Federal Benefits Law? Yes/No. When? ....

To what benefits office? ....

File number: ....

What bodily harm was recognized as damage entitled to benefits? ....

....

....

12. Did you perform army or military service domestically or abroad? Yes/No.

With what military? ....

In what time period? ....

What ailments did you contract during this period? ....

....

....

13. a) Have you made a claim under the provisions of state accident insurance?

If so, to what authority? ....

File number: ....

b) Were you invalided prematurely under social insurance provisions?

Did you make such an application?

If so, when? .... Office: ....

File number: ....

c) Do you have other claims due to damage to health (for example, under private accident insurance)? ....

If so, against whom? ....

Why? ....

....

....

14. Do you possess severely handicapped status? Yes/No.

ID card number: .... Date of issuance: ....

Issuing authority: ....

III. Personal and Economic Situation of the Persecutee: the husband: the parents:

(please cross off if not applicable)

(If the persecutee was a housewife at the start of persecution, the following questions 1 to 3 refer to the husband. For children who had not yet completed schooling or vocational training at the start of persecution, the following questions 1 to 3 refer to the parents.)

1. a) information on education:

Name and type of school	location	attended from-to	Final exams completed? Yes/No

b) Vocational training: ....

Where? ....

When? ....

What final exams completed?

    ....

2. Occupation at beginning of persecution:

    ....

Secondary and volunteer activities at beginning of persecution:

    ....

    ....

For small businesses and self-employment activities:
Number of employees, business type (branch), type of business (retail, wholesale, factory) and extent (turnover) of business:

    ....

    ....

    ....

    ....

    ....

3. Persecutee's average total <u>income</u> (not turnover!) from agriculture and forestry, small business, self-employed and non-self-employed work in the last three years prior to the beginning of the persecution that led to health damage. (If the income in the last three years before the persecution that led to health damage was diminished by prior persecution, please provide the income in the last three years before the diminution.):

from	to	type of gainful employment	name and address of firm	annual or monthly income tax (amount)	responsible tax office and identification number, if known

Please attach evidence (proof of income, tax return, etc.).

IV. If claim is made by heirs:

The persecutee died on .... ,

was pronounced dead on .... ,

has been missing since ....

Heirs are:

Family name	First name	Familial relationship to persecutee (children, widow, etc.)
....	....	....
....	....	....
....	....	....
....	....	....

Please attach proof of inheritance (inheritance certificate, other documents).

V. Remarks: ....

....

....

....

I certify that the above information is correct. I am aware of the consequences of incorrect or misleading responses (§ 7 BEG).

I agree to allow the restitution authorities access to medical documents, patient histories, and examination findings and to request information from doctors and tax authorities.

Subsequent changes in regard to information provided on this questionnaire are to be reported to the restitution authorities or restitution court immediately.

.... , date ....

....
signature

Instructions

for evaluation form in pension procedures under the Federal Law on Restitution for Victims of National Socialist Persecution

1. Under the Federal Law on Restitution for Victims of National Socialist Persecution (BEG), victims of persecution are to receive reparations if they have suffered harm to their bodies or health.

2. As the harmful events already lie a considerable number of years in the past, patient histories play a decisive role in determining individual cases. Therefore, they must be comprehensive. The patient history should provide information on the claimant's family difficulties and on health defects suffered before persecution, and should be especially detailed on the development of the claimed health damage during and after persecution. Precise information on direct effects of persecution, such as abuse, vitamin deficiencies, and other states following malnourishment, and the effects of forced labor and serious psychological hardships are thus absolutely necessary.

   The facts of persecution, as determined by the restitution authorities, to which the damage to body and health can be traced can be seen in the attached documents. It should be the basis for the report. However, should the patient history produce a deviating description of the facts of persecution, **a supplementary evaluation should be issued using this fact situation as a basis.**

3. It is necessary, in the examination to be undertaken here, to determine what damage to body or health has a cause-and-effect relationship to the persecution, in the sense both of emergence and of worsening. In many cases, precise proof of this causal relationship is very difficult, if only because of the long period of time between the time the damage appeared and the examination. It is sufficient to determine a causal relationship between the persecution, on the one hand, and the damage to body and health, on the other, if the causal connection is **probable. The causal relationship is probable if more speaks in its favor than against it. The mere possibility of a relationship is not sufficient; rather, it is necessary, using an objective standard, to determine what makes this possible relationship probable in light of medical and scientific experience.**

   In certain cases, a causal relationship between the health damage and the persecution is assumed. Such an assumption applies when the persecution consisted of deportation or deprivation of freedom and the health damage appeared during the deportation or deprivation of freedom. The assumption also applies if the health damage appeared eight months, at the latest, after the end of the deportation or the deprivation of freedom. The assumption does not apply if it can be convincingly refuted medically.

   Genetically determined ailments can also be considered to have been caused by National Socialist measures, in regard to their emergence, if these were a significant part of the cause.

   Worsening, through violent Nazi measures, of ailments that already existed prior to persecution (whether genetic, infectious, traumatic, or otherwise) is to be viewed as persecution damage depending on the worsening caused by persecution. As the extent of worsening must be determined, it is necessary to inquire more deeply into the extent of the ailment that already existed before persecution and to indicate what reduction in earning capacity exists due to this prior harm. The persecution-induced worsening may not be insignificant; it must have caused a lasting additional impairment of ability or an expectation of this in the future.

   Under the BEG and the implementing regulations still to be enacted, the following possible types of worsening may be distinguished:

   a) **distinguishable (persistent) worsening:**
      This is present when an ailment that existed prior to persecution worsens without the course of the basic ailment being altered. Here the additional illness value caused by the worsening is entitled to restitution. A **temporary** worsening will as a rule be "insignificant" and thus unable to justify a claim for restitution.

   b) **direction-setting worsening:**
      This is present when an ailment existing prior to persecution—regardless of the cause—was found in a certain constant state and, as a result of persecution, led to a progressive worsening in the ailment, that is, to its taking a course other than the one it had taken. This progressiveness does not need to continue until death. For a direction-setting worsening of an earlier ailment, this counts **in its entirety** as persecution damage.

4. In addition to the task of establishing the causality between persecution and damage to body and health, the examination should investigate the **degree** and **period of time** of the impairment of earning capacity. If the persecution-induced impairment of earning capacity reaches 25 percent or more, a pension for bodily harm will be granted. It is essential to determine **all** persecution-induced harm (even if it does not reduce earning capacity) and **any** persecution-induced reduction in earning capacity (even if minor). It is also necessary to determine persecution-induced impairment of earning capacity in the past. Where circumstances permit, therefore, it is requested that information be supplied as to when the first, and thus generally the decisive, cause of the persecution-induced impairment in earning capacity became effective. In providing this information, due regard should be paid, depending on circumstances and the state of the case, to the fact that the impairment in earning capacity may also have varied within the preceding period of time.

5. For the **assessment,** the following points are particularly important:

   a) Clear diagnosis (not list of existing ailments or symptoms).

   b) Estimate of current persecution-induced reduction in earning capacity in general working life (MdE).

   c) Amount of this MdE on 1 November 1953 (deadline).

   The estimated information is absolutely necessary for purposes of pension assessment.

   d) Detailed discussion and justification of whether a causal connection exists between the violent National Socialist measures to be taken into consideration and the established ailment, and if necessary, the estimated amount of the MdE. (Taking a position on all ailments declared by claimant.)

   e) Determination of time of emergence of persecution-induced health damage (estimates of month and year absolutely necessary).

Explanation of b

A basis for the estimate of the MdE caused by an ailment is provided by the brochure issued by the medical division of the Federal Labor Ministry in 1958, "Criteria for Medical Reporting in the Benefits System." The brochure is available from German consulates. The amounts provided in the table in Part D are minimum amounts that can be increased depending on the individual case (brief explanation necessary); estimation of the impairment of earning capacity should be reconciled with the way in which, in general working life, the reduction in earning capacity generally takes effect with health damage of the type present. The occupation practiced before persecution, or occupational training already begun or demonstrably striven for prior to this time, must always be taken into account if they work to the advantage of the persecutee in determining the extent of the MdE.

6. Thorough study of the attached supplementary questionnaire B, in which the persecutee has already provided more detailed information in the course of the restitution application for bodily harm, is advisable before issuing the evaluation.

7. Particularly for a first evaluation, a general examination and record of the ascertained prior history and findings on the attached form is necessary, even if restitution is claimed only for indeterminate organ damage. Supplementary specialist evaluations should be taken account of by the chief evaluator.

8. Expense reports are to be attached in duplicate. Supplementary evaluations, laboratory reports, hospital observations, and all extra medical services are to be reported separately.

[Instruction sheet issued by the restitution authorities for medical evaluators.]

Supplemental questionnaire

for claimants under the Law on Restitution for Victims of National Socialism

A. On the day the law went into force (2 September 1951), were you a member of one of the following parties, associations or institutions? Answer Yes or No!
(Cross-outs do not count as answers)

   1. Socialist Unity Party .... _____

   2. Communist Party .... _____

   3. Democratic Women's Union (DFB) .... _____

   4. Free German Youth (FDJ) .... _____

   5. Cultural Union for the Democratic Renewal of Germany .... _____

   6. Association for Mutual Peasants' Assistance (VdgB), including Peasants' Secretariat .... _____

   7. Peoples' Congress .... _____

   8. Peoples' Council .... _____

   9. Social Assistance .... _____

  10. Committee for Unity and Just Peace .... _____

  11. Social Democratic Action .... _____

  12. Society for German-Soviet Friendship .... _____

  13. All-German Working Group for Agriculture and Forestry .... _____

  14. Committee of Fighters for Peace .... _____

  15. Committee of Young Peace Fighters .... _____

  16. Organization of Victims of the Nazi Regime .... _____

  17. Socialist Reich Party .... _____

  18. So-called "Black Front" (Otto Strasser movement) .... _____

  19. "National Front" (umbrella organization) .... _____

B. On the day this law went into force (2 September 1951), did you belong to the Free German Trade Union Association or its subsidiaries or institutions? .... _____

C. Have you been active as a communist since 2 August 1951, or have you promoted the purposes of communist or other so-called "people's democratic" organizations in any way or belonged to such an organization? .... _____

?_____ , _____ 1952

      place

[Supplemental questionnaire on membership in "anticonstitutional" organizations from the period during which the Berlin State Law of 1951 was in force.]

Appendix B

Tables

Table 1. Settlement of Claims for Harm to Body and Health

	I. Completely resolved	II. Approved	III. Approved by court	IV. Denied	V. Otherwise resolved
383,192 petitions submitted by 31 Dec. 1960	176,897 (46.2%)	80,317 (45.5% of I)	—	65,395 (37% of I)	31,185 (17.6% of I)
550,000 petitions submitted by 31 Dec. 1966	440,000 (80%)	198,000 (45% of I)	83,000 (29.5% of II and III)	159,000 (36.1% of I)	—

Source: Die Beurteilung von Gesundheitsschäden nach Gefangenschaft und Verfolgung, ed. H. J. Herberg (Herford, FRG, 1967), pp. 7f.

Table 2. Ratio of Claim Denials in Health Damage Cases for Each of the Reparations Offices, as of 31 December 1960

Reparations Office	Denial ratio (%)	Reparations Office	Denial ratio (%)
Berlin	15	Lower Saxony	40
Bremen	19	Bavaria	42
Saarland	30	Rhineland-Palatinate	42
Hesse	32	Schleswig-Holstein	54
Hamburg	33	Baden-Württemberg	66
North Rhine–Westphalia	34		

Source: Die Beurteilung von Gesundheitsschäden nach Gefangenschaft und Verfolgung, ed. H. J. Herberg (Herford, FRG, 1967), pp. 7f.

Table 3. **Claims Processed Under the Federal Restitution Law (BEG) of 1956**

	I. All claims, not resolved on 30 June 1956 and made between 1 July 1956 and 17 Sept. 1965	II. Total resolved	III. Total approved	IV. Total denied	V. Total otherwise resolved
Foreign	2,292,504	2,040,569 (89%)	1,113,302 (54.6% of II)	466,413 (22.9% of II)	460,854 (22.6% of II)
In Germany	824,217	801,052 (97.2%)	323,229 (40.4% of II)	309,391 (38.6% of II)	168,432 (21% of II)
Total	3,116,721	2,841,621 (91.2%)	1,436,531 (50.6% of II)	775,804 (27.3% of II)	629,286 (22.1% of II)

Source: Statistischer Bericht Bundesstatistik über Anträge und Entschädigungsleitstungen.
For comparison, under the Federal Supplementary Law of 1953, a total of 1,354,486 claims were submitted between 1 Oct. 1953 and 30 June 1956, of which 272,088, or 20%, were approved.

Table 4. New Claims Under the BEG Final Law, 18 September 1965 to 31 December 1966

I. New claims	II. Resolved	III. Approved	IV. Denied	V. Otherwise resolved	VI. Payments (1,000s of DM)
480,194	295,897 (61.6%)	179,281 (60.6% of II)	42,146 (14.3% of II)	74,470 (25.1% of II)	2,398,788

Sources: Entschädigungsamt Berlin IB 6-0091/59 29.3.1967, PA Jacobs.

Table 5. Settlement of Reparations Cases, 1 July 1956 to 17 September 1965, by Type of Harm

Damages to (in, through)	I. Claims	II. Completely resolved	III. Unresolved	IV. Approved	V. Denied	VI. Otherwise resolved
Outside Germany						
Freedom	788,695	690,495	98,200 (12.4%)	478,622 (69.3% of II)	118,719 (17.2% of II)	93,154 (13.5% of II)
Professional advancement	363,696	342,339	21,357 (5.9%)	231,568 (67.6% of II)	64,434 (18.8% of II)	46,337 (13.6% of II)
Body/health	358,120	293,380	64,740 (18%)	143,806 (49% of II)	94,965 (32.4% of II)	54,609 (18.6% of II)
Assets	226,408	213,359	13,049 (5.8%)	105,247 (49.3% of II)	50,362 (23.6% of II)	57,750 (27.1% of II)
Life	171,840	144,817	27,023 (15.7%)	49,710 (34.3% of II)	52,199 (36% of II)	42,908 (29.7% of II)
Property	157,292	141,564	15,728 (10%)	26,451 (18.7% of II)	45,645 (32.2% of II)	69,468 (49.1%)
Special payments	104,679	99,632	5,047 (4.8%)	38,803 (38.9% of II)	17,227 (17.3% of II)	43,602 (43.8% of II)
Economic advancement	103,509	99,433	4,076 (3.9%)	32,175 (32.4% of II)	18,711 (18.8% of II)	48,547 (48.8% of II)

In Germany

Freedom	134,184	133,022	1,162 (0.8%)	57,635 (43.3% of II)	53,300 (40.1% of II)	22,087 (16.6% of II)
Professional advancement	223,893	218,336	5,557 (2.4%)	122,063 (55.9% of II)	68,886 (31.6% of II)	27,387 (12.5% of II)
Body/health	127,368	122,890	4,478 (3.5%)	43,064 (35% of II)	57,019 (46.4% of II)	22,807 (18.6% of II)
Assets	81,635	78,094	3,541 (4.3%)	20,595 (26.4% of II)	33,696 (43.1% of II)	23,803 (30.5% of II)
Life	50,831	49,790	1,041 (2%)	16,198 (32.5% of II)	21,124 (42.4% of II)	12,468 (25.1% of II)
Property	81,635	78,360	3,275 (4%)	13,289 (17% of II)	37,554 (47.9% of II)	27,517 (35.1% of II)
Special payments	36,884	34,950	1,934 (5.2%)	12,716 (36.4% of II)	11,420 (32.7% of II)	10,814 (30% of II)
Economic advancement	49,255	47,394	1,861 (3.8%)	12,133 (25.6% of II)	18,304 (38.6% of II)	16,957 (35.8% of II)

Source: Bundesstatistik.
Note: For greater clarity, the numerically small number of claims for immediate aid for returnees and hardship compensation has been omitted.

Table 6. Payments from 1 October 1953 to 17 September 1965, by Type of Harm

Damages to (in, through)	Total payments (in 1,000s of DM)	Recognized claims			Payments in the form of capital compensation in 1,000s of DM			Payments in the form of pensions and back pension in 1,000s of DM		
		Total	In Germany	Outside Germany	Total	In Germany	Outside Germany	Total	In Germany	Outside Germany
Freedom	2,602,064 **2,819,000**	536,251	478,622	57,635	2,602,064 **2,819,000**	2,412,458	189,606	—	—	—
Professional advancement	5,746,027 **15,921,000**	353,631	231,568	122,063	2,512,449 **3,238,000**	2,032,064	480,385	3,233,578 **12,683,000**	2,682,175	551,403
Body/health	6,105,933 **30,377,000**	186,870	143,806	43,064	1,923,668 **3,477,000**	1,464,208	459,460	4,182,265 **26,900,000**	3,139,676	1,042,589
Life	1,970,462 **5,877,000**	65,908	49,710	16,198	577,967 **659,000**	457,227	120,740	1,392,495 **5,218,000**	1,014,424	378,071
Assets	471,387 **537,000**									
Property	471,387 **422,000**									
Special payments	282,445 **302,000**									
Economic advancement	97,042 **170,500**									
Total	18,247,571* **59,878,000***									

Sources: Bundesstatistik; boldface figures (payments up to 1 Jan. 1986) from *Bericht der Bundesregierung*, 31 Oct. 1986, pp. 15ff.

* This total includes claims for immediate aid for returnees and hardship compensation, omitted from the payments listed above for the sake of clarity.

Table 7. **Settlement of Cases Before Reparations Courts, 1 October 1953 to 17 September 1965**

	I. Total registered complaints, appeals, and rehearings	II. Case pending	III. Cases resolved	IV. Cases decided in favor of claimant	V. Cases decided against claimant	VI. Cases resolved through settlement	VII. Complaints, rehearings, and appeals withdrawn or resolved for other reasons
District courts	356,102	47,249	308,853	31,783 (10.3% of III)	103,934 (33.7% of III)	90,930 (29.4% of III)	82,209 (26.6% of III)
Appeals courts, total	59,239	9,538	49,701				
Appeals by claimants			44,364	4,496 (10.1% of III)	18,656 (42.1% of III)	10,197 (23% of III)	11,015 (24.8% of III)
Appeals by states			5,337	1,519 (28.5% of III)	1,834 (34.4% of III)	804 (15.1% of III)	1,180 (22% of III)
Federal Supreme Court of Appeals, Total	2,797	341	2,456*				
Second appeals by claimants			1,904	607 (31.9% of III)	981 (51.5% of III)	43 (2.2% of III)	273 (14.3% of III)
Second appeals by states			576	163 (28.3% of III)	355 (61.6% of III)	4 (0.7% of III)	54 (9.4% of III)

Source: Bundesstatistik.
*The discrepancy of 22 between this figure and the total of appeals by claimants and the states is in the official statistics.

Table 8. **Total Reparations Payments (in DM)**

DM	Through 30 Sept. 1965	Through 1 Jan. 1986[b]	Estimated through the year 2000[b]
Under the Federal Reparations Law (BEG)	18,247,571,000[a]	59,878,000,000	82,378,000,000
Under state laws before 30 Sept. 1953 and under state regulations outside the BEG	738,183,145[a]	1,835,000,000	1,935,000,000
Under the Federal Restitution Law	2,540,517,389[a]	3,923,000,000	4,250,000,000
Under the Luxembourg Agreement with Israel and the Claims Conference	3,450,000,000[a]	3,450,000,000	3,450,000,000
Under the general treaties with twelve Western states	1,000,000,000[b]	1,000,000,000	1,000,000,000
Payments under the BWGöD and to the victims of experiments and the like[d]	2,700,000,000[c]	6,500,000,000	9,100,000,000
Final hardship arrangements	—	480,000,000	540,000,000
Total	28,676,271,534	77,060,000,000	102,653,000,000

Sources: Bundesstatistik; Kurt R. Grossmann, *Die Ehrenschuld* (Frankfurt a/M, 1967), pp. 99ff. See also *Bericht der Bundesregierung*, 31 Oct. 1986, p. 18.

[a] *Bundesstatistik.*

[b] *Bericht der Bundesregierung*, pp. 15ff.

[c] Grossmann, *Ehrenschuld*, p. 111.

[d] Payments to victims of experiments resulted from a campaign led from the United States for compensation of victims of medical experiments in the women's concentration camp at Ravensbrück. In 1951, a group of fifty-three Polish women who were former inmates of Ravensbrück had claimed reparations from Germany for this but were turned down, since they had been persecuted because of their nationality, not because of race or for political reasons. In 1958, an American publisher invited these women to the United States for half a year for free medical treatment. A publicity campaign also began in Germany, and the German government thus felt it necessary in 1960 to pay reparations to the victims of Nazi medical experiments around the world. After overcoming diplomatic hurdles (Germany did not yet have diplomatic relations with Poland at the time), and thanks to the intervention of the American lawyer Benjamin Ferencz, seventy-five Polish women also received one-time reparations payments of between $6,500 and $10,000. See Grossmann, *Ehrenschuld*, pp. 99ff, and *Bericht der Bundesregierung*, 31 Oct. 1986, p. 18.

Table 9. **Average Annual Wages and Salaries, Federal Republic of Germany, 1950–1982 (in DM)**

Year	All Industries and Handicrafts	Year	All Industries and Handicrafts*	Year	All Industries and Handicrafts*
1950	3,046	1965	9,336	1980	29,923
1955	4,475	1970	13,841	1982	32,624
1960	6,148	1975	22,063		

Source: Adapted from Volker Berghahn, *Modern Germany*, 2d ed. (New York: Cambridge University Press, 1987), p. 288.

*All workers and employees.

Appendix C

Conferences on Persecution-Induced Health Damage

1954 Paris: Congrès International de la pathologie des deportés. Reports and papers were published in medical journals in France and other countries.

1954 Copenhagen: International Social Medicine Conference on the Pathology of former Deportees and Internees. Proceedings in Max Michel, *Gesundheitsschäden durch Verfolgung und Gefangenschaft und ihre Spätfolgen* (Frankfurt on Main, 1955).

1955 Brussels: Medical conference on the occasion of the International Conference on Legislation on and Rights of Resistance Fighters. A report with the same title (in German) was published by FIR in Vienna in 1956.

1957 Moscow: International Medical Conference on the Therapy, Restoration, and Retraining of War Invalids, Resistance Fighters, and Deportees.

The proceedings of the conferences in Copenhagen and Moscow were published by FIR in three volumes: vol. 1, *Die chronische progressive Asthenie*, ed. FIR (Vienna: FIR, n.d.); vol. 2, *Andere Spätfolgen*, ed. FIR (Vienna: FIR, n.d.), and vol. 3, *Die vorzeitige Vergreisung und ihre Behandlung*, ed. L. F. Fichez and A. Klotz (Vienna: FIR, 1961).

1960 Oslo: Experts Meeting on the Later Effects of Imprisonment and Deportation. A report on this meeting was distributed in manuscript form by the World Veterans' Federation (Paris, 1961); see also H. Paul, "Erforschung der Spätfolgen von Gefangenschaft und Deportierung," *Ärztliche Praxis* 13 (1961): 1565–66.

1961 Lüttich: Third International Medical Conference of the International Federation of Resistance Fighters. There is a report on this in H. Paul, "Progressive Asthenie und vorzeitiges Altern bei Deportierten und Widerstandskämpfern," *Ärztliche Praxis* 13 (1961): 2226–30.

1961 Paris: Colloque consacré aux conséquences pathologiques tardives chez les victimes juives du Nazisme, 20–21 June 1961. *Pathologische Spätfolgen bei den jüdischen Opfern der NS-Verfolgung*, a summary report on this colloquium, in German, was published under the patronage of the Union Mondiale O.S.E., Paris (24 pp.).

1961   Baden-Baden: 77th Assembly of Southwest German Neurologists and Psychiatrists. The afternoon theme of the first day of the conference was permanent harm following Nazi persecution. Proceedings in *Zentralblatt Gesamte Neurologie und Psychiatrie* 163 (1961): 134–36; the presentations were published separately in *Nervenarzt* 32 (1961).

1961   The Hague: "Later Effects of Imprisonment and Deportation," 20–25 November 1961." An international conference organized by the World Veterans' Federation, with the participation of the government of the Netherlands, the International Committee of Military Medicine and Pharmacy, and the World Council for the Welfare of the Blind (190 pp.).

1962   Brussels: First International Doctors' Conference of the Confédération Internationale des Anciens Prisonniers de Guerre (CIAPG), Brussels, 4 November 1962. Proceedings published as *Pathologie der Kriegsgefangenschaft* (Paris: CIAPG, 1963; original reprint, Bad Godesberg: VdH, 1964; not paginated).

1963   Detroit: First Wayne State University Workshop on the Late Sequelae of Massive Psychic Trauma. Theme: Studies of concentration camp survivors.

1964   Detroit: Second Wayne State University Workshop on the Late Sequelae of Massive Psychic Traumatization, 21 February 1964. Theme: Dynamics of posttraumatic symptomatology and character changes.

1964   Bucharest: Fourth International Medical Conference on the Etiology and Therapy of the Consequences of Deportation, Internment, and Life in Hiding, held by the International Federation of Resistance Fighters in cooperation with the Romanian Committee of Former Antifascist Prisoners from 22 to 27 June 1964. A complete 2-volume report of the proceedings was published by FIR.

1964   Cologne: Second International Conference on the Pathology of Imprisonment, held by the Confédération Internationale des Anciens Prisoniers de Guerre (CIAPG) on 6–8 November 1964. Report of proceedings in H. Paul, "Vorzeitige Alterung bei ehemals Gefangenen und Internierten," *Ärztliche Praxis* 17 (1965): 918–24. Persecutees were spoken of here only in passing.

1965   Detroit: The Third Wayne State University Workshop on the Late Sequelae of Massive Psychic Traumatization, 19–20 February 1965. Themes: 1. The psychotherapy and rehabilitation of victims of massive traumatization (especially concentration camp survivors); 2. International problems of forensic psychiatry.

Proceedings of the three Wayne State University workshops in Detroit (1963, 1964, and 1965) were published in *Massive Psychic Trauma*, ed. Henry Krystal (New York, 1968).

1965   New York: Meeting held by the Provisional Committee for the Medical Rehabilitation of Victims of Man-Made Disasters, 7 March 1965. The transcript was photocopied and distributed.

1967   Cologne: International Medico-Legal Symposium. Proceedings in *Die Beurteilung von Gesundheitsschäden nach Gefangenschaft und Verfolgung*, ed. H. J. Herberg (Herford, FRG, 1967).

1969   Düsseldorf: Second International Medico-Legal Conference. Proceedings in *Spätschäden nach Extrembelastungen*, ed. H.J. Herberg (Herford, FRG, 1971).

1970   Paris: Fifth International Medical Congress of the FIR. Proceedings in *Ermüdung und vorzeitiges Altern*, ed. FIR (Leipzig, 1971).

1976   Prague: Sixth International Medical Congress of the FIR. Proceedings in *Mitteilungen der Internationalen Föderation der Widerstandskämpfer—FIR—zu medizinischen und sozialen Rechtsfragen*, no. 13 (1977).

1977   Cologne: Third Interdisciplinary Symposium on the Consequences of Extreme Hardship, Deutsches Dokumentationszentrum für Gesundheitsschäden nach Gefangenschaft und Verfolgung (German Documentation Center for Health Damage after Imprisonment and Persecution), Cologne.

1979   Fourth International Colloquium of the Deutsches Dokumentationszentrum für Gesundheitsschäden nach Gefangenschaft und Verfolgung (German Documentation Center for Health Damage after Imprisonment and Persecution), Cologne, on the current situation of former persecutees and prisoners.

Note: The unpublished presentations at its 1977 and 1979 colloquia can be obtained from the Deutsches Dokumentationszentrum für Gesundheitsschäden nach Gefangenschaft und Verfolgung e.V., Theodor-Heuss-Ring 4, Cologne, Germany

1979   Warsaw: International Medical Symposium on the occasion of the International Year of the Child. Proceedings in *Mitteilungen der Internationalen Föderation der Widerstandskämpfer—FIR—zu medizinischen und sozialen Rechtsfragen*, no. 17 (1980).

1981   Berlin, GDR: International Medical Symposium. Proceedings in *Mitteilungen der Internationalen Föderation der Widerstandskämpfer—FIR—zu medizinischen und sozialen Rechtsfragen* no. 19 (1983).

1985   Balaton Öcet, Hungary: International Medical Symposium of the FIR. Proceedings in *Mitteilungen der Internationalen Föderation der Widerstandskämpfer—FIR—zu medizinischen und sozialen Rechtsfragen* no. 20 (1985).

Notes

Note: Papers cited from the private archives of Helene Jacobs, Attorney Eberhard Fellmer, Dr. S. Pierre Kaplan, and the Hamburg-based Organization of Victims of the Nazi Regime (VVN) can now be found in the Federal Archives in Koblenz, Germany.

Preface to the U.S. Edition

1. Information supplied by an editor at Beck Verlag and by Gerold Küster, Otto Küster's son, who continues to run his father's legal practice and to handle its reparations cases, 6 Mar. 1997.

Preface to the German Edition

1. Berlin Office of Internal Affairs, letter to the author, 29 May 1985, Gesch. Z.I WG 1–0254/71.
2. Dr. Spick, head of the North Rhine–Westphalia state pension office, letter to the author, 29 Mar. 1985.
3. Dr. Spick, head of the North Rhine–Westphalia state pension office, letter to the author, 8 Nov. 1985.
4. *Käte Frankenthal: Der dreifache Fluch: Jüdin, Intellektuelle, Sozialistin,* ed. Stephan Leibfried (Frankfurt on Main, 1981), pp. 260–65.

Chapter 1: Introduction

1. *Der Spiegel* 1957, no. 51, p. 35; 1958, no. 2, p. 9; 1958, no. 5, "Leserbriefe" (Letters to the Editor).
2. Abgeordnetenhaus (House of Deputies), Berlin, Wort-Protokolle des Ausschusses für Inneres, Sicherheit und Ordnung (Records of the Committee for Internal Affairs, Security, and Order), 22d sess., 28 Apr. 1986, statement of Walter Schwarz, pp. 41, 46f.
3. Karl Heinz Roth, "Verstümmelung und Vernichtung im Dritten Reich—ein politischer Skandal seit 1945," in Evangelische Akademie Bad Boll, Protokolldienst 14/84, *Die Bundesrepublik Deutschland und die Opfer des Nationalsozialismus* (proceedings of the 1983 conference) (hereafter cited as Akademie Bad Boll, *Opfer*), pp. 68f.

4. Walter Schwarz, letter to the editor, *Die Zeit*, 1984, no. 44, p. 40.

5. On 14 September 1985, on the fiftieth anniversary of the promulgation of the Nuremberg racial laws, the Greens in the Bundestag held a public meeting of their parliamentary deputies in Bonn. The meeting took the form of a hearing of victims of persecution, in connection with the Greens' proposed law for reparations for all victims. The fact that this event was held on the Saturday before Rosh Hashanah, the Jewish New Year, and that the invited Jewish guests were thus unable to attend, was later judged self-critically as veiled anti-Semitism by a spokesperson for the Bundestag deputies. See Udo Knapp, "Ausschnitte aus der Anhörung der Grünen in Bonn am 14 September 1985," in *Anerkennung und Versorgung aller Opfer nationalsozialistischer Verfolgung*, ed. Die Grünen im Bundestag (Berlin: Fraktion der Alternative Liste, 1986), p. 9.

6. See Roth in Akademie Bad Boll, *Opfer* (cited n. 3 above), pp. 68f.

7. Ibid.

8. Michael Wunder, "Wieder'gut'machung—Bruch oder Kontinuität," in *NS-Opfer—Opfer der Gesellschaft noch heute*, ed. Hamburger Initiative "Anerkennung aller NS-Opfer" (Hamburg, 1986). This essay also appeared under the title "Wiedergutmachung—der Umgang mit den Opfern," in *Dr. med. Mabuse* 11 (1986).

9. Walter Schwarz, letter to the editor, *Die Zeit*, 1984, no. 44, p. 40.

10. Schwarz statement (see n. 2 above), pp. 42, 57.

11. *Die Tageszeitung* (newspaper), 3 Sept. 1987.

12. *Rechtsprechung zum Wiedergutmachungsrecht* (hereafter cited as *RzW*) began in 1949 as a supplement to the legal journal *Neue Juristische Wochenschrift* and ceased publication in 1981.

13. Otto Küster, "Walter Schwarz zum 70. Geburtstag," *RzW* 27 (1976): 1.

14. K. Heßdörfer, "Die Wiedergutmachung nationalsozialistischen Unrechts durch die Bundesrepublik Deutschland," *RzW* 32 (1981): 111.

15. *Die Wiedergutmachung nationalsozialistischen Unrechts durch die Bundesrepublik Deutschland*, ed. Bundesminister der Finanzen (federal minister of finance) in collaboration with Walter Schwarz (hereafter cited as BMF, *Wiedergutmachung*): vol. 1, *Rückerstattung nach den Gesetzen der Alliierten Mächte*, ed. Walter Schwarz (Munich, 1974); vol. 2, *Das Bundesrückerstattungsgesetz*, ed. Friedrich Biella et al. (Munich, 1981); vol. 3, *Der Werdegang des Entschädigungsrechts*, ed. Ernst Féaux de la Croix and Helmut Rumpf (Munich, 1985); vol. 4, *Das Bundesentschädigungsgesetz*, pt. 1, ed. Walter Brunn, Hans Giessler, Heinz Klee, Willibald Maier, and Karl Weiss (Munich, 1981); vol. 5, *Das Bundesentschädigungsgesetz*, pt. 2, ed. Hans Giessler, Otto Gnirs, Richard Hebenstreit, Detlev Kaulbach, Heinz Klee, and Hermann Zorn (Munich, 1983); vol. 6, *Entschädigungsverfahren und sondergesetzliche Entschädigungsregelungen*, ed. Hugo Finke, Otto Gnirs, Gerhard Kraus, and Adolf Pentz (Munich, 1987). The imminent appearance of vol. 7 has been announced for years by the publisher (see Preface to the U.S. edition).

16. Walter Schwarz, letter to the editor, *Die Zeit*, 1984, no. 44, p. 40.

17. Küster quotes Schwarz as saying this in *RzW* 27 (1976): 1.

18. Otto Küster, "Wiedergutmachung: Sprache, Geste, Geist" (MS, written in 1984; hereafter cited as Küster, "Geste und Geist"). This text, after being rejected at first by the Federal Ministry of Finance, is expected to appear in vol. 7 of BMF,

Wiedergutmachung (cited n. 15 above). Schwarz passionately denied to Küster that he wished to express anything like gratitude (Küster, communication to the author, 9 Sept. 1987).

19. Walter Schwarz, "Zum fünfundsiebzigsten Geburtstag von Kurt May," *RzW* 22 (1971): 388; id., "Dem 80jährigen Kurt May," *RzW* 27 (1976): 171; Franz Calvelli-Adorno, "Die Dokumentationsarbeit der URO," *RzW* 16 (1965): 198.

20. Otto Küster, communication to the author, 9 Sept. 1987.

21. Walter Schwarz on Otto Küster, *RzW* 18 (1967): 7.

22. *Freiburger Rundbrief* 7, nos. 25–28 (1954–55): 3. The *Freiburger Rundbrief*, which is still published, first appeared in 1949 "to encourage friendship between the old and the new people of God, in the spirit of both Testaments." Starting with the 6th series in 1953–54, it was called the *Freiburger Rundbrief: Beiträge zur Förderung der Freundschaft zwischen dem alten und dem neuen Gottesvolk im Geiste der beiden Testamente.*

23. See *Freiburger Rundbrief*, esp. 1949–56.

24. Walter Schwarz, "Otto Küster zum Siebzigsten," *RzW* 27 (1976): 207f.

25. Franz Böhm, "Zerfällt die freie Welt oder zerfällt der Kommunismus?" in Franz Böhm, *Reden und Schriften* (Karlsruhe, 1960), pp. 305ff. This volume contains a bibliography of all of Böhm's writings. Wallmann's speech is published, along with others, in *Recht und Gesittung in einer freien Gesellschaft: Zur Erinnerung an Franz Böhm aus Anlaß seines 90. Geburtstages,* ed. Ludwig-Erhard-Stiftung (Frankfurt on Main, 1985).

26. Adolf Arndt, *Politische Reden und Schriften* (Berlin, 1976).

27. Otto Küster, "Grundlinien der deutschen Wiedergutmachung," in Akademie Bad Boll, *Opfer* (cited n. 3 above), pp. 87f.; Walter Schwarz, "Anmerkungen zur Vorlage von Herrn Otto Küster," in ibid., pp. 90f.

28. Martin Hirsch, communication to the author, 28 Apr. 1985.

29. An interesting biography of Fritz Schäffer can be found in the register accompanying Schäffer's files in the Federal Archives.

30. Ernst Klee, *Was sie taten—was sie wurden* (Frankfurt on Main, 1986), pp. 90, 206f.

31. BA B 126/9863, List of organizations joined with the Claims Conference; Nana Sagi, *Wiedergutmachung für Israel: Die deutschen Zahlungen und Leistungen* (Stuttgart, 1981), p. 80.

32. *RzW* 29 (1978): 94f.

33. The German émigré newspaper *Aufbau* was founded in 1934 in New York by émigré journalists from the *Frankfurter Zeitung* and is still published today. Starting in September 1957, it regularly contained a special supplement every two weeks entitled "Die Wiedergutmachung" (Reparations), which reported on the current status of legislation and jurisprudence.

34. Walter Schwarz, "Dem 80jährigen Kurt May," *RzW* 27 (1976): 171f.

35. Archive of the URO in Berlin, files on the decisions of the 13th Civil Panel of the Kammergericht, Kammergericht Berlin 13 U Entsch. 2128/53, 13 U Entsch. 1099/54.

36. Jürgen Flicke, in "Ausschnitte aus der Anhörung der Grünen im Bundestag" (see n. 5 above).

37. Although the Frankfurt URO was formally subordinate to the so-called head office in London, May was the organization's chief executive; he led the

URO with a "wonderfully gentle hand" (Küster, communication to the author, 9 Sept. 1987).

38. Two laudable exceptions were Professor Wilhelm Wengler, Berlin, in the area of restitution, and Professor Ludwig Raiser in Tübingen, who taught a seminar on the original provisions of the occupation laws on restitution of businesses, drafted by the great Jewish legal scholar Max Hachenburg.

39. A. Krackhard-Schönau, book review, "Erfahrungen in der deutschen Wiedergutmachung von Otto Küster," in *RzW* 19 (1968): 159.

40. Otto Küster, "Höchstrichterliche Rechtsprechung zum Wiedergutmachungsrecht," *RzW* 32 (1981): 97.

41. Kurt May, communication to the author, 27 Nov. 1986.

42. The newsletter of the VVN presidium in Frankfurt was called the *Antifaschistische Rundschau*. It appeared monthly. The newsletter put out by the West Berlin VVN was the *Antifaschistisches Magazin* (previously known as *Aktion* and *Der Mahnruf*.). It appeared every three months. The paper of the AvS is *AVS-Info* and is published in Bonn (formerly known as *Die Gemeinschaft* and published in Cologne). The newspapers of the BVN are *Die Mahnung*, published in Berlin, and *Freiheit und Recht* (formerly *Das freie Wort*), published in Düsseldorf.

43. A. Stobwasser, *Die den roten Winkel tragen* (Hamburg, 1983).

44. For a few examples among many, see the archive of the Hamburg VVN, files of E.H., H.R., B.F., L.D., and F.D.

45. Kilian Stein, "Die Benachteiligung von antifaschistischen Widerstandskämpfern in der 'Wiedergutmachung,'" in *Anerkennung und Versorgung* (cited n. 5 above), p. 48.

46. Abgeordnetenhaus (House of Deputies), Berlin, Wort-Protokolle des Ausschusses für Inneres, Sicherheit und Ordnung (Records of the Committee for Internal Affairs, Security, and Order), 22d sess., 9 Apr. 1986.

47. In the 1950s, an organization of victims of forced sterilization, the Interest Association of Those with Physical and Health Damage, was formed, headquartered in Alsdorf-Aachen. It tried in vain, through petitions to the Federal Ministry of Finance, to have all victims of forced sterilization included under the Federal Restitution Law. See AB 126/12545, Eingaben des Interessenverbandes der Körper- und Gesundheitsgeschädigten e.V. an das Bundesfinanzministerium vom 21.2 und 18.5.1954.

48. See report of a victim of forced sterilization, Fritz Niemand, in *Anerkennung und Versorgung* (cited n. 5 above), p. 56; and see also 11th German Bundestag, Innenauschuß, *Auschußdrucksache* 11/8, 15 June 1987, opinion of experts on reparations, opinion of Professor Klaus Dörner, p. 24.

49. The Berlin Alternative List (West Berlin's Green Party) was able, in June 1986, to achieve creation of a hardship fund. See "Fonds für Opfer des Naziregimes," *Volksblatt Berlin*, 27 June 1986; and see also Christian Pross, "Härtefonds für NS-Opfer," in *Biedermann und Schreibtischtäter*, vol. 4 of *Beiträge zur nationalsozialistischen Gesundheits- und Sozialpolitik*, ed. Götz Aly et al. (Berlin, 1987), p. 191.

50. Interview with Federal Finance Minister Fritz Schäffer, in *Deutsche National- und Soldatenzeitung*, 31 Mar. 1963, quoted in Kurt R. Grossmann, *Die Ehrenschuld* (Frankfurt on Main, 1967), p. 89 (hereafter cited as Grossmann, *Eh-*

renschuld); Franz-Josef Strauss, "Wirtschaftliche Auswirkungen politischer Verträge," *Chemische Industrie* 5, no. 1 (1953): 3–6.

51. Küster, "Geste und Geist" (see n. 18 above).

52. Martin Hirsch, communication to the author, 28 Apr. 1985.

53. Hermann Steinitz, "Wiedergutmachung aus der Sicht eines ärztlichen Gutachters in Israel" (MS).

54. BMF, *Wiedergutmachung* (cited n. 15 above), vol. 1, *Rückerstattung nach den Gesetzen der Alliierten Mächte,* ed. Schwarz (hereafter cited as Schwarz, *Rückerstattung*).

55. BMF, *Wiedergutmachung,* vol. 3, *Der Werdegang des Entschädigungsrechts,* ed. Féaux de la Croix and Rumpf (hereafter cited as Féaux de la Croix, *Werdegang*).

56. Ibid., pp. 10f.

57. Ibid., p. 124.

58. Ibid., p. 149.

59. Ibid., pp. 151f. The reference is to Adenauer's declaration on a German admission of guilt, which he made on 27 September 1951 before the Bundestag, ushering in the negotiations on a reparations treaty with Israel.

60. Ibid., p. 158.

61. Ibid., p. 159.

62. Ibid. The deputy head of the German negotiating team at the time, Otto Küster, believed that right-wing German groups could just as easily have been responsible for this attack (Küster, communication to the author, 22 Feb. 1986).

63. BA R 22/3276, pp. 96–100; R 22/3194, pp. 131–166; R 22/2916, pp. 27-38.

64. ZSTAP, film no. 1058 J, Akademie für Deutsches Recht, Rasse, Volk, Staat und Raum in der Begriffs- und Wortbildung, Berlin, June 1938. Féaux de la Croix was also a member of the committee for colonial law and the committee for nationalities law of the Academy of German Law (U.S. National Archives, Washington, D.C., T 82, roll R 23).

65. ZSTAP, Rechnungshof, no. 6584.

66. *Die Bundesrepublik, 1953: Taschenbuch für Verwaltungsbeamte,* 63d year (Cologne, 1953), pp. 44, 47. See also Féaux de la Croix's numerous publications on war-related issues (*Kriegsfolgelasten*), including "Die Problematik der Reichsverbindlichkeiten," in *Juristische Studiengesellschaft Karlsruhe,* 1955, no. 15, pp. 3–21; "Die rechtliche Neuordnung des Reichsvermögens," *Archiv des öffentlichen Rechts* 77 (1951–52): 35–46; and "Betrachtungen zum Londoner Schuldenabkommen," in *Carl Bilfinger zum 75. Geburtstag, Beiträge zum ausländischen öffentlichen Recht und Völkerrecht,* no. 29 (Heidelberg: Max-Planck-Institut für ausländisches öffentliches Recht und Völkerrecht, 1954), pp. 27–70.

Chapter 2: History

1. The text of the law can be found in Weißstein, Riedel, *Kommentar zum Militärregierungsgesetz no. 59 für die amerikanische Zone* (Koblenz: Humanitas-Verlag, 1953), or in the official newsletter of the U.S. Military Government, 10 Nov. 1947.

2. The lawyer Walther Roemer (1902–) was an official in the Bavarian Ministry of Justice after 1945 and in the federal Ministry of Justice after 1949.

3. Schwarz interpreted this as reflecting the southern German state prime ministers' fear of the public reaction, which led them to refrain from signing the law themselves (Schwarz, *Rückerstattung* [cited ch. 1, n. 54, above]), but Küster writes: "The four heads of states forming the southern German council of states were quite willing to enact the experts' draft from the Ministry of Justice as a state council law. It deviated in only a few particulars, open to compromise, from the draft by the advisors to the military government. However, the military government resolved the German attempt to reach unity once and for all; in an act of impatience, it issued its draft as a military government law" (Küster, communication to the author, 9 Sept. 1987).

4. Schwarz, *Rückerstattung*, p. 54.

5. Ibid., pp. 71f.

6. Law on Compensation of Reparations, Restitution, Destruction and Compensation Harm (Reparations Harm Law), *Bundesgesetzblatt* 1969, no. 13, p. 105.

7. Otto Küster, *Erfahrungen in der deutschen Wiedergutmachung* (Tübingen, 1967), pp. 11f. (hereafter cited as Küster, *Erfahrungen*); Martin Hirsch, communication to the author, 28 Apr. 1985; and see also *Die Welt*, 8 Mar. 1965, p. 22.

8. Küster, *Erfahrungen*; Martin Hirsch, "Folgen der Verfolgung, Schädigung—Wiedergutmachung—Rehabilitierung," in Akademie Bad Boll, *Opfer* (cited ch. 1, n. 3, above), pp. 19 f.

9. Schwarz, *Rückerstattung*, p. 385.

10. On this, see BMF, *Wiedergutmachung*, vol. 2, *Das Bundesrückerstattungsgesetz*, ed. Friedrich Biella et al. (Munich, 1981).

11. For the text of the law, see "Gesetz Nr. 951 zur Wiedergutmachung nationalsozialistischen Unrechts vom 16.8.1949," *Regierungsblatt der Regierung Württemberg-Baden* 1949, no. 20, p. 187.

12. Féaux de la Croix, *Werdegang*, p. 37f.

13. "Vertrag zur Regelung aus Krieg und Besatzung entstandener Fragen" (Treaty to Settle Questions Arising from the War and Occupation), pt. 4, excerpted from H. G. van Dam, *Das Bundesentschädigungsgesetz*, pt. 2 (Düsseldorf, 1953), p. 22; cited in Féaux de la Croix, *Werdegang*, p. 130.

14. Féaux de la Croix, *Werdegang*, p. 46.

15. "Gesetz zur Regelung der Wiedergutmachung für Angehörige des Öffentlichen Dienstes vom 11. Mai 1951" (Law to Settle Reparations for Members of the Public Service), in *Bundesentschädigungsgesetz* 2d ed. (Munich: Beck'sche Textausgaben, 1955), pp. 145ff.

16. E. Landau, "Das Fiasko der Entnazifizierung," *Aufbau*, 10 June 1949, p. 25.

17. Hans Dieter Heilmann, "Das Ansehen der Stadt ist langsam wieder im Wachsen begriffen," *Asthetik und Kommunikation*, Dec. 1982, p. 50.

18. Martha Mierendorff, "Wiederverwendung ehemals belasteter Angehöriger des öffentlichen Verwaltungsapparates des NS-Staates" (Reuse of formerly tainted members of the public administrative apparatus of the Nazi state), memorandum, 1 Oct. 1985, in a letter to Berlin AL deputy Hilde Schramm.

19. Grossmann, *Ehrenschuld*, p. 79.

20. Féaux de la Croix, *Werdegang*, p. 151.

21. 2d German Bundestag, 165th sess., 27 Sept. 1951, pp. 6697f. Féaux de la Croix gives the impression that the contents of this declaration had been dictated

to Adenauer by "World Jewry" or the "headquarters of the Jewish organizations" (Féaux de la Croix, *Werdegang*, pp. 151 f.).

22. Kai von Jena, "Versöhnung mit Israel? Die deutsch-israelischen Verhandlungen bis zum Wiedergutmachungsabkommen von 1952," in *Vierteljahreshefte für Zeitgeschichte* 34 (1986): 457–80.

23. Ibid.

24. Féaux de la Croix, *Werdegang*, pp. 151 ff.

25. Von Jena, "Versöhnung mit Israel?"

26. Franz Böhm, *Freiheit und Ordnung in der Marktwirtschaft* (Baden-Baden, 1980), pp. 613ff.

27. BA B 126/51544, Hermann Josef Abs, letter to Chancellor Konrad Adenauer, 22 Feb. 1952.

28. Ibid., Hermann Josef Abs, letter to Finance Minister Fritz Schäffer, 25 Feb. 1952.

29. See Von Jena, "Versöhnung mit Israel?"

30. Grossmann, *Ehrenschuld*, pp. 33, 37.

31. See Böhm, *Freiheit und Ordnung*; Von Jena, "Versöhnung mit Israel?"

32. BA B 126/51544, Undersecretary Alfred Hartmann, letter to Finance Minister Fritz Schäffer, 9 Apr. 1952, and appendices I, II, and III.

33. Féaux de la Croix, *Werdegang*, p. 158. In the Third Reich, Abs played an important part in the "Aryanization" of Jewish property and the plundering of banks in the occupied countries. On this, see O.M.G.U.S., *Ermittlungen gegen die Deutsche Bank, 1946–47* (Investigation of the Deutsche Bank, 1946–47), ed. Karl Heinz Roth (Nördlingen, 1985).

34. BA B 126/51544, Friedrich Bracker, letter to Finance Minister Fritz Schäffer, 21 Feb. 1952.

35. BA B 126/51544, Finance Minister Fritz Schäffer, letter to Undersecretary Westrick of the federal Economics Ministry, 18 Apr. 1952.

36. BA B 126/51544, notes by the director of Dept. II, Dr. Oeftering, on a discussion among Schäffer, Böhm, Küster, and himself, 7 May 1952.

37. Féaux de la Croix, *Werdegang*, pp. 163f.

38. See Böhm, *Freiheit und Ordnung*.

39. Otto Küster, radio address, Süddeutscher Rundfunk, 20 May 1952.

40. Otto Küster, letter to Helene Jacobs, 6 June 1952 (private archive of Helene Jacobs, Berlin; hereafter cited as PA Jacobs).

41. PA Jacobs.

42. Otto Küster, communication to author, 22 Feb. 1986.

43. Finance Minister Fritz Schäffer, radio address, Süddeutschen Rundfunk, Stuttgart, 23 May 1952.

44. BA B 126/51544, Georg Löw, Schwäbisch-Gmünd, letter to Finance Minister Fritz Schäffer, 23 May 1952.

45. BA B 126/51544, L. Hohmeister, Stuttgart, letter to Finance Minister Fritz Schäffer, 23 May 1952.

46. BA B 126/51544, *Ministerialrat* O. Gurski, Dept. V, letter to Finance Minister Fritz Schäffer, 12 May 1952.

47. BA B 126/51544, *Ministerialrat* Magen, Dept. VI, statement of position on the letter cited in n. 46 above, 21 May 1952.

48. BA B 126/51544, Finance Minister Fritz Schäffer, letter to Undersecretary Walter Hallstein, 24 May 1952.

49. See Von Jena, "Versöhnung mit Israel?"

50. Féaux de la Croix, *Werdegang*, p. 164; see also Böhm, *Freiheit und Ordnung*.

51. BA B 126/51544, Assistant Secretary Bernhard Wolff to Finance Minister Fritz Schäffer, 4 July 1952.

52. Ernst Féaux de la Croix, "Gedenkworte für Bernhard Wolff," *RzW* 22 (1971): 3.

53. BA B 126/51544, Finance Minister Fritz Schäffer, letter to Privy Councillor Vocke, 11 July 1952.

54. BA B 126/9863, minutes of cabinet meeting, 11 July 1952.

55. BA B 126/51544, Assistant Secretary Bernhard Wolff, letter to Franz Böhm, 4 July 1952.

56. BA B 126/51544, position of federal Ministry of Finance delegation members on the global claims of the conference delegation, 2 July 1952.

57. BA B 126/9863, excerpts from the short minutes (*Kurzprotokoll*) of the 235th cabinet meeting, 15 July 1952.

58. BA B 126/51544, Chancellor Konrad Adenauer, letters to Finance Minister Fritz Schäffer, 26 July, 5 Aug., and 19 Aug. 1952; Undersecretary Alfred Hartmann, letter to Adenauer, 24 July 1952; Schäffer, letters to Hartmann, 22 Aug. and 30 Aug. 1952.

59. K. R. Grossmann, "Rückerstattung—'loyal' oder aufrichtig?" *Das Freie Wort*, 17 Aug. 1951, p. 8.

60. Franz Böhm, "Schacht betreibt private Außenpolitik," *Frankfurter Rundschau*, 19 Dec. 1952.

61. Féaux de la Croix, *Werdegang*, p. 172.

62. *Welt am Sonntag*, 23 Nov. 1952.

63. See Böhm, "Schacht betreibt private Außenpolitik."

64. Franz-Josef Strauss, "Wirtschaftliche Auswirkungen politischer Verträge," *Chemische Industrie* 5, no. 1 (1953): 3–6.

65. *Freiburger Rundbrief* 5, nos. 19–20 (1952–53): 9.

66. 2d German Bundestag, 254th sess., 18 Mar. 1953, pp. 12 273ff.

67. Féaux de la Croix, *Werdegang*, pp. 145f., 153, 189–91, 198.

68. Martin Hirsch, communication to the author, 28 Apr. 1985.

69. See Fritz Moser, *Aus der Geschichte der Wiedergutmachung: Zu Bruno Weils siebzigsten Geburtstag* (New York: Axis Victims' League, 1953), passim.

70. The "Auerbach Affair" was described in reports in *Aufbau* between 16 Feb. 1951 and 29 Aug. 1952, in the *Süddeutsche Zeitung* and *Berliner Allgemeine Wochenzeitung der Juden in Deutschland* newspapers of the same period, as well as in Raul Hilberg, *The Destruction of European Jews*, rev. ed. (New York, 1985). See also "Auerbach als Mahner," *Freiburger Rundbrief* 5, nos. 19–20 (1952–53): 29.

71. Interview with H. Jacobs, 23 Sept. 1986; see also *Freiburger Rundbrief* 7, no. 25–28 (1954): 5.

72. Féaux de la Croix, *Werdegang*, p. 54.

73. Ibid., p. 70.

74. Ibid., p. 73.

75. BA B 126/51549, Referat VI/5, *Ministerialrat* Friedrich Kuschnitzky, letter

to Finance Minister Fritz Schäffer, 17 Dec. 1952; see also Féaux de la Croix, *Werdegang*, p. 76. A comparative presentation of the November draft of the Bundesrat bill, the version of the Bundesrat bill that was later distorted, the U.S. occupation zone law, and the Hague Protocols is to be found in the so-called Black Book, Landesregierung Baden-Württemberg, *Unterlagen zum Bundesentschädigungsgesetz* (Stuttgart, 1953) (hereafter cited as Black Book).

76. Féaux de la Croix, *Werdegang*, pp. 74f.

77. Referat IV/5, BA B 126/51549, "Schätzung der finanziellen Gesamtaufwendungen . . . ," mimeographed letter, signed by *Ministerialrat* Friedrich Kuschnitzky, 14 Dec. 1952.

78. BA B 126/51549, Undersecretary Alfred Hartmann, letter to Finance Minister Fritz Schäffer, 19 Dec. 1952.

79. Referat VI/5, BA B 126/51549, letter, signed by *Ministerialrat* Friedrich Kuschnitzky, to Finance Minister Fritz Schäffer, 24 Feb. 1954; Féaux de la Croix, *Werdegang*, pp. 71f.

80. Elections to the second German Bundestag were scheduled for 6 Sept. 1953.

81. BA B 126/51549, Justice Minister Thomas Dehler, letter to Finance Minister Fritz Schäffer, 28 Mar. 1953 and Schäffer's answer, 31 Mar. 1953; see also Féaux de la Croix, *Werdegang*, p. 74.

82. BA B 126/12522, Finance Minister Fritz Schäffer, letter to Wilhelm Laforet and Franz-Josef Strauss, 19 Mar. 1953; Referat IV/5, 7 Apr. 1953, note on meeting of the Ausschuss für Rechtswesen und Verfassungsrecht (Committee for the Judicial System and Constitutional Law), 27 Mar. 1953.

83. BA B 126/51649, Schäffer, letter to CDU/CSU parliamentary party head, von Brentano, 19 June 1953; *Ministerialrat* Friedrich Kuschnitzky letter to Schäffer, 1 July 1953; Féaux de la Croix, *Werdegang*, p. 79.

84. Féaux de la Croix, *Werdegang*, pp. 79–81; Otto Küster, "Das Gesetz der unsicheren Hand," *Freiburger Rundbrief* 6, nos. 21–24 (1953–54): 3 (hereafter cited as Küster, "Gesetz der unsicheren Hand").

85. Black Book, p. 86; Féaux de la Croix, *Werdegang*, p. 80.

86. Féaux de la Croix, *Werdegang*, p. 83.

87. Küster, "Gesetz der unsicheren Hand," p. 4; Black Book, p. 19. In regard to his view at the time, Küster later said (communication to the author, 9 Sept. 1987) that he recalled having written "that the strange notion had its good side: in this way, the persecutees automatically enjoyed all the improvements for civil servants, the people our politicians always think of first. In addition, it was not a far-fetched idea that persecutees were, as it were, the actual public servants during the Hitler period (because of such ideas, after all, we did not extend reparations to victims of sterilization, the anti-social, etc., who are presented today as the forgotten victims). The state government here was also the first to enact one (of my) statutes, which more precisely determined categorization of persecutees in classes of civil servants. Later, a clever man simply used the four career paths for the final regulation."

88. Féaux de la Croix, *Werdegang*, p. 89; Black Book, p. 20.

89. Otto Küster, *Die Wiedergutmachung als elementare Rechtsaufgabe* (Frankfurt on Main, 1953), pp. 11f.

90. Küster, "Gesetz der unsicheren Hand."

91. Ibid.

92. BA B 126/51549, Finance Minister Fritz Schäffer, letter to Dr. Wolfgang Haußmann, 26 Feb. 1954.

93. Quoted from a letter from Otto Küster to Franz Böhm, 11 July 1954, in supplement to *Freiburger Rundbrief* 7, nos. 25–28 (1953–54): 7f. All the events surrounding Küster's dismissal are documented in this supplement.

94. Müller wanted to classify Küster as a *Ministerialrat* (section head), although his position was actually equal to the more senior one of undersecretary. This in itself was a provocation. See *Freiburger Rundbrief* 7, nos. 25–28 (1953–54).

95. Küster told the author the following about this "investigation" on 9 September 1987: "He [Teufel] was not an 'investigation head' in the correct sense of the phrase. I was not even told of his appointment, let alone questioned by him. He traveled all over the country and operated on the basis of spiteful, foolish tips from a colleague I had let go for incompetence."

96. "Der Landtag billigt Entlassung Küsters," *Stuttgarter Nachrichten* (newspaper), 6 Aug. 1954.

97. Supplement to *Freiburger Rundbrief* 7, nos. 25–28 (1953–54); Otto Küster, communication to the author, 9 Sept. 1987. Not all press commentators sided with Küster. See, e.g., "Das Streiflicht," *Süddeutsche Zeitung*, 6 Aug. 1954, and "Der Brief Otto Küsters," *Stuttgarter Nachrichten*, 6 Aug. 1954.

98. Information to author from Küster, 22 Feb. 1986.

99. See Féaux de la Croix, *Werdegang*, pp. 68 ff.

100. In a context different from his office's, Küster dealt thoroughly with the lack of courage among German civil servants:

I am totally convinced that our public service has taken a disastrous turn, and that the roots of this disaster are formed by what the former assistant secretary in the Reich and then the Prussian Ministry of the Interior, currently a professor in the United States, Dr. Brecht, called the German civil servant's "benefits obedience." In a nation that has two inflations behind it, a man who can only give up his job in such a way that his and his family's entire old-age and survivors' benefits are taken away is not only a depressing picture, but a poisonous cell. In 1951, at the German Lawyers' Conference on the status of civil servants, I was the spokesman of the reformers. Naturally there are groups that noticed this, such as Herr Teufel [the "investigation head" who helped fire Küster; see n. 95 above], but overall, reason is quite bravely represented among our civil servants; only, while they admire those who dare to contradict, they would never themselves go beyond a subdued muttering.

See *Freiburger Rundbrief* 7, nos. 25–28 (1953–54), suppl.

101. Féaux de la Croix, *Werdegang*, p. 83.

102. 2d German Bundestag, 32d sess., 28 May 1954, pp. 1532f.

103. Ibid.

104. Excerpt from a Bundestag debate, 15 Oct. 1954, reprinted in *Wiedergutmachung!—Aber wann?* ed. SPD Bundesvorstand (Bonn, n.d. [1954]).

105. 2d German Bundestag, 119th sess., 14 Dec. 1955, p. 6325.

106. Ibid., 32d sess., 28 May 1954, pp. 1532f.

107. "Härtefonds nach den Richtlinien der Bundesregierung vom 26.8.1981," in 10th German Bundestag, Drucksache 10/6287, 31 Oct. 1986, *Bericht der Bundesregierung über Wiedergutmachung und Entschädigung für nationalsoziali-*

stisches Unrecht sowie über die Lage der Sinti, Roma und verwandter Gruppen (Federal Government Report on Reparations and Restitution for Nazi Injustice and on the Situation of Gypsies and Related Groups; herafter cited as *Bericht der Bundesregierung,* 31 Oct. 1986), pp. 42ff.

108. See 2d German Bundestag, 119th sess., 14 Dec. 1955, p. 6325.

109. Ibid., 68th sess., 22 Feb. 1955, p. 3488.

110. Ibid, p. 3490. In the first decision of the Stuttgart office whose responsibility this was, Küster made sure that survivors received a pension. According to Küster, this did not involve, as in the decision cited by Arndt, the families of the 20 July 1944 conspirators, but the relatives of the commander of Königsberg, who had disobeyed orders by capitulating (interview, 9 Sept. 1987).

111. See excerpt reprinted in *Wiedergutmachung!—Aber wann!* (cited n. 104 above).

112. Ibid.

113. A similar description of day-to-day reparations practices is found in "Der Skandal der Wiedergutmachung," *Süddeutsche Zeitung,* 11 Nov. 1954.

114. See 2d German Bundestag, 119th sess., 14 Dec. 1955, p. 6330.

115. Ibid.

116. See Ibid., 68th sess., 22 Feb. 1955, p. 3488.

117. Ibid., 119th sess., 14 Dec. 1955, p. 6324.

118. *Aufbau,* 17 Sept. 1954.

119. See 2d German Bundestag, 119th sess., 14 Dec. 1955, p. 6327.

120. Féaux de la Croix, *Werdegang,* p. 87.

121. BA B 126/12530, Jewish Agency for Palestine, memo, no. 56, 9 Apr. 1956.

122. Féaux de la Croix, *Werdegang,* p. 85.

123. Ibid., pp. 88ff.

124. Grossmann, *Ehrenschuld,* p. 76.

125. Cf. *Bundesentschädigungsgesetz,* 2d ed. (Munich: Beck'sche Textausgaben, 1955), and *Bundesgesetzblatt,* no. 31 (29 June 1956): 559ff.; Féaux de la Croix, *Werdegang,* p. 89.

126. *Bundesgesetzblatt,* no. 31 (29 June 1956): 559ff.

127. Küster, "Geste und Geist" (see ch. 1, n. 18, above).

128. *Bundesgesetzblatt,* no. 31 (29 June 1956): 559ff.

129. Of the concept "harm to life," listed in the first paragraph of the law as the first type of harm, Küster observed: "As a discordant flourish, for starters, § 1, para. 1, determines compensation for murder: 'Under this law, anyone has a claim to reparations who . . . was persecuted and thereby . . . suffered harm to life.' Thus the corpse has the claim. Aside from the atrocious German and the superfluity of the sentence, in this way, with such an unworthy blunder, begins the law that is supposed to be the German people's legal response to the murders, as the toleraters of which they now go down in history" (Küster, "Gesetz der unsicheren Hand," p. 6). Küster called this an "ugly consequence of thinking in types of harm" (*Erfahrungen,* p. 13).

130. *Bundesgesetzblatt,* no. 31 (29 June 1956): 559 ff.

131. Otto Küster, "Deutsche Wiedergutmachung, betrachtet 1957," *Freiburger Rundbrief,* no. 49 (1959–60): 4.

132. Persecutees from the countries listed were compensated in the 1950s and 1960s under comprehensive agreements with the Western nations. The sums

then paid out to their citizens by the respective governments were only a fraction of what a persecutee received through individual reparations under the Federal Restitution Law. There were no such agreements with the East Bloc countries. See Féaux de la Croix, *Werdegang*, pp. 201ff., and Grossmann, *Ehrenschuld*, pp. 91ff.

133. Benjamin Ferencz, *Lohn des Grauens* (Frankfurt on Main, 1981); Position of the Interest Association of Former Forced Laborers under the Nazi Regime of 21 June 1987 on the catalogue of questions and experts for an open hearing on 24 June 1987, *Bundestagsausschußdrucksache* 11/5.

134. Norbert Schmacke and Hans-Georg Güse, *Zwangssterilisiert—Verleugnet—Vergessen* (Bremen, 1984), pp. 156ff.

135. Wolfgang Ayaß, "'Asozialen'-Verfolgung und Wiedergutmachung," in *Anerkennung und Versorgung aller Opfer nationalsozialistischer Verfolgung*, ed. Die Grünen im Bundestag (Berlin: Fraktion der Alternative Liste, 1986), p. 83. And see also id., "Die Verfolgung von Bettlern und Landstreichern im Nationalsozialismus. 'Es darf in Deutschland keine Landstreicher mehr geben!'" in *Wohnsitz: Nirgendwo*, ed. Künstlerhaus Bethanien (Berlin, 1981); id., "Die Verfolgung der Nichtseßhaften im Dritten Reich: Der ZVAK im Dritten Reich 1933–1945," in *Ein Jahrhundert Arbeiterkolonien*, ed. Zentralverband Deutscher Arbeiterkolonien (Bielefeld, 1984); id., "Bettler, Landstreicher, Vagabunden, Wohnungslose und Wanderer," in *Mitteilungen der Dokumentationsstelle zur NS-Sozialpolitik*, 1, nos. 9–10 (1985): 57–78; and id., "Vom 'Pik As' ins 'Kola-Fu': Die Verfolgung der Bettler und Obdachlosen durch die Hamburger Sozialverwaltung," in *Verachtet, verfolgt, vernichtet*, ed. Projektgruppe für die vergessenen Opfer des NS-Regimes (Hamburg, 1986).

136. See *Bundesentschädigungsgesetz*, 2d ed. (Munich: Beck'sche Textausgaben, 1955), and *Bundesgesetzblatt*, no. 31 (29 June 1956): 559ff.; Féaux de la Croix, *Werdegang*, p. 89.

137. Rudolf Schottlaender, *Trotz allem ein Deutscher* (Freiburg, 1986), pp. 72–92; Landgericht Berlin, Gesch. Nr. 196.0 (Entsch.) 326, 59 PrV.

138. Kilian Stein, "Die Benachteiligung von antifaschistischen Widerstandskämpfern in der 'Wiedergutmachung,'" in *Anerkennung und Versorgung* (cited n. 135 above), pp. 48f.

139. Cited in Heinz Düx, "Zur Geschichte der Wiedergutmachungspraxis," in *Anerkennung und Versorgung* (cited n. 135 above), pp. 37ff.

140. Ibid.; Franz Calvelli-Adorno, "Die rassische Verfolgung der Zigeuner vor dem 1. März 1943," *RzW* 12 (1961): 529–39; id., "Die Dokumentationsarbeit der URO," *RzW* 16 (1965): 198.

141. See Hans-Georg Stümke, "Verfolgung von Homosexuellen und Wiedergutmachung," and Ilse Kokula, "Die Verfolgung von lesbischen Frauen," both in *Anerkennung und Versorgung* (cited n. 135 above), pp. 84, 85.

142. *Bundesgesetzblatt*, no. 31 (29 June 1956): 559ff.

143. Cited in Uschi Körber, "Auschlußgrund: Straffälligkeit," in *Anerkennung und Versorgung* (cited n. 135 above), pp. 81f.

144. Milton Kestenberg, "Die diskriminierende Praxis in der Wiedergutmachung," in *Arbeitshefte Kinderpsychoanalyse*, vol. 2, ed. Wissenschaftliches Zentrum II, Gesamthochschule Kassel (Kassel, 1987), pp. 183–214.

145. See Stein, "Die Benachteiligung von antifaschistischen Widerstands-kämpfern" (cited n. 138 above).

146. *Bundesgesetzblatt*, 29 June 1956, BEG § 189.

147. *Bundesentschädigungsgesetz* (Munich: Beck'sche Textausgaben, 1972) § 189 (version amended by BEG Final Law).

148. Paul Matussek, *Die Konzentrationslagerhaft und ihre Folgen* (Berlin 1971), p. 43.

149. Cited in Grossmann, *Ehrenschuld*, pp. 159, 157.

150. From the middle of the 2d electoral period (1955) to the end of the 4th electoral period (1965), the Bundestag had a Reparations Committee. During the 2d and 3d periods, its chairmen were the SPD deputies Otto-Heinrich Greve, Alfred Frenzel, and Gerhard Jahn; in the 4th electoral period, it was also headed by an SPD deputy, Martin Hirsch. Following passage of the BEG Final Law in 1965, no Reparations Committee was formed in the 5th German Bundestag; instead, the issue of reparations was dealt with by the Committee for War and Persecution Harm, together with the question of compensation for ethnic German expellees from eastern Europe.

151. Deputy Martin Hirsch (SPD), speech, 4th German Bundestag, 96th sess., 14 Nov. 1963, pp. 4420f.

152. Finance Minister Fritz Schäffer, speech at the University of Frankfurt, 14 June 1957, cited in Grossmann, *Ehrenschuld*, pp. 85f.

153. Grossmann, *Ehrenschuld*, p. 86.

154. Ibid., p. 83. The basic reason for reasonable contingency fees was that the lawyer demanded no advance payments from poor persecutees and no fee if a case was lost. Thus it was considered, at least by the URO, to be a socially conscious form of calculating fees. See W. Schwarz, "Dem 80jährigen Kurt May," *RzW* 27 (1976): 171.

155. Grossmann, *Ehrenschuld*, p. 87.

156. Probst Heinrich Grüber, letter to the editor, *Die Welt*, 31 Dec. 1957, p. 5.

157. "Conference on Reparations Problems," *Aufbau*, 1 May 1959, p. 17.

158. Georg Heuser's crimes under the Third Reich did not become known until a year later. In 1959, he was arrested, and he was sentenced to fifteen years' imprisonment by a Koblenz court on 21 May 1963 for participation in the murder of thousands of Jews (AZ: 9 Ks 2/62). Heuser, who illegitimately claimed a doctorate after the war, had been an SS *Obersturmbannführer* with the Security Police and SD in White Ruthenia (Grossmann, *Ehrenschuld*).

159. Jakob Diel's machinations are also mentioned in "Es geht wieder los: Dunkle Machenschaften gegen die Wiedergutmachung," *Aufbau*, 21 Feb. 1958, p. 1.

160. Letters from Jakob Diel to members of the Bundestag, 31 Jan. and 5 Feb. 1958 (PA Jacobs).

161. "Ist das Eisen der Wiedergutmachung wirklich so heiß?" *Aufbau*, 1 May 1959, p. 18.

162. Féaux de la Croix, *Werdegang*, p. 97.

163. 4th German Bundestag, 96th sess., 14 Nov. 1963, pp. 4406–26.

164. This provision was intended to assist with the burden of proof for health damage. If a 25 percent reduction in earning capacity was found by a doctor, it was

enough to allow an assumption of a link to persecution, and the doctor did not need to show this link specifically.

165. Grossmann, *Ehrenschuld*, p. 139; Féaux de la Croix, *Werdegang*, p. 108.

166. 4th German Bundestag, 96th sess., 14 Nov. 1963, pp. 4406ff.

167. Cited in *Die Wiedergutmachungsfrage am Kreuzweg: Zur Information für Journalisten, Politiker und Interessierte* (New York and Frankfurt on Main: Conference on Jewish Material Claims Against Germany, 1964), pp. 59 ff.

168. See 4th German Bundestag, 96th sess., 14 Nov. 1963, pp. 4406ff.

169. Ibid.

170. Ibid.

171. Interview with Finance Minister Fritz Schäffer in *Deutsche National- und Soldatenzeitung*, 31 Mar. 1963, cited in Grossmann, *Ehrenschuld*, p. 89.

172. *Deutsche Zeitung*, 21 Mar. 1963, cited in Grossmann, *Ehrenschuld*, p. 165.

173. Ernst Ehrmann, "Wiedergutmachung—Wie lange noch, zu welchem Preis?" *Die Zeit*, no. 10 (6 Mar. 1964): 16.

174. See "Zur Verjährung nationalsozialistischer Verbrechen, Dokumentation der parlamentarischen Bewältigung des Problems, 1960–1979," pts. 1–3, in *Zur Sache 3–5/80, Themen parlamentarischer Beratung*, (Bonn: Deutscher Bundestag, Presse- und Informationszentrum, 1980); see also *Die Welt*, no. 124 (1968), p. 5, and *Berliner Allgemeine Jüdische Wochenzeitung*, no. 23, 1968, p. 2.

175. Féaux de la Croix, *Werdegang*, pp. 99 & 102.

176. Hermann Zorn, representing the federal Finance Ministry, rejected all Küster's suggestions; whenever Zorn said anything, the representative of the CDU, Georg Böhme, jumped to his feet and assured him of his party's support (Otto Küster, communication to the author, 22 Feb. 1986).

177. According to Martin Hirsch (personal communication to the author), as chairman of the committee, he asked Adenauer to use his influence within the governing coalition to achieve an expansion of the government draft. Shortly after this meeting, in a meeting with Bundestag President Eugen Gerstenmaier, the finance minister made the very suggestions for change that Hirsch had made to Adenauer. It may however be assumed that these changes, negotiated behind the scenes, can be credited not only to Hirsch and Adenauer, but to Nahum Goldmann. See also Féaux de la Croix, *Werdegang*, p. 104, and Grossmann, *Ehrenschuld*, p. 144.

178. Grossmann, *Ehrenschuld*, p. 144.

179. Féaux de la Croix, *Werdegang*, p. 109.

180. Walter Schwarz, "Auf die Auftragsfrist kommt es an," *Aufbau*, 15 July 1966.

181. See *RzW* 20 (1969): 358; Otto Küster, "Über das Zweitbescheidsverfahren," *RzW* 24 (1973): 41; report on judgment of the Constitutional Court, 16 Dec. 1969, in *RzW* 21 (1970): 160.

182. BGH, 2 July 1958, cited in *RzW* 9 (1958): 400.

183. "Beschluß der Länderkonferenz vom 22/23. Juni 1960 in Bremen," *RzW* 11 (1960): 353. It is noteworthy in this case that the authorities, on their own, disregarded the restrictive jurisprudence of the BGH.

184. Kurt May, communication to the author, 27 Jan. 1986; on this, see the old version of § 150 in the BEG of 1956, in *Bundesgesetzblatt*, no. 31 (1956): 31, and

the new version, following adoption of the 1965 BEG Final Law, in *Bundes-entschädigungsgesetz* 16th ed. (Munich: Beck'sche Textausgaben, 1972).

185. Federal Constitutional Court judgment, 23 Mar. 1971, in *RzW* 22 (1971): 309.

186. For more detailed information on the privileged science of reparations law, see Heinz Klee, "Die besonderen Gruppen von Verfolgten," in BMF, *Wiedergutmachung*, 5: 393–451, esp. pp. 444ff., Otto Küster, "Höchstrichterliche Rechtsprechung zum Wiedergutmachungsrecht," *RzW* 32 (1981): 97ff.; and Küster, "Geste und Geist" (see ch. 1, n. 18, above).

187. Otto Küster, "Wirklichkeitsfremde Wiedergutmachung," *RzW* 31 (1980): 50.

188. Küster, "Geste und Geist" (see ch. 1, n. 18, above).

189. Gerold Küster (the son of Otto Küster), speech at the Stuttgart Privatstudiengesellschaft, Mar. 1990 (MS).

190. Küster used the word *Gesslerhüten* (Gessler hats), echoing the legend of William Tell: in the early fourteenth century, the Austrian bailiff Gessler (at whose command the famous apple was put on the head of Tell's son), is said to have had hats bearing his insignia hung up and to have required people to bow to them as a way of forcing them to show obedience.

191. Otto Küster, "Grundlinien der deutschen Wiedergutmachung," in Akademie Bad Boll, *Opfer* (cited ch. 1, n. 3, above), pp. 87ff.

192. Walter Schwarz, "Schlußbetrachtung," in BMF, *Wiedergutmachung*, suppl. to vol. 6, p. 15.

193. See Küster, "Grundlinien" (cited n. 191 above), pp. 87ff.

Chapter 3: Damage to Body and Health

1. BA B 126/9862, report of the consulate general of the Federal Republic of Germany in New York on "Organizations of victims of National Socialism who believe they are being robbed of their restitution by unjust medical assessments," 4 Mar. and 22 Apr. 1960.

2. § 6 of the 2d BEG implementation law reads: "(1) The persecutee is to undergo the medical examination or observation prescribed by the reparations body. The medical examination or observation should serve to determine the causality between persecution and harm to body and health, as well as the degree and probable duration of the impairment of earning capacity. (2) The reparations authorities determine whether and when a follow-up medical examination is to be carried out. If the persecutee is over 60 years of age, a follow-up exam takes place only at his request."

3. § 34 of the BEG reads: "If the earning capacity of the persecutee is diminished by causes other than the impairment through persecution-induced harm, only the impairment caused by the persecution-induced harm can be the basis for measuring the amount of pension." See also 2 DV-BEG, § 3 and § 4.

4. *Anhaltspunkte für die ärztliche Gutachtertätigkeit im Versorgungswesen*, ed. Bundesminister für Arbeit und Sozialordnung (federal minister of labor and social order) (Bonn, 1973). *Anleitung für die ärztliche Gutachtertätigkeit im Rahmen des Bundesentschädigungsgesetzes*, ed. Bayerischer Staatsministerium der Finanzen (Bavarian Ministry of Finance) (Munich, 1967).

5. Kurt May, communication to the author, 27 Jan. 1986.

6. Merkblatt zum Gutachtenformular im Rentenverfahren nach dem Bundesgesetz zur Entschädigung für Opfer der nationalsozialistischen Verfolgung. Merkblatt A 3/4 68 000 I 57 BBA Berlin A.S., and 2 DV-BEG, § 3 and § 4.

7. Düsseldorf district court, reparations evaluation no. 80, in the private archive of Dr. S. Pierre Kaplan, Paris (hereafter cited as PA Kaplan). The directive went out on 16 Feb. 1968.

8. PA Kaplan; Kurt May, communication to the author, 27 Jan. 1986.

9. Willibald Maier, "Entschädigung für Schaden an Körper und Gesundheit aus ärztlicher Sicht," in BMF, *Wiedergutmachung*, 4: 371f. (hereafter cited as Maier, "Ärztliche Sicht").

10. Ibid., p. 394.

11. Karl Weiss, "Gesundheitsschaden aus rechtlicher Sicht," in BMF, *Wiedergutmachung*, 4: 216 (hereafter cited as Weiss, "Rechtliche Sicht").

12. Maier, "Ärztliche Sicht," pp. 371 f.

13. W. G. Niederland, communication to the author, 27 Aug. 1987.

14. *International Biography of Central European Emigrés, 1933–1945*, ed. Herbert A. Strauss and Werner Röder, vol. 2, pt. 2, L–Z, *The Arts, Sciences and Literature*; W. G. Niederland, communication to the author, 27 Aug. 1987.

15. *Psychische Spätschäden nach politischer Verfolgung*, ed. Hans-Joachim Herberg and Helmut Paul (1963; 2d ed., Basel, 1967), p. 246 (hereafter cited as Herberg and Paul, *Psychische Spätschäden*). Officially, it was said that "the acknowledgement of party-commissioned evaluation [counts] as a source of information," but for the author of such a party evaluation, the legal consequences were not the same as for an expert appointed by the restitution authorities; see Weiss, "Rechtliche Sicht," p. 214.

16. Maier, "Ärztliche Sicht," p. 372.

17. PA Kaplan, minutes of a discussion between the Paris Medical Committee and *Obermedizinalrat* (chief medical officer) Professor Dr. Trüb, Dr. Hand of the state pension authorities in Düsseldorf, *Oberregierungsrat* (senior executive officer) Gross from the North Rhine–Westphalian Ministry of the Interior, and *Legationsrat* Wagner of the Foreign Office (n.d.); Robert M. W. Kempner, "Bearbeitung von Gesundheitsschäden und Heilkosten," in *Aufbau*, 8 Apr. 1986.

18. See Max Michel, *Gesundheitsschäden durch Verfolgung und Gefangenschaft und ihre Spätfolgen* (Frankfurt on Main, 1955) for the proceedings of the International Social Medicine Conference on the Pathology of Former Deportees, Copenhagen, 5–7 June 1954, summarizing inter alia the findings of the Danish psychiatrists Henrik Hoffmeyer and Paul Thygesen, the French internists Charles Richet, Louis-François Fichez, and Gilbert Dreyfus, and the French psychiatrist René Targowla.

19. Otto-Heinz Hurdelbrink, former head of the medical service of the Berlin reparations office, communication to the author, 15 May 1985.

20. Walter Schwarz, "Schlußbetrachtung," unpublished supplement to BMF, *Wiedergutmachung*, 4: 7.

21. Ibid.

22. PA Kaplan, passim; S. Pierre Kaplan, communication to the author, 28 Jan. 1985.

23. PA Kaplan, file no. 46.

24. G. Ott, "Die gegenwärtige Situation der Wiedergutmachung der Gesundheitsschäden," in *Spätschäden nach Extrembelastungen*, ed. Hans-Joachim Herberg (proceedings of the Second International Medico-Legal Symposium, Düsseldorf, 1969) (Herford, FRG, 1971), p. 317f. (hereafter cited as Herberg, *Extrembelastungen*).

25. Ernst-Günter Schenck (1904–?) a member of the leadership of the Nazi Lecturers' Union after 1935, wrote a memo in 1937 at the behest of Reich Physicians Leader Wagner on creation of "health houses" as model facilities for the "new German medicine." Later, he became nutrition inspector in the SS Economic Administrative Headquarters, responsible for administration of all concentration camps. He directed nutrition experiments on healthy and sick prisoners in Mauthausen concentration camp in 1943 and 1944. See BDC Ernst-Günter Schenck; *Ärzte im Nationalsozialismus*, ed. Fridolf Kudlien (Cologne, 1985), pp. 148ff., 285; Walter Wuttke-Groneberg, *Medizin im Nationalsozialismus: Ein Arbeitsbuch* (Würmlingen, 1982), p. 324.

26. V. A. Kral, "Psychiatric Observations Under Severe Chronic Stress," *American Journal of Psychiatry* 108 (1951): 191.

27. Maier, "Ärztliche Sicht," p. 397.

28. René Targowla, "Les Données de la narcose intraveineuse liminaire dans les états "neuropathiques": Le Syndrome d'hypermnésie emotionelle tardif," *Annales des Médicine* 51 (1950): 223.

29. Eugène Minkowski, "L'Anesthésie affective," *Annales médico-psychologique* 104 (1946): 80.

30. G. Dreyfus, L.-F. Fichez, C. Richet, and H. Uzan, "Les sequelles des états de misere physiologique," *Bulletin de l'Académie nationale de médecine*, no. 37 (1948): 649.

31. P. Thygesen and J. Kieler, "The Muselmann," in *Famine Disease in German Concentration Camps* (1949; Copenhagen, 1952).

32. M. Michel, *Gesundheitsschäden durch Verfolgung und Gefangenschaft und ihre Spätfolgen* (Frankfurt on Main, 1955).

33. V. A. Kral, "Beobachtungen bei einer grossen Enzephalitisepidemie," *Schweizer Archiv für Neurologie, Neurochirurgie und Psychiatrie* 64 (1949): 281–328.

34. V. A. Kral, "Psychiatric Observations Under Severe Chronic Stress," *American Journal of Psychiatry* 108 (1951): 185–192.

35. Alfred Wolff-Eisner, *Über Mangelerkrankungen* (Würzburg, 1947).

36. P. Friedman, "The Effects of Imprisonment," *Acta Medica Orientalia* 7 (1948): 163; id., "Some Aspects of Concentration Camp Psychology," *American Journal of Psychiatry* 105 (1949): 601.

37. Maier, "Ärztliche Sicht," p. 413. Maier refers to Karl Bonhoeffer, "Vergleichende psychopathologische Erfahrungen aus den beiden Weltkriegen," *Nervenarzt* 18 (1947): 1.

38. L.-F. Fichez and A. Klotz, *Die vorzeitige Vergreisung und ihre Behandlung* (Vienna, 1961).

39. See, e.g., L.-F. Fichez, *Die chronische progressive Asthenie* (Vienna, 1957).

40. Karl Bonhoeffer, "Beurteilung, Begutachtung und Rechtsprechung bei der sogenannten Unfallneurose," *Deutsche Medizinische Wochenschrift* 52 (1926): 179; Ewald Stier, *Über die sogenannten Unfallneurosen* (Leipzig, 1926).

41. Karl Bonhoeffer, "Vergleichende psychopathologische Erfahrungen aus den beiden Weltkriegen," *Nervenarzt* 18 (1947): 1.

42. G. Bodechtel, Fred Dubitscher, Hirt, Friedrich Panse, and Gustav Störring, *Die "Neurose"—Ihre versorgungs- und sozialmedizinische Beurteilung*, (Bonn, 1960); Samuel Gringanz, "Neueste Entwicklungen auf dem Gebiete der Entschädigung von Gesundheitsschäden," *Aufbau*, 18 Dec. 1964.

43. BDC Friedrich Panse; R. Valentin, *Die Krankenbataillone* (Düsseldorf, 1981), p. 135; F. Panse, *Angst und Schreck* (Stuttgart, 1952), p. 118; *Heilen und Vernichten im Nationalsozialismus*, ed. Kölnischen Gesellschaft für Christlich-Jüdische Zusammenarbeit (Cologne Society for Christian-Jewish Cooperation) (Cologne, 1985), pp. 88ff.

44. Walther von Baeyer, "Die Freiheitsfrage in der forensischen Psychiatrie mit besonderer Berücksichtigung der Entschädigungsneurosen," *Nervenarzt* 28 (1957): 337; Kurt Kolle, "Die Opfer nationalsozialistischer Verfolgung in psychiatrischer Sicht," *Nervenarzt* 29 (1958): 462; Hans Strauss, "Besonderheiten der nichtpsychotischen Störungen bei Opfern der nationalsozialistischen Verfolgung und ihre Bedeutung bei der Begutachtung," *Nervenarzt* 28 (1957): 344; Ulrich Venzlaff, *Die psychoreaktiven Störungen nach entschädigungspflichtigen Ereignissen* (Berlin, 1958).

45. Walther von Baeyer, in *Psychiatrie in Selbstdarstellungen*, ed. L. J. Pongartz (Bern, 1977), pp. 9ff.; Regine Lockot, *Erinnern und Durcharbeiten* (Frankfurt on Main, 1985), pp. 230ff.; Walther von Baeyer and W. Binder, *Endomorphe Psychosen bei Verfolgten* (Berlin, 1982).

46. H. Pohlmeier, E. Deutsch, and H. L. Schreiber, *Forensische Psychiatrie heute: Prof. Dr. med. Ulrich Venzlaff zum 65. Geburtstag gewidmet* (Berlin, 1986), pp. 1–6.

47. Landgericht Bremen, Az: OH 2088/1951 (E); Ernst Kretschmer, "Sachverständigengutachten in einem Entschädigungsverfahren vom 24.10.1955," cited in Bodechtel et al., *Die "Neurose"* (see n. 42 above); Ammermüller-Wilden, *Gesundheitliche Schäden in der Wiedergutmachung* (Stuttgart, 1953), pp. 24f; "Die Neurosen in der Wiedergutmachung, Eine Erwiderung von Hans Strauss," *Aufbau*, 18 Apr. 1958, p. 18.

48. Ernst Kretschmer, "Konstitutionslehre und Rassenhygiene," in *Erblehre und Rassenhygiene im völkischen Staat*, ed. Ernst Rüdin (Munich, 1934), p. 184; id., "Genie und Rasse," in W. Goetz et al., *Rasse und Geist: Vier Vorträge* (Leipzig, 1932), p. 59; Hans-Ulrich Brändle, "Aufartung und Ausmerze: NS-Rassen- und Bevölkerungspolitik im Kräftefeld zwischen Wissenschaft, Partei und Staat am Beispiel des 'angeborenen Schwachsinns,' " in *Heilen und Vernichten im Nationalsozialismus*, ed. Projektgruppe "Volk und Gesundheit (Tübingen, 1983), p. 164.

49. See conference contributions by Walther von Baeyer, Paul Matussek, Wolfgang Jacob, and Edgar Trautmann, *Nervenarzt* 32 (1961): 534–51.

50. H. Witter, "Erlebnisbedingte Schädigung durch Verfolgung," *Nervenarzt* 33 (1963): 509.

51. Kurt R. Eissler, "Die Ermordung von wie vielen seiner Kinder muß ein Mensch symptomfrei ertragen können, um eine normale Konstitution zu haben?" *Psyche* 17 (1963): 241.

52. Leo Eitinger, "The Incidence of Mental Disease Among Refugees in Nor-

way," *Journal of Mental Science* 105 (1959): 326; Jan Bastiaans, *Psychosomatische Gevolgen van Onderdrukking en Verzet* (Amersterdam: N.V. Noord-Hollandsche Uitgevers, 1957).

53. *Rzw* 11 (1960): 453.

54. Archive of the URO in Frankfurt on Main (hereafter cited as URO Frankfurt), folder on "Gutachten Nerven" (evaluations on nerves).

55. Private archive of attorney Eberhard Fellmer (hereafter cited as PA Fellmer).

56. Ulrich Venzlaff, "Erlebnishintergrund und Dynamik seelischer Verfolgungsschäden," in Herberg and Paul, *Psychische Spätschäden*, 1st ed., p. 107.

57. Remarks by Ulrich Venzlaff at the Second International Medico-Legal Conference, Düsseldorf, 1969, in Herberg, *Extrembelastungen*, p. 107.

58. See *RzW* 19 (1968): 504, 549.

59. Paul gives an overview in Herberg and Paul, *Psychische Spätschäden*, 2d ed., pp. 131–38.

60. *Die Beurteilung von Gesundheitsschäden nach Gefangenschaft und Verfolgung*, ed. H. J. Herberg (Herford, FRG, 1967); Herberg, *Extrembelastungen*; Herberg and Paul, *Psychische Spätschäden*, 2d ed., pp. 231ff.

61. Herberg, *Extrembelastungen*, pp. 106f.

62. Ibid.

63. Ernst Kluge, "Über die Defektcharakter von Dauerfolgen schwerer Haftzeiten," *Med. Sachverst.* 57 (1961): 185.

64. Walther von Baeyer, Heinz Häfner, and Karl Peter Kisker, *Psychiatrie der Verfolgten* (Berlin, 1964) (hereafter cited as von Baeyer et al., *Psychiatrie der Verfolgten*).

65. Compilation of the most important characteristics of "survivors' syndrome" or "concentration camp syndrome" from W. G. Niederland, *Folgen der Verfolgung: Das Überlebenden-Syndrom. Seelenmord* (Frankfurt on Main, 1980); H. Krystal and W. G. Niederland, "Clinical Observations on the Survivor Syndrome," in *Scientific Proceedings of the 121st Annual Meeting of the American Psychiatric Association 1965* (Washington, D.C.: American Psychiatric Association, 1965), pp. 136–38; L. Eitinger, *Concentration Camp Survivors in Norway and Israel* (Oslo, 1964), p. 90.

66. Von Baeyer et al., *Psychiatrie der Verfolgten*, p. 19.

67. Henry Krystal, "Trauma: Considerations of Its Intensity and Chronicity," in Henry Krystal and W. G. Niederland, *Psychic Traumatization* (Boston, 1971), pp. 11ff.

68. Henry Krystal, *Massive Psychic Trauma* (New York, 1968), pp. 17, 33, 41.

69. Antoni Kępiński, "Das sogenannte 'KZ-Syndrom': Versuch einer Synthese," in *Die Auschwitz-Hefte: Texte der polnischen Zeitschrift "Przegląd Lekarski" über historische, psychische und medizinische Aspekte des Lebens und Sterbens in Auschwitz* (Weinheim, 1987), 2: 7–13.

70. Wanda Półtawska, Andzej Jakoubik, Jozef Sarnecki, and Julian Gatarski, "Ergebnisse der Untersuchungen der in den nazistischen Konzentrationslagern geborenen oder in den Kinderjahren inhaftierten Personen," in International Auschwitz Committee, *Anthology*, vol. 2, pt. 3 (Warsaw, 1970), p. 89.

71. Kępiński, "Das sogenannte 'KZ-Syndrom' " (cited n. 69 above).

72. Ibid.

73. Ibid.

74. Stanisław Kłodziński, "Ein charakteristischer Krankheitszustand nach dem Aufenthalt in Nazi-Lagern," *Mitteilungen der FIR zu medizinischen und sozialen Rechtsfragen*, no. 2 (1974): 3.

75. S. Kłodziński, "The Purpose and Methology of Medical Examinations of Former Prisoners of Nazi Concentration Camps." International Auschwitz Committee, *Anthology*, vol. 3, pt. 1 (Warsaw, 1971), p. 70.

76. Z. Jagoda, S. Kłodziński, and J. Masłowski, "Das Überleben im Lager aus der Sicht ehemaliger Häftlinge von Auschwitz-Birkenau," in *Die Auschwitz-Hefte* (cited n. 69 above), 1: 13ff.

77. Z. Jagoda, S. Kłodziński, and J. Masłowski, "Verhaltensstereotype ehemaliger Häftlinge des Konzentrationslagers Auschwitz," in *Die Auschwitz-Hefte* (cited n. 69 above), 2: 25–59.

78. W. G. Niederland, "The Psychiatric Evaluation of Emotional Disorder in Survivors of Nazi Persecution," in Krystal, *Massive Psychic Trauma* (cited n. 68 above), pp. 8ff.

79. Wolfgang Jacob, "Zur Beurteilung der Zusammenhangfrage körperliche und seelischer Verfolgungsschäden in der gutachtlichen Praxis der Entschädigungsverfahrens," in *Die Beurteilung von Gesundheitsschäden*, ed. Herberg (cited n. 60 above), p. 68.

80. Hermann Witter, "Erlebnisbedingte Schädigung nach Verfolgung," *Nervenarzt* 33 (1962): 509.

81. Walther von Baeyer, "Wissenschaftliche Erkenntnisse oder menschliche Wertung der erlebnisreaktiven Schäden Verfolgter?" (With a response by Witter), *Nervenarzt* 34 (1963): 120.

82. BDC Hermann Witter; Tilman Moser, *Repressive Kriminalpsychiatrie*, (Neuwied, 1971); Hermann Witter, "Kritik am Gerichtsärztlichen Ausschuß des Landes NRW?" *Spektrum* 5 (1976): 189–195; *Das Komplott zwischen Gerichtspsychiatern und Justiz: Dokumentation der Roten Hilfe Westberlin* (Berlin, 1973). The Red Army Faction, also known as the Baader-Meinhof Gang, was a violent underground leftist organization; members were kept in solitary confinement for years in West German prisons, in violation of normal basic rights.

83. Rainer Luthe, " 'Erlebnisreaktiver Persönlichkeitswandel' als Begriff der Begutachtung im Entschädigungsrecht," *Nervenarzt* 39 (1968): 465–67.

84. Ulrich Venzlaff, "Erlebnisreaktiver Persönlichkeitswandel: Fiktion oder Wirklichkeit?" *Nervenarzt* 40 (1969): 539–41.

85. As a few examples among many, see URO Frankfurt, "Gutachten Nerven" folder (consultant reports on nerves), F.S., R.E., I.R., M., L. and PA Fellmer, file F.K.; Hermann Witter, "Zur Begutachtung erlebnisbedingter Verfolgungsschäden," *Deutsches Ärzteblatt* 1964, pp. 61, 187; id., "Zur medizinischen und restlichen Beurteilung von Neurosen," *Neue Juristische Wochenschrift* 1964, pp. 11, 66.

86. Ulrich Venzlaff, "Erlebnishintergrund und Dynamik seelischer Verfolgungsschäden," in Herberg and Paul, *Psychische Spätschäden*, 1st ed., p. 107.

87. Herberg and Paul, *Psychische Spätschäden*, 1st ed., p. 77.

88. J. M. Fitzek and H. H. Herberg, "Auslesegesichtspunkte und allgemeine Erfahrungen bei den Untersuchungen des Kölner Arbeitskreises," in Herberg and Paul, *Psychische Spätschäden*, 1st ed., p. 169.

89. H. J. Herberg, communication to the author, 23 Apr. 1986.

90. Proceedings of the main medical conference of the top restitution offices on 13 May 1964, TO-Punkt 4, p. 5, appendix 4.

91. Ibid.

92. BDC Helmuth Lotz; "Bestechung eines Entschädigungsmedizinalrates," *Aufbau,* 27 Nov. 1959, p. 30.

93. Helmuth Lotz, "Psychische Spätschäden nach politischer Verfolgung: Eine Stellungnahme zu dem Buch von H. Paul und H. J. Herberg," *RzW* 15 (1964): 349f.

94. Günter Hand, retired chief government medical officer (*Regierungsmedizinaldirektor*), Düsseldorf state pension office, communication to the author, 24 Apr. 1986; H. J. Herberg, communication to the author, 23 Apr. 1986; see also correspondence on the Herberg case in URO Frankfurt, "Gesundheitsschaden 1972–1978" (Health Damage, 1972–78) folder.

95. H. J. Herberg, communication to the author, 23 Apr. 1986; internal memo, 21 May 1969, PA Fellmer.

96. H. J. Herberg, communication to the author, 23 Apr. 1986.

97. The state restitution law, before adoption of the Federal Supplementary Law in Hamburg, was called the Special Supplementary Pension Law (SHRG).

98. Wolfgang Meywald and Eberhard Fellmer, communication to the author, 29 Aug. 1985.

99. H. Huebschmann, communication to the author, 1 May 1986; URO Frankfurt, "Innere Krankheiten I" (Internal Illness, I) folder.

100. Heinrich Huebschmann, *Krankheit als Konflikt* (Freiburg, 1974).

101. See proceedings of the FIR congress, Vienna.

102. Christian Pross, "Das Krankenhaus Moabit, 1920, 1933, 1945," in *Nicht mißhandeln,* ed. Christian Pross and Rolf Winau (Berlin, 1984), pp. 242ff.

103. Kilian Stein, Berlin District Court judge, communication to the author, 30 Jan. 1986.

104. Hans Strauss, "Besonderheiten der nichtpsychotischen seelischen Störungen bei Opfern der nationalsozialistischen Verfolgung und ihre Bedeutung bei der Begutachtung," *Nervenarzt* 28 (1957): 344–50; Hans Strauss, "Psychiatric Disturbances in Victims of Racial Persecution," in *Proceedings of the Third World Congress of Psychiatry* (Montreal, 1961); Richard Dyck, "Die Neurosen in der Wiedergutmachung," *Aufbau,* 7 Mar. 1958; "Die Neurosen in der Wiedergutmachung: Eine Erwiderung von Dr. Hans Strauss," *Aufbau,* 26 May 1961; Samuel Gringanz, "Neueste Entwicklungen auf dem Gebiete der Entschädigung für Gesundheitsschäden," *Aufbau,* 4 Dec. 1964; "Nochmals 'Hysterie oder Depression,'" *Aufbau,* 7 Apr. 1967; K. D. Hoppe, "The Aftermath of Nazi Persecution Reflected in Recent Psychiatric Literature," in *Psychic Traumatization,* ed. Henry Krystal and W. G. Niederland (Boston, 1971), pp. 172f.; URO Frankfurt, "Gutachten Nerven 1.4.1955 bis 30.11.1963" folder; letter signed by seventeen persecutees to Harald Graf von Posadowski-Wehner, consul general of the German Federal Republic in New York, 21 Dec. 1974, in William G. Niederland, Collection, Library of Congress, Washington, D.C.

105. Paul Matussek, *Die Konzentrationslagerhaft und ihre Folgen* (Berlin, 1971).

106. Paul Matussek, "Die Konzentrationslagerhaft als Belastungssituation," *Nervenarzt* 32 (1961): 538–42.

107. See Jagoda, Kłodziński, and Masłowski, "Das Überleben im Lager" (cited n. 76 above), 1: 13ff.

108. Closing remarks by Paul Matussek in Herberg, *Extrembelastungen*, p. 243.

109. L. Eitinger, "Psychiatrische Untersuchungsergebnisse bei KZ-Überlebenden," in Herberg, *Extrembelastungen*, p. 144.

110. Contribution to the discussion by Eitinger, in Herberg, *Extrembelastungen*, pp. 237f.

111. See Matussek, *Die Konzentrationslagerhaft* (cited n. 105 above), p. 11.

112. Ibid.

Chapter 4: Examiners and Victims

1. Kurt R. Eissler, "Die Ermordung von wievielen seiner Kinder muß ein Mensch symptomfrei ertragen können, um eine normale Konstitution zu haben?" *Psyche* 17 (1963): 279.

2. W. G. Niederland, *Folgen der Verfolgung: Das Überlebenden Syndrom. Seelenmord* (Frankfurt on Main, 1980).

3. Klaus D. Hoppe, "The Emotional Reactions of Psychiatrists when Confronting Holocaust Survivors of Persecution," in *Psychoanalytic Forum*, vol. 3, ed. J. Lindon (New York: Science House, 1969), p. 187.

4. Klaus D. Hoppe, "Psychotherapie bei Konzentrationslageropfern," *Psyche* 19 (1965): 289ff.

5. "Unfähig, eine Sprache zu finden," interview with W. G. Niederland, in *Die Tageszeitung* (newspaper), 3 Aug. 1985, p. 3.

6. According to Otto Küster (communication to the author, 22 Feb. 1986), it was easier to work with "repentant National Socialists" in reparations than with many others, except that there were hardly any of them.

7. K. D. Hoppe, "Psychotherapie bei Konzentrationslageropfern," *Psyche* 19 (1965): 290.

8. Z. Jagoda, S. Kłodziński, and J. Masłowski, "Verhaltensstereotype ehemaliger Häftlinge des Konzentrationslagers Auschwitz," in *Die Auschwitz-Hefte* (cited ch. 3, n. 69), 2: 25–29.

9. Ulrich Brost, "Zur Praxis der Wiedergutmachung," in *Die Beurteilung von Gesundheitsschäden*, ed. Herberg (cited ch. 3, n. 60), p. 74.

10. Files of the Düsseldorf District Court (hereafter cited as LG Düsseldorf), Az. 26 0 (Entsch.) 112/65; PA Kaplan, no. 41.

11. BDC Paul Trüb; Paul Trüb, *Die Mitwirkung des Arztes bei der Durchführung des Bundesentschädigungsgesetzes und in der Paxis des Entschädigungsrechts* (Koblenz, 1955); BA B 126/9862, proceedings of the conference of officials of the top reparations authorities, 9–10 Apr. 1959 in Düsseldorf, TOP 12 b; testimony of A. Wödl of 1 Mar. 1946, LG Vienna Vg 2 b Vr 2365/45; PA Kaplan.

12. BDC Hanns Bücken.

13. Christian Pross, "Das Krankenhaus Moabit, 1920, 1933, 1945," in *nicht mißhandeln*, ed. Christian Pross and Rolf Winau (Berlin, 1984), p. 176.

14. PA Fellmer, Az VRZ 860/64.

15. The etiology of the Bechterev syndrome, which chiefly affects young people, is, in fact, still unexplained. It is interesting, however, that it occasionally appears together with classic psychosomatic illnesses, such as Crohn's disease and ulcerative colitis; see Gotthard Schettler, *Innere Medizin* (Stuttgart, 1980), p. 464.

16. BDC Gotthard Schettler; Gotthard Schettler, *Arteriosklerose* (Stuttgart, 1961), p. 512; URO Frankfurt, "Innere Krankheiten I und II" folder; Frantisek Blaha, "Arteriosklerose, Hypertension und Herzinfarkt bei Kriegsbeschädigten," in Herberg, *Extrembelastungen*, pp. 109–14.

17. URO Frankfurt, LG Hamburg (trial court), Az 82 0 (Entsch.) 10/76.

18. Joachim Luwisch, letter to the author, 28 Oct. 1987.

19. These details are taken from Wellbrock's dissertation.

20. These details are taken from Jannasch's dissertation.

21. URO Frankfurt, LG Hamburg, Az 82 0 (Entsch.) 107/70.

22. PA Fellmer, Az. VR 3/73.

23. These details are taken from Liebermann's dissertation.

24. BDC Armin Schütt; Wolfgang Meywald, communication to the author, 29 Aug. 1985.

25. PA Fellmer, Az. VRZ 5/74.

26. URO Frankfurt, "Gutachten Nerven 1979ff." folder; PA Fellmer, Az. LG Hamburg 82 0 (Entsch.) 68/70; Milton Kestenberg, Child Development Research, New York, letter to the author, 3 Jan. 1986.

27. Hilel Klein, "Wiedergutmachung—Ein Akt der Retraumatisierung," in Akademie Bad Boll, *Opfer* (cited ch. 1, n. 3, above), p. 51. The American psychiatrist Martin Wangh described the same situation in a detailed review of evaluations at the Second International Medico-Legal Symposium in Düsseldorf in 1969; see Martin Wangh, "Die Beurteilung von Wiedergutmachungsansprüchen der als Kleinkinder Verfolgten," in Herberg, *Extrembelastungen*, pp. 270ff.

28. PA Kaplan, no. 65.

29. These details are taken from Hand's dissertation.

30. Archive of the VVN Hamburg, LG Hamburg, Az. 82 0 (Entsch.) 217/72. The punctuation and wording of this quotation are as close to the original as possible.

31. The "concentration camp assumption" (BEG § 31, para. 2), intended to ease the burden of proof for persecutees and spare them the torment of repeated medical examinations, was undermined in practice by some doctors from the reparations authorities and courts through use of wording in their reports saying that a 25 percent (or higher) reduction in earning capacity could not be attributed to persecution "with a probability bordering on certainty." Such a comment in the evaluation "refuted" the concentration camp assumption, taking the actual point of the law ad absurdum; after all, for a persecutee who had spent a year in concentration camp and suffered a 25 percent reduction in earning capacity, it was supposed to be "assumed in his favor" that the reduction in earning capacity was persecution-induced. The Federal Supreme Court of Appeals gave its blessing to this misuse of the law in a judgment on 7 February 1968. In 1969, at the second congress on long-term harm organized by the Cologne documentation center, A. N. Simmedinger of the VVN acknowledged that the BGH had manipulated § 31, para. 2, out of the law (BGH decision of 7 Feb. 1968, in *RzW* 19 [1968]: 313; Herberg, *Extrembelastungen*, pp. 326f.).

32. PA Kaplan, no. 149; LG Düsseldorf 21 0 (E) 590/60.

33. Ulrich Venzlaff, "Nachruf für Dr. Eugène Minkowski," *RzW* 24 (1973): 205.

34. PA Fellmer, Az. VRZ 974/64.

35. These details are taken from Piepgras's dissertation.

36. BDC Paul Bünger.

37. PA Fellmer, Az. VRZ 11/77.

38. PA Fellmer, Az. VR 870/65.

39. URO Frankfurt, Oberlandesgericht, Koblenz, Az. 7 U (WG) 56/75.

40. BDC, Fritz Struwe file.

41. PA Fellmer, Az. VRZ 1841/64.

42. K. H. Roth, "Großhungern und Gehorchen," in *Heilen und Vernichten im Mustergau Hamburg*, ed. Angelika Ebbinghaus et al. (Hamburg, 1984), pp. 130ff.

43. These details are taken from Wunnenberg's dissertation.

44. BDC Werner Lungwitz.

45. Gerd Karl Döring, "Spezifische Spätschäden der weiblichen Psyche," in Herberg and Paul, *Psychische Spätschäden*, 1st ed., p. 155.

46. D. Klebanow, "Hunger und psychische Erregungen als Ovar- und Keimschädigungen," *Zeitschrift für Geburtshilfe und Gynäkologie* 7–8 (1948): 812.

47. See Döring, "Spezifische Spätschäden der weiblichen Psyche" (see n. 45 above).

48. See the description of the inventor of these experiments, the gynecologist Carl Clauberg, in *Heilen und Vernichten im Nationalsozialismus*, ed. Projektgruppe "Volk und Gesundheit" (Tübingen, 1983), pp. 189ff.

49. Kurt May, communication to the author, 27 Jan. 1986. In concentration camp literature, the subject of rape is discussed by Karol Cetynski, *House of Dolls* (New York, 1955).

50. Henry Krystal and W. G. Niederland, "Clinical Observations on the Survivor Syndrome," in Henry Krystal, *Massive Psychic Trauma* (New York, 1968), pp. 341f.

51. Walther von Baeyer, H. Häfner, and K. P. Kisker, *Psychiatrie der Verfolgten* (Berlin, 1964), pp. 252ff.

Chapter 5: Taking Stock

1. As Franz-Josef Strauss put it in a campaign speech in Jan. 1987.

2. VVN, *Anträge zur Novellierung 1. des Bundesentschädigungsgesetzes (BEG), 2. des Gesetzes zur Wiedergutmachung nationalsozialistischen Unrechts in der Sozialversicherung (WGSVG), vorgelegt vom Präsidium des VVN-Bund der Antifaschisten* (Frankfurt on Main, 1973).

3. "Beschluß des Petitionsausschusses des Deutschen Bundestages vom 7.8.1974 über den Antrag der Arbeitsgemeinschaft für Wiedergutmachungsrecht im Deutschen Anwaltsverein, Landesgruppe NRW, auf Novellierung des § 150 BEG," *RzW* 26 (1975): 44.

4. Féaux de la Croix, *Werdegang*, pp. 111–13.

5. H. Klee, "Die besonderen Gruppen von Verfolgten," in BMF, *Wiedergutmachung*, 5: 447.

6. "Richtlinien für die Vergabe von Mitteln an jüdische Verfolgte zur Abgeltung von Härten in Einzelfällen im Rahmen der Wiedergutmachung vom 3.10.1980," *Bundesanzeiger*, no. 192 (14 Oct. 1980): 1.

7. "Richtlinien für die Vergabe von Mitteln an Verfolgte nicht jüdischer Abstammung zur Abgeltung von Härten in Einzelfällen im Rahmen der Wiedergutmachung vom 26.8.1981," *Bundesanzeiger*, no. 160 (29 Aug. 1981): 1.

8. *Bericht der Bundesregierung*, 31 Oct. 1986 (cited ch. 2, n. 107, above), pp.

42ff.; U. Körber, "Die Unzulänglichkeit der bestehenden Härteregelung," in *Anerkennung und Versorgung aller Opfer nationalsozialistischer Verfolgung*, ed. Die Grünen im Bundestag (Berlin: Fraktion der Alternative Liste, 1986), pp. 54f.

9. Private archive of Joseph Lautmann, Berlin, *Entschädigungsakte* (reparations file) Landgericht Munich, Gesch. No. 22 Ek 82/83.

10. *Die Tageszeitung*, 9 Nov. 1985.

11. Ibid., 26 June 1986; the draft law is reprinted in *Anerkennung und Versorgung* (cited n. 8 above), p. 10.

12. 10th Berlin House of Deputies (Abgeordnetenhaus von Berlin), Bericht des Ausschusses für Inneres, Sicherheit und Ordnung, Drucksache 10/839, 23 June 1986; "Fonds für Opfer des Naziregimes," *Volksblatt Berlin* (newspaper), 27 June 1986; Christian Pross, "Härtefonds für NS-Opfer," in *Biedermann und Schreibtischtäter*, vol. 4 of *Beiträge zur nationalsozialistischen Gesundheits- und Sozialpolitik*, ed. Götz Aly et al. (Berlin, 1987), p. 191.

13. 11th German Bundestag, Innenausschuß, Auschußdrucksache 11/8, Stellungnahmen der Sachverständigen, Bonn 15 June 1987; Klaus Hartung, "Anerkennung der 'Zweiten Verfolgung,'" *Die Tageszeitung*, 26 June 1987; id., "Neue Härte gegen NS-Opfer," ibid., 6 Nov. 1987; id., "Kompromiß für zwangssterilisierte NS-Opfer," ibid., 15 Jan. 1988.

14. Grossmann, *Ehrenschuld*, pp. 104–13.

15. *Bericht der Bundesregierung*, 31 Oct. 1986 (cited ch. 2, n. 107, above), 31 Oct. 1986, pp. 14ff.

16. Ibid., p. 15.

17. Otto Küster, "Grundlinien der deutschen Wiedergutmachung," in Akademie Bad Boll, *Opfer* (cited ch. 1, n. 3, above), p. 87.

18. Küster, *Erfahrungen*, p. 12.

19. Grossmann, *Ehrenschuld*, pp. 107f.

20. Landesverwaltungsamt Berlin, Gesch. Z. I J 1a Reg. no. 150 350.

21. BA B 126/12549, letter from the federal Press and Information Office to the federal Minister of Finance, 19 Nov. 1954 regarding inquiry by *Business Week*; ibid., report of the consulate general of the FRG, Los Angeles, 28 Feb. 1955, on danger to pro-German public opinion through unsatisfactory settlement of reparations and restitution claims.

22. O.M.G.U.S., *Ermittlungen gegen die Deutsche Bank, 1946–47* (Investigation of the Deutsche Bank), ed. Karl Heinz Roth (Nördlingen, 1985).

23. Féaux de la Croix, *Werdegang*, pp. 151f.

24. See continuing reports in *Aufbau* in the late 1940s and early 1950s.

25. A. Stobwasser, *Die den roten Winkel tragen* (Hamburg, 1983), pp. 44f.

26. Küster later admitted that this greatly concerned him. He said the reason for the introduction of the exclusionary clause in the Berlin reparations law was the situation in Berlin after the city was divided, with the conflict between the SEW (the West Berlin arm of East Germany's ruling party, the SED) and SPD in the western sector. See contribution to discussion by Küster, in Akademie Bad Boll, *Opfer* (cited ch. 1, n. 3, above), pp. 157f.

27. Interview with federal Finance Minister Fritz Schäffer in *Aufbau*, cited in Grossmann, *Ehrenschuld*, p. 86.

28. Féaux de la Croix, *Werdegang*, pp. 185f.

29. S. Pierre Kaplan, communication to the author, 28 Jan. 1985.

30. Walther von Baeyer tells of only 16 "classic pension neuroses" among the 535 persecutees he examined and reported on; see id., H. Häfner, and K. P. Kisker, *Psychiatrie der Verfolgten* (Berlin, 1964), p. 117.

31. Gerhard Kloos, *Grundriß der Psychiatrie und Neurologie* (1944; repr., Munich, 1968), p. 115 (by the 1970s, this handy short textbook had gone through ten reprints). On this, see Karl Friedrich Masuhr and Götz Aly, "Der diagnostische Blick des Gerhard Kloos," in *Reform und Gewissen*, vol. 2 of *Beiträge zur nationalsozialistischen Gesundheits- und Sozialpolitik*, ed. Götz Aly et al. (Berlin, 1985), pp. 81–106.

32. Von Baeyer et al., *Psychiatrie der Verfolgten*, p. 347.

33. PA Fellmer, Az VR 769/64.

34. Hilel Klein, "Wiedergutmachung—Ein Akt der Retraumatisierung," in Akademie Bad Boll, *Opfer* (cited ch. 1, n. 3, above), p. 51.

35. Ibid.

36. Kurt R. Eissler, "Pervertierte Psychiatrie?" *Psyche* 21 (1967): 553-75; see also id., "Die Ermordung von wievielen seiner Kinder muß ein Mensch symptomfrei ertragen können, um eine normale Konstitution zu haben?" *Psyche* 17 (1963): 241–91.

37. Walther von Baeyer and W. Binder, *Endomorphe Psychosen bei Verfolgten* (Berlin, 1982); *30 Jahre Schutzkommission, Zivilschutzforschung*, vol. 13, ed. Bundesamt für Zivilschutz (Berlin, 1981).

38. Max Mikorey became a member of the Nazi Party in 1933 and was cofounder of the Nazi Academy of German Law, where he was a lecturer in criminal psychiatry; he was known for authoring anti-Semitic tracts against liberal Weimar criminal law reformers. See BDC Max Mikorey; M. Mikorey, "Das Judentum in der Kriminalpsychiatrie," in *Das Judentum in der Rechtswissenschaft* (Berlin, 1936), vol. 3, p. 61; *Panik: Erkennen-Verhüten-Bekämpfen*, Schriftenreihe Innere Führung, Reihe Erziehung, no. 8, ed. Bundesministerium der Verteidigung (Defense Ministry), 1962; Christian Pross, "Panikforschung im Zweiten Weltkrieg und heute, in Herrenmensch und Arbeitsvölker," in *Beiträge zur nationalsozialistischen Gesundheits- und Sozialpolitik*, vol. 3 (Berlin, 1986), p. 181.

39. Von Baeyer and Binder, *Endomorphe Psychosen* (cited n. 37 above), p. 146.

40. On this, see DGSP, *Panikpersonen sofort eliminieren!* (Loccum, 1983).

Making Good Again

1. There are a number of works dealing specifically with the role of the Vatican and the OSS in hiding Nazi war criminals after World War II. The Vatican had assigned a Bishop Hudal (from Graz) that task. The fate of these escaped Nazis is likewise described in many well-documented books and papers. Among others, see M. Linklater, I. Hilton, and N. Ascherson, *The Fourth Reich* (London: Hodder & Stoughton, 1984); T. Bower, *Blind Eye to Murder* (London: André Deutsch, 1981), p. 501; L. Hunt, "U.S. Cover Up of Nazi Scientists," *Bulletin of the Atomic Scientists* 41 (Apr. 1985): 16–24; and R. Sherrill, "The Golden Years of an Ex-Nazi," *The Nation* 242 (June 1968): 790–96.

2. See, inter alia, E. Dabringhaus, *Klaus Barbie* (Washington, D.C.: Acropolis Books, 1984), and T. Bower, *Klaus Barbie: The Butcher of Lyon* (New York: Pantheon Books, 1984).

3. "Foreign Letters: The Refugees from Germany," *JAMA* 102 (1934): 1860-61.

4. Cited in D. S. Wyman, *Paper Walls* (Boston: University of Massachusetts Press, 1968).

5. The attempts of Jews under Hitler to emigrate anywhere and the attempts of the rest of the world to keep them out have been well described. Despite this, there persists the fiction that the reason so many perished was their own failure to leave the country. While some most certainly and for various reasons remained behind voluntarily, most desperately tried to escape anywhere and by any means. The obstacles willfully created by Western countries (especially by the United States) and the sometimes ingenious hurdles (or actual lies) created by the bureaucracies of these countries have been well documented. See, inter alia, D. S. Wyman, *The Abandonment of the Jews* (New York: Pantheon Books, 1984); id., *Paper Walls*; Secretary of Labor, *Report* (Washington, D.C.: U.S. Government Printing Office, 1933–42); K. Drobisch, *Juden unterm Hakenkreuz* (Berlin, 1973); A. D. Morse, *While Six Million Died: A Chronicle of American Apathy* (New York: Random House, 1968).

6. The atmosphere in the United States during the mid to late 1930s and up to the entrance of the United States into World War II was one marked by isolationist and often jingoist sentiment, as well as anti-Semitic, anticommunist (and then as now, communism was persistently conflated with socialism), and, at times, anti-British feeling. It was an atmosphere the Nazis and their adherents in America knew how to turn to good advantage. See, inter alia, Grossman, *Emigration* (Frankfurt on Main: Europaische Verlagsanstalt, 1969); "Editorial: Refugees Unlimited," *Medical Economics* (1939): 24–28, 96–102; E. H. Loewy, "The Fate of Jewish Physicians During the Nazi Era" (MS); G. H. Shuster, "The Conflict Among Catholics," *American Scholar* 10 (Winter 1940–41): 6–15; C. H. Stember et al., *Jews in the Minds of America* (New York: Basic Books, 1966); and Wyman, *Paper Walls*.

7. The story of Allied neglect of the Holocaust has been amply recorded. There is impeccable evidence that the Vatican knew about the extermination program and that shortly thereafter, the British and U.S. governments were informed. Furthermore, the Holocaust was merely the tip of the iceberg, the culmination of the persistent violation of humans that exemplified the Third Reich. See, inter alia, Morse, *While Six Million Died*.

8. The story of Americans of Japanese extraction during World War II has been largely downplayed. The internment of the Japanese and their resulting loss of liberty and property was not only a violation of all principles of human rights but in direct violation of the U.S. Constitution. See R. Daniels, *Concentration Camps USA: Japanese Americans and World War II* (New York: Holt, Rinehart & Winston, 1972); B. Hosokawa, *Nisei: The Quiet Americans* (New York, 1969); J. Hersey, "A Mistake of Terrifically Horrible Proportions," in *Manzanar*, ed. J. Armor and P. Wright (New York: Random House, 1988).

9. The story of black Americans in the Army Air Corps is one that has only recently been written and is not well enough known. See Billie A. Day, *The Afro-American Airmen in World War II* (Washington, D.C.: Department of Transportation, Federal Aviation Administration, Office of General Aviation Affairs), GA 20–85.

Glossary

Amenorrhea—absence of regular menstruation.

Aryanizers—Germans who confiscated or obtained Jewish property during the Nazi period.

Asthenia—weakness, lack of strength.

Asthenic-leptosomic disposition—type of physical constitution, according to Ernst Kretschmer, that included a narrow head, narrow shoulders, and flat chest.

BEG Final Law—the second reform of the Federal Restitution Law, enacted in 1965.

Bridge symptoms—symptoms of illness that emerged in the period between the end of persecution and the manifestation of persecution disorders, the so-called latency period.

Capital restitution—compensation of harm in the form of a one-time monetary settlement, as opposed to ongoing payment of compensatory pension.

Chronic progressive asthenia—progressive weakness and fatigue in survivors of the concentration camps (as described by Louis Fichez).

Civil servant classes (separation into)—the four salary groups for civil servants—junior, mid-level, upper-level, and senior. To calculate the amount of reparations pensions, persecutees were classed in one of the four civil servant groups, depending on their professional status before persecution.

Claims Conference (abbrev. of Conference on Jewish Material Claims Against Germany)—union of fifty-two Jewish organizations in western countries, formed in 1951 to represent reparations claims to West Germany for Jews living outside Israel.

Claims deadlines—also exclusionary deadlines. Deadlines under the Federal Restitution and Federal Restitution Final Laws by which claims to reparations had to be registered with the offices.

Concentration camp assumption—provision of the BEG Final Law (§ 31, para. 2) under which the assumption is made, for persecutees who had spent at least one year in a concentration camp and suffered a reduction in earning capacity of 25 percent or more, that the reduction in earning capacity was persecution-induced, without further proof. This provision was included in the law to ease the burden of proof.

Concentration camp syndrome—also deportees' syndrome, survivors' syndrome.

Characteristic complex illness in surviving concentration camp prisoners (see ch. 3, "Survivors' Syndrome")

Conversion reaction, conversion neurosis—neurosis with physical symptoms.

Coronary phobia—attacks of heart palpitations, combined with fear that the heart will stop.

Damage to career (or professional advancement)—damage suffered due to restrictions on professional practice, layoffs from public service or private businesses, reduction in income, forced breaking off of training, and so on.

Damage to life—harm to the survivors of a persecutee through the death of their breadwinner.

Dissimulation—playing down, hiding symptoms.

DPs—short for displaced persons. Survivors of the concentration camps and forced labor, mainly East European Jews who had no homes to go back to and who lived following liberation in camps in the Western-occupied zones of Germany.

Endoradiogram—method by which abnormal changes in vessels can be seen, for example by injecting a dye visible in an X ray.

Evaluators, doctors attached to consulates abroad—doctors engaged by consulates and embassies abroad to examine and report on persecutees.

Exclusionary clause—§ 6, para. 1, no. 2, of the BEG, based upon which no one who opposed the free democratic basic order had a claim to reparations.

Federal Restitution Law (BEG)—first legal reform of reparations law, enacted in 1956.

Federal Supplementary Law—first national reparations law, enacted in 1953.

Hypermnesia—frequent, tormenting recall of the horrors of the camps.

Hypertonia—high blood pressure.

Hypomanic condition—slightly manic excitement, abnormally positive mood and busyness.

Late emigrants; also "post-fifty-three-ers"—persecutees from the eastern European areas from which ethnic Germans had been expelled who emigrated to western countries after the deadline, that is, the date the BEG went into force, 1 October 1953.

Latency period—symptom-free interval between the end of the persecution and the manifestation of the persecution disorder.

Leucocytosis—increase in white blood cell count.

London Debt Conference—conference held in London in 1952 at which the amount and method of payment of the total debt of the former Third Reich to the victorious powers was negotiated.

Luxembourg Treaty—reparations agreement between Israel, the Claims Conference, and West Germany, signed in Luxembourg on 10 September 1952.

Mastoidectomy—removal of the mastoid process behind the ear.

Muselmann stage—state of complete physical emaciation and debilitation following hunger, cold, and illness in the concentration camps, accompanied by complete apathy.

Neurodystonia—outdated phrase for the following symptoms, caused by faulty regulation of the autonomic nervous system: heart palpitations, restlessness, sleeplessness, dizziness, head and stomach aches, and cold, damp extremities. Before the offices and courts recognized psychological damage as persecution harm, such neurodystonia often served as an alternative diagnosis, as a physical illness was more likely to be recognized.

November version of the Bundesrat draft—draft of a federal restitution law written by Otto Küster and presented to the Bundesrat in November 1952. It was defeated by the federal minister of finance and his allies.

Pectanginous disorders—attacks of heart pain caused by contractions or reduced circulation of the coronary blood vessels.

Pension neurosis—also tendentious neurotic, purposeful reaction. Neurosis whose purpose is to demonstrate disorders and symptoms of illness in order to gain a pension. This concept was developed by German psychiatrists following World War I.

Persecutees from the areas of expulsion—persecutees from eastern Europe, that is, the same areas from which ethnic Germans were expelled, who emigrated to the West after the war.

Persecution-induced reduction in earning capacity—percentage of the reduction in earning capacity caused by persecution disorder.

Postcommotional encephalopathy—continuing disruption of brain function after a concussion.

Property damage—damage suffered as a result of losses caused by boycotts, liquidation of businesses, and so on.

Psychasthenia, neurasthenia—outdated terms for states of psychological or nervous exhaustion.

Psychopath—abnormal personality (as described by Kurt Schneider).

Reduction in earning capacity—medical-insurance jargon for a diminished capacity to work caused by accident or illness, expressed as a percentage of total earning capacity.

Reparations—in the strict legal sense, this is the umbrella term for restitution of property and compensation for harm.

Residency requirements—under the BEG, persecutees only received compensation if they had resided within the 1937 borders of the German Reich or had taken up residency in West Germany by the deadline date of 31 December 1952. Special rules covered persecutees from the areas of expulsion (eastern Europe).

Residual damage—damage remaining after acute illness has abated.

Restitution (*Rückerstattung*)—return of real estate, houses, businesses, factories, and so forth stolen during the "Aryanization" of the economy.

Reviewing doctors—doctors who verify the medical examination reports issued in the course of a restitution proceeding, at the behest of the restitution offices.

Scar pterygium—growth of hypervascular connective tissue between the corner of the eye and the cornea following an eye injury.

Special Supplementary Pension Law (Sonderhilfsrentengesetz; or SHRG)—Hamburg state restitution law before enactment of the Federal Supplementary Law.

Survivors' guilt—persecutees' feelings of guilt toward their murdered families and comrades, including a belief that because they survived, they share the guilt for the death of others.

Tightrope walk—test of impaired balance. The patient must walk a straight line.

Toxic liver damage—liver cell damage caused by poison, medication, and so on.

Transitional treaty—treaty concluded between West Germany and the Western Allies on 26 February 1952 on an end to occupational status and return of sovereignty to Germany. Part IV of this treaty included guidelines for a national reparations arrangement.

Traumatic epilepsy—attacks occurring following skull injury.

United Restitution Organization (URO)—Jewish legal assistance organization whose offices in West Germany and other Western countries represented less-well-off persecutees in reparations cases.

Worsening—

1. Worsening of a hereditary disorder by external harm
   • distinguishable worsening: partially worsened by the harm, therefore only partially entitled to pension
   • direction-setting worsening: the disorder took a completely new course as a result of the harm, and is thus entirely entitled to a pension.
2. Worsening of a disorder for which a person is entitled to a pension through progression of the disease process.

Worsening application—If an illness took a serious turn for the worse in the years after a pension was granted, and this led to a greater reduction in earning capacity, an increased pension could be applied for. Such an application required a new medical examination.

Index

Library of Congress Cataloging-in-Publication Data

Pross, Christian.
    [Wiedergutmachung. English]
    Paying for the past : the struggle over reparations for surviving
victims of the Nazi terror / Christian Pross ; translated by Belinda
Cooper.
        p.   cm.
    Includes bibliographical references and index.
    ISBN 0-8018-5824-0 (alk. paper)
    1. Holocaust, Jewish (1939–1945)—Germany (West)—Reparations.
2. Jews—Germany—History—1945–   3. Holocaust survivors—Diseases—
Germany (West)   4. Holocaust survivors—Mental health—Germany
(West)   5. Germany (West)—Ethnic relations.   I. Title.
DS135.G332P7613   1998
940.53'18—dc21   97-39245
                                                                  CIP